Not
Your Mother's®
Slow Cooker
Cookbook

Also by Beth Hensperger and Julie Kaufmann

The Ultimate Rice Cooker Cookbook

Also by Beth Hensperger

Bread

Baking Bread

Bread for All Seasons

Beth's Basic Bread Book

Breads of the Southwest

The Bread Bible

The Pleasure of Whole Grain Breads

Bread Made Easy

Bread for Breakfast

The Best Quick Breads

The Bread Lover's Bread Machine Cookbook

Not Your Mother's® Slow Cooker Cookbook

Beth Hensperger

and Julie Kaufmann

The Harvard Common Press
Boston, Massachusetts

For Agra: Thank you for sharing your
understanding of the cosmos that flows through you,
dear friend and gentle heart.

—BH

o o o

For Ben, who supports me in everything I do

—JK

The Harvard Common Press
535 Albany Street
Boston, Massachusetts 02118
www.harvardcommonpress.com

Printed in the United States

Library of Congress Cataloging-in-Publication Data
Hensperger, Beth.
    Not your mother's slow cooker cookbook / Beth Hensperger and Julie Kaufmann.
        p.   cm.
    Includes index.
    ISBN 1-55832-244-2 (hc : alk. paper) — ISBN 1-55832-245-0 (pb : alk. paper)
        1. Electric cookery, Slow.   I. Kaufmann, Julie.   II. Title.
    TX827.H39 2005
    641.5'884—dc22   2004018564

ISBN-13: 978-1-55832-245-5

Special bulk-order discounts are available on this and other Harvard Common Press books. Companies and
organizations may purchase books for premiums or resale, or may arrange a custom edition, by contacting the
Marketing Director at the address above.

25 24 23 22 21 20 19 18 17 16 15

Cover and interior design by RLF Design
Cover photography by Eskite Photography
Food styling by Andrea Lucich
Prop styling by Carol Hacker

Cover photographs--front: Thai Pork with Peanut Sauce, page 360; spine: Crock-Roasted Root Vegetables,
page 135; back: Orange Hoisin Chicken, page 271 and Hot Fudge Spoon Cake, page 425.

Not Your Mother's is a registered trademark of The Harvard Common Press.

Contents

Introduction

We started this project because we love to cook, and we both are advocates of quick cooking—making our favorite recipes as easy and effortless as possible. Since food writing and editing are our professions, we are both in the kitchen a great deal, but the dilemma we face of coming up with tasty, healthful meals in a short amount of time every day is the same one that challenges any working person or busy parent. We love ethnic and traditional American cooking, but we take

a very flexible approach. We like to play with our favorite seasonings and flavor combinations. We like to experiment, substitute ingredients as needed, and enjoy our time in the kitchen, rather than have it be a chore. We don't want to save our favorites for guests; we want to eat them when we choose. The slow cooker, to our surprise, fit into our culinary lives with perfection.

As its name implies, cooking in the slow cooker takes longer than conventional stove-top or oven cooking. But we found it was quick in other ways: the no-fuss assembly was efficient, we could still be imaginative in our choice of ingredients, and the slow-cooking process took virtually no hands once the cooker was loaded and turned on. This method was a return to truly traditional cooking and was extremely useful in our busy lives.

We collected recipes—the nostalgic and the new, the exotic and homey—over two years of testing with the one requirement being that they taste good. We found the slow cooker style of cooking is designed to complement the way we live—it is time conscious, economical, energy conscious, and reliable. We cooked from scratch with fresh ingredients, and we could cook the same dishes as easily for a dinner party as for a family supper. It was simple to make enough so we had leftovers and extras for the freezer.

We ended up appreciating our slow cooker meals and the appliance's ability to enhance our daily lives. We found that wonderful food does not need to be complicated. The goal of this cookbook is not only to give you lots of ideas for recipes and ways to use your slow cooker, but to enhance your time in the kitchen with home-cooked dishes you may have forgotten or have never known. Since most of the recipes constitute one-dish meals, all you need is some bread or a salad and dinner is on the table. Happy slow cooking!

Acknowledgments

We offer a special thank you to Pam Hoenig, our meticulous and painstaking editor, for guiding this book project with sensitivity, intelligence, and good humor. Her support made this book a pleasant experience. Also thank you to Deborah Kops, our copyeditor and much more, and to Valerie Cimino and the staff at The Harvard Common Press.

Additional thanks go to all our friends and other cookbook writers who have been generous enough to share their slow cooker recipes and food philosophies with us—we have acknowledged them individually in the recipes.

And we want to thank our friends Nancyjo Rieske, Batia Rabec, and Vivien "Bunny" Dimmel, who were diligent with testing, tasting, and giving us advice. We appreciate the help.

It is the happiest of circumstances that we have had Martha Casselman as the same literary agent for all our books except one way back when. Now well into retirement, she will be remembered for three loves—the love of the craft of writing, which she inherited from her father, the old newspaper man; her generous love of community, from the food bank to nonprofit fundraising benefits; and, of course, her love of good food.

Cooking in
Slow Motion

Americans are known throughout the modern world for their love of new technology in the mechanical and electronic realms. Any piece of equipment or tool that can do the job better and faster is immediately embraced and touted. So who could have predicted the success of a kitchen appliance that does the job more slowly? In 1971, the Rival Company, known for manufacturing home kitchen electric appliances and for its invention of the electric can opener (in 1955), introduced a revolutionary countertop appliance (originally designed to be an electric bean cooker called the Beanery), which it dubbed the Crock-Pot. And what a smash hit it was.

Originally marketed as a boon to the busy working woman who still wanted to serve her family homemade food, the appeal of the slow cooker has broadened considerably, reaching across gender and generational lines. The pot itself has become something of a phenomenon, with sales to date of more than 80 million units in 350 different models. To some, the slow cooker became unfashionable over time, and its avocado green and harvest gold colors seemed to be hopelessly out of tune with current style. But the slow cooker's devotees just went right along cooking in slow motion, assembling savory one-pot meals in their trusty cookers and sitting down to eat the delicious results hours later.

The slow cooker, a fat tub on short legs, is actually the modern embodiment of a centuries-old method of preparing food: enclosed cooking in earthenware. Today's slow cookers are made by a bevy of manufacturers that market worldwide from the Far East to Mexico and Europe, but the cookers share certain characteristics. They have a thick stoneware insert housed in a metal casing. Electrical heating elements within the metal casing carry the heat up and all around the stoneware as it sits in the casing.

Incorporating elements of stove-top and oven cooking methods, a slow cooker works by keeping the food constantly simmering at the lowest possible temperature for a very long period of time. Once you have mastered the skill of cooking in it, you can assemble and cook a dish that does not require any tending. In fact, you can leave the house or go to bed without worry. Today's heavy, fully glazed stoneware cooking vessels are so versatile and attractive that you can, in most instances, assemble and refrigerate the ingredients in the insert (if you have a removable one) at night, and in the morning, place it directly in the metal housing containing the heating elements. Turn on the cooker, let it cook for hours, then serve the meal directly from it. Think of it as a large oven-to-table casserole or soup tureen. It permits you to cook back-to-basics cuisine at its best—simple and economical, yet sumptuous and hearty.

The slow cooking of food is not just a technique, a piece of equipment, or place in the kitchen, but a frame of mind as well. On one hand, it is simplicity itself and allows for the most basic of foods to be cooked to perfection. But for good results, you must start with the best available ingredients (and "best" does not mean "most expensive") and take care in their preparation. Time-honored techniques like measuring with care, cutting ingredients to a uniform size, soaking beans, browning meats and vegetables to bring out their full flavor, and deglazing sauté pans are the touches that all pay big dividends in flavor.

Slow cooking is a method of cooking that invites the blending of lots of ingredients: meats (including sausage), vegetables, greens, beans and legumes, grains and noodles, wine or beer, broth and water. Flavor enhancers—salt, spices, herbs, and the like—are adjusted at the end of the cooking to prevent an overconcentration from occurring because of the long cooking time. More delicate ingredients—seafood, dairy products, and some vegetables—are also added at the end of the cooking period to keep their integrity.

What You Will Find in This Book

When we began this recipe collection, we were programmed to think of the slow cooker as the "magic pot" that cooked while the cook was away. Well, sometimes the cook is at home. Some foods cannot cook all day and still be recognizable. Our goal was to produce good-tasting food that was prepared by a loving hand and would be enjoyed by a discerning palate. We wanted to take advantage of the global culinary melting pot with all its appetizing and contrasting flavors and also savor old-fashioned and traditional favorites. We wanted to be able to enjoy beef bourguignon or short ribs with honey barbecue sauce one day, and Mexican posole or Japanese beef curry the next. Some days we would have the time for multiple preparation steps that would further enhance the final flavor; other days there would be only enough time to throw everything into the cooker before dashing out the door.

While writing this book, we looked around the world for inspiration, seeking foods that traditionally have been cooked in closed ceramic pots or casseroles, such as the Spanish *olla*; the French *daubière*, *toup*, and *cassole*; the Italian *fagioliera*; the Moroccan tagine; the Japanese *donabe* casserole; and the Chinese sandpot. We found a wealth of wonderful, soul-satisfying recipes and adapted them to the slow cooker. The low temperature and long cooking time of such dishes allows for the toughest, often most inexpensive "country" cuts of meat (unsuitable for fast, high-heat sautés and grilling) to be cooked to a luscious tenderness without loss of their natural juices. Bean dishes, long-simmered tomato sauces, and other flavorful vegetable dishes are also slow cooker naturals. The slow cooker is one of the best ways to cook beans, lentils, and split peas to perfection.

What Is Slow Cooking?

All foods are cooked by one of two methods: moist or dry. Dry-heat cooking methods include roasting, baking, broiling, grilling, toasting, panfrying, and deep-frying. This category makes use of appliances such as the microwave, toaster, outdoor grill, and conventional oven.

Moist-heat cooking includes stewing, braising, steaming, and poaching. The slow cooker, with its even, low heat sealed in a covered pot, uses this technique. During moist-heat cooking, meat and other foods are cooked in a closed environment of constantly moving liquid or steam. This method is used for foods that are not naturally tender, such as beans and other plants with lots of fiber and meat with a lot of connective tissue. The hot, moist environment breaks down fiber, making the beans and fibrous vegetables soft and tender, and it dissolves meat's connective tissue, called collagen, into gelatin, thereby tenderizing tough meat.

The temperature that will give you the most tender meat is around 180°F, equivalent to the LOW setting on the slow cooker. It is the lowest temperature deemed safe for cooking by the United States Department of Agriculture (USDA). The very slow simmer engulfs the food, creates steam, and retains the food's natural texture and flavor. The slow cooker is the master of this style of cooking, efficiently transferring the heat from its source in the base surrounding the heat-sensitive crockery insert to the liquid, and finally, to the food.

About the Stoneware Insert in Your Slow Cooker

The stoneware insert used in the slow cooker is fully glazed, inside and out. It is fired at more than 2,000°F, a process that vitrifies the clay, hardening it so it becomes resistant to chipping and discoloring, and giving it its shiny, glassy, easy-to-clean finish. You can cook acidic ingredients like rhubarb and tomatoes in it with no worry of off flavors developing. Today's slow cooker utilizes two basic shapes, both of which encourage condensation but, with their tight-fitting lids, prevent evaporation. For this reason, the slow cooker version of a recipe will call for less liquid than the oven or stove-top original, where evaporation will occur. Cooking the slow cooker way adds an extra ½ to 1 cup of liquid during the cooking process as the ingredients exude juices, which condense under the lid and do not evaporate.

In older models, the stoneware is not removable and, hence, a hassle to clean. All the models we inspected during the writing of this book were removable for easy cleaning and were even dishwasher safe. The first cookers were only available in 3½- or 4-quart round shapes and did not have lips suitable to be used as handles. All the stoneware inserts now have handles so you can easily lift and lower the pot. An empty medium-size round crock weighs about 6 pounds.

There are also slow cookers with nonstick metal cooking vessels. These models, designed for multitasking such as popping corn and deep-frying, do not work as well as the stoneware inserts.

Stoneware cannot, under any circumstance, be placed over direct heat on the stovetop for browning or finishing off, or set in the freezer; it will crack when exposed to extremes in temperature. It can, however, be used in the oven with great success as a casserole dish or for baking bread.

Slow Cooker Shapes and Sizes

The first, and most familiar, shape is the round slow cooker. This is the best shape for cooking soups, beans, stews, and risottos. It reminds us of a classic flowerpot, with a rather small base and tall, slightly sloping sides, and a large, open "mouth" with a domed, see-through, tempered glass lid, which seals the slow cooker into an airtight container when the contents are heated. The first slow cookers had flimsy Lexan plastic lids. The current glass lids are a fabulous improvement, allowing the heat to reflect down and envelop the contents in moist heat from all sides. As for color, the poisonous colors of decades past—psychedelic orange, green, and yellow, or overly decorated cutesy styles—have been replaced with pale soft white, a simple border, or stunning stainless steel, which looks elegant with its black stoneware insert.

In the last few years, the oval roaster shape has appeared. Based on the classic

French terrine with lower, wider sides, it is a bit more shallow and compact than the round shape and is especially well suited for holding large cuts of meat, such as a pork roast, leg of lamb, or whole chicken. Available in black or a soft creamy beige, it is a handsome casserole by any definition. It has more surface area than the round model, so take that into consideration when timing; it will cook slightly faster if you are making a stew or soup in it.

The slow cooker is available in a wide range of volume capacities, from 1 to 7 quarts, increasing in 2-cup increments. It is up to you to decide what size you need, depending on the number of people you want to serve on average and what types of foods you will be making. Hard-core slow cooker users usually own two or three sizes.

The three basic size categories are small, medium, and large, which is how we specify the proper cooker to use in each of the recipes in the book. Most sizes come in a choice of round or oval, but be sure to check inside the box when purchasing; we have found that the picture on the outside of the box sometimes does not match the shape within.

Rival's smallest slow cooker is dubbed the "Little Dipper," since it is perfect for making and serving hot dips and small amounts of fondue. We prefer the 1- or 1½-quart size, as it gives a bit more room for hands to do the dipping. This size, however, is too small for cooking soups and stews. When we indicate "small" in a recipe, you can use a 1½- to 2½-quart ca-

pacity slow cooker. Many who cook for one or two people use a 2- or 2½-quart model (if you do, you can cut the recipes designed for the medium-size cooker in half).

Medium is the most popular size of slow cooker and before you even make your first dish in it, you will know why: It is easy to handle, comfortable to lift and manipulate, and fits nicely on the counter or in the dishwasher. When we indicate "medium" in a recipe, we are referring to the 3- to 4½-quart models. The 3-quart oval won us over when we tested recipes for this book. This size holds 4 to 6 servings, equivalent to a 3- to 3½-pound roast or cut-up chicken. This is also a good size for two people who like leftovers. Meatloaf can be made in either a round or oval shape of this size, but note the shape of the finished dish will reflect that of the insert.

Large cookers are the 5- to 7-quart models, the most popular being the 5- and 6-quart sizes. These are designed for families and for entertaining and are best for large cuts of meat, such as brisket and corned beef, pot roasts, whole poultry, and large quantities of stew. The large is the

What if you want to make a dish that cooks for 6 hours and you won't be home for 8 hours? Until now, you had no choice but to overcook the food or make something else. Now there is another option. Rival, maker of the Crock-Pot line of slow cookers, created Smart-Pots, which are slow cookers that are easily programmable, even by the legions of us who can't program our VCRs.

There are two styles of Smart-Pot. One type can cook on the HIGH setting for 4 or 6 hours, or on the LOW setting for 8 or 10 hours. When the cooking time is up, the Smart-Pot will automatically shift to the KEEP WARM setting (which is recommended for no more than 4 hours), so your meal is waiting for you when you are ready to eat. With this type of Smart-Pot, if you want to cook for periods of time that differ from the automated setting (for example, less time on LOW or a longer time on HIGH), you'll have to be there to turn the pot off or on. Please note that even though this is an automatic machine, you *cannot* preprogram the cooking start time with a Smart-Pot, letting food sit in the crock to begin cooking at a later time, because the food will spoil rapidly. The Smart-Pot is so named because you can program how long to cook the food.

The second type of Smart-Pot is more flexible. You can set it to cook on HIGH or LOW for anywhere from 30 minutes up to 20 hours, in half-hour increments. Here is how to use it: Fill the crock as usual, then place it into the housing and put on the cover. Plug in the Smart-Pot. The cooker's three lights—marked HIGH, LOW, and KEEP WARM—will all flash, alerting you that it is time to select the setting you wish to use. Push the round button on the left, which is marked HIGH, LOW, and KEEP WARM, top to bottom. One push selects LOW, two pushes select HIGH, and three select KEEP WARM. (If you set the Smart-Pot to KEEP WARM, you cannot set a cooking time. It will stay on KEEP WARM until you manually turn it off.) If you have chosen LOW or HIGH, you will now set the cooking time. Press the button with the up-pointing arrow. The first push puts 30 minutes on the digital display, and every subsequent push adds 30 minutes more. If you accidentally put more time on the cooker than you wanted, no matter. Just push the button with the down-pointing arrow and watch the display decrease in 30-minute increments. When the cooking time is up, the cooker will automatically switch to the KEEP WARM setting, which will keep the food hot until you are ready to eat it.

This cooker is also equipped with an OFF button, so you can easily end the cooking earlier than planned. If you wish, you may leave the cooker turned off but plugged in when you are not using it. (We don't recommend this, however. It's too easy for the empty cooker to be turned on accidentally.)

preferred size for steaming puddings and brown bread, which require a mold. If you are multiplying up a recipe designated for a medium-size cooker, increase the cooking time by 1½ to 2 hours and increase your ingredients accordingly, depending on whether you are using a 5-, 6-, or 7-quart cooker. For example, a recipe designed to feed four can be tripled or quadrupled in a larger cooker.

The Temperature Settings

Different machines have different settings. For the best results, if you are not already schooled in this method of cooking, you must experiment with different cooking times and settings to get results that appeal to you. The small slow cookers tend to have one heat setting—LOW. This is a safety precaution, because of the cooker's small size. Some have an OFF setting, while others must be unplugged to turn them off.

Standard medium-size and large slow cookers have two heat settings—LOW and HIGH. Foods will cook faster on HIGH than on LOW, but for all-day cooking or for cooking less tender cuts, the LOW setting is recommended. It's safe to cook foods on LOW the entire time. If time permits, however, turn the cooker to HIGH for the first hour of cooking to get the cooker up to temperature as quickly as possible, and then reset it to LOW.

Because of food safety considerations, the slow cooker does not allow you to pre-program the cooking start time, so you can't fill the pot with food, leave home, and have the pot go on an hour or two later. However, while the food is cooking and once it's done, it will be safe as long as the cooker is operating. The stoneware insert will retain heat for a full hour after turning off the machine.

The new Smart-Pot machines (see box, page 6) available from Rival in medium and large sizes, have a digital face and can be programmed for the designated amount of cooking time. There are HIGH and LOW buttons as well as two buttons for increasing or decreasing the cooking time. When the food has been cooked the programmed amount of time, the pot will switch automatically to a KEEP WARM setting. These pots are really a convenience for away-from-home, all-day cooking.

Your New Slow Cooker

You may be buying your very first slow cooker or replacing an old one. The new machines are a great improvement over those on the market even five years ago. Since it is such an inexpensive appliance, go ahead and upgrade, or buy a second or third machine in a different size if you wish. When shopping, do check inside the box to make sure all parts are intact and the shape, which may be different than what is pictured on the outside of the box, is the one you want to buy.

At home, after removing the slow cooker and manufacturer's booklet from the box, place the slow cooker on your countertop. Remove the lid and stoneware insert (if removable), and wash them in hot soapy water, taking care not to scratch them. Dry the insert thoroughly and return it to the base by sliding it into place. We like to line up the handles on the insert and base. Dry the lid and leave it on the counter until you are ready to cook something. Read the manufacturer's booklet, highlighting warranty information and customer service phone numbers, and fill out the warranty card. Make a note in the back of this book regarding the model and its capacity. This information will be especially useful as time goes on and you forget the size of your slow cooker.

Inspect the inside of the metal base of the cooker to familiarize yourself with the design. The low-wattage, wraparound heating coils are sandwiched between the inner and outer metal walls for indirect heat; the heat source never makes direct contact with the stoneware crock. The coils inside the base heat up, and then the space between the base wall and crock heats up and transfers that heat to the stoneware. The slow cooker cooks between 180° and 300°F.

Before you use your slow cooker, be sure to familiarize yourself with Rules of the Pot on page 10. After choosing a recipe, assemble and prepare the ingredients according to the instructions, then place them in the stoneware insert. You can do this while it is in the base, taking care not to splash liquid over the sides, or you can remove the insert and fill it outside the base. It is your choice. Do not fill the insert more than three-fourths full to avoid

spillage as the heated contents expand. The cooker works most efficiently when it is one-half to three-fourths full because of the placement of the heating coils. Put the stoneware in the base, cover with the lid, and plug it in.

If necessary, set the machine to ON, LOW, or HIGH (some models, usually smaller machines, are on when they are plugged in). Do not cook on the WARM or KEEP WARM setting, if you have one. If you have a Smart-Pot, now is the time to program the cooking time.

We recommend that you stay in the house the first time you use the appliance to assess how it works and observe the cooking process. Slow cookers do not have a thermostat, so if you are concerned about temperature, use an instant-read food thermometer inserted into the meat or cooking liquid. There will never be a specific temperature in a slow cooker recipe because the cooking process is based on the wattage and time. The contents will take 1 to 2 hours to heat up to a simmer, which is much slower than any other cooking process, so be prepared for it. Many cooks turn the cooker to the HIGH setting for 1 to 2 hours to bring the temperature up as quickly as possible to 140°F—the temperature at which bacteria can no longer proliferate in food—then switch to LOW for the remainder of the cook time. The LOW setting uses 80 to 185 watts and cooks in the temperature range of 180° to 200°F. The HIGH heat setting is double the wattage, 160 to 370 watts, and cooks at a temperature of about 280°F, with slight variations due to the size of cooker, the temperature of the food, and how full the crock is. Any time you lift the lid to check the contents or to stir, you release the accumulated steam that cooks the food, the temperature drops, and, once you put the lid back, it takes approximately 20 to 30 minutes for the temperature in the cooker to return to the original level. So keep your peeking to a bare minimum!

The first time you use the machine, be prepared for the smell, and perhaps light smoke, emitted from the heating elements as any manufacturing residues are burned off. This is normal. We found that most new machines emitted a metal-like smell for about one full hour. It is best to use your stove fan, open a window or a door, or a combination of these, to allow the smell to dissipate as rapidly as possible. During cooking, the outside of the metal base housing will become hot to the touch, so keep it away from children and walls or low cabinets. The stoneware insert will slowly reach the same temperature, although we found we could touch both briefly without oven mitts to check the temperature. If you are bringing the dish to a buffet or potluck, just carry the entire portable unit by its handles, then plug it in and set to LOW to reheat the food. (There are optional accessories available such as a lid latch, which keeps the lid in place while transporting, and a lovely insulated carrying case designed by one manufacturer.)

• • High Altitude Slow Cooking • •

There are guidelines to slow cooking at altitudes more than 3,000 feet above sea level. Just remember that the higher you go, the less compressed the air is. At high altitudes, liquids come to a boil more quickly and at a lower temperature. Figure your food will take approximately 25 percent more time to come up to the proper cooking temperature and cook.

The rule is to increase the oven temperature 1°F for every 100 feet of altitude in an oven to compensate for slower heating, but in the slow cooker the temperature is preset, so you need to cook all foods on HIGH and increase the cooking time slightly. Use the LOW heat setting for warming.

Use the following chart as a guideline. Be sure to make notes on the adjustments you have made on your recipes for future preparation.

Altitude Adjustment	3,000 feet	5,000 feet	7,000–8,000 feet
Cooking temperature	HIGH	HIGH	HIGH
Decrease in liquid per cup in recipe	1–2 tablespoons	2–3 tablespoons	3–4 tablespoons

Set a timer, make a mental note, or write down the estimated time that the food will be done according to the recipe. It is best to wait and check the food after the suggested time has elapsed. We like to use a wooden spoon or heat-resistant spoon or spatula, though metal utensils are fine as long as you are careful not to chip the crock. If you are using an immersion blender to purée, be sure to keep from hitting the sides of the crock and unplug the slow cooker unit first.

When handling the full insert, always turn off the machine and unplug it first, then use oven mitts to transfer the hot insert to a hot pad or heat-proof surface, or serve directly out of the insert while it is still in its base. After cooking, you can leave the insert in the housing until it is cool enough to handle. Once emptied, do not fill the hot insert with cold water; you could crack it. Cooled crockery inserts can be used to store leftovers in the refrigerator but not in the freezer—the extreme temperature can crack the ceramic.

Rules of the Pot

Please be sure to read these important guidelines before your first cooking forays and use it as a reference thereafter, as the slow cooker has some very important guidelines for safe cooking.

- Many instruction booklets say never to lift the lid during the cooking process. On one hand, that is a good rule; on the other hand, it's next to impossible. As the contents of the slow cooker heat up and create steam, a natural water seal is created around the rim of the lid to form a vacuum. The rim of the lid will stick in place when gently pulled. This is important for the even cooking of the food within. But the recipe might call for adding ingredients halfway or near the end of the cooking time, or you might want to check your food for doneness at some point. It is fine to do this, but always remember that by breaking the seal around the lid and allowing the steam to escape, the temperature within will drop. When you replace the lid, it takes 20 to 30 minutes for the contents to return to the proper cooking temperature. You can easily check the contents visually through the glass lid and for the most part there is no need to stir or turn the food, unless a recipe specifies it.

- The glass lid becomes quite hot during the cooking process. Use a pot holder to remove it, if necessary, and handle with care to avoid burns. The lid is dishwasher-safe.

- Unless you are cooking on the wrong temperature, have used too much or too little liquid, have let a dish cook too long, or have overfilled the crockery insert, there will be no burning, sticking, or bubbling over in the slow cooker. However, these things can occur if you have the cooker set at HIGH with the cover off to encourage evaporation of liquid, so keep an eye on it under those circumstances.

- Never preheat a crockery insert when empty. Load the crock with the ingredients, then turn on the cooker or plug it in to start the heating process.

- The cord on the slow cooker is deliberately short to minimize danger from tangling or tripping. You may use a heavy-duty extension cord *only* if it has a marked electrical rating at least as great as the electrical rating of your cooker.

- The cooking time on HIGH is about half of what it is when the setting is on LOW. One hour on HIGH is equivalent to 2 to 2½ hours on LOW, or twice as fast. Our recipes specify the best cooking temperature setting for the best results. While old recipes were often printed with both a HIGH and LOW temperature setting and two different cooking times for convenience, we have found that the new slow cookers are much more efficient and run at slightly higher temperatures than older cookers. Check the wattage of your unit; there are slight differences among manufacturers. Some recipes turn out better on LOW, with its gentle rolling simmer, than the vigorous simmer on HIGH. Many cooks start their cookers on HIGH for about an hour to get a good start on the cooking, then switch to LOW for the remainder of the cooking time.

- Most recipes need at least a bit of liquid to cook properly in the slow cooker, though there are exceptions, such as Crock-Baked Potatoes (page 123). Liquid measurements vary drastically in our recipes, from a few tablespoons to cover the bottom of the crock to submerging the food completely in liquid. Each recipe will be specific on these points. Fill the crock with the solid ingredients, place it in the base, if it is removable, then add the liquid to avoid splashing or lifting an overly heavy crock.

- Ideally, the slow cooker should be filled half full to no more than 1 full inch from the rim. The best practice is to fill the cooker one-half to two-thirds or three-fourths full because the heating elements are around the sides; this will give you the most even cooking.

- Tender vegetables overcook easily, so add them during the last 30 to 60 minutes of cooking. The same goes for seafood. For the most control over seasoning, add fresh herbs during the last hour and dried herbs and spices at the beginning, with the bulk of the

Is the Slow Cooker Safe?

Yes, the slow cooker, a countertop appliance, is very safe. Foods cook more slowly and at a lower temperature—between 180° and 300°F—than on the stove top or in the oven. However, the multi-directional heat from the pot, lengthy cooking time, and concentrated steam created within the tightly covered container combine to destroy bacteria and make the slow cooker a safe appliance for cooking foods.

The slow cooker is user-friendly and very economical, utilizing about the same amount of energy as a 75-watt light bulb. It takes much less electricity to use a slow cooker than a conventional gas or electric oven. On the HIGH setting, you will use less than 300 watts. It is an excellent alternative method of cooking on extremely hot days when energy alerts recommend reduced use of electrical appliances, and it won't heat up your kitchen like an oven does.

---

ingredients. But remember that the flavors will concentrate, so do not add too much; you can always add more at the end. More fresh herbs, salt, and pepper are often added at the end.

○ Unless otherwise noted in the recipe, thaw frozen foods before placing them in the slow cooker so that the temperature of the food can reach 140°F as soon as possible. This is very important; frozen foods can slow the heating of the cooker and leave your stew or braise at too low a temperature for too long a time to be safe to eat.

○ While the crockery insert, if removable, can be used in a conventional oven, it cannot be used on a gas or electric stove top; it will break if it comes in direct contact with a heating element. If you need to brown ingredients, such as meat, do so in a sauté pan, skillet, or saucepan as directed in the recipe, then transfer to the crock. The manufacturer's directions will specify if a crock is ovenproof, microwave-safe, or able to go under the broiler.

○ Once the dish is completely cooked, you can keep the food hot by switching to the LOW setting or, if your model has it, the KEEP WARM setting. Food can be held safely on KEEP WARM for up to 4 hours before eating. Many programmable digital cookers switch automatically to the KEEP WARM setting when the cooking time is up. Do not use the KEEP WARM setting, if you have one, for cooking; the temperature is too low to cook foods safely.

○ At the end of the cooking time, remove the lid and stir the food well with a wooden or plastic spoon. If your dish is not cooked to your preference, replace the lid, set the cooker to HIGH, and cook in increments of 30 to 60 minutes until the food is done to your liking.

○ When the food is cooked and ready to be served, turn the cooker to the OFF setting and/or unplug the unit. Many older slow cookers and small units do not have an OFF setting; OFF is when the unit is unplugged.

○ If you are not serving directly out of the cooker, use heavy oven mitts to carefully lift the hot crock, if removable, with its contents out of the cooker and set it on a trivet or folded towel.

○ Transfer leftovers to proper refrigerator or freezer storage containers within 2 hours after finishing cooking. Do not store your cooked food in the crockery insert, because it can crack with the difference in temperature.

○ Ceramic clay cookware cannot withstand quick changes in temperature. Never store the stoneware crock in the freezer. The crock can also crack if you add a lot of frozen food or submerge it in cold water while still hot from the cooking cycle. Be sure to let the crock come to room temperature before washing it; never pour cold water into a hot crock. If your crock becomes cracked or deeply scratched, contact the manufacturer for replacement instructions.

○ The crock can be washed by hand with nonabrasive dish-washing soap and a nylon scrubbie or brush or placed in the dishwasher.

○ If you were away from home during the entire cooking process and you discover that the power has gone out, throw away the food even if it looks done.

○ Cold cooked food should not be reheated in the crockery insert as it will not reach a safe internal temperature quickly enough to render the food safe to eat. However, cooked food can be heated on the stove or in a microwave and then put into a preheated slow cooker to keep it hot until serving. To preheat the crockery insert, fill it with warm, not boiling, water and let it stand a few minutes. Pour out the water and dry the insert, then add the food.

○ Never immerse the metal housing of the slow cooker in water or fill it with liquid; you must always have the crockery insert in place to cook. To clean, let the base come to room temperature, then wipe inside and out with a damp, soapy sponge, rinse, and dry with a towel so as not to damage the finish. Make sure the bottom is clean inside and free of food particles or spillage.

Safe Beginnings

A clean, organized work area makes assembling slow cooker dishes a snap and contributes to an easy cleanup. Begin with a clean cooker and utensils and a clean work surface. Wash your hands before and during food preparation. Keep perishable foods refrigerated until preparation time. If you cut up meat and vegetables in advance, store them separately, covered, in the refrigerator. The slow cooker takes up to two hours to slowly increase to a safe, bacteria-killing temperature. Constant refrigeration assures that bacteria, which multiply rapidly at room temperature, won't get a head start during the first few hours of cooking. Read the recipe carefully through to the end before preparation to be sure you have all of the ingredients, know the procedures, have assembled the utensils, and know how long the cooking time will be.

Always defrost meat or whole poultry before putting it in a slow cooker, otherwise it will not cook properly in the allotted time. Exceptions include certain recipes that require fully frozen poultry pieces, which can help keep the delicate flesh from overcooking. Do not use the wrong size slow cooker for large pieces of meat, such as a roast or whole chicken, because the food will cook so slowly and unevenly it could remain in the bacterial "danger zone" for too long. When preparing these large pieces of meat, follow the recipes and slow cooker suggestions carefully.

Filling the Slow Cooker with the Right Amount of Food

Using the proper amount of ingredients for the size of your cooker is of the utmost importance for successful results. Fill the stoneware insert no less than one-half full

Power Outages

If you are not at home during the entire slow-cooking process and you know the power has gone out during the day, throw away the food, even if it looks done. If you are at home when the power goes out, finish cooking the ingredients immediately by some other means: on the stove top or in the oven, if you have a gas stove, on an outdoor grill, or at another house where the power is on. If you are at home and if the food was completely cooked before the power went out, the food should remain safe to eat for up to two hours in the cooker with the power off.

and no more than three-fourths full to allow for expansion during cooking. The vessel needs to be at least one-half full because of the positioning of the heat coils around the walls of the cooker. Vegetables cook more slowly than meat and poultry in a slow cooker, so if you are using them, put the vegetables in first, at the bottom and around the sides of the cooking vessel, in layers. Then add the meat, then pour over the liquid, whether broth, water, or tomato or barbecue sauce. It is also important to prep your ingredients properly, namely by cutting them to the appropriate size for optimum cooking. We follow these guidelines in our recipes:

minced: $\frac{1}{16}$ inch

chopped: $\frac{1}{8}$ to $\frac{1}{4}$ inch

coarsely chopped: $\frac{1}{4}$ to $\frac{1}{2}$ inch

thinly sliced: $\frac{1}{8}$ inch thick

sliced: $\frac{1}{8}$ to $\frac{1}{4}$ inch thick

thickly sliced: $\frac{1}{2}$ inch thick

diced: $\frac{1}{2}$-inch squares

cubed (unless otherwise indicated): 1-inch squares

How to Read Our Recipes

Our recipes are designed to be easy to read. We tried to make it easy to spot important information efficiently. After the title of the recipe comes the headnote. Do not skip this; it contains information on the food or type of dish and any special points or techniques to which you need to pay particular attention. We often put

If the morning rush to get everyone out the door doesn't leave you enough time to get dinner into the slow cooker, don't despair before leaving for work or to do daylong errands. With most main dish recipes, you can shift the prep work to the night before. Prepare your ingredients as directed in the recipe. If the recipe calls for ingredients to be browned or sautéed on the stove, go ahead and do that step, too. Load the crock as directed in the recipe, then cover it with the lid and refrigerate overnight. In the morning, place the crock into the metal housing and begin cooking. For any recipe that cooks longer than four hours, you won't notice any difference in cooking time. For recipes that cook in less time, you may need an additional 20 to 30 minutes of cooking time because of the cold crock and ingredients.

---

serving suggestions or complementary food suggestions here.

The recipe's yield follows. Serving sizes are notoriously subjective; they do not take into account the big eater who has multiple helpings, nor children's portions, nor a desire for leftovers, so pay attention here and adjust the quantity to your specific needs.

Then comes the size of the slow cooker machine we feel is best suited for the recipe, based on our testing. If you are doubling the recipe, consider using a larger machine, and if you are cutting the recipe in half, downsize the machine. Remember, though, that the small slow cookers often only have a LOW setting, so if the dish must be cooked on HIGH, such as some of the bean recipes, a smaller machine will not be an option for you.

The machine setting (LOW or HIGH) and cook time are next. We suggest writing down the approximate finish time or setting a digital timer as a reminder. Check your food in the middle of and then near the end of the recommended cook time for the most control over the final texture and degree of doneness.

Slow Cooker Cook Times

Beth went nuts at first. With her background in baking, where variations in final baking times are usually within 5 to 10 minutes, the idea of a two hour or more window of doneness for the slow cooker was hard to adapt to at first. But with more experience, this anxiety disappeared. We suggest that you check the food for doneness at least once towards the middle of the cook time, then again around the minimum time suggested, especially the first time you make a dish (this can make the difference between a shapely crock-baked apple and applesauce). We encourage you to note your final cooking time in the margin of that recipe for future reference. Five people tested these recipes, all with different models and slightly different sizes of slow cookers. They lived in different regions, at a variety of altitudes, and worked through the seasons during a variety of weather conditions. Each had slightly different cook times, which fell within our recommended time window.

Guide to Internal Temperatures

There is always a bit of leeway when determining whether a particular food is completely cooked, or cooked to your preference, and this skill is usually acquired through years of cooking. But most professional chefs believe that gauging the internal temperature of meats and poultry is the most reliable way to tell when a food has reached a particular stage of doneness. When using a slow cooker, especially if you are a novice, it is important to get the cooking temperature to 140°F (out of the bacteria "danger zone") as soon as possible, and then to be sure the meat or poultry is totally cooked before eating it.

Just because it has cooked for hours does not mean it is done. Because of the lack of browning, you rely less on visual clues. You look, smell, and touch to ascertain the doneness. An instant-read thermometer or an accurate meat thermometer is the tool we recommend in every slow cooker kitchen. This is particularly important when cooking larger pieces of meat or whole poultry. A roast beef that is approximately 125°F in its interior will always be rare, whether braised in a slow cooker, grilled outdoors, or roasted in a conventional oven, regardless of how long it took to reach that temperature. Use the chart "Is It Done Yet?" on the following page as a guide for judging when your meat and poultry are done when using a slow cooker.

Handling Leftovers from the Slow Cooker

The convenience of the slow cooker allows for making extra-large batches of your favorite dishes, perfect for leftovers to refrigerate or freeze. Handle your leftover slow cooker foods as you would food cooked in the oven or on the stove top. Do not leave food in the stoneware cooker at room temperature for long periods. Remove the contents, store them in shallow, covered containers, and refrigerate or freeze them within two hours after cooking is finished. Reheating leftovers in a slow cooker is not recommended. Use the stove top or a microwave oven for the full reheat, then, if you wish, place in a slow cooker to keep hot for serving.

Adapting Conventional Recipes to the Slow Cooker

If you are an experienced slow cooker user, you will have already learned that adapting conventional recipes for use in the slow cooker requires keeping a few things in mind:

- Slow-cooker recipes require less liquid than recipes that use conventional cooking methods because evaporation is so markedly reduced. In general, we have found that slow cooker recipes require ½ to 1 cup less liquid than conventional recipes. As moisture condenses, it accumulates under the lid. These moisture droplets then fall onto the food, self-basting it. The liquid will not boil away or evaporate, so, combined with the food juices, you will end up with more liquid than when you began. When converting a recipe for the first time, we usually reduce the liquid by half, then add more as necessary at the end of cooking (for example, to thin a soup or bean dish), making the appropriate adjustment notes on the recipe.

○ Herbs and spices take on a new dimension in the slow cooker. With the long cooking times and concentration during cooking, fresh herbs tend to disintegrate and taste washed out, while dried herbs and spices can become overpowering and bitter. Start with half the amount of dried herbs and spices called for in a recipe and taste for seasoning an hour before serving, making final adjustments and seasoning with salt and pepper. Add fresh herbs at the end of cooking.

○ The big difference is timing. A stew that calls for 1 hour on the stove will take 6 to 8 hours on the LOW setting. Please refer to the Recipe Time Conversion Chart on page 18 as a guide.

Useful Cooking Techniques for the Slow Cooker

Because of the types of dishes you will be making in your slow cooker, you'll most likely find the following techniques of great use.

How to Get the Fat Out

When you've made a meat stew, a braised dish, or a stock or soup, you will often want to remove as much fat as possible from the liquid. Here are the several methods we recommend.

If you are not serving the dish until the next day, your task is simple. For stocks,

---

• • Is It Done Yet? • •

Type of Meat	Rare	Medium	Well Done
Beef	125° to 130°F	140° to 145°F	160°F
Duck and game birds	Not recommended	170° to 175°F	180°F
Veal	Not recommended	140° to 145°F	160°F
Lamb	130° to 140°F	140° to 145°F	160°F
Pork	Not recommended	145° to 150°F	160°F
Venison	125° to 130°F	140° to 145°F	160°F

Note: Cook chicken and turkey to an internal temperature of 170° to 180°F.

•• Recipe Time Conversion Chart ••

We use this handy conversion chart as a guide for translating traditional cooking times into slow cooker time. All times are approximate. When making a recipe for the first time, be sure to check for doneness halfway through and almost at the end of the cook time. We also recommend that you make notes on the recipe for future reference. Some recipes will cook just as well on HIGH, and take half the amount of time that they would on LOW. Generally, 1 hour of cooking on the HIGH setting is equal to 2 or 2½ hours on LOW. While early recipes for the slow cooker designated both LOW and HIGH cook times, we have found that most every dish cooks best on one or the other setting, so keep that in mind as you convert your favorite recipes to the slow cooker.

Conventional Recipe Time	Slow Cooker Time on LOW
15 minutes	1½ to 2 hours
20 minutes	2 to 3 hours
30 minutes	3 to 4 hours
45 minutes	5 to 6 hours
1 hour	6 to 8 hours
1½ hours	8 to 9 hours
2 hours	9 to 10 hours
3 hours	12 hours plus

refrigerate the liquid, uncovered, in a bowl. For braises, refrigerate the cooled liquid in an uncovered container separate from the meat and other ingredients. For stews with many components, this may not be possible. Just let the dish cool, then refrigerate the entire thing, covered. In each case, the next morning you can spoon off any congealed fat, which will have risen to the top and solidified. Many cooks like to leave a small amount of the fat behind for flavor instead of removing all of it.

If you are using a stock right away, pour the liquid from the hot crock into a heat-proof glass bowl or measuring cup (such as Pyrex). Wait several minutes for the fat to rise to the top of the liquid. You will be able to see a translucent, yellowish layer floating on the top of the liquid.

Now you have two options: remove the fat from the liquid or remove the liquid from the fat. To remove the fat, use a large, shallow metal spoon and carefully spoon off the clear fat, discarding it as you go. This isn't a perfect solution; you will inevitably spoon off some of the liquid you are trying to save or you will leave some fat floating on top. If there is very little fat, you can float a paper towel in the liquid for a few seconds. It will absorb the topmost layer, and then can be thrown away.

The second approach is to sneak the liquid out from under the layer of fat. One way to do this is with a turkey baster. Place a clean container large enough to hold the degreased liquid next to the container holding the liquid. Squeeze the turkey baster bulb and lower the open end straight down to the bottom of the container with the liquid. Release the bulb, and the baster will fill with the liquid from the bottom of the container. Bring the baster straight up out of the container, still holding it pointed end downward and being careful not to put pressure on the bulb, and aim the baster into the clean container. Squeeze the bulb and squirt in the liquid. Repeat until there is just fat remaining in your original container.

A brilliant little gadget called a degreaser is a worthwhile investment if you find yourself degreasing liquids often. It's like a measuring cup, but with a spout from the bottom instead of the top. To use it, pour in the liquid you are trying to degrease and wait several minutes for the fat to rise to the top. Then pour off the grease-free liquid from the bottom, stopping just before the fat layer can sneak into the spout.

How to Thicken

The slow cooker naturally produces a lot of moisture during cooking, and while we often like eating our soups, stews, and leftover liquid from roasting *au naturel,*

we like to have the option of thickening it, too. Here are the most common ways to prepare and use thickening agents and enrichments. You can use them interchangeably for the most part. Your choice may depend on dietary preferences, the type of ingredients needing to be thickened, or your own cooking style.

Flour is the most commonly used thickener. You dredge meat in it before browning or sprinkle it in the pan afterwards, then stir in liquid and pour it all into the slow cooker. You can use bleached or unbleached all-purpose, whole wheat, or whole wheat pastry flours interchangeably. Flour can also be added at the end of cooking by making a slurry, 1 to 2 tablespoons of flour mixed with an equal amount of water per cup of liquid, depending on how thick you want your dish. Turn the cooker to HIGH, stir the slurry into the hot liquid, re-cover, and cook until thick, 10 to 15 minutes, or cook a bit longer on LOW.

Roux is the term for equal parts of flour and butter cooked to form a paste. Melt the butter in a shallow pan over medium heat, then whisk in the flour. Stir for a few minutes to cook the flour slightly. Add some liquid and stir until smooth. Stir roux into your soup, stew, or leftover liquid until thickened and no longer murky. For a soup, use the ratio of 1 tablespoon each of butter and flour to 1 cup of liquid, and for a stew or sauce, 2 tablespoons each of butter and flour to 1 cup of liquid. Turn the cooker to HIGH, stir the roux into the hot liquid, re-cover, and cook until thick, 10 to 15 minutes, or cook a bit longer on LOW.

Beurre manié also utilizes flour and butter and is one of our favorite methods of thickening. It is an uncooked paste of flour and butter and it will transform the thinnest of sauces into a luscious one. To make a *beurre manié,* place an equal amount of soft butter and flour in a bowl or small food processor. Using a fork or pulsing motion, mash them together until the mixture becomes a semifirm mass. *Beurre manié* can be made ahead, divided into portions, then wrapped in plastic and stored in the refrigerator for a week, or in the freezer (it can be used frozen). For a soup, use the ratio of 1 tablespoon each of butter and flour to 1 cup of liquid, and for a stew, 2 tablespoons each butter and flour to 1 cup of liquid. Turn the cooker to HIGH, stir the *beurre manié* into the hot liquid, re-cover, and cook until thick, 10 to 15 minutes, or cook a bit longer on LOW.

Butter used alone will thicken a soup or sauce slightly and, of course, will add lots of flavor. Add at the end of cooking and stir gently a few times.

Cornstarch is used like flour and produces a glossy, clear, thickened liquid. It is notorious for lumping, so always mix with some cold liquid to form a slurry first, then stir constantly while adding it to the hot liquid. Use 1 tablespoon of cornstarch mixed with 2 tablespoons water to thicken 1 cup of liquid. Turn the cooker to HIGH, stir it into the hot liquid, recover, and cook until thick, 10 to 15 minutes, or cook a bit longer on LOW.

Arrowroot also produces a glossy, clear, thickened liquid and has double the thickening power of flour. To use, it must be mixed with a cold liquid to form a slurry. Stir constantly while adding the slurry to the hot liquid. Use 1 tablespoon of arrowroot mixed with 2 tablespoons of water to thicken 2 cups of liquid. Turn the cooker to HIGH, stir the slurry into the hot liquid, re-cover, and cook until thick, 10 to 15 minutes, or cook a bit longer on LOW.

Whipping cream, sour cream, and *crème fraîche* are considered thickening agents when added at the end of the cooking time in whatever amount produces the desired flavor and consistency. Add these within the last 20 to 30 minutes of cooking to avoid curdling.

Reduction is a process you will see quite often in our recipes. To reduce a sauce in the slow cooker, simmer the contents with the lid off until its volume decreases and the flavor concentrates. We use the HIGH setting for this. Reduction will happen a lot more slowly in the cooker than on the stove top; one benefit is that the liquid is not likely to burn, though we recommend you stay close to the kitchen while reducing it. Slow cooker reduction is not for the cook in a hurry. Sometimes we call for a liquid to be transferred from the slow cooker to a saucepan and reduced quickly on the stove top.

Egg yolks and cream are, in combination, a traditional thickener and enrichment agent that should only be used at the end of the cooking time in slow-cooked recipes. Beat the egg yolks and cream in a small bowl. Add a few tablespoons of the hot liquid and whisk to warm the mixture so it won't curdle when added to the dish. Pour this mixture into the sauce or soup and keep the setting on LOW; cook for 15 to 20 minutes. For sauces, use 1 egg yolk with 2 to 3 tablespoons of cream for 1 cup of liquid if it is already thick; use 2 to 3 yolks for the same amount of cream if the sauce is very thin. For a soup, use 2 to 3 yolks with ¼ cup of cream for every 5 to 6 cups of liquid.

Vegetable purées are one of the oldest ways to bulk up and thicken a soup or stew. Add potatoes, a few tablespoons of split peas or lentils, tomatoes, zucchini (which cooks into a nice mush in the slow cooker), okra, or carrots in an amount that will give you the desired consistency. Rice or barley can be added too. We just add the appropriate vegetable (or grain) raw with the initial ingredients. Some spices, such as filé powder, used in gumbo, are traditionally added at the end of cooking for thickening as well.

From the Porridge Pot

One of the best ways to use your slow cooker is to let familiar, and not-so-familiar, grains cook slowly into creamy, nutritious porridges. When grains are cooked in water or milk, they become a porridge, a food that has sustained humans since they first gathered wild grains. Using the slow cooker allows you to have hot porridge waiting for you when you wake in the morning. Most of these recipes can be made in a small machine and serve one to four, but feel free to double

or triple any recipe and use a larger machine. Making granola in a large slow cooker was a wonderful surprise for us when we tested recipes; it turned out better than granola baked in the oven, with much less fuss and mess.

The secret to making excellent porridges is to use very fresh whole-grain cereals, such as rolled oats and bran. Be sure to get residue-free, organically grown whole grains every chance you get for the maximum health benefit. A commercial brand such as Arrowhead Mills' Bear Mush is an excellent alternative to processed farina, and McCann's Irish Oatmeal is an excellent alternative to Quaker. Look for real old-fashioned rolled oats, rather than quick-cooking varieties, as well as barley and wheat flakes. Steel-cut oats and the chopped groats known as Irish-cut or Scotch-cut, which can be intimidating to cook properly on the stove top, are transformed into creamy cereals with no fuss in the slow cooker. The cracked grain cereal combinations—blends that might include cracked wheat, rye, oats, barley, millet,

flaxseed, and corn—cook up beautifully with slow cooking.

A key to how cereals will cook is the way they are processed. If they are processed minimally, as are cracked grains, they will need more water (because they need to absorb more to soften) and a longer cooking time. Whole grains, with their bran and germ intact, will cook more slowly and take more water than grains that have been hulled and degermed, which explains the difference between brown and white rice in their cooking times and ratios of rice to water. Processed grains, such as rolled flakes, which are first steamed, then flattened by rollers, require less time and less water to cook into a smooth cereal, though thick-cut flakes will require more water and more time than the thinner ones.

Everyone has a personal preference when it comes to cereal; some like it smooth and loose, while others prefer it a bit stiff, so that the milk poured on it becomes a moat. Adjust these recipes to fit your individual tastes.

Jook (Chinese Breakfast Rice Soup)

Jook (pronounced juk) is a soothing, savory rice porridge. It is eaten for breakfast, as a late-night snack, or anytime a creamy and sustaining dish is in order. Also known as congee, it's a staple in China and has become an increasingly popular menu item in U.S. cities with substantial Chinese-American populations. Restaurants that specialize in *jook* offer a staggering variety of choices in ingredients and condiments. A uniquely Chinese-American tradition is to make a turkey *jook* the day after Thanksgiving. This recipe, from food writer Elaine Corn, is one of her breakfast staples. It cooks on LOW from 10:00 P.M. to 6:00 A.M., so it is hot and ready for a satisfying breakfast. The magic of the slow cooker makes a *jook* so creamy you don't need to finish it off with milk, but it is an option at the end of all the cooking to add 1 cup of plain soy milk for extra whiteness and a velvety consistency. ○ *Serves 4 to 6*

COOKER: Medium or large round

SETTINGS AND COOK TIMES: LOW for 8 to 9 hours, then HIGH for 1 to 1½ hours (final HIGH period is optional)

1 cup Calrose rice (medium grain), or a premium Japanese-style rice such as Nishiki

2 tablespoons vegetable oil

10 cups chicken or turkey broth

2 teaspoons salt

About 1 tablespoon finely minced cilantro stems

1 cup plain soy milk (optional)

FOR SERVING:

Chopped fresh cilantro leaves

Minced green onions

Oyster sauce, soy sauce, and/or any hot pepper sauce, such as *sriracha* or Tabasco

1. Wash the rice in a colander until the water runs clear. Soak in water to cover about 30 minutes.

2. Meanwhile, heat the oil in the slow cooker set on HIGH. Drain, rinse, and drain the rice one last time. Add the rice to the hot oil and cook, stirring, until the rice is well coated with oil and smells toasty, about 5 minutes. Add the stock all at once, then the salt and cilantro stems. Stir well, cover, turn the cooker to LOW, and cook, 8 to 9 hours, or overnight.

3. To finish the *jook,* stir it well because the liquid and rice may have separated. If you want your *jook* thicker, turn the cooker to HIGH, cover, and cook for 1 to 1½ hours more, stirring now and then. The soup will become thick and white. Add the soy milk now, if desired, for an ultra-creamy consistency.

4. To serve, set out small bowls of chopped cilantro leaves and minced green onion with a choice of oyster sauce, soy sauce, and hot sauce.

Congee

ongee is another regional name for *jook,* a staple savory breakfast rice porridge similar to Indian *kitchari.* It is very bland on its own, but congee is usually served with all manner of savory toppings, including wontons, pork meatballs, or shredded duck. Our own recipe is served more simply, with soy sauce or hot sauce. ○ *Serves 4*

COOKER: Medium round
SETTINGS AND COOK TIMES: HIGH for 30 minutes to 1 hour, LOW for 8 to 9 hours, then HIGH for 1 to 1½ hours (final HIGH period is optional)

¾ cup Calrose rice (medium grain), or a premium Japanese-style rice such as Nishiki or Tamaki Gold
8 cups water or vegetable broth
1 teaspoon salt

FOR SERVING:
Soy sauce
Hot pepper sauce, such as Tabasco

1. Wash the rice in a colander until the water runs clear. Soak in water to cover for about 30 minutes.

2. Drain the rice, then place the rice, water or broth, and salt in the slow cooker. Stir well, cover, and cook on HIGH for 30 minutes to 1 hour to bring to a boil.

3. Turn the cooker to LOW and cook for 7 to 8 hours, or overnight.

4. Stir the congee well. If the rice is not thick and creamy, turn the cooker back to HIGH, stir well because the liquid and rice may have separated, cover, and cook for another 30 minutes. The soup will become thick and white. Serve with soy sauce and hot sauce.

Old-Fashioned Oatmeal

O atmeal made in the slow cooker overnight is creamy, nourishing, and, most importantly, ready when you are. No early-morning fumbling for the measuring cups required. The earliest riser in the family can grab a bowl full, then replace the slow cooker lid to keep the rest of the oatmeal warm for the late sleepers. Be sure to use old-fashioned rolled oats in this recipe, not the quick-cooking type. ○ *Serves 4*

COOKER: Small or medium round
SETTING AND COOK TIME: LOW for 7 to 9 hours, or HIGH for 2 to 3 hours

2 cups old-fashioned rolled oats or thick-cut rolled oats
4¾ cups water
Pinch of salt

1. Combine the oats, water, and salt in the slow cooker; stir to combine. Cover and cook on LOW for 7 to 9 hours, or overnight, or on HIGH for 2 to 3 hours.

2. Stir the oatmeal well and scoop into bowls with an oversized spoon. Serve with milk, buttermilk, or cream, a sprinkle of toasted wheat germ, brown sugar, and a sprinkle of cinnamon.

Blueberry Oatmeal: Add 1 cup of fresh blueberries, picked over for stems, or thawed and drained individually frozen blueberries, during the last 30 minutes of cooking.

Orange Oatmeal: Add ¼ cup of coarsely chopped candied orange peel and 2 tablespoons thawed orange juice concentrate to the cooker with all the other ingredients.

Mixed Grain Oatmeal: Add 1 cup of cooked white or brown rice to the oatmeal either at the beginning or during the last 30 minutes of cooking.

Cinnamon Apple Oatmeal

There is no one right way to eat oatmeal—the fun is that you can have it any ol' way you please. The combination of fresh apples and oatmeal is one delicious way to have your fruit and grains in the morning. If you cook the apple the entire time, it will blend into the oatmeal; if you prefer to have some chunks of fruit, add it during the last 30 minutes of cooking. ❍ *Serves 2*

COOKER: Small round
SETTING AND COOK TIME: LOW for 7 to 9 hours, or HIGH for 2 to 3 hours

1 cup old-fashioned rolled oats or thick-cut rolled oats
2 tablespoons light or dark brown sugar
½ to ¾ teaspoon ground cinnamon, to your taste
Pinch of salt
2½ cups water, or a combination of water and apple juice
1½ tablespoons unsalted butter
1 medium-size apple or pear, peeled, cored, and chopped

1. Combine all the ingredients in the slow cooker. Cover and cook on LOW for 7 to 9 hours, or overnight, or on HIGH for 2 to 3 hours.

2. Stir the oatmeal well and scoop into bowls with an oversized spoon. Serve with milk or cream.

Hot Oatmeal and Rice

The rolled oats make for a creamy cereal, while steel-cut oats will make it a bit heartier. ❍ *Serves 4*

COOKER: Small round
SETTING AND COOK TIME: LOW for 7 to 9 hours

1 cup old-fashioned or thick-cut rolled oats, or steel-cut oats
1 cup short-grain brown rice
2 tablespoons oat bran or toasted wheat germ

Pinch of fine sea salt

5 cups water

1. Combine all the ingredients in the slow cooker. Cover and cook on LOW for 7 to 9 hours, or overnight.

2. Stir the cereal well and scoop into bowls with an oversized spoon. Serve with milk, soy milk, or light cream and honey.

Overnight Steel-Cut Oatmeal

One of the most popular ways to use a slow cooker is to prepare steel-cut oatmeal. Steel-cut oat nibs, also marketed as Irish or Scottish oats, are whole groats cut into two or three chunks. They are notorious for the long soaking and cooking times required to soften them properly, which makes them perfect for the slow cooker. These proportions make a moderately thick porridge; if you like it thicker, cut back the water by ½ to 1 cup the next time you make it. This is the oatmeal the Scottish eat with a glass of cold ale or stout or drizzled with single-malt Scotch and brown sugar. We in America like it with a pat of butter, clover honey or pure maple syrup, and cream. ☉ *Serves 2*

COOKER: Small round

SETTING AND COOK TIME: LOW for 8 to 9 hours

1 cup steel-cut oats

4 cups water

1. Combine the oats and water in the slow cooker. Cover and cook on LOW for 8 to 9 hours, or overnight, until tender.

2. Stir the oatmeal well and scoop into bowls with an oversized spoon. Serve with milk or cream and brown sugar or maple syrup.

Overnight Nutty Steel-Cut Oatmeal: If you like to dress up your oatmeal, stir in ¼ cup of toasted sunflower seeds, chopped walnuts, pecans, or almonds at the end of cooking.

Creamy Oatmeal with Dried Fruit

Food writer John Thorne wrote a fun article called "Splendor in the Pot," a little treatise on oatmeal, for his *Simple Cooking* magazine. He calls his metal canister of McCann's Irish oatmeal the means to making an honest batch of cereal. Thorne thinks a bowl of instant oatmeal and oatmeal made from steel-cut oats are miles apart in taste, just like the taste difference between a cup of instant coffee and one that is freshly brewed. This oatmeal, chock-full of dried fruit, is so good you can refrigerate any left over, then cut it into little squares and serve it with whipped cream for dessert. ● *Serves 3*

COOKER: Small round
SETTING AND COOK TIME: LOW for 8 to 9 hours

1 cup steel-cut oats
⅔ cup dried tart cherries or sweetened dried cranberries
⅓ cup chopped dried figs
⅓ cup chopped dried apricots
4½ cups water
½ cup half-and-half or evaporated milk

1. Combine all the ingredients in the slow cooker. Cover and cook on LOW for 8 to 9 hours, or overnight, until tender.

2. Serve the oatmeal straight from the pot with no embellishment but a light sprinkling of sea salt, a pat of butter, and milk.

Maple Oatmeal with Dried Fruit and Sweet Spices

Here is another fabulous overnight oatmeal made with steel-cut oats. It is strong on the spice, so cut back to ½ teaspoon if you would like just a whisper. If you prefer a richer flavor, toast the oats on a baking sheet at 350°F for 15 minutes, stirring occasionally. ○ *Serves 2*

COOKER: Small round
SETTING AND COOK TIME: LOW for 7 to 9 hours

1 cup steel-cut oats
½ cup raisins or dried cherries, dried blueberries, or sweetened dried cranberries
1 teaspoon apple pie spice, or ground cinnamon mixed with a pinch of ground cloves, nutmeg, and allspice
4 cups water
2 tablespoons pure maple syrup or granulated maple sugar, plus extra for serving

1. Combine all the ingredients in the slow cooker. Cover and cook on LOW for 7 to 9 hours, or overnight.

2. Stir the oatmeal well and scoop into bowls with an oversized spoon. Serve with milk and maple syrup or sugar.

Rebecca's Rustic Whole Oat Porridge

Oat groats, the whole kernels of oats, are a lot more robust in flavor than rolled or steel-cut oats and make a wonderful hearty breakfast cereal. From natural foods maven and cookbook writer Rebecca Wood comes this recipe for an old-fashioned proper pot of porridge. Serve with milk and honey or maple syrup, or fresh fruit sautéed in unsalted butter with a sprinkle of sugar and lemon juice. ○ *Serves 2 to 3*

COOKER: Small round

SETTING AND COOK TIME: LOW for 7 to 9 hours

1 cup oat groats
Pinch of fine sea salt
One 4-inch cinnamon stick
4¼ cups water

1. Combine all the ingredients in the slow cooker. Cover and cook on LOW for 7 to 9 hours, or overnight. (If you have the time, set the cooker to HIGH for 1 to 2 hours to start the cooking; this is optional.)

2. Discard the cinnamon stick. Stir the porridge well and scoop into bowls with an oversized spoon.

Hot Barley Breakfast Cereal

B arley has a chewy texture and a sweet flavor with a mild malty aftertaste. Food writer Elizabeth Schneider describes it as having hints of "autumn leaves and lemon rind." Rolled barley flakes, made from toasted hulled pearl barley, are nice and thick and are best cooked for a long time over low heat, making them a satisfying alternative to rolled oats. ● *Serves 4*

COOKER: Small or medium round

SETTING AND COOK TIME: LOW for 7 to 9 hours

2 cups old-fashioned rolled barley flakes
Pinch of fine sea salt
4½ cups water

1. Combine the ingredients in the slow cooker. Cover and cook on LOW for 7 to 9 hours, or overnight.

2. Stir the cereal well and scoop into bowls with an oversized spoon. Serve with milk or soy milk and maple syrup, honey, or brown sugar.

We have learned to appreciate the subtle art of combining our own cereal mixtures. Store mixtures in quart or half-gallon spring-top jars (they look nice on the counter), or plastic buckets with airtight lids (inside the cupboard). These are breakfast cereals par excellence.

Hot Apple Granola ○ Makes about 5½ dry cups

1½ cups steel-cut oats

1 cup cracked wheat

1 cup cracked rye

1 cup barley grits

1 cup minced dried apples

¾ cup dried currants

2 teaspoons ground cinnamon or apple pie spice

In a large bowl, combine all the ingredients; mix well. Store in a covered container or plastic bag at room temperature. Use in any recipe calling for steel-cut oats.

Four-Grain Cereal Flakes ○ Makes about 5 dry cups

1 cup old-fashioned or thick-cut rolled oats (not quick cooking)

1 cup rolled wheat

1 cup rye flakes

1 cup old-fashioned rolled barley flakes

In a large bowl, combine all the ingredients; mix well. Store in a covered container or plastic bag at room temperature. Use in any recipe calling for rolled oats.

Vanilla Barley Porridge

This is a gussied-up version of our plain overnight Hot Barley Breakfast Cereal (page 32). To get at the vanilla bean seeds, use a sharp paring knife and slit the bean (which is actually the seed pod) in half lengthwise; we like to leave it attached at one end for easy handling. The flavorful seeds will leak out into the porridge. ○ *Serves 3 to 4*

COOKER: Small round

SETTING AND COOK TIME: LOW for 7 to 9 hours

1½ cups old-fashioned rolled barley flakes

2 tablespoons honey

Pinch of salt

4 cups water

1 tablespoon unsalted butter

½ vanilla bean

FOR SERVING:

Sliced bananas

Toasted almonds

1. Combine the barley, honey, salt, water, and butter in the slow cooker. Split the vanilla bean with the point of a small sharp knife; scrape out the seeds. Add the pod and seeds to the cooker and stir. Cover and cook on LOW for 7 to 9 hours, or overnight.

2. Remove the vanilla pod. Stir the cereal well and scoop into bowls with an oversized spoon. Serve with milk or cream and top with sliced bananas and toasted almonds.

Creamy Rice Porridge with Raisins

T his is an Americanized version of congee, so it is served sweet with milk and dried fruit. You must use a medium- or short-grain rice so that there is enough starch to make the cereal creamy. ○ *Serves 3*

COOKER: Small round

SETTING AND COOK TIME: LOW for 6 to 8 hours

1 cup medium-grain rice, such as Calrose, or short-grain rice, such as Arborio

2 cups water

1½ cups evaporated skim milk

½ teaspoon salt

½ cup raisins

1. Combine all the ingredients in the slow cooker. Cover and cook on LOW until tender and creamy, 6 to 8 hours or overnight.

2. Stir the porridge well and serve straight from the pot with no embellishment.

Creamy Cornmeal Porridge

C ornmeal is unique in flavor and texture, and there is no substitute for it. It bakes up into breads with a sandy texture in the form of johnnycakes, corn sticks, corn muffins, and skillet corn bread, which are the most familiar ways to eat cornmeal. Here we jump back over the centuries and make new an old-fashioned cornmeal mush, a cereal that has been sustaining peoples all over the globe for centuries. It is best moistened with tangy buttermilk and is also good with tart cheeses, such as goat cheese and Monterey Jack. Here we recommend you try mascarpone or cream cheese, stirred in until it melts; then top the porridge with berries. ❍ *Serves 2*

COOKER: Small round
SETTING AND COOK TIME: LOW for 7 to 9 hours

½ cup coarse cornmeal, polenta, or corn grits, stone-ground if possible
2 cups water
Pinch of salt
½ cup evaporated milk

1. Combine all the ingredients in the slow cooker. Cover and cook on LOW for 7 to 9 hours, or overnight. Stir a few times with a whisk or wooden spoon, if possible, during cooking.

2. Stir the porridge well and scoop into bowls with an oversized spoon. Serve with a pat of butter, milk, and a sprinkle of toasted wheat germ; or stir in cream cheese or mascarpone and top with berries.

Sweet Breakfast Grits

Sometimes called hominy grits, corn grits (or cornmeal grits) are not ground from hominy, but rather from plain dried corn. Cornmeal grits are fantastic with apples, pears, peaches, and all tart berries, from raspberries to cranberries. As a cooked mush, it is good sweetened with honey, maple syrup, or molasses. We think cornmeal goes with just about everything except chocolate.

○ *Serves 2*

COOKER: Small round
SETTING AND COOK TIME: LOW for 7 to 9 hours

½ cup corn grits, stone-ground if possible
2 cups water
Pinch of salt
3 tablespoons honey or pure maple syrup
Sliced fruit or berries for serving

1. Combine the grits, water, and salt in the slow cooker. Cover and cook on LOW for 7 to 9 hours, or overnight.

2. Stir the grits a few times during cooking with a whisk and stir in the honey just before serving. Stir well and scoop into bowls with an oversized spoon. Serve with milk and sliced fruit or berries.

Millet Porridge with Dates

Millet *(Setaria italica)* has a long history in the culinary world, though today it is almost an invisible grain. It makes a rare appearance, however, as one of the key ingredients in seven- and nine-grain whole-cereal blends. Millet has a mildly nutty taste and is very easy to digest. Food writer Elizabeth Schneider describes its flavor as having "a hint of cashew and corn." It is bright gold in color and becomes fluffy and soft when cooked. If your batch has a few dark specks, they are unhulled grains that escaped the hulling process. Millet has a natural affinity for dates, which we add here for sweetness. ○ *Serves 4*

COOKER: Small round
SETTING AND COOK TIME: LOW for 7 to 9 hours

1 cup cracked or whole millet
3½ cups water
Pinch of salt
½ cup evaporated milk, whole milk, or light cream
¼ to ½ cup chopped pitted dates, to your taste

1. Combine the millet, water, and salt in the slow cooker. Cover and cook on LOW for 7 to 9 hours, or overnight. Stir a few times with a whisk during cooking.

2. Turn the cooker to HIGH and stir in the milk and dates; cover and cook until hot, 5 to 10 minutes.

3. Stir the porridge well and scoop into bowls with an oversized spoon. Serve with milk and honey.

Cracked Wheat Porridge

C racked wheat is a fine, medium, or coarse cut of a whole wheat kernel with the bran removed. It is different from bulgur wheat, which is parboiled, and dried cracked wheat. An important ingredient in mixed grain cereals, cracked wheat is often overlooked as a breakfast porridge by itself. If you decide to substitute a multigrain blend in this recipe, you will get a mixture of wheat, rye, barley, triticale, corn, oats, flax, millet, brown rice, wheat germ, wheat bran, and soy grits, in varying proportions. But the rich, nutty flavor of plain cracked wheat is something you will want to try at least once as a hot cereal. ○ *Serves 4*

COOKER: Small round
SETTING AND COOK TIME: LOW for 7 to 9 hours, or HIGH for 2½ to 3 hours

1 cup fine cracked wheat, bulgur wheat, or a 5- or 7-grain hot cereal blend

3 cups water

Pinch of salt

1. Place the cracked wheat in a dry skillet and toast over medium heat until you can just smell the aroma, about 5 minutes.

2. Combine the wheat, water, and salt in the slow cooker. Cover and cook until tender on LOW for 7 to 9 hours (the cracked wheat will take longer to cook than the bulgur), or overnight, or on HIGH for 2½ to 3 hours. Stir a few times with a whisk during cooking.

3. Scoop into bowls with an oversized spoon. Serve with milk and brown sugar or honey.

Cracked Wheat Cereal Cooked in Apple Juice

This is a variation on plain cracked wheat cereal. It is made with apple juice (instead of water), dried apples, and sweet spices. The cereal has an excellent flavor and will fill the kitchen with an incredible aroma while slow cooking. ○ *Serves 4*

COOKER: Small round

SETTING AND COOK TIME: LOW for 7 to 9 hours

1 cup fine cracked wheat or bulgur wheat

4 cups apple juice

3 tablespoons honey

2 tablespoons unsalted butter

Pinch of salt

½ teaspoon ground cinnamon

¼ teaspoon ground cardamom

½ cup chopped dried apples

1. Put the cracked wheat in a dry skillet and toast over medium heat until you can just smell the aroma, about 5 minutes.

2. Combine the wheat, apple juice, honey, butter, salt, cinnamon, cardamom, and dried apples in the slow cooker. Cover and cook on LOW for 7 to 9 hours, or overnight, until tender (the cracked wheat will take longer to cook than the bulgur, which is parboiled). Stir a few times with a whisk during cooking.

3. Stir the cereal well and scoop into bowls with an oversized spoon. Serve with milk, cream, or soy milk.

Farina Porridge

S emolina is the ground endosperm of cream-colored durum wheat, and in its most familiar guise, it is the flour used extensively in pasta making. Durum is also a delicious, high-protein wheat used for a coarse meal, similar to coarse cornmeal, known as farina. Semolina meal may not sound familiar to you, but Cream of Wheat and Wheatina most certainly will. Cream of Wheat is ground from the endosperm only, while Wheatina is ground from whole-grain durum wheat. There are alternatives available in health food stores, such as Roman Meal and Bear Mush, which are farina ground from whole red winter wheat. When you cook farina overnight in the slow cooker, you will have the creamiest version ever. ○ *Serves 4*

COOKER: Small round
SETTING AND COOK TIME: LOW for 7 to 9 hours

½ **cup Cream of Wheat farina**
⅓ **cup wheat cereal, such as Wheatena**
4½ **cups water**
Pinch of salt

1. Combine all the ingredients in the slow cooker. Cover and cook on LOW for 7 to 9 hours, or overnight, until creamy. Stir a few times with a whisk, if possible, during cooking.

2. Scoop into bowls with an oversized spoon and serve with milk and brown sugar.

Your Own Blend Overnight Porridge

o to the health food store and pick some whole grains, maybe even ones you have never tried before, and mix them together into a hot breakfast cereal. This cooks overnight, nice and easy. ○ *Serves 6*

COOKER: Medium round
SETTING AND COOK TIME: LOW for 8 to 9 hours

½ **cup steel-cut oats**
½ **cup short-grain brown rice or mixed fancy rice blend**
½ **cup millet**
½ **cup whole-grain barley**
⅓ **cup wild rice**
¼ **cup polenta (coarse cornmeal) or corn grits**
3 **tablespoons ground or whole flaxseed**
½ **teaspoon salt**
7 **cups water**

1. Combine all the ingredients in the slow cooker. Cover and cook on LOW for 8 to 9 hours, or overnight, until tender.

2. Stir well and scoop into bowls with an oversized spoon. Serve with milk or cream and brown sugar or maple syrup.

Old-Fashioned Almond and Coconut Granola

he secret to making great tasting granola is to use very fresh, high-quality rolled oats. You will want to make a nice big batch so that you only have to do it once in a while. Granola takes a good couple of hours in a conventional oven, but plan on 4 to 6 hours in the slow cooker. Except for a bit of stirring needed at the very start, the granola, surprisingly, bakes in the crock more evenly than in the oven, without the danger of overbrowning (which does not make for good-tasting granola). Store in an airtight plastic container or jars with screw-on lids in the cupboard, where it will await breakfasters or afternoon munchers. For longer storage, freeze the granola. You will need a large slow cooker to make this recipe, or else halve the recipe for a medium-size cooker. ○ *Makes about 12 cups*

COOKER: Large round or oval
SETTINGS AND COOK TIMES: HIGH for 2 hours, then LOW for 4 to 6 hours

WET INGREDIENTS:
½ cup mild honey, warmed for easier pouring
1 cup cold-pressed organic canola oil or sunflower seed oil
2 teaspoons pure vanilla extract
1 teaspoon pure almond extract

DRY INGREDIENTS:
6 cups old-fashioned rolled oats (1 pound, not quick cooking)
1 cup raw sunflower seeds
1 cup unsweetened shredded coconut (available in health food stores; check the freezer section)
1 cup slivered blanched almonds
1 cup raw wheat germ (4 ounces)
1 cup instant nonfat dry milk
½ cup firmly packed light brown sugar

1. Place the wet ingredients in the slow cooker and set it on HIGH. Warm the mixture, uncovered, for 30 minutes to melt the honey, stirring with a whisk to combine well.

2. In a large bowl, combine all the dry ingredients and stir to evenly distribute. Add one-third of the dry ingredients to the warm mixture and stir until evenly moistened with a heat-resistant spatula or wooden spoon. Slowly add the remaining dry ingredients, stirring constantly so that all of it is evenly moistened. Continue to cook on HIGH, uncovered, for exactly 1½ hours, stirring every 30 minutes for even toasting.

3. Turn the cooker to LOW, cover, and cook the granola until dry and a very light golden color, 4 to 6 hours, stirring every hour or so for even cooking. When done, the granola will slide off a spatula or spoon.

4. Turn off the cooker, remove the lid, and let the granola cool completely at room temperature; it will become crispier as it cools. Transfer to a tightly covered container, where it will keep for up to a month.

Maple Oat Granola with Dried Cranberries

 This is a dark amber, deeply flavored, low-fat cereal.

○ *Makes about 10 cups*

COOKER: Large round or oval
SETTINGS AND COOK TIMES: HIGH for 2 hours, then LOW for 4 to 6 hours

WET INGREDIENTS:
¾ cup pure maple syrup
½ cup water
¼ cup firmly packed light brown sugar
¼ cup cold-pressed organic canola oil or sunflower seed oil

DRY INGREDIENTS:
6 cups old-fashioned rolled oats (1 pound, not quick cooking)
1 cup raw sunflower seeds
½ cup raw pumpkin seeds
½ cup raw oat bran

1 cup honey-toasted wheat germ (4 ounces)
1½ cups sweetened dried cranberries
½ cup chopped dried apricots
3 tablespoons raw sesame seeds

1. Put the wet ingredients in the slow cooker and set on HIGH; stir with a whisk to combine well.

2. In a large bowl, combine all the dry ingredients and stir to evenly distribute. Add one-third of the dry ingredients to the warm mixture; stir until evenly moistened with a heat-resistant spatula or wooden spoon. Slowly add the remaining dry ingredients, stirring constantly so that all of it is evenly moistened. Continue to cook on HIGH, uncovered, for exactly 1½ hours, stirring every 30 minutes.

3. Turn the cooker to LOW, cover, and cook until the granola is dry and a very light golden color, 4 to 6 hours, stirring every hour or so for even cooking. When done, it will slide off a spatula or spoon.

4. While the granola is hot, stir in the wheat germ, dried cranberries, apricots, and sesame seeds. Let cool completely; the mixture will become crispier as it cools. Transfer to a tightly covered container, where it will keep for up to a month.

The Slow Cooker
Soup Pot

Whether it's a hearty bean or split pea soup, an exotically smooth cream soup, or a chunky vegetable soup, everyone loves home-made soup. They "light the inner fires," says soup and bread expert Bernard Clayton. Soups are the original comfort food and almost seem made for the slow cooker. There is a soup for every culture and cuisine in the world. They can be specially concocted over a few days, with special care given to the stock as well as the other ingredients, or tossed together from what is on hand. Some soups are filling enough to be a full meal, the one-pot solution for busy cooks.

Tips for the Best
Slow Cooker Soups

- As simple and easy as it is to prepare soups in the slow cooker, it is important not to overcook them to the point of becoming a murky mess with little flavor. Pay attention to the cooking time recommended in each recipe. This does not apply to making broth (pages 93–105), which can cook for longer periods of time.

- Take advantage of what's available and looks good at your market and make soups that complement the seasons. Use the freshest ingredients. Also, soups cook best if all the ingredients are cut to a uniform size so they cook evenly, so take the time needed for their proper preparation.

- Add water or broth to at least cover the solid ingredients in the slow cooker. Add boiling liquid to adjust the consistency at any time during the cooking. Take into account how much you wish to serve. Is this a first course soup (figure about one cup of soup per serving), or a family-style main dish (which can be two cups or more per serving)?

- Unless noted, we like the LOW setting best for soups, especially in the new slow cookers where the HIGH setting is a rather intense boil. LOW gives a slow simmer with a slight low boil. Why rush?

- Use herbs and spices sparingly and always taste for the seasonings at the end of cooking. Slow cookers tend to intensify flavorings.

- If you like, you can sweat some of the vegetables, such as onions and garlic, in butter or oil before adding them to the crock. This is a nice flavor addition, although optional.

- To purée soups, either use a handheld immersion blender stick (Beth's favorite kitchen tool), taking care not to hit the sides of the crock, or transfer the soup in batches to a food processor and pulse. With the immersion blender you will not have to remove the soup from the crock. Some soups, such as artichoke or asparagus, are best put through a coarse metal sieve since they have tough fibers.

Herbed Barley and Buttermilk Soup

his tangy, low-fat soup is an old favorite, adapted from a recipe in *Diet for a Small Planet* (Ballantine, 1975), one of the culinary bibles of the hippie generation. Cultured buttermilk adds body and rich flavor; fresh herbs provide the spark that takes this from ordinary to something special. Vary the herbs based on your preference and what is in season. ○ *Serves 4 to 6*

COOKER: Medium round
SETTINGS AND COOK TIMES: LOW for 5 to 6 hours, then HIGH for 30 minutes

2 tablespoons unsalted butter
2 large yellow onions, chopped
1 cup chopped celery
¾ cup pearl barley, rinsed and drained
4 cups water
2 cups buttermilk
Salt and freshly ground black pepper to taste
¼ cup minced fresh herbs, such as cilantro, tarragon, chives, dill, thyme,
    or parsley, or a combination

1. Heat the butter in a large skillet over medium heat. When it is melted, add the onions and celery and cook, stirring occasionally, until the celery has softened and the onion is lightly browned, about 10 minutes. Transfer to the slow cooker. Add the barley and water; stir to combine. Cover and cook on LOW until the barley is very tender, 5 to 6 hours.

2. Stir in the buttermilk. Cover and cook on HIGH until the soup is thoroughly hot, about 30 minutes longer. Season with salt and pepper. Just before serving, stir in half the herbs. Sprinkle the remaining herbs over the individual bowls as a garnish.

Finishing Touches and Garnishes ·· for Slow Cooker Soups

You can choose to garnish a soup or not. Garnishes can be sprinkled or spooned on for visual effect, but they can also add another element of flavor and texture, such as toasted almonds or a chunky tomato salsa.

○ For thick soups, use croutons (page 69); grated or shredded cheese, such as Parmesan or cheddar; snipped fresh chives; chopped red or green onions; chopped fresh flat-leaf parsley, watercress, or arugula; edible, unsprayed flower blossoms, such as nasturtiums; thin slices of lemon or lime; shredded meat or poultry; chunky salsa; chopped fresh vegetables; or frizzled (fried) leeks, onions, or shallots.

○ For cream soups, use toasted almonds or pine nuts; snipped fresh chives or green onions; chopped fresh flat-leaf parsley; or dollops of sour cream, *crema Mexicana,* or crème fraîche.

○ For clear soups, choose from strips of freshly made crêpes, croutons, dumplings, or gnocchi; snipped fresh chives or green onions; chopped fresh flat-leaf parsley; chunks of tofu; or slices of avocado or lemon.

Mary Moo's Green Split Pea and Barley Soup

B eth's friend Mary Cantori is a primary school teacher, and Thursday is her day to use the slow cooker. She leaves the house at seven in the morning and returns at seven in the evening to a kitchen gratefully filled with the warm, savory aroma of ready-to-eat split pea soup. She adjusts the herbs, gathered from her prodigious backyard garden, perhaps cooks some chicken apple sausage to add, and dinner is on the table. Bragg's Liquid Aminos is a vegetarian stock substitute available in natural food stores. ○ *Serves 6*

COOKER: Medium round
SETTING AND COOK TIME: LOW for 10½ to 12½ hours; salt, pepper, marjoram, and sausage added during last 30 minutes

1 pound dried green split peas

2 tablespoons olive oil

1 medium-size yellow onion, finely chopped

1 rib celery, chopped

1 medium-size carrot, minced

¾ cup pearl barley, rinsed and drained

2 to 3 tablespoons Bragg's Liquid Aminos

2 tablespoons chicken or vegetable bouillon powder

1 teaspoon garlic powder

¼ teaspoon cayenne pepper

Salt and freshly ground black pepper to taste

1 to 2 tablespoons chopped fresh marjoram, to your taste

4 to 8 ounces chicken apple sausage (optional), to your taste, browned in
   a sauté pan or under the broiler, and sliced

1. Put the split peas in a colander and rinse under cold running water. Pick over, discarding any that are discolored. Soak them overnight in enough cold water to cover by 2 inches at room temperature; drain well and put in the slow cooker.

2. In a large skillet, heat the olive oil over medium heat. Add the onion, celery, and carrot and cook, stirring a few times, until just softened, about 5 minutes. Put in the cooker along with the barley, Bragg's Liquid Aminos, bouillon powder, garlic powder, and cayenne. Add water to come about 3 inches above the vegetables. Cover and cook on LOW for 10 to 12 hours.

3. Season with salt and pepper, then stir in the marjoram and sausage, if using. Add water to thin if the soup is too thick. Cover and continue to cook on LOW for another 30 minutes, or until the sausage is heated through. Ladle into serving bowls and serve hot.

Vegetarian Split Pea Soup

If you've ever driven California's highways, you've seen Pea Soup Andersen's restaurants, or at least the billboards advertising them. We always think of those billboards when we make this soup, which is similar to his restaurants'. It is creamy, savory, and can be cooking away in your slow cooker in no time. For a really smooth purée, put the finished soup through a fine-mesh strainer before serving. ○ *Serves 4 to 6*

COOKER: Medium or large round
SETTING AND COOK TIME: LOW for 12 to 15 hours

1 cup dried green split peas
5 cups water
⅔ cup chopped shallots (2 to 3 medium-size)
1 cup chopped carrots
1 cup chopped celery
1 bay leaf
½ teaspoon dried thyme or 1½ teaspoons chopped fresh thyme
¼ teaspoon dried sage or 1 teaspoon chopped fresh sage (optional)
Salt to taste
Dash of cayenne pepper
Warm bread or croutons for serving

1. Put the split peas in a colander and rinse under cold running water. Pick over, discarding any that are discolored. Put in the slow cooker along with the water, shallots, carrots, celery, bay leaf, thyme, and sage, if using. Stir to combine. Cover and cook on LOW until the peas are completely tender, 12 to 15 hours. Remove the bay leaf.

2. Purée the soup, using a blender, food processor, immersion blender, or the fine blade of a food mill. You may need to do this in batches. Season the soup with salt (start with about ¼ teaspoon) and a just a bit of cayenne pepper. Serve hot with warm bread or croutons.

Amy's Split and Fresh Pea Soup: Near the end of cooking, add 2 heaping cups thawed frozen petite peas. When cooked, purée everything together as directed above.

Seasonal Dal Soup

We met cooking entrepreneur and caterer Pat Li when she invited us to a catered dinner at her demonstration kitchen and private dining room. She cooked a 12-course tasting meal that featured her blend of French technique with classical Chinese dishes. Married to an Indian, she also cooks Indian food, and here is her version of dal soup. Pat keeps her soup simple. "Don't abuse ingredients," she said, "and save the complex dishes for special occasions." Pat uses different dals in winter and summer, combining two or three to blend the textures, flavors, and colors; some dals are more bland, some rather small, others larger and starchier. Nice combinations include equal parts of *moong, urad,* and *toovar* dals, or *moong* and *chana* dal (all of these split dals are prehusked and easy to cook without soaking). Look in the bins at your Indian grocery for dals of uniform color that aren't shriveled and experiment with the combinations, making sure that whatever you pick ends up equaling 1 cup for this recipe. Vary the recipe by adding a bunch of fresh spinach or Swiss chard and a clove of garlic, or 1 very small head of cauliflower and 1 cup of fresh peas, or cubed potatoes and frozen thawed petite peas or okra, or use 2 tomatoes and add some red pepper flakes and chopped fresh dill. Serve with basmati, plain Patna, Texmati, or brown rice. We like whole wheat paratha flatbread, which is flakier, richer, and more buttery than a plain chapati. This dal soup is great to cook when you have a cold or flu. ○ *Serves 4 to 5*

COOKER: Medium or Large round or oval
SETTING AND COOK TIME: LOW for 6 to 8 hours

½ cup *mansoor* dal
½ cup split *moong* dal
½ large ripe tomato, seeds squeezed out and chopped, or ¼ cup drained canned diced tomato
7 cups water
3 tablespoons olive oil, or half olive and half soy oil
1 medium-size red onion, chopped
1 jalapeño, seeded and chopped

1½ teaspoons cumin seeds
2 to 4 tablespoons minced fresh cilantro or
    fresh flat-leaf parsley, to your taste
Salt to taste

FOR SERVING:
Plain yogurt
Pure New Mexican chile powder
Lime wedges

1. Rinse the dals and remove any stones or debris. Combine the dals, tomato, and water in the slow cooker.

2. Add the olive oil to a medium-size warm skillet over medium heat and cook the onion, jalapeño, and cumin seeds, stirring, until the onion is softened and the cumin seeds are browned, about 5 minutes; add to the cooker. Cover and cook on LOW for 6 to 8 hours. The mixture will have the consistency of thin oatmeal.

3. Stir in the cilantro and taste for salt. Serve the soup in bowls poured over rice or alongside whole wheat flatbread. You can garnish with a dollop of yogurt, a sprinkle of red chile powder, and lime wedges if you like.

Kitchari

K itchari is a favorite Indian vegetarian breakfast porridge, although it is also often eaten after a fast, or with extremely simple foods to rest the digestive tract, clean out the accumulated toxins, and rejuvenate tissues. Recipes for it are included in every Indian cookbook. In Ayurvedic cuisine, it is known for restoring a systemic balance in all three *dosha* body types, the *vata, pitta,* and *kapha,* as it can be grounding, calming, and warming all at once. Call it the Indian version of mom's chicken soup, tasting like a cross between lentil soup and rice cereal. It is delicious, simple to make, and especially nice in winter. **o** *Serves 4*

COOKER: Medium round or oval
SETTING AND COOK TIME: LOW for 5 to 6½ hours; ginger-coconut purée
    and rice added at 4 to 5 hours

1¼ cups yellow split *moong* dal

6½ cups water

3 tablespoons unsalted butter

½ teaspoon ground cinnamon

¼ teaspoon ground cardamom

¼ teaspoon freshly ground black pepper,

¼ teaspoon ground cloves

¼ teaspoon turmeric

1 bay leaf

1 heaping tablespoon chopped fresh ginger

2 tablespoons unsweetened shredded coconut (available in health food stores; check the freezer section)

⅓ bunch chopped fresh cilantro

1 cup white basmati rice, rinsed

Salt to taste

Whole wheat tortillas or chapatis for serving

1. Rinse the dal and remove any stones or debris. Combine the dal and 6 cups of the water in the slow cooker.

2. In a medium-size skillet, melt the butter over medium heat. Add the ground spices; cook 1 to 2 minutes, stirring constantly, just to heat and gently toast them. Stir into the dal and add the bay leaf. Cover and cook on LOW for 4 to 5 hours. The mixture will be soupy.

3. In a blender or small food processor, combine the ginger, coconut, cilantro, and remaining ½ cup of water and process until smooth. Add to the cooker along with the rice, cover, and cook on LOW until the rice is tender, 1 to 1½ hours longer.

4. Remove the bay leaf and season with salt. Serve the soup hot in bowls with some warm whole wheat tortillas or chapatis.

Red Lentil Soup

D ried red lentils, also called Egyptian lentils, are a staple in Middle Eastern and Muslim Indian cooking. Since the delicate-looking dark pink lentil does not have its seed coat, the small lens-shaped pulse disintegrates into a smooth purée all on its own in cooking. Look for red lentils in well-stocked super-markets, natural food stores, and specialty stores. If you are shopping in an Indian grocery, look for *masoor* dal. Serve this spooned over a couple of tablespoons of hot basmati rice. ○ *Serves 6*

COOKER: Medium round
SETTINGS AND COOK TIMES: HIGH for 1 hour, then LOW for 5 to 6 hours

2 tablespoons olive oil
1 medium-size yellow onion (optional), finely chopped
2 ribs celery, chopped
2½ cups dried red lentils, picked over and rinsed (about 1 pound)
1 teaspoon ground cumin
1 teaspoon turmeric
¾ teaspoon ground coriander
2 tablespoons fresh lemon juice
6 cups chicken or vegetable broth
Salt and freshly ground black pepper (optional) to taste

1. In a large skillet, heat the olive oil over medium heat. Add the onion and celery and cook, stirring often, until just softened, about 5 minutes. Transfer to the slow cooker, along with the lentils, spices, and lemon juice. Add the broth and enough water to come about 3 inches above the vegetables. Cover and cook on HIGH for 1 hour.

2. Turn the cooker to LOW and cook the soup for 5 to 6 hours. Season with salt and pepper, if desired. Add water to thin if the soup is too thick. Ladle into bowls and serve hot.

Italian Lentil Soup

his is a brown lentil soup from our friend, Sharon Jones, fine sous chef and catering chef from Beth's old restaurant days at St. Michael's Alley in Palo Alto, California. It has the unusual addition of a bit of molasses to gently sweeten the pot at the end. ○ *Serves 6*

COOKER: Medium round

SETTING AND COOK TIME: LOW for 7 to 9 hours; onion, celery, carrots, and garlic added at 3 to 4 hours; wine, lemon juice, molasses, salt, and pepper added during last 30 minutes

3 cups dried brown lentils, picked over and rinsed

7 cups water or vegetable broth

2 tablespoons olive oil

2 tablespoons unsalted butter

1 medium-size yellow onion, finely chopped

2 ribs celery, finely chopped

2 medium-size carrots, finely chopped

2 teaspoons minced garlic

2 tablespoons dry red wine

2 tablespoons fresh lemon juice

1½ tablespoons light molasses or brown sugar

Salt and freshly ground black pepper to taste

FOR SERVING:

Chopped green onions

Red wine vinegar

1. Put the lentils and water in the slow cooker, cover, and cook on LOW for 3 to 4 hours.

2. In a medium-size skillet over medium heat, heat the oil and butter together until the butter melts. Add the onion, celery, and carrots and cook, stirring a few times, until just softened, about 5 minutes. Add the garlic and cook, stirring, another 2 minutes. Stir into the partially cooked lentils, cover, and continue to cook on LOW for another 3 to 4 hours.

3. Stir in the wine, lemon juice, and molasses. Season with salt and plenty of fresh black pepper. Add water to your taste to thin if the soup is too thick. Cover and continue to cook on LOW another 30 minutes.

4. Ladle into bowls and serve hot topped with chopped green onions and a drizzle of vinegar.

Lentil and Red Pepper Soup

This is a soup Julie first made when she was vacationing in the cool region of northwestern Spain called Galicia. It was the height of pepper season, and the heavy red globes were piled temptingly in all of the markets. After a long day of walking or enjoying the beach, this soup and a ring-shaped loaf of the chewy local bread were a warming supper. Use your best olive oil and fresh paprika for this: you want to taste both flavors. ○ *Serves 4 to 6*

COOKER: Medium or large round
SETTING AND COOK TIME: LOW for 7 to 9 hours

2 tablespoons extra virgin olive oil
1 small onion, finely chopped
4 to 6 cloves garlic, to your taste, finely chopped
1 teaspoon sweet paprika or *pimentón* (smoked paprika)
1 large or 2 medium-size red bell peppers, seeded and finely chopped
1 cup dried brown lentils, picked over and rinsed
5 cups water
2 teaspoons salt, or to taste
½ teaspoon freshly ground black pepper, or to taste
1 to 2 tablespoons sherry vinegar or red or white wine vinegar, to your taste

1. In a medium-size skillet, heat 1 tablespoon of the oil over medium heat. Add the onion and garlic and cook, stirring a few times, until they begin to soften, about 3 minutes. Reduce the heat if they begin to brown. Stir in the paprika and allow it to cook for about a minute more. Add the bell pepper and cook for 2 to 3 minutes, stirring a few times, until it just begins to soften. Use a heat-resistant rubber spatula to scrape the vegetables and oil into the slow cooker. Add the lentils and water and stir to combine. Cover and cook on LOW until the lentils are completely soft, 7 to 9 hours.

2. Season the soup with the salt and pepper and the remaining 1 tablespoon of olive oil. Stir in 1 tablespoon of the vinegar, adding more if needed. Serve hot ladled into soup bowls.

Old-Fashioned Bean and Lentil Soup from a Mix

T he supermarket bean section has an astonishing array of aromatic dried bean soup mixes packaged in boxes or pouches by various industrious culinary entrepreneurs. They are 12 to 16 ounces each and contain a variety of beans, split peas, lentils, and dried vegetables. The idea is you dump the contents into a medium-size stockpot or covered stoneware French *poterie,* add water, and *voilà,* in a few hours you have soup. No muss, no fuss. This recipe is suitable for one of those mixes. You can certainly use just the mix, but we like to add a bit more to the pot. ○ *Serves 4*

COOKER: Medium round

SETTINGS AND COOK TIMES: HIGH for 1 hour, then LOW for 8 to 10 hours; kale added at 4 to 5 hours

One 12- to 16-ounce commercial dried bean soup mix, picked over and rinsed
8 cups water or chicken or vegetable broth
¼ cup chopped fresh flat-leaf parsley
1 bouquet garni: 4 sprigs fresh flat-leaf parsley, 1 bay leaf, 1 or 2 sprigs fresh thyme, 1 sprig fresh tarragon, 10 black peppercorns, and 1 clove peeled garlic, wrapped up in cheesecloth and tied with kitchen twine
2 tablespoons olive oil
1 medium-size yellow onion, finely chopped
1 bunch kale, stems removed and leaves chopped
2 tablespoons dry white wine
2 tablespoons cider vinegar
1 teaspoon hot pepper sauce, such as Tabasco
Salt and freshly ground black pepper to taste

1. Combine the bean mix, water, parsley, and bouquet garni bag in the slow cooker. Cover and cook on HIGH for 1 hour.

2. Meanwhile, in a medium-size skillet, heat the oil over medium heat. Add the onion and cook, stirring a few times, until just softened, about 5 minutes. Add to the cooker, cover, turn the cooker to LOW, and cook the soup for 4 to 5 hours.

3. Add the kale and stir to incorporate (if you need to let the soup cook all day while you are gone, just add the kale at the beginning or substitute spinach and add at serving time). Cover and continue to cook on LOW until the beans are tender, another 4 to 5 hours.

4. Discard the bouquet garni. Stir in the wine, vinegar, and hot pepper sauce. Season with salt and plenty of fresh black pepper. If the soup is too thick, add boiling water to thin. Ladle into soup bowls and serve hot.

Old-Fashioned Black Bean Soup

Whereas black bean chili is a stick-to-your-ribs thick bean stew, black bean soup, made from scratch, is quite a bit thinner in consistency but every bit as soul satisfying. Black beans have a black skin, but after cooking there is a sweet, creamy interior that is so good you often cannot stop with one bowl full.

○ *Serves 6*

COOKER: Medium or large round
SETTINGS AND COOK TIMES: HIGH for 1 hour, then LOW for 7 to 8 hours;
 salt, pepper, and sherry added during last 15 minutes

1 pound dried black turtle beans, picked over, soaked overnight in water to cover, and drained
1 ham bone or ham hock
6 cups chicken broth or water
3 tablespoons unsalted butter
2 medium-size yellow onions, chopped
2 cloves garlic, minced
1 cup chopped celery, including some leaves
1 teaspoon dried marjoram
1 bay leaf
Salt to taste
¼ teaspoon freshly ground black pepper
½ cup dry sherry (optional)

1. Combine the drained beans, ham bone or hock, and broth in the slow cooker. Cover and cook on HIGH until boiling, about 1 hour.

2. Meanwhile, in a large skillet over medium heat, melt the butter. Add the onions, garlic, and celery and cook, stirring a few times, until softened, about 5 minutes. Add to the cooker along with the marjoram and bay leaf. Cover, turn the cooker to LOW, and cook the soup for 7 to 8 hours.

3. Stir in the salt, pepper, and sherry, cover, and continue to cook on LOW 15 minutes longer.

4. Discard the bay leaf and ham bone or hock, returning any bits of meat left on the bone to the soup. Purée in batches in a food processor or in the cooker with a handheld immersion blender. Taste to adjust the seasonings. Add some boiling water to thin, if desired. Ladle into soup bowls and serve hot.

Tomato–Black Bean Soup

his is a recipe from Beth's sister Amy, who loves black beans in any form, from chili to cold salad. She makes this thick, hearty soup in her 3-quart slow cooker. Toss it in the cooker early in the morning and it is ready for lunch. ○ *Serves 4 to 6*

COOKER: Medium round
SETTING AND COOK TIME: LOW for 5 to 7 hours

Two 15-ounce cans black beans, rinsed and drained
Two 4.5-ounce cans chopped roasted green chiles
One 14.5-ounce can Mexican stewed tomatoes with green chiles
One 14.5-ounce can diced tomatoes, with their juice
One 11-ounce can whole kernel corn, drained; 1½ cups frozen yellow or white baby corn,
    thawed; or 3 to 4 ears fresh corn, kernels cut off the cobs
4 green onions (white part and 2 inches of the green), sliced
2 cloves garlic, pressed
1 to 1½ tablespoons chili powder, to your taste
1 teaspoon ground cumin

FOR SERVING:
Shredded cheddar cheese
Sour cream

1. Put all the ingredients in the slow cooker and stir to combine. Cover and cook on LOW for 5 to 7 hours.

2. Add some boiling water to thin, if desired. Ladle into individual bowls and serve hot with a sprinkling of shredded cheddar cheese and a dollop of sour cream.

U.S. Senate Bean Soup

Hard to believe, but the U.S. Senate has its own dining room concession, and some of the dishes made there have been around for decades. This is one of the best. ○ *Serves 6*

COOKER: Large round
SETTINGS AND COOKING TIMES: HIGH for 1 hour, then LOW for 8 to 10 hours; parsley and pepper added during last 15 minutes

1 pound dried navy beans, picked over, soaked in water to cover overnight, and drained
1 large ham hock
10 cups water
2 medium-size yellow onions, minced
3 medium-size baking potatoes, peeled and cubed
6 ribs celery, including some leaves, finely chopped
⅓ cup chopped fresh flat-leaf parsley
¼ teaspoon freshly ground black pepper, or to taste
Salt to taste

1. Put the drained beans and ham hock in the slow cooker and cover with fresh cold water. Cover and cook on HIGH for 1 hour.

2. Drain, taking care not to splash yourself with the hot water, and add the 10 cups of water. Add the onions, potatoes, celery, and half the parsley. Cover, turn the cooker to LOW, and cook for 8 to 10 hours.

3. Stir in the remaining parsley and the pepper, season with salt, cover, and continue to cook on LOW 15 minutes longer.

4. Remove the ham hock, returning any bits of meat left on the bone to the soup; discard the bone. Ladle into soup bowls and serve hot with garlic bread.

White Bean Soup with Bacon

White bean soup is a staple main-course soup in Italian gastronomy and New England kitchens. Use navy or great northern beans, which are easily found on supermarket shelves. ○ *Serves 4 to 6*

COOKER: Medium or large round
SETTING AND COOK TIME: LOW for 8 to 9 hours; seasonings and
  cream added during last 15 minutes

2 cups dried navy or great northern beans, picked over, soaked in water
  to cover overnight, and drained
2 to 3 strips bacon, cooked until the fat is rendered but not crispy,
  drained on paper towel, and chopped; or 1 ham bone
1 small yellow onion, finely chopped
1 rib celery, minced
1 small carrot, minced
1 bouquet garni: ½ teaspoon dried oregano, 3 sprigs fresh flat-leaf parsley,
  ½ fresh sage leaf, and 1 bay leaf, wrapped in cheesecloth and tied with kitchen twine
6 cups chicken broth or water
Salt or tamari or another soy sauce to taste
¼ teaspoon freshly ground black pepper, or to taste
½ cup heavy cream (optional)

1. Combine the beans, bacon, onion, celery, carrot, bouquet garni, and broth in the slow cooker. Cover and cook on LOW for 8 to 9 hours.

2. Remove the bouquet garni and bone, if using, and discard. Purée about one-third of the soup in a food processor or with a handheld immersion blender. Season with salt, then add the pepper and cream, if using, cover, and continue to cook on LOW 15 minutes longer. Ladle into soup bowls and serve hot.

White Bean and Kale Tomato Soup

Beans and kale have a natural affinity for each other in soups and stews, and they are the basis for many Old World preparations. Since kale consists mostly of water, you can add it directly to the soup at the end of cooking. Kale leaves have lots of curly surfaces where grit can hide, so wash them well, as you would spinach. They have a wonderful sweet flavor that does not become bitter, as many greens do when added to soup broth. Remember that you might need a bit more cooking time if the kale is older and the leaves larger; kale will reduce to about one quarter of its volume when cooked. This soup is equally good with or without the sausage. ○ *Serves 4 to 6*

COOKER: Medium or large round
SETTING AND COOK TIME: LOW for 5½ to 7½ hours; kale and sausage added during last 20 to 30 minutes

Three 14-ounce cans vegetable broth
One 15-ounce can tomato purée
One 15-ounce can white, cannellini, or great northern beans, rinsed and drained
½ cup converted rice
1 medium-size yellow onion, chopped
2 cloves garlic, minced
2 teaspoons dried basil
Salt and freshly ground black pepper to taste
1 pound kale, stems removed and leaves coarsely cut on the diagonal
    into wide ribbons and coarsely chopped (8 packed cups)
1 pound sweet Italian sausage (optional), cooked all the way through
    in a sauté pan, cooled, and thickly sliced

FOR SERVING:
Finely shredded Parmesan cheese
Extra-virgin olive oil

1. Combine the broth, tomato purée, beans, rice, onion, garlic, and basil in the slow cooker, season with salt and pepper, and stir to blend. Cover and cook on LOW for 5 to 7 hours.

2. Stir in the kale and sausage, if using, cover, and continue to cook on LOW until the kale is limp and tender, another 20 to 30 minutes. When you add the kale, it will fill the cooker at first; you can add it in batches if you need to.

3. Ladle the soup into bowls and serve hot with Parmesan cheese and a drizzle of olive oil.

Zuppa Bastarda

Z uppa bastarda is one of the simplest and most traditional soups of Tuscany. It is essentially a modest, filling soup you could make if you didn't have much in the cupboard. The bread that is at the bottom of the bowl is usually a Tuscan saltless variety, but any chewy artisan bread will do. In the winter, use borlotti beans; in the summer, use cannellini beans. If you cannot find borlotti beans, one of the most beloved and oft used beans in Italy, substitute dried cranberry beans. ◦ *Serves 8*

COOKER: Medium or large round
SETTING AND COOK TIME: LOW for 7 to 9 hours; sage added at 5 to 7 hours

1 pound dried borlotti beans, picked over, soaked overnight
    in cold water to cover, and drained
1 large white onion, coarsely chopped
3 cloves garlic, minced
2 tablespoons finely chopped fresh sage, plus a few whole leaves
Salt and freshly ground black pepper to taste
8 thin slices stale or toasted chewy whole grain country bread

FOR SERVING:
Extra virgin olive oil
Shredded or shaved Parmesan or Asiago cheese

1. Put the drained beans in the slow cooker and add water to cover by 4 inches. Add the onion and garlic. Cover and cook on LOW for 5 to 7 hours.

2. Stir in the sage, cover, and continue to cook on LOW until the beans are tender, another 2 hours.

3. Season with salt and pepper. The soup will be very thick. Place a toasted slice of bread in each of 8 shallow soup bowls and drizzle liberally with the olive oil. Ladle the soup over the bread, sprinkle with Parmesan cheese, and pass the pepper grinder. Eat hot with an oversized spoon.

Minestrone

Minestrone is the Italian catch-all name for "everything in the kitchen" soup. It has as many variations as there are cooks and days in a year. It is an excellent winter soup. ○ *Serves 6*

COOKER: Medium round or oval

SETTINGS AND COOK TIMES: LOW for 7 to 8 hours (Swiss chard and wine added at 5 hours), then HIGH for 30 minutes; the pasta is added during last 30 minutes

3 tablespoons olive oil

1 medium-size yellow onion, chopped

2 small carrots, diced

2 ribs celery, chopped

2 small zucchini, ends trimmed, and cubed

One 15-ounce can red kidney beans, rinsed, drained, and half the beans mashed

1 teaspoon salt

1 bay leaf

Freshly ground black pepper to taste

¼ cup packed fresh flat-leaf parsley leaves, chopped

One 28-ounce can whole tomatoes, mashed, with their juice,

One 10-ounce package frozen baby lima beans

2½ cups chicken broth

5 leaves Swiss chard, chopped, or ½ small head Napa cabbage, cored and chopped

½ cup dry red wine, such as Chianti, Merlot, or Pinot Noir

⅓ cup elbow macaroni or little shells

Freshly grated Parmesan cheese for serving

1. In a large skillet, heat the olive oil over medium heat. Add the onion, carrots, celery, and zucchini and cook, stirring often, until just softened, about 5 minutes. Transfer to the slow cooker and add the kidney beans, salt, bay leaf, pepper, parsley, tomatoes and their juice, limas, and broth. Add water to come about 1 inch above the vegetables. Cover and cook on LOW for 5 hours.

2. Add the Swiss chard and wine, cover, and continue to cook on LOW for another 2 to 3 hours. Remove the bay leaf.

3. Stir in the pasta, cover, and cook on HIGH until the pasta is just tender, about 30 minutes. Ladle into soup bowls and serve hot with lots of Parmesan.

Crock-Baked Italian Bread Soup

his is an old-fashioned peasant soup that is simply a layering of broth, greens, and bread. While it is cooking, the bread absorbs the liquid to make a *panada,* or filling "dry" soup. Use homemade broth, if possible, because homemade really makes this soup amazing. Serve with grilled sausages and a simple salad. ○ *Serves 4*

COOKER: Medium round or oval
SETTING AND COOK TIME: HIGH for 2½ to 3 hours

4 cups homemade hot rich Beef Broth (page 98) or Roasted Vegetable Broth
    (page 102) or canned broth
2 bunches Swiss chard, leaves and stems chopped
2 to 3 thick slices chewy white country bread, such as ciabatta or baguette
Salt and freshly ground black pepper to taste
1 cup finely shredded Parmesan cheese for serving

1. Combine the broth and chopped chard in the slow cooker and set on HIGH; stir to wilt the greens. Tear the slices of bread into large pieces and cover the greens in a single layer; push down to moisten the bread. Cover and continue to cook on HIGH until most of the broth is absorbed, 2½ to 3 hours. The soup will be very thick.

2. With a large spoon, scoop into shallow soup bowls. Season with salt and pepper and sprinkle with the Parmesan. Eat the soup hot with an oversized spoon.

The Easiest French Onion Soup

Beth's mom's neighbor was raving about her favorite onion soup and how easy it was. When we got the recipe, one she clipped from her local newspaper, we had to agree; it is a wonderful recipe. The onions cook a very long time and end up delightfully brown and caramelized on the bottom. Get the real Gruyère cheese, the rich, nutty Swiss cheese with the little holes that melts so perfectly atop a slice of toasted French bread soaked with savory soup. ○ *Serves 4 to 6*

COOKER: Medium round or oval
SETTING AND COOK TIME: HIGH for 9 to 10 hours

6 large yellow onions
3 tablespoons olive oil, plus extra for brushing
One 14-ounce can chicken broth
One 10.5-ounce can beef broth
2 tablespoons Marsala or red wine (optional)
Four to six 1-inch-thick slices French bread
8 ounces Gruyère cheese, cut into thin slices

1. Peel and thinly slice the onions by hand or in a food processor. Put in the slow cooker and toss with the olive oil. Cover and cook for 9 to 10 hours on HIGH.

2. Add both the broths and Marsala, if using; add *no* water or salt. Cover and continue to cook on HIGH until hot, 15 to 30 minutes.

3. Meanwhile, preheat the oven to 400°F. Put the bread slices on a baking sheet and brush with olive oil or leave plain. Bake until golden brown around the edges, about 10 minutes. Set aside.

4. Ladle the soup into individual ovenproof soup bowls and place on a baking sheet to prevent the bowls from tipping over. Top each bowl full of soup with a toasted bread slice and cover with a slice of the Gruyère. Adjust the oven rack to comfortably fit the bowls under the broiler with at least 4 inches to spare. Turn on the broiler and slide the soups under the flame; broil until the cheese is melted and bubbly, 1 to 2 minutes. Serve immediately.

Onion soup is made all over Europe, and the ingredients reflect the region in which it is made. In Chartres, you will find *beauceronne,* onion soup made with white wine, chives, and tomatoes with a poached egg floating on top. In Italy, they serve *acqua a sale,* a vegetarian onion soup made with parsley, tomatoes, and water. In Switzerland, there is *gebrannte Mehlsuppe,* a burnt flour/beef broth soup with bay leaf and a large clove-studded onion that is removed before serving. But the granddaddy of all onion soups is *soupe à l'oignon gratinée,* also known simply as cheese soup, which has fortified millions of Frenchmen for centuries, in both lean or grand times. Beth made her first onion soup vegetarian style, with only water and white wine as the liquid, and served the soup the next day, after the onions had a chance to flavor the broth. It was fabulous.

The ingredients for onion soup are simple but each is significant, since there are so few. The onions, broth, wine, and garnishes are all traditional.

o **The onions:** The best onions for onion soup are the big red ones, sometimes called Italian or torpedo onions. They are pungent and powerful, with enough perfume to give the soup the strength it needs. The next best onion is the white Bermuda, whose delicate taste is pungent nevertheless. Yellow onions are passable, but we like to mix them, half-and-half, with red Italians. Leave plenty of time to cook the onions perfectly. It is this technique that makes the soup. What looks like a lot of onions, filling the slow cooker, will collapse during cooking and become caramelized and golden brown from the natural sugars inherent in the onions. This is what you are looking for.

o **The broth:** Some old French recipes call for half beef and half chicken broth, but the chefs we talked to like their onion soup with 100 percent beef broth. Homemade is best, but canned works fine.

o **The wine:** A dry white wine, including Champagne, is the most common choice. Many versions use white wine in combination with brandy, Cognac, or port.

o **The cheese:** Mozzarella and Gruyère top the list, with Parmesan cheese third.

Julie's French Onion Soup for Two

C ooked by conventional methods, onion soup is big-batch food. In other words, it's just not practical to make one or two servings at a time. A small slow cooker changes all that. Many of the smaller slow cookers have only one heat setting, which is equivalent to LOW on the larger cookers, so that's the way we designed this small-batch onion soup recipe. You can use high-quality canned broth for convenience, but by all means use homemade if you have it. ● *Serves 1 to 2*

COOKER: Small round
SETTING AND COOK TIME: LOW for 11 to 13 hours; wine and broth added at 10 to 11 hours

1½ teaspoons unsalted butter, cut into 4 pieces
1½ teaspoons flavorful olive oil
1 large or 2 medium-size onions
¼ teaspoon sugar
¼ teaspoon salt
2 tablespoons dry white wine
2 cups homemade Beef Broth (page 98) or one 14.5-ounce can high-quality beef broth
One or two ¾-inch-thick slices French, Italian, sourdough, or another rustic white bread, small enough to fit inside the rim of the soup bowl, for each serving
2 teaspoons Cognac
Freshly ground black pepper to taste
About ½ cup shredded Gruyère cheese for each serving

1. Combine the butter and oil in the slow cooker and cover. Turn on the cooker and allow the butter to melt and the oil to heat while you slice the onion.

2. Peel the onion, slice it in half lengthwise, then slice it thinly into half-moons. You should have about 2 heaping cups of onion slices. Add them to the cooker. Sprinkle the sugar and salt over the onions. Use 2 forks to toss the onion slices with the oil, butter, sugar, and salt to coat them. Cover and cook on LOW until the onions are dark brown and caramelized, but not burned, 10 to 11 hours. They will have cooked down to a fraction of their former volume and most of the liquid will be evaporated. If you are home, stir the onions once or twice during the cooking period to help them cook evenly. (If you stir them more often, you will need to increase the cooking time.)

3. When the onions are done, add the wine and broth. Cover and continue to cook on LOW until hot and aromatic, 1 to 2 hours longer.

4. Meanwhile, toast the bread. Preheat the oven to 350°F. Put the bread slices on a baking sheet and bake until dry and toasted, 10 to 15 minutes. Increase the oven temperature to 400°F.

5. When you are ready to serve the soup, stir in the Cognac, pepper, and more salt, if needed. Pour the soup into 1 or 2 ovenproof soup bowls; place on a baking sheet to prevent spills. Drop a bit of the shredded cheese into the soup. Top each bowl with a piece of bread, or two if they are small. Pile the rest of the cheese on top of the bread. Return the baking sheet to the oven and bake until the cheese is melted and browned, about 10 minutes. Serve immediately.

Provençal Garlic Soup

There is a restaurant in Tijuana, Mexico, known for its superb Mediterranean-style cuisine. One of the specialties is this tomato garlic soup, which is served as a first course with hot pita triangles, local olive oil for dipping, and a tapenade spread. Garlic may be pungent when raw, but after braising it is surprisingly mellow. Since peeling the individual little cloves is an arduous task at best, be sure to use our technique of blanching the garlic; when you peel it, the skin will slip right off. In Provence, garlic soup is considered a great restorative. ● *Serves 4*

COOKER: Medium round
SETTING AND COOK TIME: LOW for 6 to 7 hours

4 heads garlic
1 large yellow onion, chopped
Three 14-ounce cans chicken broth
One 6-ounce can tomato paste
3 tablespoons extra virgin olive oil
Hot fresh crusty bread for serving

1. Fill a small deep saucepan with water and bring to a boil. Separate the garlic heads into cloves and toss them into the boiling water; blanch for 1 minute exactly.

Drain the garlic cloves in a colander and rinse under cold running water; peel with a paring knife.

2. Combine the garlic cloves, onion, broth, and tomato paste in the slow cooker and stir to blend. Cover and cook on LOW for 6 to 7 hours.

3. Purée the soup with a handheld immersion blender or transfer to a food processor or blender and purée in batches,. Before serving, add the olive oil. Ladle into soup bowls and serve hot with fresh crusty bread. You can drizzle the top of the soup with a bit more olive oil if you like.

•• Bread Croutons for Soups ••

Any good day-old bread, from a baguette to pumpernickel or whole wheat, makes great soup croutons. Basic soup croutons, which are cubes, are tossed into soups, while larger ones are either placed in the bottom of the bowl or floated in the soup.

Oven Soup Croutons: Preheat the oven to 375°F. If the bread is soft, cut into ¾-inch-thick slices, then cut into thick cubes. If the bread is dense, like rye bread, cut into thinner slices and smaller cubes. Place on an ungreased baking sheet. Drizzle the bread cubes with melted butter or olive oil (the French love to drizzle the bread with the fat skimmed off their *pot au feu*) and bake until crisp and dry, stirring about every 5 minutes to keep from burning. Remove from the oven when just golden and drizzle with more melted butter or olive oil. Leave plain or sprinkle with a few tablespoons of grated Parmesan or top with fresh soft goat cheese. The croutons are best used the same day they are made.

Large Skillet Croutons: Cut day-old bread into slices ½ to ¾ inch thick, or split day-old rolls in half horizontally. In a sauté pan or skillet over medium heat, heat butter, olive oil, or an equal combination of the two; when melted, arrange the slices in the pan. Turn them as necessary, until crisp and golden brown. Remove with tongs to drain on paper towels, and serve immediately. These can also be made under a broiler or over a charcoal fire.

Herb Croutons for Soup: These are excellent floated in plain or cream soups, such as asparagus, carrot, broccoli, pumpkin, potato-leek, and zucchini. Sprinkle in bowls of hot soup just before serving. Preheat the oven to 400°F. Cut the bread into 1-inch-thick slices and then into cubes. Place on an ungreased baking sheet. Drizzle the bread cubes with olive oil. Toast until dry, stirring about every 5 minutes to keep from burning. While hot, sprinkle with 2 tablespoons minced fresh or dried herbs, such as dill, and some grated Parmesan cheese. The croutons are best used the same day they are made.

Corn Chowder

This recipe is adapted from one that Linda Lingg of Palo Alto, California, contributed to a class cookbook when Linda's son and Julie's daughter were in preschool together; Julie has been making it ever since. It's hearty and chunky and works so well in the slow cooker. If you have some leftover chicken, it's easy to turn it into chicken corn chowder. ● *Serves 4 to 6*

COOKER: Medium or large round

SETTINGS AND COOK TIMES: LOW for 5 to 6 hours, then HIGH for 1 hour; milk, corn, and chicken added during last hour

1 tablespoon unsalted butter

1 small onion, finely chopped

3 ribs celery, finely chopped

2 medium-size russet potatoes, peeled and cut into ½-inch dice

2 cups chicken broth

½ bay leaf

⅛ teaspoon paprika

1 teaspoon dried thyme or 1 tablespoon chopped fresh thyme

¼ teaspoon freshly ground black pepper

½ teaspoon salt (optional)

2 cups milk

3 cups frozen corn kernels

1 to 2 cups diced (½ inch) cooked chicken (optional)

1. In a medium-size skillet, melt the butter over medium-high heat. Add the onion and celery and cook, stirring a few times, until the onion is transparent but not browned, 2 to 3 minutes. While the onion and celery are cooking, put the potatoes in the slow cooker. Scrape the onion and celery into the cooker along with any remaining butter. Add the broth, bay leaf, paprika, thyme, and pepper. If the broth is unsalted, add the salt. Stir the top layer of the ingredients very gently, trying not to disturb the potatoes, which should stay submerged. Cover and cook on LOW until the potatoes are tender, 5 to 6 hours.

2. Add the milk, corn, and chicken, if using. Stir, cover, and cook on HIGH until the chowder is heated through, about 1 hour. Taste and, if necessary, add more salt and pepper. Remove the bay leaf before serving.

Potato-Leek Soup

Potato-leek soup is the workhorse of the French kitchen and has sustained many a soul on a cold night. This was the first recipe Beth made in the 1970s out of her copy of *Mastering the Art of French Cooking* by Julia Child. It is so simple it is embarrassing and it is the base for many variations (see below) that are just as tasty. If you want to make a classic French soup called *potage à la bonne femme,* "the good wife's soup," just add a handful of chopped fresh chervil at the end of cooking. Leeks are milder in taste than regular onions. Be sure to clean them well under running water; there can be sand between the layers. You really don't have to worry about proportions, though we use a leek for every potato. It tastes just as good made with water as with broth. You just cook the vegetables, purée, and *voilà!* Your soup is prepared for dinner. ○ *Serves 6*

COOKER: Medium round or oval
SETTING AND COOK TIME: LOW for 5 to 7 hours

4 medium-size leeks (white part only), washed well and thinly sliced (about 4 cups)
4 medium-size to large russet potatoes, peeled and diced
4 to 6 cups water or vegetable or chicken broth
Salt to taste
2 tablespoons unsalted butter
French bread for serving

1. Put the leeks and potatoes in the slow cooker. Add enough of the water or broth to just cover them. Cover and cook on LOW until the potatoes are tender, 5 to 7 hours.

2. Purée the soup with a handheld immersion blender or transfer to a food processor or blender and purée in batches. Add the salt and butter, swirling until it is melted. Ladle the hot soup into bowls and serve immediately with French bread.

Pea and Watercress Potato-Leek Soup: Follow the recipe as directed. One hour before the soup is done, add the leaves and tender stems of 1 bunch of watercress and one 12-ounce package frozen petite peas, thawed, to the crock and cover. When done, purée the soup and serve immediately; it will become dull as it sits. We never strain this; we love the bits of green vegetables.

Potato-Leek Soup with Sorrel or Spinach: Follow the recipe as directed. One hour before the soup is done, add 2 cups of firmly packed sorrel or spinach leaves to the crock and cover. When done, purée the soup, stir in 1 cup of heavy cream, and serve immediately.

Beth's Cream of Celery Soup: Put 1 bunch of celery, ends trimmed off and ribs chopped with the leaves, in the slow cooker along with the leeks and potatoes. Cover and cook as directed. Purée the soup, stir in 1 cup heavy cream, and serve immediately.

Potato-Leek-Fennel Soup: Add 1½ pounds fennel (2 bulbs), quartered, bases cut off, and tough lower core cut out, to the crock along with the leeks and potatoes. Cover and cook as directed. Purée the soup, swirl in ¼ cup of sour cream, and serve immediately.

Gina's Baked Potato Soup

W hat do we all love about baked potatoes? Well, there is the oozing melted butter for starts, then the dollop of cold sour cream, and, of course, the chopped chives. This simple soup combines all that into a remarkable savory taste treat. This is a soup from pastry chef Gina DiLeone-Dodd; she made this for the Black Cat Cafe in rural New Hampshire to serve with her foccacia and sandwiches. She always made it in the slow cooker and let it stay warm all day long on the LOW setting. ○ *Serves 12*

COOKER: Large round
SETTING AND COOK TIME: HIGH for about 5 hours; butter, half-and-half, sour cream, salt, and pepper added during last 30 minutes

5 pounds russet potatoes, peeled and cut into 1-inch cubes
½ cup (1 stick) butter
1 cup half-and-half
½ cup sour cream (don't use nonfat)
Salt and freshly ground black pepper to taste
8 ounces bacon, cooked until crisp, drained on paper towels, and crumbled
6 green onions (white and green parts), sliced, or 3 tablespoons minced fresh chives

1. Put the potatoes in the slow cooker and add water to cover. Cover and cook on HIGH until the potatoes are cooked and falling apart, about 5 hours.

2. Turn the cooker to LOW, add the butter, half-and-half, and sour cream, and season with salt and pepper. Cover and cook until hot, about 20 minutes.

3. Stir in the crumbled bacon and sliced green onions. Serve immediately or keep warm on LOW, adding water or milk to thin if necessary.

Cream of Artichoke Soup

I n the rural coastal town of Pescadero, California, in the midst of the local artichoke fields, there is a small clapboard restaurant on the one street that is the town. Duarte's is known all the way to San Francisco for its cioppino, fruit pies, and cream of artichoke soup. This is a quick and easy soup—the sweet fresh cream is a must. ○ *Serves 6*

COOKER: Medium round or oval
SETTINGS AND COOK TIMES: HIGH for 30 minutes, LOW for 6 to 7 hours; cream added during last 20 minutes

6 tablespoons (¾ stick) unsalted butter, cut into 4 or 5 pieces
1 small white onion, chopped
3 leeks (white part and 1 inch of the green), washed well and thinly sliced
Three 10-ounce packages frozen artichoke hearts, thawed
6 cups chicken broth
Salt and white pepper to taste
1 cup heavy cream
Croutons (optional) for serving

1. Place the butter, onion, and leeks in the slow cooker. Turn to HIGH, cover, and sweat the vegetables for 30 minutes.

2. Add the artichoke hearts and broth, cover, and cook on LOW for 5 to 6 hours.

3. Purée with a handheld immersion blender or transfer to a food processor or blender and purée in batches. Strain the soup by pushing it with a spatula through a large-mesh strainer to remove any fibers. Season with salt and pepper.

Return the soup to the cooker, stir in the cream, cover, and cook on LOW until heated through, about 20 minutes; do not boil.

4. Ladle the hot soup into bowls and garnish with croutons, if desired.

Slow-Cooked Broccoli Soup with Garlic and Olive Oil

(B)roccoli is usually cooked very quickly in a steamer or a wok. But it works beautifully in this simple Italian peasant soup by James Peterson. The soup is a testament to how a very few ingredients can add up to a full, satisfying flavor. While most people go for the florets, we love the flavor and texture of the stems as well. Remember that the thinner the stem, the more tender it is; the thinnest may not need to be peeled. Don't even consider using less garlic than called for; you want its flavor to balance out that of the broccoli. Serve with toast and Parmesan cheese or top with a dollop of crème fraîche or sour cream with a bit of grated lemon zest stirred in. ○ *Serves 6*

COOKER: Medium round
SETTING AND COOK TIME: LOW for 5 to 6 hours

2 bunches broccoli (about 3 pounds)
½ cup olive oil
8 cloves garlic, sliced
2 teaspoons chopped fresh thyme or marjoram, or ½ teaspoon dried
6 cups vegetable or chicken broth
¼ cup dry white wine
2 tablespoons fresh lemon juice
Salt and freshly ground black pepper to taste

FOR SERVING:
Toasted slices of French bread
Freshly grated Parmesan cheese

1. To prepare the broccoli, cut off the florets and chop them. Trim off the bottom 2 inches of each stem, peel the stems, and thinly slice. Combine the broccoli, oil, garlic, thyme, broth, wine, and lemon juice in the slow cooker. Cover and cook on LOW for 5 to 6 hours.

2. With the back of a large spoon, mash some of the broccoli against the side of the cooker; the soup will be chunky. Or for a smooth soup, purée with a handheld immersion blender or transfer to a food processor or blender and purée in batches. Season with salt and pepper. Serve in bowls, passing the toast and Parmesan.

Winter Red Cabbage Soup with Roots

T his is a delicious main-course beef soup made with red cabbage; you need to plan ahead and make the broth one day before you make the soup. For the two days of cooking, you will be rewarded with a satisfyingly thick and flavorful dish that is also quite low in calories. The red cabbage gives up all of its color to the soup, so you are left with a beautifully rosy broth and what appears to be green cabbage. If you have extra soup bones stashed in the freezer, pull them out and toss them in to enrich the broth. This is a generous recipe, so it needs the large capacity cooker; for a medium slow cooker, cut the amounts in half. ○ *Serves 10 to 12*

COOKER: Large round or oval
SETTINGS AND COOK TIMES: Broth, LOW for 8 to 10 hours; Soup, HIGH for 1 hour, then LOW for 10 to 12 hours (beef added during last 1 to 2 hours)

BROTH:
1 large or 2 small slices beef shank (about 1½ pounds)
Additional beef soup bones (optional)
1 small onion, quartered
1 small carrot, quartered
1 rib celery with leaves, cut into chunks
1 or 2 sprigs fresh flat-leaf parsley
4 to 5 black peppercorns

SOUP:

1 tablespoon olive oil

1 large yellow onion, chopped

2 medium-size to large carrots, sliced into rounds or half-moons

3 large ribs celery, chopped into bite-sized pieces

1 medium-size turnip, peeled and chopped into bite-sized pieces

½ medium-size red cabbage, cored and cut into ribbons about ⅓ x 1 inch (about 5 cups)

One 28-ounce can chopped tomatoes, with their juice

1 large all-purpose or baking potato, peeled and diced

6 cups beef broth

2 tablespoons chopped fresh flat-leaf parsley

1 teaspoon dried thyme

1 teaspoon dried savory

1½ cups diced cooked beef, reserved from making the broth

1 teaspoon salt, or to taste

⅛ teaspoon freshly ground black pepper, or to taste

1 to 2 tablespoons red wine vinegar (optional), to your taste

Pinch of sugar (optional)

1. To make the broth, preheat the oven to 375°F. Put the beef shank and soup bones, if using, in a shallow roasting pan in the oven and roast until nicely browned, turning once, 30 to 45 minutes. Transfer the beef, bones, and any juices from the roasting pan to the slow cooker. Add the onion, carrot, celery, parsley, and peppercorns. Add water to cover everything. Cover and cook on LOW for 8 to 10 hours.

2. Using tongs or a slotted spoon, transfer the beef shank and bones to a plate and allow to cool. Strain the broth into a container and allow it to cool a bit before refrigerating, uncovered. Discard the vegetables. When the meat and bones are cool enough to handle, separate the meaty pieces and refrigerate them. Discard the bones.

3. The next day, with a spoon, skim the congealed fat from the top of the broth and discard. Dice the lean portion of the meat. You will have about 1½ cups. Cover and refrigerate until making the soup.

4. To make the soup, in a large skillet, heat the oil over medium-high heat. Add the onion and cook, stirring a few times, until softened, 3 or 4 minutes. Add the carrots, celery, and turnip and continue to cook, stirring occasionally, until the onion and the celery are transparent. Do not allow the onion to burn. Transfer the vegetables to the slow cooker. Add the cabbage, tomatoes, potato, and broth. Add the parsley, thyme, and savory and stir to combine. Cover and cook on HIGH for 1 hour.

5. Turn the cooker to LOW and cook 10 to 12 hours longer. (If you will be leaving the house immediately, just cook on LOW for 10 to 12 hours and skip the cooking on HIGH step). One to two hours before serving, stir in the diced beef.

6. Before serving, add the salt and pepper, and add the vinegar, if desired. Taste the soup and add additional salt, pepper, sugar, or vinegar if needed. Ladle the hot soup into bowls and serve.

Butternut Squash Soup

This creamy orange soup made from the sturdy butternut squash seems to grow more popular every year, and no wonder. It is sustaining but not heavy, slightly sweet and warming, a fall and winter favorite for many. Using your slow cooker, it's deliciously easy to make. Just find a squash that will fit completely inside your slow cooker, with the lid all the way down.

You will find this soup is a delightful canvas for your creativity. It's easy to vary the flavor: Omit the brown sugar and season the soup with 1 teaspoon of curry powder. Gently sauté a grated apple or pear and a bit of minced ginger with the onion, adding them after the onion is about halfway cooked. Instead of broth, use half water and half apple cider. Or sauté about 2 teaspoons of minced fresh sage with the onions. Serve the soup with buttery croutons and more minced sage.

If you are really pressed for time, you can simplify the preparation still further. Instead of chopping and sautéing the onion, leave the peel on, wash it, and place it, whole, in the slow cooker with the squash. When the squash is tender, the onion will be, too. Halve it, peel away the skin, and purée it along with the squash.

We like to serve this soup with a dollop of something creamy on top, sprinkled with a few cumin seeds or *pepitas* (pumpkin seeds). Toast the seeds if you have time. ● *Serves 6*

COOKER: Medium or large round or oval
SETTINGS AND COOK TIMES: LOW for 7 to 9 hours, then HIGH for 1 hour

1 butternut squash that will fit in your slow cooker
2 tablespoons water
1 large yellow onion
1 tablespoon olive or vegetable oil or unsalted butter
4 cups chicken or vegetable broth
1 teaspoon light brown sugar
Salt and freshly ground black pepper to taste

FOR SERVING:
Sour cream, plain yogurt, or crème fraîche
Pinch of cumin seeds or *pepitas,* toasted in a dry skillet
    over medium heat until fragrant

1. Wash and dry the squash and place it in the slow cooker. Add the 2 tablespoons of water. Cover and cook on LOW until the squash is tender, 7 to 9 hours. When the squash is done, a wooden skewer or a paring knife will pierce it easily and slip through to the center. If the squash is not done, replace the cover and continue to cook on LOW, checking every 30 minutes. Allow the cooked squash to cool. Do not discard any liquid in the slow cooker.

2. While the squash is cooking, peel and chop the onion. In a medium-size nonstick skillet, heat the oil over medium heat. Add the onion and cook, stirring, until softened, about 5 minutes. Set aside.

3. Slice the squash in half lengthwise. Use a soup spoon to scrape out the seeds and strings. Discard them. Scoop out the cooked flesh and discard the shell. In a blender or food processor, purée half the squash with half the onion and about 2 cups of the broth. Pour the purée into the slow cooker and stir to dissolve any caramelized squash juices that have stuck to the bottom. Purée the remaining squash and onion with the remaing 2 cups of broth and add to the cooker. Add the brown sugar and season with salt and pepper. Cover and cook on HIGH until the soup is hot, about 1 hour.

4. Taste and correct the seasonings, if needed. Serve the soup hot, topped with a dollop of sour cream, yogurt, or crème fraîche and a few toasted cumin seeds or *pepitas.*

Zucchini Bisque

Zucchini is a favorite vegetable that becomes very soft with slow cooking. It makes a delightful light soup. The bit of rice added is for body; it will be puréed, so your diners will never know it is in the mix. If you can find organic half-and-half, do use it; the soup is so simple that the flavor of the fresh cream will really come through. ○ *Serves 4*

COOKER: Medium round or oval
SETTINGS AND COOK TIMES: HIGH for 30 minutes, then LOW for 5½ to 6½ hours; half-and-half added during last 20 minutes

6 tablespoons (¾ stick) unsalted butter, cut into 3 or 4 pieces
1 large yellow onion, chopped
½ teaspoon curry powder
1½ pounds zucchini, ends trimmed, and cut into chunks
2 heaping tablespoons white basmati rice or long-grain white rice
1 tablespoon chopped fresh basil
3 cups chicken or vegetable broth
Salt and freshly ground black pepper to taste
1 cup half-and-half
Croutons (optional) for serving

1. Put the butter, onion, curry powder, and zucchini in the slow cooker, cover, and cook on HIGH to sweat the vegetables for 30 minutes.

2. Add the rice, basil, and broth, cover, and cook on LOW for 5 to 6 hours.

3. Purée with a handheld immersion blender or transfer to a food processor or blender and purée in batches. Season with salt and pepper. Stir in the half-and-half, cover, and continue to cook on LOW until heated through, 20 minutes; do not boil.

4. Ladle the hot soup into bowls and garnish with croutons, if desired.

Beth's Vegetarian Borscht

T he beet, *Beta vulgaris*, is native to the Mediterranean coast. It is in the same family as Swiss chard and the white sugar beet. Its earthy flavor comes from a microorganism in the soil that it naturally absorbs to create a compound called geosmin, which is also found in blue-green algae, the super food. This soup is prepared for the slow cooker in minutes; it turns ruby red as soon as the water hits the beets and deepens in color as it cooks. Serve it hot or cold—it's delicious either way. You can use ¼ cup of chopped fresh dill or tarragon in place of the dried. ○ *Serves 6 to 8*

COOKER: Medium round or oval
SETTINGS AND COOK TIMES: HIGH for 1 hour, then LOW for 4 to 5 hours

1 bunch red beets, trimmed, peeled and chopped, and their greens, rinsed
1 large yellow onion, chopped
2 to 3 medium-size red or white potatoes, left unpeeled and chopped
2 large carrots, thickly sliced
1 heaping teaspoon dillweed, dried tarragon, or a salt-free herb blend,
    such as Mrs. Dash or McCormick
3 tablespoons dry red wine, such as Merlot
¼ teaspoon freshly ground black pepper, or to taste
Sea salt to taste
Cold sour cream or plain yogurt for serving

1. Put the beets, onion, potatoes, carrots, and herbs in the slow cooker. Chop about half of the beet greens and add to the cooker (reserve the rest for another use). Add the wine and enough water to cover everything by 1 inch (you can add some chicken broth if you prefer). Cover and cook on HIGH for 1 hour.

2. Turn the cooker to LOW and cook until the vegetables are tender but not falling apart, 4 to 5 hours longer.

3. Stir in the pepper and season with salt. Ladle the hot soup into bowls and top with a spoonful of cold sour cream or yogurt.

Winter Tomato Soup

T his is one of those surprise soups: it's absolutely delicious and will leave you craving more. Use home-canned tomatoes if you have them, but tinned tomatoes will still give you a wonderful soup. It's definitely worth getting a bottle of dry vermouth, such as Martini & Rossi, to keep in the fridge for this. The soup was originally published decades ago in an exceptional cookbook, *The American Table* (Silver Spring, 2000), by award-winning poet Ronald Johnson, and is one of those cookbooks that is popular with food professionals and Johnson's literary peers. Beth has been making it every year since it was reviewed by Jim Wood in the San Francisco *Examiner* in December 1986; it even looks good in the photograph. The recipe serves four, but you might not want to share. Serve with baguettes. ○ *Serves 4*

COOKER: Medium round
SETTING AND COOK TIME: LOW for 5 to 6 hours

½ **cup (1 stick) unsalted butter**
1 large or 2 medium-size yellow onions, chopped
1 quart home-canned tomatoes or one 28-ounce can imported Italian whole or
    chopped plum tomatoes, with their juice
½ **cup dry vermouth or dry white wine**
1 tablespoon sugar
1 heaping teaspoon dried tarragon
Sea salt to taste
Cold sour cream for serving

1. In a large skillet over medium heat, melt the butter. Add the onion and cook until golden, about 15 minutes, stirring often to cook evenly.

2. Combine the tomatoes, vermouth, sugar, and tarragon in the slow cooker; add the onion and butter, scraping out the pan. Cover and cook on LOW for 5 to 6 hours.

3. Purée in batches in a food processor or with a handheld immersion blender. If you don't like the seeds, push the soup through a strainer set over the slow cooker. Season with salt. Keep warm on LOW without letting it come to a boil until serving. Ladle the hot soup into bowls and top with a spoonful of cold sour cream.

Hot Tomato Consommé

T his is an unusual, light-bodied soup adapted from one of Beth's favorite pamphlets, *Home for the Holidays* by Irena Chalmers (Potpourri Press, 1980). It is perfect for a first course or light lunch. Don't skip the avocado garnish; it is delicious. Try serving this with bruschetta or grilled cheese sandwiches.

o *Serves 4*

COOKER: Medium round
SETTING AND COOK TIME: HIGH for 2 to 2½ hours

4 cups tomato juice
4 cups good-quality canned chicken or vegetable broth
2 tablespoons tomato paste
3 large shallots, cut into chunks
¼ teaspoon garlic powder
¼ teaspoon ground allspice
½ teaspoon dried basil
2 tablespoons fresh lemon juice
2 tablespoons Madeira or dry sherry
2 tablespoons minced fresh chives
2 tablespoons minced fresh flat-leaf parsley

FOR SERVING:
Thin lemon slices
2 plum tomatoes, diced
1 firm, ripe avocado, peeled, pitted, and diced

1. Combine the tomato juice, broth, tomato paste (mix with a bit of broth to loosen it up), shallots, garlic powder, allspice, and basil in the slow cooker. Cover and cook on HIGH for 2 to 2½ hours.

2. Discard the shallots. Stir in the lemon juice, Madeira, chives, and parsley. Serve immediately or let stand on LOW for as long as 2 hours. Serve in soup bowls with a lemon slice on the side and a little diced tomato and avocado on top.

Carrot Soup with Honey and Nutmeg

Carrot soup was the house soup served with falafel in pita bread at a tiny vegetarian eatery off Castro Street, the main drag known as Restaurant Row, in Mountain View, California. When it closed, Beth was so addicted to the thick vegetable soup that she got the recipe from Rick, the owner, who moved to Oregon to get married. Of course he rattled it off from memory. Try to get carrots with their tops still on; the carrots will be sweeter. If you want a garnish, top with chopped cilantro and plain yogurt, but it is fine without. ● *Serves 8*

COOKER: Large round
SETTINGS AND COOK TIMES: HIGH for 1 hour, then LOW for 5 to 7 hours

¼ **cup olive oil**

2 medium-size yellow onions, chopped

2 large russet potatoes, peeled and chopped

3 pounds carrots (about 15 medium-size), scrubbed, tops cut off, and chopped

1 or 2 small cloves garlic, to your taste, pressed

½ **teaspoon** *each* **dried thyme and marjoram, or 1 teaspoon Spike natural salt-free seasoning**

4 to 6 cups water or chicken broth, as needed

2 heaping tablespoons honey

½ **to 1 teaspoon freshly grated nutmeg, to your taste**

Sea salt and freshly ground black pepper to taste

1. Heat the oil in a large skillet over medium heat. Add the onions and cook until softened, 6 to 8 minutes, stirring often to cook evenly.

2. Put the potatoes, carrots, garlic, and herbs in the slow cooker; add the onions and oil, scraping them out of the pan. Add enough of the water to cover everything. Cover and cook on HIGH for 1 hour.

3. Turn the cooker to LOW and cook until the vegetables are soft, 5 to 7 hours. Purée in batches in a food processor or right in the slow cooker with a handheld immersion blender; the soup will be nice and thick. Stir in the honey and grate the nutmeg right over the crock. Season with salt and pepper. Keep warm on LOW without letting it come to a boil until serving. Ladle the hot soup into bowls and enjoy.

Japanese Soup with Mushrooms and Tofu

his is so quick and impressive. Mirin is a sweet rice wine available in the Asian food section of the supermarket. If you shop at specialty food stores or your local Asian market, look for nonalcoholic mirin; it is just as tasty. Pair this with pot stickers or spring rolls, or serve as a first course. ○ *Serves 12*

COOKER: Medium or large round
SETTING AND COOK TIME: HIGH for 2 to 3 hours

3 quarts homemade (page 95) or good-quality canned chicken broth, Vegetable Dashi for
    Miso Soup (page 103), or Asian Vegetarian Broth (page 104)
½ cup mirin
3 tablespoons tamari or another soy sauce
8 ounces mushrooms, sliced
½ head Napa cabbage, cored and coarsely shredded
Two 12-ounce blocks extra-firm tofu, cut into ½-inch cubes
1 bunch green onions (white and green parts), sliced on the diagonal in
    ¼-inch-thick slivers, for serving
¼ cup toasted sesame oil for serving

1. Combine the broth, mirin, tamari, mushrooms, and cabbage in the slow cooker. Cover and cook on HIGH for 2 to 3 hours.

2. Stir in the tofu. Serve immediately or let stand on LOW for as long as 1 hour before serving. Ladle into Japanese soup bowls and garnish each serving with 1 tablespoon of the green onions and drizzle with 1 teaspoon of sesame oil.

Chicken Tortilla Soup

n Baja, California, and elsewhere in Mexico, every restaurant has a version of tortilla soup. The soup is usually quite thin, almost a consommé, with some crisp tortilla strips and shreds of chicken meat in a homemade tomato or chicken broth. This is based on one of the best versions, which Beth had in La

Paz in a small dinette on the harbor. The cilantro leaves make the broth very fresh tasting, so don't leave them out. ○ *Serves 4 to 5*

COOKER: Medium round or oval

SETTING AND COOK TIME: LOW for 5 to 6 hours, or HIGH for 3 to 3½ hours; chicken and corn added during last hour of cooking at either setting

One 28-ounce can diced tomatoes, with their juice

One 10-ounce can red or green enchilada sauce

2 medium-size yellow or white onions, chopped

One 4-ounce can chopped green chiles, drained

1 clove garlic, minced

3 tablespoons chopped fresh cilantro

2 cups water

One 14.5-ounce can chicken or vegetable broth

1 teaspoon ground cumin

1 teaspoon chili powder

½ teaspoon salt

A few grinds of black pepper

1 bay leaf

¾ teaspoon dried oregano

1½ pounds boneless, skinless chicken breasts, cooked through in gently simmering water, drained, and shredded

One 10-ounce can Mexican corn, drained

8 yellow or white soft corn tortillas

3 tablespoons light olive oil

FOR SERVING:

Finely shredded sharp cheddar cheese, such as longhorn

Sour cream thinned with a few tablespoons milk, or *crema Mexicana*

Sliced avocado

Sprigs fresh cilantro

1. Combine the tomatoes, enchilada sauce, onions, chiles, garlic, cilantro, water, broth, cumin, chili powder, salt, pepper, bay leaf, and oregano in the slow cooker. Cover and cook on LOW for 5 to 6 hours or on HIGH for 2 to 2½ hours.

2. Add the shredded chicken and corn, cover, and continue to cook on LOW for another hour. Discard the bay leaf.

3. Meanwhile, preheat the oven to 400°F. Lightly brush both sides of each tortilla with some of the oil. With a knife, cut the tortillas into 2½ x 1-inch strips. Spread out the tortilla strips on a parchment paper–lined baking sheet. Bake until crisp but not browned, turning once halfway through baking, 8 to 12 minutes.

4. To serve, ladle the soup into bowls. Sprinkle each serving with tortilla strips and grated cheese. Top with a tablespoon of sour cream or *crema Mexicana,* then with a few slices of avocado and cilantro sprigs. Serve immediately.

Gumbo

G umbo, almost a thick stew, is delightfully complex in flavor. It is served with filé (pronounced FEE-lay), made of dried ground sassafras leaves, which is what gives it that unique flavor and frequently serves as a thickener, too. You never reheat a dish once filé has been added; it is to be sprinkled on at the table like salt or pepper. Sassafras is the familiar flavoring in root beer. The roots of the sassafras plant are dug in the spring and stripped of their bark, and are then boiled for an herbal tea "to thin the blood." Gumbo is considered a nourishing restorative in Louisiana, much like *menudo* is in Mexico. ○ *Serves 4*

COOKER: Medium round or oval

SETTINGS AND COOK TIMES: HIGH for 30 minutes, then LOW for 6 hours; tomatoes, rice, and okra added during last hour

2 strips bacon, cooked until crisp, drained on paper towels, and crumbled

1 large onion, finely chopped

1 pound boneless, skinless chicken breasts, any fat trimmed

2 large ribs celery, chopped

½ green bell pepper, seeded and diced

1 bay leaf

4 cups chicken broth

One 14.5-ounce can whole tomatoes, with their juice, chopped

1 cup frozen sliced okra, rinsed under cool water and drained, or
    fresh okra, ends trimmed and sliced

⅓ cup converted white rice

2 tablespoons chopped fresh flat-leaf parsley

¼ teaspoon dried thyme

¼ teaspoon freshly ground black pepper

Salt to taste

1 to 2 teaspoons gumbo filé powder for serving

1. Put the bacon, onion, chicken, celery, bell pepper, bay leaf, and chicken broth in the slow cooker. Cover and cook on HIGH for 30 minutes.

2. Turn the cooker to LOW and cook for 5 hours.

3. Remove the chicken breast, cut the meat into bite-sized pieces, and return to the cooker. Discard the bay leaf. Add the tomatoes and their juice, okra, rice, parsley, thyme, and pepper; cook on LOW until the soup is heated through and the rice cooked, about 1 hour longer.

4. Season with salt. Serve in shallow soup bowls and sprinkle with filé powder.

Cock-a-Leekie Soup

C ock-a-leekie is a simple and comforting Scottish soup. It has its place in the pantheon of kettle soups with wild names such as cullen skink, feather fowlie, neep broase, hotchpotch, and powsowdie. It is said the early versions of cock-a-leekie were made with the stewed loser of the local cockfight. The soup became a favorite French meal as well. This version, from Brit Susie Dymoke, is as economical as it is delicious. It uses a few tablespoons of barley as a thickener, but oatmeal is not unheard of. Leek and potato soups do not need exact ratios as long as you include all the basic ingredients. While an unusual garnish, the chopped pitted prunes are a traditional touch. The recipe calls for a Turkish bay leaf, which is smaller and more subtle in flavor than the more common California leaf. ○ *Serves 4 to 5*

COOKER: Medium round or oval
SETTING AND COOK TIME: LOW for 6 to 8 hours

1 bunch leeks (about 1 pound, white part and about 2 inches of the green)

1½ pounds boneless, skinless chicken thighs, diced

2 medium-size russet potatoes, peeled and diced

2 tablespoons pearl barley

2 small white or yellow onions, diced

5 sprigs fresh flat-leaf parsley

1 Turkish bay leaf, or ½ California bay leaf

3 cups chicken broth or water

Salt and freshly ground black pepper to taste

FOR SERVING:

4 ounces pitted prunes, chopped

Chopped fresh flat-leaf parsley

Worcestershire sauce

1. Rinse the leeks under cool running water. Halve them lengthwise, and peel off the tough outer layer. Rinse them again to remove all sand. Thinly slice.

2. Combine the leeks, chicken, potatoes, barley, onions, parsley, bay leaf, and broth in the slow cooker; stir to combine. Cover and cook on LOW for 6 to 8 hours.

3. Season with salt and pepper. Ladle into bowls and serve hot, garnished with some chopped prunes and parsley. Have the Worcestershire sauce bottle nearby for a little splash.

Poached Chicken in Tomato Broth

T his is just the kind of warming, nourishing, simple dish that tastes so good when you are under the weather, or even when you are not. We use a couple of short cuts that make the preparation a snap. First of all, we remove most of the skin from the chicken before cooking. This makes it possible to serve a lean broth without the extra step of skimming. And we use canned tomatoes so we don't have to take the time to peel fresh ones. Serve the chicken and its broth in soup plates, with some cooked rice or egg noodles added to every dish.

○ *Serves 4 to 5*

1 medium-large onion, chopped

3 medium-size carrots, chopped

3 ribs celery, chopped, plus leaves and top from 1 medium-size rib

1 medium-size chicken (about 3½ pounds)

A few sprigs of fresh flat-leaf parsley

1 bay leaf

One 14.5-ounce can chopped tomatoes, with their juice

2 cups chicken broth

4 cups water

1 teaspoon salt

½ teaspoon freshly ground black pepper

FOR SERVING:
Steamed white rice or boiled egg noodles
Minced fresh flat-leaf parsley (optional)

1. Put the onion, carrots, and chopped celery in the slow cooker.

2. Remove and discard as much of the skin and fat from the chicken as possible. To do this, use a paring knife or pair of shears to slit the skin down the center of the breast. Pull away the skin from the flesh, cutting as necessary as you go. You will probably be able to remove all but the wing skin. Put the celery stalk and leaves, parsley, and bay leaf in the chicken cavity. Truss the chicken, tying the legs together and tying an extra loop of string around the center of the chicken crosswise to catch the wings. Put the chicken in the cooker. Pour the tomatoes and their juice over the chicken. Add the broth, water, salt, and pepper. Cover and cook on LOW for 6 to 8 hours. The chicken will be very tender and the broth richly flavored.

3. To serve, remove the lid from the cooker and carefully transfer the chicken to a cutting board. Be careful and use the string to help you if necessary, because the chicken will be so tender that it may fall apart. Taste the broth and add more salt and pepper if needed. Cover the cooker and leave it on LOW to keep the broth hot. Carve, shred, or disjoint the chicken as desired, discarding the aromatics from the chicken cavity. For each person, place some hot cooked rice or noodles in a flat soup plate or a shallow bowl. Add a piece of chicken or some shredded or sliced chicken. Ladle some of the broth and vegetables over the chicken. Top with minced parsley, if desired. Any leftover chicken can be shredded or chopped and added to the broth to make a really outstanding chicken soup.

Scotch Broth

A favorite winter soup, this is also called barley broth, and is made from scratch with cracked lamb shanks for the stock. No old mutton here! Beth got this recipe when she was in her late teens and working on the line at a small upscale lingerie factory, nicknamed "the underwear factory." Amid the whirl of sewing machines, bolts of fabric, and racks of nighties in Monet pastels was posted an old photograph of a lounging Paul Newman in the movie *Hud*. All ages of women worked sorting and inspecting, all the while talking about life, love, movie stars, and, of course, food. One of the women, a real soup maven, gave her this recipe, which she still makes to this day. The rich stock cooks first for 6 to 8 hours and it can be made the day ahead, so plan accordingly. ○ *Serves 6*

COOKER: Medium or large round
SETTINGS AND COOK TIMES: Stock, HIGH for 1 hour, then LOW for 6 to 8 hours; Soup, LOW for about 7 hours (meat is added during the last hour)

STOCK:
1½ pounds cracked lamb shanks
10 cups cold water
1 teaspoon salt

SOUP:
1 large yellow onion, chopped
2 large carrots, chopped
3 ribs celery with leaves, chopped
½ cup pearl barley
¼ cup chopped fresh flat-leaf parsley
Pinch of dried thyme
Salt to taste
A few grinds of black pepper

FOR SERVING:
Homemade soda bread
Butter

1. To make the stock, put the lamb shanks, water, and salt in the slow cooker. Cover and cook on HIGH for 1 hour.

2. Skim off the foam on the surface. Cover, turn the cooker to LOW, and cook for 6 to 8 hours.

3. Uncover and let cool to lukewarm. Set a large colander lined with cheesecloth or a fine-mesh strainer over a large bowl and pour the broth through to strain. Cut the meat off the bones. Discard the bones and set aside the meat, in the refrigerator, for the soup.

4. To make the soup, put all the ingredients, except the salt and pepper, in the cooker. Add the stock, cover, and cook on LOW for about 6 hours.

5. Add the reserved meat, cover, and continue to cook on LOW for another hour. Season with salt and pepper. Ladle into bowls and serve hot with homemade soda bread and butter.

Hamburger Steak Soup

T his soup, made from humble hamburger (ground round steak or sirloin steak), is thick, hearty, and warming, the perfect antidote to a chilly day. It's worth seeking out the Maggi seasoning, which may be found in the Asian or Latin American sections of the supermarket. ● *Serves 8*

COOKER: Medium or large round
SETTING AND COOK TIME: HIGH for 4 to 6 hours

½ **pound lean ground beef**
1 **large yellow onion, chopped**
2 **cloves garlic, chopped**
½ **cup olive oil**
1 **cup all-purpose flour**
Two 14-ounce cans beef broth
3 **ribs celery, chopped**
2 **medium-size carrots, chopped**
One 14.5-ounce can chopped tomatoes, with their juice
¼ **teaspoon Maggi seasoning or** ½ **teaspoon soy sauce**
½ **teaspoon freshly ground black pepper**
Salt to taste
One 10-ounce package frozen mixed vegetables

1. In a large, heavy skillet, brown the ground beef, onion, and garlic over medium-high heat until no longer pink, breaking up any clumps of meat. Drain off as much fat as possible. Transfer to a bowl.

2. Wipe out the skillet with a paper towel. Add the oil and heat over medium-high heat. Add the flour and stir to combine. Cook the roux, stirring constantly with a wooden spoon, until it turns a rich brown, about the color of cocoa powder or a light milk chocolate. Don't rush this; it will take 10 to 15 minutes. If the flour burns, discard it and try again with more oil and flour.

3. Add 1 can of the broth and stir with a whisk until the mixture is smooth. Add the remaining can of broth and stir until smooth. Transfer the mixture to the slow cooker. Stir in the meat-and-onion mixture, celery, carrots, tomatoes, Maggi seasoning, and pepper. Season with salt. (If you have used canned broth, you may not need any salt at all.) Put the still-frozen mixed vegetables in the cooker and submerge the frozen block. Cover and cook on HIGH for 4 to 6 hours. Serve hot.

·· About Bouquet Garni ··

The aromatic combination of fresh parsley, thyme, bay leaf, and peppercorns tied up in a piece of cheesecloth is a classic Mediterranean herbal bouquet, known as a bouquet garni. Instead of tossing herbs into the broth by themselves to float around, they are neatly placed in the center of a 10-inch square of cheesecloth and tied with some kitchen twine. If you don't have any cheesecloth, just gather up the herbs in a small bunch and wrap with the twine. A small bouquet garni will suffice in each of the following recipes for broth.

You can improvise with any combination of herbs you like—rosemary, sage, marjoram, curly or flat-leaf parsley, a crushed garlic clove, even dried mushrooms and a hot little dried chile pepper. Or try Indian spices, such as whole cloves, cinnamon stick, fennel seeds, and some brown mustard seeds. A favorite is *herbes de Provence.* When you turn down the heat to LOW, toss in the bouquet garni. During the skimming, you will easily be able to discard it by just fishing around and pulling out the soggy bag.

The Slow Cooker Stockpot

One of the most wonderful food preparations that a slow cooker can create is homemade stock, also called broth. Food writer Shirley O. Corriher calls homemade stock "a real treasure for cooks." Why make homemade stock or broth? Simply put, there is no substitute. The purpose is to provide a depth of flavor and nutrition in your soups and stews that are just not obtainable from water. Our recipes all suggest a canned alternative, but if you make your own stocks, you will taste the difference. And beyond that, making stock is not difficult, especially with our recipes. You just put bones, vegetables, and some herbs in the cooker, add cold water, and simmer away. Proportions are flexible.

There are four classic stocks or broths: white stock, made from chicken or other poultry; brown stock, made from beef and veal; fish stock; and vegetable stock. Pork and lamb, unless used for specific soups or *chile verde,* are rather sweet and therefore not good for all-purpose stocks. Meat and poultry stocks are best made with knuckles, backs, legs, necks, and wings because they have the highest collagen content, which, after long, slow simmering, turns into gelatin. It is gelatin that gives homemade stock its rich, velvety consistency.

The slow cooker is the perfect medium for making low-simmering essences of poultry and meat, as they do not yield a nice stock if left to boil. Also, there is little evaporation in the slow cooker, so you don't have to replenish liquid at any time, as you do in stove-top cooking. The following recipes make a moderate amount of broth, so a large 6- to 7-quart capacity slow cooker will do nicely and be easy to lift when full.

A few minutes are needed to combine all the ingredients in the pot and to add enough water to just cover the bones. Then the broth is left alone to simmer for part of the day, until it develops its own sweet aroma and rich color. Cold water produces a broth with a deeper color and more intense flavor. It also prevents the bones from coagulating their proteins, which makes for a cloudy broth. Instead the proteins will float to the top and you can skim off the foamy residue.

For making broth, vegetables from the supermarket produce section are as good as ones harvested from a home garden. Frankly, the simpler the ingredients, the better the broth, so resist throwing every kind of vegetable scrap into the pot, although slightly over-the-hill vegetables (but not moldy) are great because they are soft and flavorful. Add the so-called aromatic vegetables, the basic combination of chopped onions, celery, and carrots known as *mirepoix.* You want these vegetables to fall apart and dissolve into the broth. After an initial hour on HIGH in the slow cooker to quickly bring up the temperature of the liquid, the long simmering time allows all the flavors to be extracted by the water. No salt is added so that you can taste and season at the end.

When the broth is done, strain it, then transfer it to storage containers and refrigerate or freeze. Don't leave out your broth at room temperature; it's a perfect warm bath for bacteria. If broth has spoiled, it will smell fermented; in that case, discard immediately.

What looks like a lot of broth in the slow cooker when you start will be a bit less after you cook it down and strain it. Use a small saucepan or large ladle to transfer the still-warm broth (ideally around 160°F) into a cheesecloth-lined colander sitting in a larger bowl. Do this procedure over the sink, since during the process of straining there is the chance of splashing. The solids will catch in the colander and, when you lift it out, you can admire your beautiful, clear broth. After straining, refrigerate until cold. The fat will coagulate on top if you are making a meat or poultry broth, and it will be easy to remove by scooping it right off with a spoon. Leave on the fat while you store the broth in the refrigerator (it actually seals the broth from exposure to the air), but remove it when freezing. Some people do not skim off all the fat; you can leave a few tablespoons to contribute to the overall flavor.

Buy a variety of 2- and 4-cup freezer containers at the supermarket that stack easily in the freezer. Then you are ready to toss together a stew or soup in your slow cooker at a moment's notice. Always reboil broth in whatever recipe you use it. Add a bit of salt and pepper and you can savor a bowl of it on its own or poured over toasted country bread for a great lunch!

Chicken Broth

H omemade chicken broth is an essential ingredient in soup making, risottos, and stews. We like cutting up a whole chicken and adding some extra parts (you can keep them in the freezer), but if you have a large cooker, you can just put in the whole chicken and cook for the maximum time with little fuss. The cooking time is very flexible. ○ *Makes about 2½ quarts*

COOKER: Large round or oval
SETTINGS AND COOK TIMES: HIGH for 1 hour, then LOW for 6 to 16 hours

3½ pounds chicken parts with bones, such as backs, necks, legs, wings, and carcass;
   or one 3- to 4-pound whole chicken, cut up, fat trimmed and liver removed
1 large yellow onion, quartered
1 large carrot, cut into chunks
2 to 3 ribs celery with leaves
8 sprigs fresh flat-leaf parsley with stems
A few grinds of black pepper or a few black peppercorns
Salt (optional) to taste

1. Combine all the ingredients in the slow cooker, except the salt. Add cold water to cover by 2 to 3 inches. Cover and cook on HIGH for 1 hour.

2. Skim off any surface foam with a large spoon. Cover, turn the cooker to LOW, and cook for 6 to 16 hours. If the water cooks down below the level of the ingredients, add a bit more boiling water.

3. Uncover and let cool to lukewarm. Set a large colander lined with cheesecloth or a fine-mesh strainer over a large bowl and pour the broth through to strain. Press on the vegetables to extract all the liquid. Discard the vegetables, skin, and bones. If desired, reserve the meat for soup, salad, or another purpose. Taste the broth and season with salt if needed, or wait to salt until you are using the broth. Refrigerate.

4. The broth is ready for use and can be refrigerated, tightly covered, for up to 2 to 3 days. Or remove the congealed fat from the surface and pour into airtight plastic freezer storage containers, leaving 2 inches at the top to allow for expansion. Freeze for 3 to 4 months. Whether refrigerated or frozen (and defrosted), make sure the broth is brought to a boil when using it.

Extra-Rich Chicken Broth

Also known as white stock, this can be used in place of plain chicken broth in risottos and veal or poultry stews. Buy chicken breasts for dinner, debone them, and keep the meaty raw bones in plastic freezer bags until you are ready to make broth. This one is really delicious. ○ *Makes about 3 quarts*

COOKER: Large round or oval
SETTINGS AND COOK TIMES: HIGH for 1 hour, then LOW for 8 to 10 hours

2 medium-size yellow onions, quartered
2 medium-size carrots, cut into chunks
2 leeks (white part only), washed well and chopped
3 ribs celery with leaves, cut into chunks
1 or 2 veal knuckles, cracked
6 chicken breast bones (left over from deboning the breast halves) and
    a few wings; or 1 whole chicken (3½ to 4 pounds), fat trimmed
1 bouquet garni: 4 sprigs fresh parsley, 1 bay leaf, 1 or 2 sprigs fresh thyme,
    1 sprig fresh tarragon, 10 black peppercorns, and 1 clove peeled garlic,
    wrapped up in cheesecloth and tied with kitchen twine
1 cup dry white wine
Salt (optional) to taste

1. Put the vegetables, veal, chicken, and bouquet garni in the slow cooker. Add cold water to cover by at least 3 inches and the wine. Cover and cook on HIGH until hot, about 1 hour.

2. Skim off any surface foam with a large spoon. Cover, turn the cooker to LOW, and cook for 8 to 10 hours. If the water cooks down below the level of the ingredients, add a bit more boiling water.

3. Uncover and let cool to lukewarm. Set a large colander lined with a double layer of cheesecloth or a fine mesh strainer over a large bowl and pour the broth through to strain. Press the vegetables to extract all the liquid. Discard the vegetables, bouquet garni, bones, and meat. Season with salt, if desired, or leave unsalted. Refrigerate the broth.

4. Use immediately or refrigerate for 2 to 3 days, tightly covered. Or remove the congealed fat from the surface and pour into airtight plastic freezer storage containers, leaving 2 inches at the top to allow for expansion. Freeze for 3 to 4 months. Whether refrigerated or frozen (and defrosted), make sure the broth is brought to a boil when using it.

Turkey Broth

The next time you have roast turkey, make a nice rich broth out of the carcass. If you have a round cooker, you will have to break it up (separate the ribs from the backbone; it won't fit whole into the pot). If the broth is not strong enough after cooking, add some canned chicken broth. Use this recipe for making broth with cooked leftover rabbit, pheasant, or duck as well. This broth is good for soups and stews, as well as for Jook (page 25). ◦ *Makes about 3 quarts*

COOKER: Large round or oval
SETTINGS AND COOK TIMES: HIGH for 1 hour, then LOW for 8 to 10 hours

1 roast turkey carcass with some meat left on, including the wings and skin, broken up
2 medium-size yellow onions, quartered
2 leeks (white part only), washed well and chopped
5 medium-size carrots, cut into large chunks
3 ribs celery with leaves, cut into chunks
6 sprigs fresh flat-leaf parsley with stems
1 teaspoon dried thyme or 2 sprigs fresh thyme
A few grinds of black pepper
Salt (optional) to taste

1. Put the broken-up turkey carcass in the slow cooker. Add cold water to cover by at least 4 inches. Cover and cook on HIGH until hot, about 1 hour.

2. Skim off any accumulated surface foam with a large spoon. Add the remaining ingredients, except the salt, turn the cooker to LOW, cover, and cook for 8 to 10 hours. If the water cooks down below the level of the ingredients, add a bit of boiling water.

3. Uncover and let cool to lukewarm. Set a large colander lined with a double layer of cheesecloth or a fine-mesh strainer over a large bowl and pour the broth through to strain. Press the vegetables to extract all the liquid. Discard the vegetables and bones, reserving the meat for soup or another use, if desired. Season with salt, if desired, or leave unsalted. Refrigerate.

4. The broth will keep, tightly covered, for 2 to 3 days. Or remove the congealed fat from the surface and pour into airtight plastic freezer storage containers, leaving 2 inches at the top to allow for expansion. The broth will keep, frozen, for 3 to 4 months. Whether refrigerated or frozen (and defrosted), make sure the broth is brought to a boil when using it.

Beef Broth

The secret to getting deep beef flavor and rich color in a broth is to roast the bones in the oven before popping them in the slow cooker. You can skip that step, but the flavor just won't be the same. ● *Makes about 2 quarts*

COOKER: Large round or oval
SETTINGS AND COOK TIMES: HIGH for 1 hour, then LOW for 10 to 16 hours

4 pounds raw meaty beef bones, such as shanks, sawed in a few places;
    or 2 pounds bones and 2 pounds cubed stewing beef
2 medium-size yellow onions, quartered
2 medium-size carrots, cut into chunks
4 ribs celery with leaves, cut into chunks
¼ bunch fresh flat-leaf parsley
1 bay leaf, broken in half
4 cloves
10 black peppercorns
½ cup dry white wine
2 tablespoons tomato paste
10 cups cold water

1. Preheat the oven to 450°F. Put the bones, meat, onions, and carrots in a roasting pan and roast for 30 minutes, turning once.

2. Meanwhile, combine the celery, herbs and spices, wine, tomato paste, and 8 cups of the water in the slow cooker. Cover and cook on HIGH until hot, about 1 hour.

3. Add the bones, meat, onions, and carrots to the slow cooker. Pour off the fat from the roasting pan, add the remaining 2 cups of water, and scrape up the brown bits from the bottom; add to the cooker. Cover, turn the cooker to LOW, and cook for 10 to 16 hours. If the water cooks down below the level of the ingredients, add a bit of boiling water. Skim off any surface foam with a large spoon.

4. Uncover and let cool to lukewarm. Set a large colander lined with a double layer of cheesecloth or a fine-mesh strainer over a large bowl and pour the broth through to strain. Press the vegetables to extract all the liquid. Discard the vegetables, bones, and meat. This is best left unsalted. Refrigerate.

5. The broth will keep, tightly covered, for 2 to 3 days in the refrigerator. Or remove the congealed fat from the surface and pour into airtight plastic freezer storage containers, leaving 2 inches at the top to allow for expansion. The broth will keep, frozen, for 3 to 4 months. Whether refrigerated or frozen (and defrosted), make sure the broth is brought to a boil when using it.

Smoky Meat Broth

This is the broth to make with your leftover smoked or honey cured ham. This is a must for making lentil, bean, and split pea soups, cabbage soup, borscht, and baked beans. ○ *Makes about 3 quarts*

COOKER: Large round or oval
SETTINGS AND COOK TIMES: HIGH for 1 hour, then LOW for 8 to 10 hours

One 1- to 2-pound ham bone, or 1 to 2 pounds smoked pork chop bones, or 2 large ham hocks
2 medium-size yellow onions, quartered
2 leeks (white part only), washed well and chopped
2 ribs celery with leaves, cut into chunks
1 medium-size carrot, cut into chunks
1 medium-size parsnip, peeled and cut into chunks
1 bay leaf
8 black peppercorns

1. Put all the ingredients in the slow cooker. Add cold water to cover by at least 3 inches. Cover and cook on HIGH until hot, about 1 hour.

2. Skim off any accumulated surface foam with a large spoon. Cover, turn the cooker to LOW, and simmer for 8 to 10 hours. If the water cooks down below the level of the ingredients, add a bit of boiling water.

3. Uncover and let cool to lukewarm. Set a large colander lined with a double layer of cheesecloth or a fine-mesh strainer over a large bowl and pour the broth through to strain. Press the vegetables to extract all the liquid. Discard the vegetables, bones, and meat. This is best left unsalted. Refrigerate.

4. The broth will keep, tightly covered, in the refrigerator for 2 to 3 days. Or remove the congealed fat from the surface and pour into airtight plastic freezer storage containers, leaving 2 inches at the top to allow for expansion. The broth will keep, frozen, for 3 to 4 months. Whether refrigerated or frozen (and defrosted), make sure the broth is brought to a boil when using it.

Vegetable Broth

Known in French as *fond de légumes,* vegetable broth is a wonderfully old-fashioned, aromatic combination of mild herbs and vegetables with a decidedly neutral taste. Note that vegetables with strong flavors, such as cabbage, turnips, Brussels sprouts, green peppers, broccoli, and cauliflower, should be used with care; they will flavor your broth distinctly, and even make it bitter. And save potatoes and beets for your soup instead of your broth. The starch in potatoes will make a broth murky, while beets will instantly tint it a brilliant, earthy color, which is undesirable for an all-purpose broth. Use leek tops, tomato ends, spinach, parsley stems, carrot peelings, and green bean strings. We like to use fresh vegetables for this broth; old vegetables just do not cook up into a nice vegetable broth.

We make two different kinds of vegetable broths: one with roasted vegetables (page 102) for use in recipes that require a fuller bodied broth, and this one, in which we sweat the primary vegetables in a little oil before adding the liquid; it is for use with more delicate dishes. In the summer you can add the juice from home-canned fruit for a fruity flavor, which is very nice in cold fruit soups or as a poaching liquid for fish. ○ *Makes about 2 quarts*

COOKER: Large round or oval

SETTINGS AND COOK TIMES: HIGH for 1 hour, then LOW for 4 to 6 hours

3 yellow onions, peeled

3 or 4 cloves

3 tablespoons olive oil

2 leeks (white and green parts), washed well and chopped

2 medium-size carrots, cut into chunks

1 medium-size parsnip, peeled and cut into chunks

1 small bunch celery with leaves, cut into chunks

1 or 2 leftover corn cobs (optional), broken into hunks (after you have cut off the kernels)

3 cloves garlic, smashed

6 sprigs fresh flat-leaf parsley with stems

1 bay leaf

1 sprig fresh thyme or marjoram

1 tablespoon black peppercorns

2 to 3 teaspoons salt, to your taste

1. Coarsely chop 2 of the onions; leave 1 onion whole and stud with the cloves. Heat the oil over medium-high heat in a large soup pot; add the chopped onions, leeks, carrots, parsnip, and celery and cook, stirring, for 10 to 15 minutes. (This step is optional, but the initial sweating makes for a more flavorful broth.)

2. Put the sautéed vegetables, corn cobs, if using, garlic, parsley, bay leaf, thyme, and peppercorns in the slow cooker. Add cold water to cover by 2 to 3 inches. Cover and cook on HIGH until hot, about 1 hour.

3. Turn the cooker to LOW and cook for 4 to 6 hours. If the water cooks down below the level of the ingredients, add a bit of boiling water.

4. Uncover and let cool to lukewarm. Set a large colander lined with a double layer of cheesecloth or a fine-mesh strainer over a large bowl and pour the broth through to strain. Press the vegetables to extract all the liquid. Discard the vegetables. Season with salt; you may need quite a lot, 2 teaspoons to 1 tablespoon. The broth is ready for use and can be refrigerated for up to 1 week or frozen for 3 to 4 months.

Flavor Variations for Vegetable Broth

- 2 to 3 plum tomatoes, cut up, add color, flavor, and acidity to the broth and are very appropriate for many summer soups.

- 1 fennel bulb, diced, is bold and adds great flavor to seafood dishes; use the bulb, stalk, and outer leaves.

- 4 to 6 ounces of fresh mushrooms or a few dried mushrooms can be added to the broth as it simmers; dried mushrooms add a deep, woodsy flavor, while fresh ones are a bit tamer.

Roasted Vegetable Broth

For a fuller bodied broth, roast the vegetables first in the oven. You will not believe how much more aromatic a broth you will get. Note that onions and leeks are basics in vegetable broths. Don't use onion skins, though; they make a broth bitter. This is a classic winter vegetable broth, good for chunky vegetable or bean soups. ● *Makes about 2 quarts*

COOKER: Large round or oval
SETTINGS AND COOK TIMES: HIGH for 1 hour, then LOW for 4 to 6 hours

2 medium-size leeks (white part only), washed well and diced
2 large yellow onions, chopped
3 garlic cloves, pressed
2 ribs celery with the leaves, chopped
3 medium-size carrots, cut into chunks
½ butternut squash, peeled, seeded, and cut into chunks
1 medium-size red bell pepper, seeded and cut into chunks
1½ tablespoons olive oil
1 to 2 green Swiss chard leaves (not ruby chard; optional)
¼ cup dried lentils, picked over and rinsed
½ bunch fresh flat-leaf parsley
¼ cup sun-dried tomatoes (not oil packed)
1 large bay leaf
Salt (optional) to taste

1. Preheat the oven to 400°F. Place the leeks, onions, garlic, celery, carrots, squash, and bell pepper in a large bowl and toss with the oil to lightly coat. Roast in the oven on a baking sheet until caramelized, 50 to 60 minutes.

2. Place the roasted vegetables in the slow cooker along with the chard, lentils, parsley, tomatoes, and bay leaf and add cold water to cover by 2 to 3 inches. Cover and cook on HIGH until hot, about 1 hour.

3. Turn the cooker to LOW and cook 4 to 6 hours more.

4. Uncover and let cool to lukewarm. Set a large colander lined with a double layer of cheesecloth or a fine-mesh strainer over a large bowl and pour the broth through to strain. Press the vegetables to extract all the liquid. Discard the vegetables. Season with salt or leave unsalted. The broth is ready for use and can be refrigerated for up to 1 week. Or pour into airtight plastic freezer storage containers, leaving 2 inches at the top to allow for expansion, and freeze for 3 to 4 months.

Vegetable Dashi for Miso Soup

Beth is constantly complaining about having to make dashi broth with bonito flakes every time she wants a bowl of clear miso soup. Well, thanks to food wiz Victoria Wise, here is the vegetarian alternative adapted from her book *The Vegetarian Table: Japan* (Chronicle Books, 1998). Vegetarian dashi is quite common, especially in monastery food; it is made from simmered roots, stems, and miscellaneous available produce. This mild broth is fast and easy and does not cook all day. ○ *Makes about 2 quarts*

COOKER: Medium round
SETTINGS AND COOK TIMES: HIGH for 1 hour, then LOW for about 3 hours

1 bunch green onions (white and green parts), cut into 2-inch lengths
8 ounces daikon, cut into ½-inch-thick rounds
A few sprigs of fresh cilantro with stems
4 large dried or fresh shiitake mushrooms, rinsed
2 ribs celery, chopped, plus ½ cup chopped celery leaves
1 long strip kombu seaweed, wiped clean
Pinch of sea salt

1. Put all the ingredients in the slow cooker. Add cold water to cover by at least 3 inches. Cover and cook on HIGH until boiling hot, about 1 hour.

2. Turn the cooker to LOW and simmer until the daikon is soft, about 3 hours.

3. Uncover and let cool slightly. Set a large colander lined with a double layer of cheesecloth or a fine-mesh strainer over a large bowl and pour the broth through to strain. Press the vegetables to extract all the liquid. Discard the solids. The broth is ready for use and can be refrigerated for up to 3 days. Or pour into airtight plastic freezer storage containers, leaving 2 inches at the top to allow for expansion, and freeze for up to 3 months.

Making Miso Soup

To make miso soup, use 2 teaspoons to 1 tablespoon of red miso per cup of Vegetable Dashi (page 103) and whisk it into the hot dashi. (Use double the amount if using the milder white miso, or a combination of half white and half red miso.) Do not let the mixture boil. Add chopped green onions, cilantro, or mitsuba (a Japanese herb sometimes called trefoil), cubed silken or firm tofu, and your choice of slivered fresh shiitake mushrooms, some shredded Napa cabbage or spinach, or a few canned azuki or black soybeans. Simmer for 30 minutes and serve.

Asian Vegetarian Broth

his is an aromatic variation on plain Vegetable Broth (page 100). The addition of fresh-tasting cilantro (known as Chinese parsley or fresh coriander), dried shiitake mushrooms, a few broken points of licorice-scented star anise (a favorite seasoning for Asian broths), and slices of spicy fresh gingerroot make for a broth that is still quite delicately flavored. Aromatic Szechuan peppercorns, used in place of black peppercorns, are pan-toasted to bring out their flavor and fragrance. If you can't find them, just use regular black peppercorns. The dried shiitake mushrooms are called black mushrooms when sold with Asian ingredients. Star anise is another Asian ingredient, but it is also sold with Latin American foods as *anis estrella*. ◦ *Makes about 2 quarts*

COOKER: Large round or oval
SETTINGS AND COOK TIMES: HIGH for 1 hour, then LOW for 5 to 6 hours

2 medium-size yellow onions, quartered

1 bunch green onions (white and green parts), cut crosswise into several lengths each

1 head Napa cabbage, cored and coarsely shredded

2 medium-size carrots, cut into chunks

3 ribs celery or bok choy leaves, cut into pieces

½ bunch fresh cilantro with stems

3 to 4 large dried shiitake mushrooms

1 head garlic, left unpeeled and cut in half crosswise so that each clove has been halved

8 thin slices fresh ginger, left unpeeled

3 tablespoons tamari or another soy sauce

1 star anise

1 teaspoon Szechuan peppercorns, toasted in a dry skillet over medium heat until fragrant

1 teaspoon Chinese 5-spice powder

1. Put the vegetables, garlic, and ginger in the slow cooker. Add cold water to cover by at least 3 inches, and add the tamari and spices. Cover and cook on HIGH until hot, about 1 hour.

2. Turn the cooker to LOW and cook for 5 to 6 hours.

3. Uncover and let cool to lukewarm. Set a large colander lined with a double layer of cheesecloth or a fine-mesh strainer over a large bowl and pour the broth through to strain. Press the vegetables to extract all the liquid. Discard the solids. The broth is ready for use and can be refrigerated for 3 to 4 days. Or pour into airtight plastic freezer storage containers, leaving 2 inches at the top to allow for expansion, and freeze for up to 3 months.

Slow-Cooked Side Dishes, Vegetable Stews, and Stuffings

Vegetables are the trickiest to cook in the slow cooker because of their wide variations in textures and cooking times. Generally the key to success with vegetables in the slow cooker is to remember that they cook a lot faster than meat or bean stews, so you're probably not going to be cooking all day. Please pay close attention to our recommended cooking times; they vary widely. The best vegetables for braising are ones with a lot of cellulose so that they will retain their flavor essence even when soft and mushy. Roots, tubers, and winter squashes are really stars in the slow cooker, but, surprisingly, long-cooked greens and green beans are excellent, as are artichokes and beets. Be sure to try making your own fresh stewed tomatoes and roasted garlic in the crock.

Slow-Steamed Artichokes

he oval cooker is the best shape for cooking whole artichokes. If you only have a round one, buy artichokes of a comparable size and fit them tightly side by side in the cooker. ○ *Serves 4 to 6*

COOKER: Medium or large round or oval
SETTING AND COOK TIME: LOW for 6 to 7 hours

4 to 6 large artichokes
1½ cups water
2 tablespoons olive oil
3 slices lemon
2 cloves garlic, peeled; or 1 slice onion

1. Cut the stem flush with the bottom of the artichoke so it can stand flat. Cut off the top 1 inch and, with kitchen shears, snip the tip off each exposed leaf. Arrange the artichokes stem end down and packed together in the slow cooker; add the water, oil, lemon, and garlic. Cover and cook on LOW until a leaf is very tender and separates with no resistance when pulled off, 6 to 7 hours.

2. Remove the chokes from the cooker with tongs. Eat hot immediately, leave at room temperature, or cool, wrap in plastic, and chill before serving.

Soy-Sake Asparagus

resh asparagus is one of the glories of springtime; the season runs from mid-February through June. Here's a way to enjoy it that goes much beyond steaming in the flavor department. If you can find them, buy Japanese sesame seeds; they are usually sold in a tall plastic cylinder and come conveniently already toasted. Light brown in color and larger, they are more flavorful than the usual kind. If you have a spare moment, retoasting them in a small skillet over medium heat for a couple of minutes will intensify the flavor even more.
○ *Serves 4 to 5*

COOKER: Medium or large oval

SETTING AND COOK TIME: HIGH for 1¼ to 1½ hours

1¼ to 1½ pounds medium to thick asparagus
1 tablespoon olive oil
1 tablespoon sake
1 teaspoon soy sauce
Pinch of brown sugar
Pinch of salt
1 to 2 teaspoons toasted sesame seeds (optional) for garnish

1. Wash and drain the asparagus. One by one, hold each spear in both of your hands. Bend the spear at the stem end until the end snaps off. Discard the stem end. Put the asparagus in the slow cooker. Drizzle in the olive oil, sake, and soy sauce. Sprinkle with the brown sugar and salt. With your hands, gently toss the asparagus to coat them lightly with the seasonings. Cover and cook on HIGH until tender when pierced with a sharp knife, 1¼ to 1½ hours.

2. Use a pair of tongs to place the asparagus on a serving platter. Pour the liquid from the crock over the asparagus. Sprinkle with the toasted sesame seeds just before serving.

Braised Peas with Lettuce

The French have a unique method for preparing those tough large peas that tend to show up at the end of the season, either fresh or frozen; slow cooking them under a blanket of lettuce, where they stay nice and green. Don't worry if they look a bit wrinkled after cooking; they will taste delicious. This is particularly good with chicken dishes. ○ *Serves 8*

COOKER: Medium round

SETTINGS AND COOK TIMES: HIGH for 30 minutes, then LOW for 2 to 3 hours

1 medium-size head Boston lettuce
1 sprig fresh thyme, savory, or mint

8 white boiling onions (16 if they are really tiny), peeled

½ cup (1 stick) unsalted butter, softened

½ teaspoon sugar

½ teaspoon salt

½ teaspoon ground white pepper

3½ to 4 pounds fresh peas in the pod (5 to 6 cups shelled peas of a uniform size),
   or two 12-ounce bags frozen garden peas (not petites), thawed

¼ cup water

1. Coat the slow cooker with nonstick cooking spray or butter; line the bottom and sides with the outer lettuce leaves. Reserve some leaves for the top. Open the lettuce heart, place the single herb sprig inside, and tie with kitchen twine. Put it in the cooker and add the onions.

2. In a small bowl, mash together the butter, sugar, salt, and pepper. Add to the bowl of shelled peas and, with your hands, gently squeeze the butter into the mass of peas to coat them; it is okay if some peas are bruised, but try not to crush any. Pack the peas around the heart of lettuce in the cooker and top with more lettuce leaves. Add the water. Cover and cook on HIGH for 30 minutes to get the pot heated up.

3. Reduce the heat setting to LOW and cook until the peas are tender, 2 to 3 hours. At 2 hours, lift the cover to check their progress. Remove the lettuce leaves and the lettuce heart, and serve the hot peas from the crock.

Braised Fresh Shell Beans

W e decided to put the fresh shell beans here with the vegetables instead of in the bean chapter. They are a rarity in regular supermarkets, but are in their glory in the summer at regional farmers markets or roadside produce stands. Freshly picked beans still in their long pods are a real treat for vegetable lovers. Use any type fresh bean you come across, from limas and cranberries to white beans. The small beans can cook as fast as 1½ hours; the large ones take 3 to 4 hours. Serve with some of your favorite extra virgin olive oil for drizzling and fresh bread. ○ *Serves 6*

COOKER: Medium round

SETTING AND COOK TIME: HIGH for 1½ to 4 hours, depending on the type of bean

3 tablespoons olive oil

2 shallots, minced

3 pounds fresh shell beans, shelled (you will have 1 to 1½ cups per pound of beans, depending on the size)

1 cup water, vegetable broth, or chicken broth

Salt and freshly ground black pepper to taste

2 to 3 teaspoons fresh chopped herbs, such as thyme, parsley, marjoram, or basil

2 to 3 teaspoons dark or white balsamic vinegar

1. In a small skillet over medium heat, warm the olive oil and cook the shallots, stirring, until softened. Put in the slow cooker along with the beans and water. Cover and cook on HIGH for 1½ to 4 hours, depending on the size of the bean.

2. Season with salt and pepper and stir in the herbs and vinegar. Serve immediately, or refrigerate and eat cold.

•• Crocked-Baked Beets in •• Warm Raspberry Vinaigrette

This is one of our favorite ways to serve freshly cooked beets. The raspberry fruit flavor is a natural complement for the ruby beets. ○ *Serves 4*

⅓ cup olive oil

1 small shallot, chopped

¼ cup raspberry vinegar

8 small or 3 large beets, cooked, with 1 tablespoon of the crock liquid

Butter lettuce for serving

Salt and freshly ground black pepper to taste

In a small skillet over medium heat, heat 1 tablespoon of the olive oil and cook the shallot, stirring, until softened. Add the vinegar and the tablespoon of beet liquor and heat just to warm. Add the remaining olive oil and pour over the beets in a bowl; toss to coat. Arrange the lettuce in a serving dish and spoon the beets onto the bed of lettuce. Season with salt and pepper, and serve.

Southern-Style Barbecue Green Beans with Bacon

Green beans, the long, slender, slinky pods, are surprisingly good slow cooked, especially Blue Lake beans that are a bit older than the young 'uns. These are braised, and are good to serve with plain roasted or barbecued meats, or even a hamburger. ○ *Serves 4 to 6*

COOKER: Medium round or oval
SETTING AND COOK TIME: LOW for 6 to 7 hours

2 strips pork or turkey bacon
1 small yellow or white onion, chopped
1 pound fresh green beans, stem ends snapped off
¾ cup barbecue sauce of your choice

1. In a small skillet over medium-high heat, cook the bacon until crisp. Drain on paper towels, crumble, and set aside.

2. Grease the inside of the slow cooker with some of the bacon drippings.

3. Add the onion to the skillet and cook, stirring, until softened, about 5 minutes.

4. Put the beans, crumbled bacon, and onion in the cooker. Pour over the barbecue sauce, cover, and cook on LOW until the beans are tender and glazed, 6 to 7 hours. Serve hot.

Crock-Baked Beets

So many diners stick their noses up about beets, but roasted beets bear little resemblance to their canned cousins. The timing will vary somewhat; small beets will cook more quickly. In addition, if you fill the cooker with beets, plan on additional cooking time. Serve the beets whole, cut into wedges, or mashed.

They are good hot, with butter, salt, and pepper. To serve them cold, let them cool in a vinaigrette (see page 112). ◦ *Serves 4*

> **COOKER:** Small or medium round or oval
> **SETTING AND COOK TIME:** HIGH for 4 to 6 hours

2 small or 1 large bunch beets (4 to 10 beets, depending on the size), scrubbed

1. Prepare each whole beet by leaving the root intact and trimming the stem to a 1-inch stub to prevent bleeding. Wrap each whole beet in aluminum foil and pile into the slow cooker. If your beets are small, wrap three together. Cover and cook on HIGH for 4 to 6 hours, depending on the size of the beets. (To check for doneness, pierce a beet with the tip of a sharp knife through the foil. When it goes in with no resistance, the beet is done.) The more beets in the cooker, the longer the cook time.

2. Remove the beets from the cooker with tongs, unwrap, and slip off the skins with a paring knife. Leave whole if small, or slice or cut into chunks. Serve immediately, or refrigerate and eat cold.

Red Cabbage and Apples

R ed cabbage lights up the table with color and lends a sweeter flavor than its all-green cousin. Braising intensifies that sweetness. Pair red cabbage with apples and vinegar and you have one of the traditional dishes of northern European cuisines. When shopping, choose heads that are tight and firm and feel heavy for their size. A variation of this dish, a favorite with children for generations, has the apples stuffed with sautéed onions and ham, then set on top of the cabbage to cook like baked apples. Serve this hot or chill and serve cold alongside sausages and pork. ◦ *Serves 6 to 8*

> **COOKER:** Medium or large round or oval
> **SETTING AND COOK TIME:** LOW for 5 to 6 hours

1 to 2 heads red cabbage, cored and shredded (12 to 14 cups)
2 tart firm apples, peeled, cored, and diced

½ **cup red wine vinegar**

2 tablespoons light brown sugar

1½ teaspoons salt

½ **teaspoon freshly ground black pepper**

1. Put the cabbage and apples in the slow cooker and stir to mix. Combine the vinegar and brown sugar; pour over the top and toss the cabbage to coat. Cover and cook on LOW until the cabbage is tender, 5 to 6 hours.

2. Sprinkle the cabbage with the salt and pepper and toss to distribute the seasonings evenly. Serve hot or refrigerate for up to 24 hours, covered with plastic wrap.

Sauerkraut and Onions

 his dish is simplicity itself. Use fresh sauerkraut, sold in plastic bags, not canned. Serve this hot with roasted pork or sausages. ○ *Serves 6 to 8*

COOKER: Medium round or oval
SETTING AND COOK TIME: LOW for 4 to 6 hours

2 pounds fresh sauerkraut, rinsed and drained

1 large yellow onion, sliced ¼ inch thick

2 tablespoons light or dark brown sugar

1 tablespoon unsalted butter

Combine all the ingredients in the slow cooker. Cover and cook on LOW for 4 to 6 hours.

Collard Greens and Kale

nless you were born in the South, collard greens are an almost mystical dish—how to make those bunches of oversized smooth leaves into a palatable mess o' greens that everyone raves about it? Even though many recipes say you can use greens interchangeably, collards are really in a taste class of their own, with a much more muted, downright mild flavor, but they mix well with other greens. You must wash the greens carefully, since they tend to be sandy. What starts out as a mountain of greens will cook down to a fraction of their volume; in this recipe, about 4½ cups cooked greens. The cooking liquid is known as pot liquor and can be served with the greens or drunk separately. For a full meal, increase the broth to 3 cups and add one or two 15-ounce cans of white beans in the last hour of cooking. Or use this recipe with all collards and nestle two smoked turkey wings in the center for that wonderful smoky flavor. ○ *Serves 4 to 6*

COOKER: Medium round or oval
SETTING AND COOK TIME: LOW for 4 to 5 hours

1 bunch collards (1½ pounds)
1 bunch kale (1½ pounds)
3 tablespoons olive oil
4 cloves garlic or 2 small shallots, chopped
1 cup chicken, beef, or vegetable broth
1 canned chipotle pepper in adobo sauce or small dried hot pepper (optional)
Salt and freshly ground black pepper to taste
Juice of 1 lemon
1 tablespoon cider vinegar

FOR SERVING:
Unsalted butter
Cornbread

1. Rinse the greens well in the sink. Drain and trim off the tough stems. Cut the leaves crosswise into ½-inch-wide strips; you will have about 12 to 14 cups.

2. In a deep saucepan, heat the olive oil over medium heat. Add the garlic and cook, stirring, just 30 seconds to 1 minute. Add the greens in handfuls and toss to coat with the oil. With each addition, cover for a minute until wilted, then add some more. Transfer to the slow cooker once they've all been wilted and add the broth. If using the chipotle pepper, nestle it down in the center of the grains. Cover and cook on LOW until tender, 4 to 5 hours.

3. Season with salt and pepper and stir in the lemon juice and vinegar. Serve nice and hot with a pat of butter and some cornbread.

Hominy and Corn

H ere is one of Beth's favorite veggie dishes. It is especially nice made with fresh corn and whole milk mozzarella cheese, and is so easy in the slow cooker. The recipe may be doubled or tripled; make it in a large slow cooker and add an extra hour or two to the cooking time. ○ *Serves 6 as a main dish*

COOKER: Medium round or oval
SETTINGS AND COOK TIMES: HIGH for 1 hour, then LOW for 3 to 5 hours

One 7-ounce can roasted whole green chiles, drained;
    or 4 large Anaheim chiles, roasted, peeled, and seeded (see Note)
Two 16-ounce cans yellow or white hominy, drained
4 cups frozen white baby corn kernels, thawed; or
    two 16-ounce cans corn kernels, drained; or
    7 to 8 ears fresh white corn, kernels cut off the cob
2 cups shredded cheddar, Monterey Jack, or mozzarella cheese
Warm tortillas or French rolls for serving

1. Coat the slow cooker with nonstick cooking spray. If using canned chiles, cut them in half and rinse inside and out. Pat dry and cut into thick strips. Or pat the freshly roasted chiles dry and cut into strips.

2. In layers add one-third of the hominy, one-third of the corn, one-third of the chile strips, and one-third of the cheese to the cooker. Repeat the layers two more times, ending with the cheese. Cover and cook on HIGH for 1 hour.

3. Reduce the heat to LOW and cook for 3 to 5 hours. Serve hot with warm tortillas or French rolls.

Note: To roast, peel, and seed fresh chiles or bell peppers, first char them over a flame, under the broiler, or on the surface of a grill, turning them, until the skin is blackened. Place in a closed paper bag for 10 minutes to loosen the skins. Peel off the skins under cold running water. Slit each pepper in half, remove the seeds, and cut off the stem end.

Crock-Roasted Fresh Corn on the Cob

T he best corn to eat is either just picked or just bought from your roadside produce stand. As soon as corn is harvested, the sugar in the kernels begins to turn into starch, so supermarket corn on the cob will take longer to cook and be a bit tougher after cooking, since it is usually days old. If you must keep fresh corn, be sure to refrigerate until ready to cook. We think you will be surprised at what a nice job the slow cooker does with corn on the cob (and no big pot of boiling water to hassle with), even though it needs an hour or two to cook. For this recipe, be sure to get corn still in its fresh green husk; you will be steaming it slowly in the husk. ○ *Serves 4 to 8*

COOKER: Medium or large round
SETTING AND COOK TIME: HIGH for 1 to 2 hours

4 to 8 ears fresh yellow or white corn in their husks
½ to ¾ cup water
Butter for serving

1. Carefully pull back the husk, but leave it attached at the stem end. Remove the silk from each ear and rinse under cold running water. Rewrap the corn in the husk and tie the top with kitchen twine or a strip of husk. Trim the stem flat so the ears can stand upright in the slow cooker (do not stack horizontally).

2. Arrange the ears with the stem ends down, packed together so they are standing up in the cooker; add ½ cup water for a medium cooker, ¾ cup for a large one. Cover and cook on HIGH until the corn is very tender (pull back the husk and pierce with the tip of a knife to check), 1 to 2 hours, depending on the age of the corn.

3. Remove the corn from the cooker with tongs, peel back the husk, and slather with butter. Eat immediately.

Old-Fashioned Creamed Corn

reamed corn is a dish that shows up during the holidays, and here it is conveniently prepared with frozen corn. This recipe can also be made with fresh corn in the summer. ○ *Serves 4 to 6*

COOKER: Medium round or oval
SETTING AND COOK TIME: HIGH for 3 to 3½ hours

2 cups half-and-half
1 tablespoon sugar
¼ cup instant flour, such as Wondra
Three 1-pound bags baby white or yellow corn kernels, thawed and drained
Salt and freshly ground black pepper to taste
2 tablespoons unsalted butter

1. Whisk the half-and-half, sugar, and flour together in the slow cooker until smooth. Add the corn and stir to combine. Cover and cook on HIGH until thickened and bubbly, 3 to 3½ hours, stirring every hour.

2. Season with salt and pepper and stir in the butter until melted.

Succotash

uccotash is a northeastern Native American word and a dish that has survived from Colonial America. With the staples of beans and corn, succotash was made year round. In the winter, it was made with dried corn and beans; in the summer, cooks used fresh corn and fresh shell beans. Modern cooks use frozen lima beans and fresh or frozen corn, whichever is more convenient. If you can get fresh lima beans, they are great, but the frozen baby limas are still a treat. ○ *Serves 6*

COOKER: Medium round
SETTING AND COOK TIME: LOW for 2¾ to 4¼ hours; salt, pepper, and corn added during last 15 minutes

4 ears white or yellow corn, or 3 cups frozen corn kernels, thawed

2 cups shelled fresh lima beans (about 2 pounds unshelled), or
    one 10-ounce package frozen baby limas, thawed

¼ cup water

¼ cup (½ stick) unsalted butter, cut into pieces

Salt and freshly ground black or white pepper to taste

⅓ cup heavy cream

1. If using fresh corn, cut the kernels off the cobs and scrape the cobs to extract the milk. Place the corn and limas in the slow cooker with the water and butter. Cover and cook on LOW until the vegetables are tender, 2½ to 4 hours. The time will vary with fresh or frozen vegetables, so test at 2½ hours for doneness.

2. Season with salt and pepper and stir in the cream. Cover and cook 15 minutes longer. Serve out of the crock with an oversized spoon.

Southwest Succotash: In a large skillet, cook 3 strips of bacon, chopped, with 1 chopped yellow onion until softened. Put in the crock. Add the corn, limas, water, and butter, as well as 8 ounces of okra, sliced, 1 seeded and minced jalapeño, and 1 tablespoon of chopped fresh basil. Cook as directed. At the end of cooking, add 1 pint of cherry tomatoes, cut in half, or 1 large seeded and chopped tomato. Omit the cream.

Crock-Roasted Garlic

R oasted garlic is a supporting actor in so many wonderful dishes, as well as a star in its own right. Roasting garlic heads whole changes the character of the inner cloves completely, from crisp, white, and tongue-burningly pungent to creamy, brown, and sweet, with just a hint of the garlic punch they pack when raw. We love it spread on crusty bread instead of butter, or tossed with steamed green beans or asparagus. Try it smeared over the dough as a first layer on pizza or puréed in dips, dressings, or earthy mashed potatoes. Use instead of raw cloves in stove-top sautés or our slow cooker braises, simply adding them with the liquid. ○ *Serves 4 to 6*

2 or more heads of garlic
Extra virgin olive oil for drizzling
Fresh or dried herbs such as rosemary, thyme, oregano, or marjoram (optional)

1. Remove the loose outer, papery skins from the garlic heads, leaving the cloves attached. Put the heads, in pairs, on squares of aluminum foil large enough to hold them. Over each 2 garlic heads, drizzle 2 teaspoons of olive oil. If desired, add one or more herbs. If using dried, crumble a pinch of the herb between your fingers over the garlic. If using fresh herbs, place small sprigs into each packet. Try a ½-inch sprig of rosemary, two or three 2-inch sprigs of thyme, or a 2-inch sprig of oregano or marjoram (or use a combination of two or more herbs). Fold the foil around the garlic and herbs, sealing the edges tightly. Place the packets in the slow cooker. Cover and cook on LOW until the garlic is very tender (squeeze a head with your fingers to check for the degree of softness), about 5 hours.

2. To use the cloves, cut the heads of garlic in half, or simply cut off the pointed end of each head. Squeeze out the cloves. To serve with bread, break the heads into sections and offer one section to each person; squeeze the soft cloves out of their skins. The garlic will keep, refrigerated, for up to 3 days.

Braised Leeks and Onions

his is a satisfying, complex vegetable braise. Serve with grilled, broiled, or roasted meats and poultry. ○ *Serves 4 to 6*

COOKER: Medium or large round or oval
SETTING AND COOK TIME: HIGH for 1½ to 2 hours

8 medium-size leeks (white part and about 2 inches of the green)
2 medium-size yellow onions
2 tablespoons olive oil
3 medium-size plum tomatoes, peeled, seeded, and chopped
½ cup vegetable or chicken broth
Salt and freshly ground black pepper to taste

1. Rinse the leeks under cool running water. Halve them lengthwise, peeling off the tough outer layer. Rinse them again to remove all the sand. Slice the onions ¼ inch thick.

2. In a large skillet over medium-high heat, heat the oil, then cook the onions, stirring a few times until just limp, about 2 minutes. Transfer to the slow cooker and arrange the leeks on top. Sprinkle with the tomatoes and pour the broth over. Cover and cook on HIGH until the leeks are tender, 1½ to 2 hours.

3. Season with salt and pepper and serve hot.

Stuffed Bell Peppers

J ulie's good friends Karin Schlanger and David Winsberg own Happy Quail Farms, a pepper farm in urban East Palo Alto, California. David grows a rainbow of beautiful bells, and a few hot peppers as well. And believe us, if there is something to know about peppers, they know it! For the most beautiful presentation, Karin suggests buying a variety of colors: red, yellow, orange, and chocolate (a deep purple-brown), as well as green. We have adapted one of Karin's excellent pepper recipes for the slow cooker. With easy access to the bounty of several of the Bay Area's finest farmers markets, David and Karin make the sauce with flavorful, fresh tomatoes as long as the season lasts, but it's fine to use canned tomatoes, too. ● *Serves 6*

COOKER: Medium oval or large round or oval
SETTING AND COOK TIME: LOW for 5 to 6 hours, or HIGH for 2½ to 3 hours

2 tablespoons olive oil or butter
2 medium-size onions, chopped
4 cups peeled, seeded, and chopped fresh tomatoes or
    one 28- or 29-ounce can whole tomatoes, drained and chopped
2 tablespoons minced fresh mint or 2 teaspoons dried
1 pound lean ground beef
1½ cups cooked converted rice

2 tablespoons minced fresh flat-leaf parsley

¾ teaspoon salt, plus extra for seasoning

⅛ teaspoon freshly ground black pepper, plus extra for seasoning

6 large bell peppers, in a variety of colors, tops cut off and seeds removed

1. In a large skillet, heat the oil over medium-high heat, then add half of the onion and cook, stirring a few times, until softened, about 5 minutes. Add the tomatoes, bring to a boil, and continue boiling, stirring occasionally, until some of the liquid has evaporated and the sauce has thickened somewhat, 5 to 7 minutes. Stir in half of the mint. Season with salt and pepper, then pour the sauce into the slow cooker.

2. Add the ground beef and remaining onion to the same skillet (no need to wash it) and cook the meat over medium heat, breaking it up with a spatula as it cooks. When it is no longer pink and the onion has begun to soften, 5 to 7 minutes, remove the skillet from the heat. Drain any excess fat from the meat. Stir in the rice, the remaining mint, and the parsley. Add the ¾ teaspoon of salt and ⅛ teaspoon of pepper, or more to taste.

3. Use a spoon to fill each pepper with some of the meat mixture. Do not pack it tightly. As the peppers are filled, arrange them so they are standing up in the cooker, side by side. Do not stack them; the peppers must be in a single layer. Cover and cook on LOW for 5 to 6 hours, or on HIGH for 2½ to 3 hours. The peppers will be tender when done.

4. Serve the peppers with some of the tomato sauce spooned over or alongside them.

Crock-Baked Potatoes

T his recipe uses "mature" potatoes, the big lumpy brown potatoes sold loose or in 10-pound cellophane sacks that look as if they were just dug up out of the earth. These all-purpose potatoes, available year-round, are used for baking, roasting, mashing, and French fries. Don't buy any that have a green cast, indicating they have been exposed to sunlight for an extended amount of time during storage and are bitter. Be sure to puncture the skin before cooking to avoid bursting. You can most certainly skip the step of rubbing the outside with the butter or oil, but this makes for a delicious skin. ○ *Serves 4 to 10*

COOKER: Medium or large round or oval
SETTING AND COOK TIME: HIGH for 3 to 5 hours, or LOW for 6 to 9 hours

4 to 10 medium-size Idaho or russet baking potatoes, scrubbed under running water and dried
1 to 2 tablespoons unsalted butter or margarine, softened, or olive oil

FOR SERVING:
Butter or sour cream
Minced fresh chives

1. Prick each potato several times with a fork or the tip of a sharp knife and rub with the butter. Pile into the slow cooker; do not add water. Cover and cook on HIGH for 3 to 5 hours, or LOW for 6 to 9 hours (pierce with the tip of a knife to check for doneness). The more potatoes in the cooker (you may fill the crock if you wish), the longer the cook time.

2. Remove the potatoes from the cooker with tongs and serve split open and piping hot with butter or sour cream and minced fresh chives. Eat immediately.

Roasted New Potatoes with Garlic and Herbs

(F)or this dish, bypass the baking potatoes and big red and white boilers. Seek out the smaller waxy and flavorful varieties, such as Yellow Finns, fingerling, Yukon Gold, baby new red or white potatoes, or even the little purple potatoes. During testing, we loved the creaminess and rich flavor of the Yukon Gold. This is one case where fresh herbs are not the best choice because they tend to burn; use dried. You can increase the quantities somewhat from those given here, especially if you have a very large cooker, but do not pack the crock full of potatoes. You can peel the garlic easily if you place the individual unpeeled cloves in a cup of cold water for a few minutes. ○ *Serves 4 to 6*

COOKER: Medium or large round or oval
SETTING AND COOK TIME: HIGH for 2½ to 3½ hours

1½ to 2 pounds small, waxy boiling potatoes (see varieties suggested above)
4 to 5 cloves garlic, to your taste, peeled
1 tablespoon olive oil
½ teaspoon dried rosemary
¼ teaspoon kosher or coarse sea salt
Pinch of dried thyme

Scrub the potatoes and drain them. Put them in the slow cooker with the garlic. Drizzle with the olive oil and sprinkle with the rosemary, salt, and thyme. With a spoon or your hands, toss the potatoes and garlic to coat them lightly with the oil and herbs. Spread out the potatoes as evenly as possible in the crock. Cover and cook on HIGH until the potatoes are tender when pierced with a sharp knife, 2½ to 3½ hours. Serve immediately.

Twice-Crocked Stuffed Potatoes with Cheddar and Chives

or your best pot roast or meatloaf, serve these stuffed potatoes nice and hot. ● *Serves 6*

COOKER: Medium or large round or oval
SETTINGS AND COOK TIMES: HIGH for 4 to 6 hours, or LOW for 6 to 8 hours;
    then HIGH for 45 to 60 minutes

6 large Idaho or russet baking potatoes, scrubbed and left dripping wet
4 to 6 tablespoons (½ to ¾ stick) unsalted butter, softened
One 8-ounce container sour cream
About ¼ cup milk, or as needed
Salt to taste
1 cup shredded mild or sharp cheddar cheese
2 tablespoons snipped fresh chives (optional) for serving

1. Prick each dripping-wet potato with a fork or the tip of a sharp knife and pile into the slow cooker; do not add water. Cover and cook on HIGH for 3 to 5 hours, or on LOW for 6 to 8 hours (pierce with the tip of a knife to check for doneness).

2. Remove the potatoes from the cooker with tongs and cut in half. Scoop out the center of each potato half with a large spoon, leaving enough potato to keep the shell intact. Put the potato flesh in a bowl and add the butter, sour cream, and milk; beat until smooth with a fork, electric mixer, or potato masher. You want it quite thick. Season with salt. Spoon the filling back into the shells, mounding each. Return the potatoes to the slow cooker, arranging them in a single layer so they are touching each other, and sprinkle with the cheese. Cover and cook on HIGH 45 to 60 minutes.

3. Remove carefully from the cooker and eat immediately, sprinkled with the chives, if desired.

Hot German Potato Salad

Versions of this classic appeared in the very first slow cooker cookbooks and it is still an excellent way to prepare one of the best potato salads. The secret to the good flavor of the finished dish is to make sure the potatoes are hot when they are tossed with the vinegar. Here in the slow cooker, they are cooked in the vinegar to achieve that necessary tartness. ○ *Serves 4*

COOKER: Medium round or oval
SETTING AND COOK TIME: LOW for 4 to 4½ hours

2 pounds baking potatoes (5 to 6), such as russet, sliced ¼ inch thick
1 small red onion, chopped
3 ribs celery, chopped
½ green bell pepper, seeded and finely chopped
¼ cup cider vinegar
½ cup water
¼ cup canola or light olive oil
2 tablespoons sugar
½ teaspoon celery seeds
¼ cup chopped fresh flat-leaf parsley

6 strips bacon or turkey bacon, cooked until crisp, drained on paper towels, and crumbled; or
   3 tablespoons veggie bacon bits
Salt and freshly ground black pepper to taste

1. Put the potatoes, onion, celery, and bell pepper in the slow cooker; toss to mix. Pour over the vinegar, water, oil, sugar, and celery seeds. Cover and cook on LOW for 4 to 4½ hours.

2. Add the parsley and bacon and stir gently to combine; season with salt and pepper. Serve hot.

Rough Mashed Potatoes with Garlic

 You cook the potatoes and garlic together, then mash them together with a potato masher or pastry blender. Excellent. The potatoes can sit in the cooker for a few hours until serving, as well. ❍ *Serves 4*

COOKER: Medium round or oval
SETTING AND COOK TIME: HIGH for 3½ to 4½ hours

2 pounds baking potatoes (5 to 6), such as russet, peeled and cut into chunks
4 cloves garlic, chopped
1 bay leaf
2 cups chicken broth, vegetable broth, or water
½ cup hot whole milk or buttermilk
2 tablespoons unsalted butter
Salt and freshly ground black or white pepper to taste

1. Put the potatoes, garlic, and bay leaf in the slow cooker. Add enough broth to completely cover the potatoes. Cover and cook on HIGH for 3½ to 4½ hours, depending on size of potato chunks.

2. Drain in a colander over a bowl, reserving the liquid and discarding the bay leaf. Return the potatoes to the cooker, add the milk and butter, and mash, adding some cooking liquid to adjust the consistency to your preference. Season with salt and pepper. If you like, press a pat of butter into the top. Cover and keep on KEEP WARM or LOW until serving. Serve at the table right from the slow cooker.

Crock-Baked Sweet Potatoes or Yams

T his is the basic recipe for cooking whole sweet potatoes and yams. They will hold in the hot cooker for an hour or two before serving. Serve steaming hot right out of the cooker with butter. ○ *Serves 5*

COOKER: Medium or large round or oval
SETTING AND COOK TIME: LOW for 4 to 6 hours

5 medium-size sweet potatoes or yams, scrubbed and left dripping wet
Butter for serving

1. Prick each potato with a fork or tip of a sharp knife to prevent bursting. Pile into the slow cooker; do not add water. Cover and cook on LOW until tender (pierce with the tip of a knife to check for doneness), 4 to 6 hours, depending on the size of the potato. The more potatoes in the cooker, the longer the cook time.

2. Remove the potatoes from the cooker with tongs, and serve split open and piping hot with butter. Eat immediately.

Yams with Coconut and Pecans

W hile we love sweet potatoes, the ruby yam with its dark orange flesh is an all-time favorite for fall. Please do not skip the coconut extract, which helps accent the sweet flavors of this holiday side dish. ○ *Serves 6 to 8*

COOKER: Medium or large round or oval
SETTING AND COOK TIME: LOW for 6 to 7 hours

2 pounds yams or sweet potatoes, peeled and sliced ½ inch thick
¼ teaspoon coconut extract
¼ teaspoon vanilla extract
¼ cup (½ stick) unsalted butter, melted
½ cup firmly packed light or dark brown sugar
¼ cup sweetened shredded coconut
¼ cup broken pecans

¼ teaspoon ground cinnamon

2 tablespoons cold unsalted butter, cut into pieces

Coat the slow cooker with butter or nonstick cooking spray. Arrange the slices of yams in overlapping layer. Stir the extracts into the melted butter and drizzle over the yams. Combine the brown sugar, coconut, pecans, and cinnamon in a small bowl; sprinkle over the yams in a layer. Dot with the cold butter. Cover and cook on LOW until the yams are tender (to check for doneness pierce with the tip of a knife), 6 to 7 hours.

Old-Fashioned Stewed Tomatoes

W hat would life be without the tomato? Serve this in bowls alongside macaroni and cheese, or use in recipes as you would the canned version. The recipe can be doubled and still fit in a medium slow cooker. ○ *Serves 4 to 6*

COOKER: Medium round or oval

SETTING AND COOK TIME: LOW for 8 to 10 hours

8 large firm ripe tomatoes

1 small white onion, thinly sliced

½ cup finely chopped celery

¼ cup seeded and minced green bell pepper

½ teaspoon sugar

½ teaspoon dried basil

1 small bay leaf

Salt and freshly ground black pepper to taste

2 to 3 tablespoons fresh lemon juice, to your taste

2 tablespoons unsalted butter

1. Dip each tomato in boiling water and transfer to a double layer of paper towels. Slip off the skin and halve the tomato; squeeze out the seeds and cut out the core.

2. Put the tomatoes, onion, celery, bell pepper, sugar, basil, and bay leaf in the slow cooker. Cover and cook on LOW for 8 to 10 hours.

3. Remove the bay leaf, season with salt and pepper, and stir in the lemon juice. Stir in the butter until melted. Serve hot.

Crock-Steamed Winter Squash

L arge winter squash—so creamy and delicious—can be a nuisance to cook by conventional methods. The dry heat of the oven can dry out and toughen the cut side of the squash, leaving a skin that is hard to break through with a fork. A steamer or the microwave will do a credible job, but one can hardly leave the house with a pot on the stove or the microwave running. Let your slow cooker come to the rescue. Because you add no liquid to the slow cooker, your squash will be intensely flavored. Take a tip from Julie's mother-in-law, a prolific gardener in Vermont who is always faced with a pile of squash at season's end, and freeze the cooked pulp in meal-sized amounts in plastic freezer bags. Then you can have puréed squash or a treat of muffins or pies made with your own cooked pumpkin anytime.

• • Cooking Winter Squash in the Slow Cooker • •

The slow cooker is a real boon to winter squash lovers—especially those who don't enjoy hacking apart a big winter squash, laboriously scraping out the tenacious strings and slippery seeds, and trimming away the peel. With your slow cooker, the only trick is choosing a squash—or several small ones—that will fit completely into your cooker and still allow the lid to close. If the squash fits in whole, just wash and dry it and place it in the crock along with 2 tablespoons of water. Cover and cook on LOW until the squash is tender enough to be easily pierced through to the center with a skewer or paring knife, 4 to 9 hours, depending on the type and quantity of squash and size of your cooker. Allow the squash to cool, then slice it in half from stem to base. The seeds and strings will be oh-so-easy to scoop out with a soup spoon. Discard them and spoon out the flesh from the hard, outer shell. Discard the shell. The cooked squash can be eaten as is, used in recipes, or frozen for future use.

If you wish to cook a squash that is too large for your slow cooker, the technique is slightly different. Wash the squash, cut it into pieces, and scrape out the seeds and strings. Pour 2 tablespoons of water in the crock, then stack the squash pieces in the inside, hard shell side down. Cover and cook on LOW until the squash is tender, 2 to 6 hours, depending on the squash and your cooker. When the squash is cool enough to handle, scoop out the flesh with a spoon and discard the skin.

Typical jack-o-lantern pumpkins can be quite watery and do not have the intense flavor of squash varieties that are grown for eating. Many people just discard jack-o-lanterns after Halloween. We have found that the cooked flesh, drained of excess liquid, is quite palatable and fine for baking or other uses if it is well seasoned. Scoop the cooked and puréed pumpkin flesh into a strainer set over a large bowl. Allow the pumpkin to drain for about an hour, then discard the liquid in the bowl.

COOKER: Large round or oval
SETTING AND COOK TIME: LOW for 7 to 9 hours

1 large or 2 smaller hard-shelled winter squash or pumpkins

1. Wash and dry the squash. Cut in half and use a metal spoon to scoop out the seeds and strings from the center. Cut the unpeeled squash into pieces that will fit into your slow cooker. Stack the pieces in the cooker, hard shell side down. (If you have too many to fit at one time, cook them in batches, refrigerating the remaining uncooked squash pieces in a plastic bag until you are ready for them.) Cover and cook on LOW until tender, 8 to 10 hours. When the squash is cool enough to handle, scoop out the flesh with a spoon and discard the skin. The squash may be served right away or puréed for use in other recipes.

2. To serve as is, top with a bit of butter. Add a sprinkling of salt and pepper or brown sugar and ground ginger or cinnamon. To serve mashed squash, when the squash is cool enough to handle, use a large metal spoon to scoop out the flesh. Purée the squash in a food processor or by passing it through a food mill. Flavor it with fresh orange juice and grated fresh or ground ginger.

Summer Squash Enchilada Casserole with Three Cheeses

ere is a vegetarian main dish that will delight all lovers of tender summer squash—those who grow them and those who simply eat them. You don't have to use the varieties we've specified here; just choose two types that are different colors. In greengrocers and farmers markets, you'll find yellow zucchini, yellow crookneck, pale green zucchini, and green scalloped squash, for instance. But please use tender young squash. The zuke someone overlooked in the garden until it was the size of a rolling pin will be too bitter for this casserole. If you can't find the crumbly Mexican-style cheese *queso fresco,* use a mild feta instead. If you use feta, which can be quite salty, rinse it in cold water (and drain well) to remove some of the salt first. If you can't find green chile enchilada sauce in a can (we like Las Palmas brand), purchase green chile salsa instead. ○ *Serves 8*

COOKER: Large, oval preferred
SETTING AND COOK TIME: HIGH for 2 hours, or LOW for 4 hours

1 tablespoon olive oil
1 large onion, chopped
4 cloves garlic, minced
1 pound green zucchini or other summer squash, ends trimmed, and cut into ¾-inch-thick rounds
1 pound yellow scalloped squash, or other summer squash, cut into ¾-inch rounds
1 teaspoon dried oregano or 2 tablespoons minced fresh oregano
½ teaspoon ground cumin
1 cup fresh corn kernels, or frozen corn, thawed
2 cups finely shredded Monterey Jack cheese
2 cups finely shredded cheddar cheese
3 to 4 cups canned green chile enchilada sauce
1 dozen soft corn tortillas, each cut into 4 strips
8 ounces *queso fresco* or rinsed and well drained mild feta cheese, crumbled

1. In a large nonstick skillet, heat the oil over medium-high heat, then add the onion and cook, stirring a few times, until softened, about 5 minutes. Add the garlic, zucchini, yellow squash, oregano, and cumin and cook, stirring a few times, until the vegetables begin to brown, 4 to 5 minutes. Add the corn and cook another minute or two. Remove the skillet from the heat.

2. Mix the Jack and cheddar cheeses together. Pour about ½ cup of the enchilada sauce into the slow cooker and tilt to spread it around. In layers add one-quarter of the tortilla strips, one-quarter of the remaining enchilada sauce, one-third of the sautéed vegetables, and one-quarter of the cheese blend. Sprinkle with one-quarter of the *queso fresco*. Repeat the layers two more times, ending with the *queso fresco*. Finish the casserole with the remaining tortilla strips, sauce, cheese blend, and *queso fresco*. Cover and cook on HIGH for 2 hours or on LOW for 4 hours. The casserole will begin to brown around the edges, but do not allow it to burn.

3. Let cool for a few minutes before cutting into squares or wedges to serve.

Ratatouille

R atatouille, a regional vegetable stew from Provence, is summer incarnate to us. When Beth taught French cooking out of her minute apartment kitchen, the first menu was always ratatouille, a classic salad with vinaigrette, and apple tart. This stew tastes even better the day after it is made, so you might want to plan ahead. Serve hot sprinkled with crumbled goat cheese, at room temperature with lemon wedges and freshly grated Parmesan cheese, or cold drizzled with balsamic vinegar. ○ *Serves 4 to 6*

COOKER: Medium or large round or oval
SETTING AND COOK TIME: HIGH for 2½ to 3 hours, or LOW for 4 to 5½ hours; zucchini added at 1½ to 3 hours, and basil, salt, and pepper added during last hour

1 large eggplant (1½ pounds), peeled and cut into 1-inch cubes
Salt
1 medium-size yellow onion, coarsely chopped
2 medium-size or large bell peppers (green, red, orange, or yellow),
    seeded and cut into big squares
10 plum tomatoes, peeled and chopped; or one 14.5-ounce can diced plum tomatoes, drained
2 to 3 cloves garlic, to your taste, minced
½ cup olive oil
5 zucchini or summer squash, ends trimmed, and cut into thick rounds
1 to 2 tablespoons chopped fresh basil, to your taste
Freshly ground black pepper to taste

1. Put the cubed eggplant in a colander and sprinkle with salt. Let stand 1 hour to drain. Press out the excess moisture with the back of a spatula and pat dry with paper towels.

2. Combine the eggplant, onion, bell peppers, tomatoes, and garlic in the slow cooker. Pour over the olive oil and toss to coat. Cover and cook on HIGH for 1 to 1½ hours, or on LOW for 2 to 3 hours.

3. Stir in the zucchini. Cover and continue to cook on HIGH for another 1½ hours or LOW for 2 to 2½ hours. The last hour, add the basil and season with salt and black pepper. The vegetables will be cooked but will still hold their shape.

Calabacitas

alabacitas, or "little squash," is a vegetable stew rather like a Southwestern succotash. It contains green chiles, corn, onion, and zucchini, which can become slush in the slow cooker. Well, with *calabacitas,* that is what you are going for; you want the squash to break down a bit. This is incredibly delicious.

○ *Serves 4*

COOKER: Medium round or oval
SETTING AND COOK TIME: LOW for 3 to 4 hours

2 tablespoons unsalted butter or olive oil
2 medium-size yellow or white onions, chopped
6 mild green chiles, such as Anaheim, roasted, peeled, seeded, and cut into large pieces
1 pound zucchini, ends trimmed, and cut into 2- to 3-inch hunks
2 to 3 ears yellow or white corn, kernels cut off the cob; or one 10-ounce package frozen corn, thawed
½ cup water
1 cup shredded cheddar or Monterey Jack cheese

1. In a small skillet, melt the butter over medium heat and cook the onions, stirring a few times, until softened, about 5 minutes.

2. Transfer to the slow cooker along with the chiles, zucchini, corn, and water. Cover and cook on LOW until the zucchini begins to break down and make a stew, 3 to 4 hours.

3. Sprinkle with the cheese and serve out of the crock with an oversized spoon.

Crock-Roasted Root Vegetables

The root vegetables and squashes of late fall and winter lend themselves well to slow cooking, emerging soft, but not mushy, and deeply flavored. While you can do this in a round cooker just fine, we like the oval cooker because it has more surface area. This combination of root vegetables is downright soul satisfying to eat on a wintry night with roasted meats or broiled seafood. ○ *Serves 6*

COOKER: Medium or large round or oval
SETTING AND COOK TIME: HIGH for 3½ to 4 hours

One 2½- to 3-pound butternut squash, peeled, seeded, and cut into 1-inch cubes

1½ pounds new red or white potatoes, cut into 1-inch cubes

2 small or 1 large bunch beets, scrubbed, trimmed, and peeled

2 medium-size turnips or rutabagas, peeled and cut into 1-inch cubes

2 large carrots, cut into thick rounds, or 20 whole baby carrots

1 medium-size to large red onion, cut in half, then cut into ½-inch wedges

6 cloves garlic, peeled

2 to 3 tablespoons olive or walnut oil

Salt and freshly ground black pepper to taste

About 3 tablespoons chopped fresh flat-leaf parsley

1. Turn the slow cooker on HIGH with the insert empty and preheat for 3 to 5 minutes. Meanwhile, put the vegetables in a large bowl, add the oil, season with salt and pepper, and toss gently. Transfer to the cooker. Cover and cook on HIGH until the vegetables are just tender and still hold their shape, 3½ to 4 hours.

2. Serve with plenty of fresh parsley sprinkled on top.

Crock-Roasted Root Vegetable Soup: Add 2 large tomatoes, quartered, to the cooker along with all the other vegetables. When done, remove the vegetables from the cooker and blend in batches with 4½ cups of vegetable or chicken broth and 2 tablespoons of fresh lemon juice. Pour back into the cooker, cover, and heat on LOW for 20 minutes. Serve with cheese croutons (see page 69).

Crock-Roasted Summer Vegetables

S ummer vegetables are so tender that usually they are not roasted, but this combination of vegetables with herbs and a touch of olive oil is stupendous. Serve hot, at room temperature, or cold along with grilled meat or fish, sausages, or a quick chicken sauté. ○ *Serves 6*

COOKER: Medium or large round or oval
SETTING AND COOK TIME: HIGH for 1½ to 2 hours

2 large red bell peppers, or 1 red and 1 yellow, seeded and cut into strips
2 large red onions, cut into 8 wedges each
3 medium-size yellow crookneck or pattypan summer squash,
    ends trimmed and sliced ½ inch thick
3 medium-size zucchini, ends trimmed, and cut into thick matchsticks; or
    1 pound baby zucchini with blossoms attached, left whole
5 ounces fresh green beans, stem end snapped off
4 cloves garlic, peeled
2 to 3 tablespoons olive oil
1 tablespoon chopped fresh basil or savory
Salt and freshly ground black pepper to taste
About 3 tablespoons chopped fresh flat-leaf parsley
2 to 4 tablespoons white or dark balsamic vinegar

1. Put all the vegetables in the slow cooker. Add the oil and basil, season with salt and pepper, and toss to coat evenly. Cover and cook on HIGH until the vegetables are just tender and still hold their shape, 1½ to 2 hours.

2. Serve sprinkled with the parsley and vinegar.

Zuni Stew

W hen the Greens restaurant vegetarian cookbook came out in 1987 (*The Greens Cookbook,* by Deborah Madison with Edward Espe Brown, Broadway Books), it was greeted with a big sigh of relief. Finally, a book from the Bay

Area's most innovative vegetarian restaurant, run by the members of the Tassajara Zen community. It was a smash hit. The first recipe most of our friends made was the Zuni Stew, a simple and satisfying Southwest-style vegetable stew. Here we have adapted it a bit for the slow cooker, since the original recipe used only fresh ingredients. If you have cumin and coriander seeds in your pantry, just grind them in a mortar with a pestle. If you love chiles, add a second ancho chile. Serve with warm tortillas and a nice fresh salsa plopped on top. ○ *Serves 6*

COOKER: Large round or oval
SETTING AND COOK TIME: LOW for 5½ to 6½ hours;
    zucchini added at 2½ to 3 hours

One 28-ounce can chopped tomatoes, with their juice
4 ears fresh white or yellow corn, kernels cut off the cob;
    or 2½ cups frozen corn, thawed
8 ounces fresh green beans, stem end snapped off, and cut into 1-inch pieces
Two 15-ounce cans pinto beans, with their liquid
1 ancho chile, seeds and veins removed, and cut into narrow strips
Pinch of dried oregano or marjoram
2 to 3 tablespoons olive or corn oil
2 medium-size yellow onions, diced
2 cloves garlic, minced
2 tablespoons chili powder
½ teaspoon ground cumin
¼ teaspoon ground coriander
1 pound zucchini or mixed summer squash, ends trimmed, and sliced ½ inch thick
Salt and freshly ground black pepper to taste
Leaves from about ½ bunch fresh cilantro, chopped
1½ cups shredded Monterey Jack or Muenster cheese

1. Combine the tomatoes and their juice, corn, green beans, pinto beans with their liquid, ancho chile, and oregano in the slow cooker. We turn the cooker on HIGH for about 15 minutes at this point, but this is optional.

2. In a large skillet, heat the oil over medium heat and cook the onions, stirring a few times, until softened. Add the garlic, chili powder, cumin, and coriander; cook, stirring, for 1 minute and add to the cooker. The stew will be thick, but you can add some water if you like. Cover and cook on LOW for 2½ to 3 hours.

3. Add the zucchini. Cover and continue to cook on LOW until the vegetables are just tender and still hold their shape, another 3 to 3½ hours.

4. Season with salt and pepper. Stir in the cilantro and cheese and serve hot.

Vegetarian Oden
(Japanese Root Vegetable Stew)

Oden is a well-loved Japanese stew made with vegetables, hard-boiled eggs, and fish balls and served out of large steaming kettles in little street restaurants called *oden-yas*. The fish version, however, is not to everyone's taste. Here we have a vegetarian rendition with the classic flavors of Japan—kombu, tamari, ginger, and mirin rice wine, adapted from the *Angelica Home Kitchen* (Ten Speed Press, 2003). Look for burdock root, daikon—a large white mild radish—and the thickener kuzu, or arrowroot, at an Asian grocery. Burdock root requires some special handling. Try to buy it the day you will use it, or at most one or two days ahead. When you get it home, if you are not going to use it right away, wrap it tightly in a plastic bag and refrigerate. To prepare burdock, also called *gobu,* scrub it very well under cold running water with a stiff vegetable brush. Trim off any discolored parts. As you cut the burdock, drop the pieces into a bowl of cold water. This will keep them from discoloring. When cutting the vegetables, try to make all of them almost equal in size for even cooking. Serve this with buckwheat soba noodles, baked marinated tofu, and a kimchee relish. ● *Serves 4 to 6*

COOKER: Large round or oval
SETTING AND COOK TIME: HIGH for 3½ to 4 hours, or LOW for 6 to 7 hours; tofu and kuzu added during last 15 minutes

1 tablespoon olive oil
1 large yellow onion, cut in half, then cut into ½-inch wedges
1 pound new white potatoes, cut into 1-inch cubes
1½ cups cubed burdock root (see headnote above)

1½ cups peeled and cubed daikon

2 medium-size rutabagas or white turnips, peeled and cut into 1-inch cubes

3 large carrots, cut into thick rounds

2 large parsnips, peeled and cut into thick rounds

6 dried shiitake mushrooms, rinsed and broken into pieces

One 3- to 4-inch piece kombu seaweed, wiped clean and cut into strips

5 to 8 slices peeled fresh ginger, bruised with the side of a large knife

½ cup tamari or another good-quality soy sauce

2 tablespoons mirin (nonalcoholic is fine)

One 14-ounce block firm or extra-firm tofu, drained very well on paper towels
and cut into 1-inch cubes

¼ cup kuzu (arrowroot)

¼ cup cold water

FOR SERVING:

2 tablespoons toasted sesame oil

About 3 tablespoons chopped fresh green onions
(white part and 2 inches of the green)

1. Coat the slow cooker with the olive oil. Place all the vegetables in the cooker. Add the mushrooms, kombu, ginger, tamari, mirin, and enough of the water to just cover the vegetables. Cover and cook on HIGH for 3½ to 4 hours, or LOW for 6 to 7 hours, until the vegetables are just tender and still hold their shape.

2. Add the tofu and stir gently to combine. Dissolve the kuzu in the ¼ cup cold water; stir into the hot stew and simmer on HIGH until the liquid is slightly thickened, about 15 minutes.

3. Serve with a drizzle of sesame oil and a sprinkling of green onions.

Stuffings

One of the most surprisingly successful foods to prepare in the slow cooker is bread stuffing. Instead of stuffing the turkey, many food purists and food professionals now cook the stuffing outside the bird. Well, casserole cooked stuffing was always too dry for us, but not in the slow cooker. It turns out like a moist, dense souffle.

While the turkey fills the oven, let the stuffing cook to perfection on the counter in the slow cooker.

•• Tips for Good Slow Cooker Stuffings ••

- A 1-pound loaf of bread will yield about 6 cups of cubed bread, a 1½-pound loaf will yield about 10 cups of cubed bread, and a 2-pound loaf will yield about 12 cups of cubed bread. White bread will give a lighter textured stuffing than whole wheat or whole grain. You can use anything from French bread to focaccia. Around the holidays, small bakeries will often bag their day-old bread, in delightful combinations, for use in stuffings; keep an eye out for them. If you use cornbread, make it the day before. You can also use packaged stuffing mix, if desired.

- Never use raw meats or fish, especially pork products or oysters, in stuffings. Loose pork sausage or any type of raw sausage must be cooked completely, whether sautéed, baked, boiled, or grilled, before adding it to the stuffing mix.

- If you are using really stale bread, you need to soak it in chicken broth or milk to soften a bit. Fresh bread doesn't soak up the same amount of liquid. You can use fresh bread cubed and dried in the oven, day-old bread cut into cubes and air-dried overnight, or a package of seasoned commercial stuffing mix.

- Adding leafy vegetables, such as Swiss chard or parsley, lightens the texture of a stuffing.

- We give a guideline for the amount of liquid needed to moisten each recipe, but you can add more or less, depending on how moist or crumbly you like your stuffing.

- Spoon the stuffing loosely into the crock, rather than packing it in, to allow room for the stuffing to expand as it heats up.

- You will serve about ½ to 1 cup of prepared stuffing per person. Take into account your love of leftovers when deciding how much to make.

- Let leftover portions cool to room temperature, then transfer to a covered storage container, and refrigerate.

Old-Fashioned Sage Stuffing Casserole

 his simple stuffing recipe is for those who don't want anything other than the traditional onion-celery-sage trinity. ● *Serves 6*

COOKER: Medium round or oval
SETTINGS AND COOK TIMES: HIGH for 1 hour, then LOW for 5 to 6 hours

½ cup (1 stick) unsalted butter, or ½ cup olive oil

2 large yellow onions, minced

4 ribs celery, chopped

1 tart apple, peeled, cored, and chopped; or 1 large carrot, chopped

1 small loaf French bread, cut into small cubes

One 7-ounce package seasoned stuffing mix, or 2 cups crumbled day-old cornbread

½ cup chopped fresh flat-leaf parsley

1½ teaspoons dried sage

1½ teaspoons dried thyme

1½ teaspoons dried marjoram

1 teaspoon salt

A few grinds of black or white pepper

1 large egg (optional), beaten

1½ to 1¾ cups turkey or chicken broth, as needed

2 tablespoons unsalted butter, cut into pieces

1. In a large skillet, heat the butter until melted over medium-high heat. Add the onions, celery, and apple and cook, stirring occasionally, until softened, about 5 minutes.

2. Put the bread and stuffing mix in a large bowl. Add the parsley, dried herbs, salt, and pepper and toss to combine. Pour the sautéed vegetables over the bread cubes and mix together. Add the egg and enough of the broth, stirring, until the ingredients are evenly moistened. Taste to adjust the seasonings.

3. Coat the slow cooker with butter, olive oil, or nonstick cooking spray. Pack the stuffing lightly into the cooker. Dot with the butter pieces and sprinkle with a few more tablespoons of chicken broth. Cover and cook on HIGH for 1 hour.

4. Reduce the heat to LOW and cook until puffy and nicely brown around the edges, 4 to 5 hours. The dressing can sit in the cooker, covered, on KEEP WARM for 2 to 3 hours before serving. Serve hot right out of the crock.

Dried Fruit and Nut Bread Stuffing

E veryone has their favorite all-purpose stuffing. Here is ours, with lots of dried fruit and nuts. Any of your homemade breads; bakery bread, such as a nice French loaf; or supermarket bread, can be the base. The bread cubes will need to dry out overnight, so plan accordingly. ○ *Serves 6*

COOKER: Medium or large round
SETTINGS AND COOK TIMES: HIGH for 1 hour, then LOW for 4 to 5 hours

One 1½-pound loaf white, whole wheat, or French bread, cubed (about 10 cups)
½ cup (1 stick) unsalted butter
2 medium-size yellow onions, chopped
4 ribs celery, chopped
½ cup chopped fresh flat-leaf parsley
1 to 2 tablespoons minced fresh sage leaves, to your taste
2 teaspoons poultry seasoning; or ¾ teaspoon *each* dried thyme, marjoram,
    and rosemary, crumbled
8 ounces mixed dried fruit, plumped in hot water and chopped, or moist-pack dried fruit bits
½ cup raisins, dried cherries, or sweetened dried cranberries
½ cup chopped pecans
1 to 1½ cups chicken or turkey broth, as needed
2 tablespoons unsalted butter, cut into pieces

1. Cover the cubed bread with a clean dish towel and let stand at room temperature overnight to dry out.

2. In a large skillet over medium heat, melt the butter. Add the onion and celery and cook, stirring a few times, until softened, about 5 minutes. Remove from the heat.

3. Put the bread in a large bowl. Add the parsley, dried herbs, dried fruit, and nuts and toss to combine. Pour the sautéed vegetables over the bread cubes and mix together. Add just enough of the broth, stirring, so the ingredients are evenly moistened. Taste to adjust seasonings.

4. Coat the slow cooker with butter, olive oil, or nonstick cooking spray. Pack the stuffing lightly into the cooker. Dot with butter and sprinkle with a few more tablespoons of chicken broth. Cover and cook on HIGH for 1 hour.

5. Reduce the heat to LOW and cook until puffy and nicely brown around the edges, 4 to 5 hours. The dressing can sit in the cooker, covered, on KEEP WARM for 2 to 3 hours before serving. Serve hot right out of the crock.

Slow Cooker Buttermilk Dumplings

B oiled dumplings are little round balls, spheres, or small fat sausage shapes that are cooked in soups, stews, or a pot of boiling water. They are eaten at dinner as a side or main dish, like noodles, with butter or gravy. This recipe is designed to be cooked on top of the stew in your slow cooker. Dumpling connoisseurs agree that the secret to good dumplings is to slide them into the gently boiling water; they shouldn't be jostled or overcrowded, otherwise, even the toughest dumpling will disintegrate or collect in clumps on the bottom of the pot. Be sure to drop the dough on top of something solid, like a chunk of meat or vegetable, so it can steam on top of the bubbling stew, and always make the dumplings right before serving. If you can find a soft white flour, such as White Lily, use it; Beth combines unbleached all-purpose with cake flour to approximate a nice pastry flour. For variety, add a tablespoon of chopped fresh parsley or basil, or a large pinch of minced dried herbs, such as sage or marjoram. ○ *Makes 6 servings*

COOKER: Medium or large round or oval
SETTING AND COOK TIME: HIGH for 25 to 30 minutes

1 cup all-purpose flour
¾ cup cake flour, such as Softasilk, or whole wheat pastry flour
2 teaspoons baking powder
½ teaspoon baking soda
¾ teaspoon salt
3 tablespoons margarine or solid vegetable shortening
1 large egg
⅔ to ¾ cup cold buttermilk, as needed

1. In a medium-size bowl, whisk together the flours, baking powder, baking soda, and salt. Cut in the margarine with a fork until the mixture is crumbly. Stir in the egg and ⅔ cup of the buttermilk and blend until a lumpy, thick, soft dough is formed, adding the remaining buttermilk if it is too dry. Do not overmix.

2. Using an oversized spoon, scoop up some dough and drop immediately on top of the finished simmering stew in the slow cooker, taking care to place each dumpling on top of something. Cover and cook on HIGH until the dumplings are cooked through, 25 to 30 minutes. Pierce the dumplings with a toothpick, bamboo skewer, or metal cake tester; it should come out clean. Serve immediately.

Slow Cooker Dumplings from a Mix: If you have a biscuit mix, you can have dumplings ready to steam 1-2-3: Combine 2 cups of biscuit mix, such as Bisquick, and ⅔ to ¾ cup of whole milk or buttermilk. Mix and cook as directed above.

Rice and Other Grains

Low-fat, low-sugar, low-sodium, and high-fiber grains are nutritionally sensible foods. Most people have become well acquainted with the virtues of whole grains through the highly advertised need for more fiber in today's modern diet. Grains have the lowest percentage of chemical and inorganic residues found in foods today. Cholesterol free and low in fat, they contain pacifarins, natural antibiotics that help protect the body against disease. Starchy grains make us feel satisfied

and well fed. They taste good and have a long history in every cuisine of the world. Everyone eats some type of grain food every day.

What is a grain? Grains have the same simple yet sophisticated structure. Each grain is a tiny dry fruit that contains a single seed capable of reproducing itself. An inedible, hard outer shell protects the seed. The seed is surrounded by a layer of starchy carbohydrates designed to feed a developing embryo. The embryo, or germ, contains a powerhouse concentration of micronutrients, fat, and proteins. The outer coating, the bran, provides the renown water-soluble fiber, a major source of complex carbohydrates and a gold mine of minerals. In varying amounts, grains contain all 10 essential amino acids. During the digestion process, grains provide an even flow of energy and stamina as well as balancing body chemistry by releasing glucose slowly into the bloodstream. They absorb water in the digestive system, creating that full feeling. The natural substance auxin helps rejuvenate cells, playing a part in preventing

premature aging. Grains also contain phytic acid, which is thought to neutralize radioactive and chemical toxins.

In short, grains are a complete food. Once the domain of a minority of health-conscious folks, a wide range of grains is now in evidence on supermarket shelves and in bins. Grains in the form of wheat berries, whole wheat flour, corn, hominy, rye berries, barley, millet, wild rice, regular rices, buckwheat, and oats all fall into this category. What follows is a short chapter on some of the best grains to make in the slow cooker machine, but there are many more recipes throughout the entire book (check the index). For example, The New-Fashioned Bean Pot and From the Porridge Pot contain delicious recipes made with whole grains. We encourage you to use our recipes as a template for creating more grain-based dishes.

One of the nice surprises with the slow cooker is that you can make a good risotto in it without any stirring, eliminating the need to ladle in the broth in small amounts. And yes, you can prepare regular rice successfully in the slow cooker, but you can't reach for just any type of rice on the shelf. Converted rice is the kind to use. It has been steamed before hulling, which makes for a firmer grain. That firmness is what allows it to stand up to long, slow cooking without getting sticky or gummy. Actually, the slow cooker is a wonderful solution for those times when you want to serve rice to a large group. You can start the slow cooker well ahead of time and know that your rice will be hot and ready when you want it to be. However, we do call for other rices in recipes, such as brown rice, to achieve a desired consistency or flavor, so please follow our suggestions carefully.

Risotto

Risotto is known as the most time-consuming rice dish to make because of all the stirring and the need to add boiling broth in small portions over the half hour of cooking time. In the slow cooker, you can make really fabulous risotto, but do watch the time closely so that it is not overcooked.

Risotto is described in literature as "gilded grains of gold," in reference to *risotto milanese,* where the cooked rice is bathed in a pale golden sheen of saffron. It is traditionally a first course dish in Italian meals, not an accompaniment like American rice, except when paired with osso bucco. We like it with all types of beef stews.

Arborio medium-grain rice is labeled *fino or superfino* and is the right size grain for risotto. Lesser grades are labeled *fino, semi-fino,* and *commune,* and are fine to use in soups. The Lundberg rice company of California has a domestic California Arborio on the market that they have been developing for ten years. RiceSelect has Texas Arborio (called risotto rice), and there is another domestic called CalRiso, all of which you can substitute, cup for cup, for their imported Italian cousins, to make lovely, less expensive, risottos, although gourmets insist the Italian rices make the most authentic risottos. A 500-gram bag, a little over one pound, yields about 2 cups of raw rice.

There is a little family of Italian medium-grain rices grown for risotto that include Carnaroli and Vialone nano along with the Arborio. Carnaroli is grown alongside Arborio in Piedmont and Lombardy. The newest hybrid of Italian Carnaroli is just starting to be exported from Argentina by Lotus Foods and is considered equal, or even superior to, to Arborio. In Venice and Verona, Vialone nano is cooked until *all' onde,* or "wavy," which is a bit looser in texture than the other risotto recipes; the rice is available now through Williams-Sonoma (800-541-2233; www.williams-sonoma.com).You can use all of these rices interchangeably in risotto recipes.

Risotto is best served immediately (it thickens dramatically as it stands at room temperature), but in a pinch, it will keep on the KEEP WARM setting for an hour or less. A warm shallow soup bowl and a soup spoon is nice to use for eating, but the correct etiquette is to eat risotto with a fork.

Of course, Italians are sticklers for the right cheese to use in risotto: Parmigiano-Reggiano. Buy a chunk of this imported Parmesan if you can; otherwise, domestic is okay. You can use sheep's milk Pecorino Romano in place of the Parmesan (it is quite a bit stronger), Asiago (poor man's Parmesan), or a Parmesan-Romano combination if you like. We like them shredded as well as finely grated.

·· Risotto in the Slow Cooker Basics ··

There are three distinct steps to making risotto: cooking the onion and rice, adding the broth and other ingredients, and adding the butter and cheese to finish, known as "creaming."

1. Risotto must be made by first sautéing chopped onion in butter (or half butter and half olive oil), then adding the rice. Put the butter, in pieces, in a sauté pan over medium-high heat on the stove top. The butter will melt in 1 to 2 minutes. Add the chopped onion, leek, or shallot; cook until soft and any liquid it exudes is evaporated. If using wine, add and cook to evaporate, a minute or so.

2. Add the measured amount of rice to the hot butter and onion; stir with a wooden spoon. The rice will gradually heat up and gently sizzle. Stir occasionally and gently to coat all the grains. Give the rice a full 1 to 2 minutes to cook. This precooks the outer coating of the rice to keep the grains separate and helps them to release their starchy amylopectin while they slowly absorb and cook in the aromatic broth.

3. Scrape the hot rice mixture into the slow cooker with a heat-proof rubber spatula. Add the broth (never water) and any other ingredients, as specified in the recipe. Stir a few times. Cover and cook on HIGH. You can open the slow cooker once or twice and stir gently, but this is optional. Use a light broth, such as chicken. You will have three to four times as much liquid as rice and there will be less evaporation with the cover closed than when you cook on the stove top. You don't have to fuss about the exact amount, and you add all the broth at once (with no preheating of the broth).

4. Check the rice for tenderness at 2 hours; continue cooking or turn off the machine. When it is done, with a plastic or wooden spoon, stir the risotto a few times, adding the butter and cheese, or cream. The bit of butter swirled in at the end of cooking is very traditional, but optional. Never add wine at the end; it will taste too bitter, spoiling the delicate flavor of your risotto. The risotto can stand on the KEEP WARM setting, if your machine has it, for about an hour. Serve immediately in shallow soup bowls with more Parmesan cheese for sprinkling (use as much as you like) and pass the pepper grinder.

Parmesan Risotto

This simple risotto is creamy and comforting. Try it with roast chicken.
● *Serves 3 to 4*

COOKER: Medium or large round
SETTING AND COOK TIME: HIGH for 2 to 2½ hours

¼ **cup olive oil**
2 medium-size shallots, minced
¼ **cup dry white wine**
1¼ **cups Arborio, Vialone nano, or Carnaroli rice**
3¾ **cups chicken broth**
½ **teaspoon salt**
¾ **cup freshly grated Parmigiano-Reggiano cheese**

1. In a small skillet over medium heat, warm the oil. Cook the shallots until softened, 3 to 4 minutes; do not brown. Add the wine and cook, stirring, for a minute or so. Add the rice and cook, stirring, until it turns from translucent to opaque (do not brown), about 2 minutes. Scrape with a heat-proof rubber spatula into the slow cooker. Add the broth and salt. Cover and cook on HIGH until all the liquid is absorbed, but the rice is still moist, 2 to 2½ hours. The risotto should be only a bit liquidy, and the rice should be *al dente,* tender with just a touch of firmness.

2. Stir in ½ cup of the cheese and pass the remainder for sprinkling. Serve immediately, spooned into bowls. Risotto will keep on the KEEP WARM setting for an hour or so.

Risotto with Edamame

Edamame are young, green soybeans. They are a favorite snack in Japan, where they are boiled, then served in the pod, lightly salted. You pick one up, squeeze the fuzzy pod to open it, eat the tender green beans inside, and discard the pod. Just the thing to go with a cold glass of beer! Once a rarity in the United States, edamame are now easy to find in supermarket freezer sections. You can sometimes buy them already boiled in tubs in the produce department, but we find these edamame are sometimes not as fresh as they should be, so we prefer to buy them frozen. In our stores, we can choose from frozen shelled or in-the-pod edamame. To cook them, follow the directions on the bag. They are usually boiled for just a few minutes—about 3 to 5 minutes, typically—then quickly drained before they overcook. We've used them in risotto here to echo a more typical, but labor-intensive, Italian choice—fava beans. ○ *Serves 3 to 4*

COOKER: Medium round
SETTING AND COOK TIME: HIGH 1¾ to 2¼ hours

3 cups chicken broth, or one 15-ounce can low-sodium broth plus water to equal 3 cups
1 pound in-the-pod edamame, or 1 cup shelled edamame
1 tablespoon olive oil
2 tablespoons unsalted butter
1 small yellow onion, chopped
1 cup Arborio, Vialone nano, or Carnaroli rice
⅓ cup freshly grated Parmesan cheese, plus more for serving
Salt and freshly ground black pepper to taste

1. In a large saucepan, bring the broth to a boil. Add the edamame and cook as long as specified on the package, generally about 5 minutes. Remove the beans from the broth with a slotted spoon and spread them out on a large plate. Reserve the broth. If you are using in-the-pod edamame, as soon as they are cool enough to handle, pinch the pods to remove the beans. Discard the pods.

2. In a small skillet over medium heat, warm the oil and 1 tablespoon of the butter, add the onion, and cook, stirring, until softened, 3 to 4 minutes. Then add the rice, stirring, until it turns from translucent to opaque (do not brown), about 2 minutes. Scrape the rice with a heat-proof rubber spatula into the slow cooker. Add the warm broth. Cover and cook on HIGH for 1¾ to 2¼ hours. The risotto should be only a bit liquidy and the rice should be *al dente,* tender with just a touch of firmness.

3. Stir in the edamame and the remaining 1 tablespoon of butter. Cover and wait about 5 minutes for the edamame to warm up and the butter to soften. Stir in the cheese and season with salt and pepper. Serve immediately, spooned into a bowl, with more Parmesan for sprinkling. The risotto can stand on the KEEP WARM setting for an hour or so.

Rice in the Slow Cooker

Over the course of testing, we found that, in general, converted rice cooks better on the HIGH setting. Small amounts (up to 2 cups) cook almost as well on LOW, so you can make 1 or 1½ cups of raw rice in a larger small cooker, such as a 2½ quart. Any larger quantity should always be cooked on HIGH; when cooked on LOW, the rice on the bottom tends to get squashed by the weight of the rice on top of it. Take care not to overfill your slow cooker. Larger quantities (4 to 5 cups of raw rice) should *only* be prepared in a 4½-quart or larger slow cooker to allow plenty of room for expansion during cooking.

Here is the basic method for preparing

converted rice in the slow cooker. Following the recipe on page 152 is a chart showing the amount of water and cooking time for larger quantities. We generally prepare our rice plain and season it after cooking, but, if you wish, add ½ teaspoon of salt and up to 1 tablespoon of butter per cup of rice to the cooking water. Add no salt if substituting salted broth for water and note that the ratio of water to rice decreases as the volume of rice increases. The cooked rice will stay warm and ready to serve in a turned-off slow cooker for up to 1 hour (with the lid on, of course, and the insert kept in the slow cooker base).

Converted Rice in the Slow Cooker

Y es, you can cook rice quickly on the stove or in an electric rice cooker, but sometimes a busy schedule or a crowded stove top makes it more convenient to cook rice in your slow cooker. ◦ *Serves 4*

COOKER: Medium round
SETTING AND COOK TIME: HIGH for 1½ hours, or LOW for 2½ hours

1 cup converted white rice (such as Uncle Ben's)
2 cups water
½ teaspoon salt (optional)
1 tablespoon unsalted butter (optional)

1. Combine the rice, water, and salt, if using, in the slow cooker and stir to combine. Use your fingers or a spoon to smooth the rice into as even a layer as possible. Add the butter pat, if using. Cover and cook on HIGH for 1½ hours or on LOW for 2½ hours.

2. Turn off the cooker. Use a fork to gently stir and fluff the rice, breaking up any clumps. Serve immediately. Or, if you are not ready to eat, cover the rice. It will stay hot for about 1 hour. (Leave the insert in the cooker to help conserve the heat.)

• • Cooking Converted Rice • •

Amount of Rice	Serves	Amount of Water	HIGH	LOW
1 cup	4	2 cups	1½ hours	2½ hours
2 cups	8	3½ cups	1¾ hours	2½ hours
3 cups	12	4½ cups	2 hours	
4 cups	16	5½ cups	2 hours	
5 cups	20	7 cups	2¾ hours	

Spanish Brown Rice with Spicy Sausage

ere is a one-pot meal that is a snap to assemble—you put everything in the cooker and push the button. Be sure the sausage is fully cooked—never raw. ○ *Serves 6*

COOKER: Medium round
SETTING AND COOK TIME: LOW for 8 to 9 hours

½ cup diced yellow onion
1 clove garlic, minced
1 medium-size red bell pepper, seeded and coarsely chopped
One 15- to 16-ounce can crushed tomatoes with their juice
1½ cups water
2 teaspoons chili powder
2 teaspoons Worcestershire sauce
¾ cup short-grain brown rice
1 tablespoon chopped jalapeño: *en escabeche,* nacho-style, or fresh
1 pound Santa Fe-style sausage or any other fully cooked spicy sausage, diced

Combine all the ingredients in the slow cooker and stir to evenly distribute. Cover and cook on LOW for 8 to 9 hours. Serve hot. The dish will remain warm in a turned-off slow cooker for up to 30 minutes.

Mujedrah

eemingly every region of the world has its nutritious, cheap, and beloved dish featuring rice and legumes; this one is from the Middle East. *Muje-drah* (also spelled *mujadarra* or *megadarra*) is a simple stew of lentils and rice that gets its personality from mounds of well-browned onions. The cucumber-yo-gurt sauce is a nice addition but is not essential. Serve *mujedrah* (pronounced ma-JED-rah) as a vegetarian main dish or side dish. It is good hot or at room temperature. In stove-top versions of *mujedrah*, the rice must be added when the lentils are almost cooked; in this convenient slow cooker version, the rice and lentils cook together. The only rice to use is converted rice, which holds its shape beautifully during slow cooking. ○ *Serves 3 to 4 as a main dish, 6 as a side dish*

COOKER: Medium or large round
SETTING AND COOK TIME: HIGH for 1½ to 2 hours

¾ **cup dried brown or green lentils**
¾ **cup converted white rice (such as Uncle Ben's)**
3 cups water
¾ **to 1 teaspoon salt, to your taste**
Freshly ground black pepper to taste

ONION TOPPING:
3 medium-size or 2 large red onions, sliced ¼ inch thick
2 tablespoons olive oil

YOGURT SAUCE:
1 cup plain yogurt
½ **cup finely diced or coarsely grated cucumber (peel first if skin is bitter and scoop out seeds)**
1 tablespoon chopped fresh mint
¼ **teaspoon salt, or to taste**

1. Pick over the lentils and discard any damaged ones. Rinse in a fine-mesh strainer under cold running water and drain. Combine them in the slow cooker with the rice and water, cover, and cook on HIGH until the lentils and rice are tender, 1½ to 2 hours; almost all of the water will have been absorbed. Add ¾ teaspoon of the salt and 1 grind of pepper, then stir the rice and lentils gently with a wooden or plastic spoon, taking care not to mash the lentils. Taste and adjust the seasonings if necessary.

2. While the lentils and rice are cooking, prepare the onion topping and the yogurt sauce. To make the onion topping, in a large skillet, heat the oil over medium-high heat. Add the onions, reduce the heat to medium-low, and cook, stirring occasionally, until they are very browned but not burned; this will take at least 20 minutes.

3. To make the yogurt sauce, stir together the yogurt, cucumber, mint, and salt in a small bowl. Refrigerate and cover until serving.

4. To serve, place the lentil-and-rice mixture on individual plates or a large serving platter. Top with the onions and offer the yogurt sauce alongside.

Double-Corn Spoonbread

S poonbread is a soul-satisfying Southern specialty served with savory foods, just like mashed potatoes. The cooked cornmeal mush is also known as batter bread and can contain cooked rice, hominy, different cheeses, and vegetables, such as the corn in this recipe. Scoop it up piping hot right out of the cooker and serve with roasted meat and poultry. ○ *Serves 4 to 6*

COOKER: Medium round
SETTING AND COOK TIME: HIGH for 3 to 3½ hours

3 cups milk
½ cup medium-grind yellow cornmeal
1¼ teaspoons salt
¼ cup (½ stick) unsalted butter, cut into pieces
2 cups fresh yellow or white corn kernels or thawed frozen baby corn
1 teaspoon hot pepper sauce, such as Tabasco
1 tablespoon baking powder
6 large eggs
1 cup thinly shredded cheddar cheese

1. Whisk together the milk, cornmeal, and salt in a large saucepan over high heat until the mixture comes to a boil. Reduce the heat to a simmer and cook until thickened, about 1 minute. Stir in the butter until melted, the corn, and hot pepper sauce. Sprinkle with the baking powder and whisk in the eggs until completely smooth. Fold in the cheese.

2. Coat the slow cooker with nonstick cooking spray. Pour in the batter. Cover and cook on HIGH until the spoonbread looks set but is not quite firm, 3 to 3½ hours. Serve immediately, scooped onto plates.

Polenta

Polenta is the traditional and versatile Italian dish served alongside a nice beef braise or with a red sauce over the top. The slow cooker makes an admirable, gloriously simple job of a task that usually requires the cook to stand and stir for an hour. You will be surprised at how fluffy and delectably creamy this polenta is with only a few stirs to avoid lumping. Please note the higher water-to-grain ratios needed in the slow cooker; it is 5:1 instead of 4:1. If you are doubling the recipe for a group, be sure to use a large cooker; the crock should never be more than three-quarters full. While the grain called polenta is a particularly coarse grind of dried cornmeal, you can make the dish from regular medium-grind yellow cornmeal. If it is allowed to cool and firm up, it is also great browned in butter or olive oil, or grilled with sausages. ○ *Serves 8*

COOKER: Medium or large round
SETTINGS AND COOK TIMES: HIGH for 30 minutes to 1 hour, then LOW for about 5 hours

7½ cups water
1½ cups coarse-ground yellow polenta
1½ teaspoons salt
Freshly ground black pepper to taste
½ cup (1 stick) unsalted butter
1 cup grated or shredded Parmesan or Italian fontina cheese

1. Whisk the water, polenta, and salt together in the slow cooker for a few seconds. Cover and cook on HIGH for 30 minutes to 1 hour to heat the water.

2. Stir again, cover, turn the cooker to LOW, and cook for about 5 hours, stirring occasionally with a wooden spoon. The polenta will thicken quite quickly after 2 hours, sort of expand magically in the cooker, and look done, but it will need the extra time to cook all the grains evenly. At 5 hours, taste and make sure the desired consistency has been reached and all the grains are tender. The longer the polenta cooks, the creamier it will become. When done, it will be smooth, very thick (yet pourable), and a wooden spoon will stand up by itself without falling over (the true test). The polenta will be fine on LOW for an additional hour, if necessary. Add a bit more hot water if it gets too stiff. Stir before serving.

3. To serve as a mound of soft polenta, portion out with an oversized spoon onto plates or into shallow soup bowls. Top each serving with a pat of the butter and sprinkle with some of the cheese. Serve immediately.

Fried Polenta: You can also pour out the polenta onto a marble board or into a greased pan to cool; it will stiffen, yet be quite tender. Refrigerate if not using within a few hours. Then you can fry slices of it in butter or olive oil and serve alongside roasted meats or egg dishes.

Green Chile Grits

Similar to polenta, grits should be served right away in a low mound topped with some grated cheese or a pat of butter, alongside grilled or roasted meats, sausage, or poultry. You can also refrigerate the mixture in a buttered loaf pan for a few hours or overnight, covered with plastic wrap. Unmold, cut into ½-inch-thick slices, and fry in butter until browned, turning once. It makes a wonderful accompaniment for omelets. ○ *Serves 6 to 8*

COOKER: Medium round
SETTING AND COOK TIME: HIGH for 3 to 3½ hours, or LOW for 7 to 9 hours

2 cups regular grits, stone-ground if possible
6 cups water
½ teaspoon sweet paprika
½ to 1 teaspoon salt, to your taste
One 4-ounce can chopped mild green chiles, drained
1 jalapeño, seeded and minced
Pinch of cayenne pepper or other pure red chile powder

Combine all the ingredients in the slow cooker. Cover and cook on LOW for 7 to 9 hours or on HIGH for 3 to 3½ hours, stirring occasionally. If cooking on HIGH, check for consistency; when it is almost done, add ¼ to ½ cup boiling water to thin if it is too thick.

Pumpkin Cheddar Grits

his is an adaptation of a recipe from our rice cooker book; we love this combination for a fall side dish. Grits have become fashionable outside the South, so finally there are creative recipes circulating that use all sorts of different ingredients. Here you add mashed pumpkin purée, fresh if you can manage it, for a nice accompaniment to roast pork, turkey, duck, or chicken. ○ *Serves 4*

COOKER: Medium round
SETTING AND COOK TIME: HIGH for 3 to 3½ hours, or LOW for 7 to 9 hours

⅔ cup coarse, stone-ground grits
1½ cups water
1 cup evaporated milk
1 teaspoon salt
1 cup mashed cooked pumpkin or another winter squash, such as
    Blue Hubbard or butternut; or 1 cup canned pumpkin purée
A few grinds of black pepper
¼ cup (½ stick) unsalted butter
½ cup finely shredded cheddar cheese

1. Combine the grits and some cold water in a bowl; the husks will rise to the top. Drain in a mesh strainer.

2. Combine the grits, 1½ cups of water, evaporated milk, and salt in the slow cooker. With a wooden or plastic spoon, stir for 15 seconds. Add the pumpkin and pepper, cover, and cook on HIGH for 3 to 3½ hours or on LOW for 7 to 9 hours, until thick and creamy.

3. Stir in the butter and cheese, cover, turn off the cooker, and let the mixture rest for 10 minutes to melt the butter and cheese. Serve immediately.

Fresh Hominy

H ominy is whole corn kernels that have been soaked in a lime bath, and then hulled, a method of preservation that gives the corn a distinctive flavor. Dried, this is the corn that is ground to make masa harina, used for making corn tortillas. Many of our recipes call for canned hominy, but this is how to prepare the fresh, frozen, or dried hominy you would use instead of canned in soups, chili, and posole stew. Fresh or partially cooked frozen hominy needs to be cooked before using, even though the grains look cooked and plump. Fresh hominy is usually available in the meat department of supermarkets, especially around holidays, and it is worth the trouble to cook it up. Do not add any salt while cooking, however, or the kernels will never soften properly. If you are using dried hominy, a Southwest staple, please note you will need double the amount of water and double the cooking time. Hominy is great served hot with Jacquie Higuera McMahan's Red Chile Sauce (see page 269) and cheddar cheese. ◦ *Makes about 4 cups*

COOKER: Medium round
SETTINGS AND COOK TIMES: HIGH for 1 hour, then LOW for 5 to 6 hours for fresh or frozen hominy or 9 to 12 hours for dried hominy

1 pound fresh hominy; or frozen hominy, defrosted overnight in the refrigerator; or 2 cups dried hominy (see headnote)

1. Put the hominy in the slow cooker and cover with a full 2 inches of cold water. Cover and cook on HIGH for 1 hour to bring to a boil.

2. Turn the cooker to LOW and cook until the hominy is tender and the kernels burst open, but are still slightly firm to the bite, 5 to 6 hours for fresh or frozen hominy, or 9 to 12 hours for dried hominy.

3. Drain off most of the liquid by pouring the hominy through a colander. Rinse with cool water, and let cool to room temperature. Use immediately in a soup or posole, or store, covered, in the refrigerator for up to 2 days.

Orange Barley Casserole

A good alternative to rice, pearl barley is hulled, so it looks nice and white, kind of like a little pearl seed. It needs no soaking, and cooks in under an hour. Pearl barley is not the same as quick barley, which is precooked and dried and and becomes very mushy when cooked, so we don't use it. You want barley to still be chewy. This dish is wonderful alongside poultry or game. ● *Serves 4*

COOKER: Medium round
SETTING AND COOKING TIME: LOW for 3 to 4 hours

1 cup orange juice
1 cup vegetable or chicken broth
⅓ cup pearl barley
¼ cup dried currants
¼ cup dried apricots cut into strips
¼ cup chopped pitted dates
1 tart apple, peeled, cored, and chopped
2 tablespoons chopped pecans

Combine all the ingredients in the slow cooker and stir to distribute them evenly. Cover and cook on LOW for 3 to 4 hours. Serve hot.

Kasha

K asha is roasted buckwheat, a low-fat, high-protein food with a distinctive nutty flavor. Despite its name, buckwheat is not a type of wheat; in fact, it is not really a grain at all. Triangular in shape, buckwheat "grains" are the edible seeds of the buckwheat plant. Left whole, they are called groats, but more commonly found are the fine, medium, and coarse granulations. We've used the three types interchangeably, though cooking times vary slightly. If you've never cooked kasha before, you may wonder why it is coated with egg and sautéed before cooking. It is a technique that keeps the pieces of kasha from sticking together. (If you cook with whole kasha, you do not need to do this.) This easy and delicious pilaf is an adaptation of a back-of-the box recipe from Wolff's kasha. If you can't find kasha in a local market, you can order it online from www.thebirkettmills.com.

○ *Serves 4*

COOKER: Medium round
SETTING AND COOK TIME: HIGH for about 1½ hours

1 large egg or 1 large egg white
⅛ teaspoon salt
⅛ teaspoon freshly ground black pepper
1 cup kasha, coarse, medium, or fine (not groats)
2 tablespoons unsalted butter or olive oil
¼ cup chopped shallots
1¾ cups homemade (page 95) or one 15-ounce can low-sodium chicken broth
1 to 2 tablespoons chopped fresh parsley or thyme, or a combination (optional)

1. Coat the slow cooker with nonstick cooking spray.

2. Beat the egg in a small bowl with the salt and pepper. Add the kasha and stir to coat with egg. Set aside.

3. In a medium-size skillet, heat the butter over medium-high heat until melted. Add the shallots and cook, stirring, until softened, 3 to 4 minutes. Add the kasha and cook, stirring, until it appears dry and smells toasty, 5 to 7 minutes. Add the broth and raise the heat to high.

4. When the liquid boils, transfer the mixture to the cooker. Cover and cook on HIGH until the liquid is absorbed and the kasha is tender, about 1½ hours,.

5. Fluff the kasha with a fork, taste, and season with salt and pepper if needed. (If you used canned broth, you will probably not need additional seasoning.) If using fresh herbs, stir them in with the fork. Serve hot.

Basic Wheat Berries

Wheat berries—whole-grain wheat with all its natural bran and germ intact—are well known to health-food enthusiasts and people who grind their own flour. Sadly, this form of wheat is little known to many otherwise well-versed cooks. Wheat berries are chewy, with a lovely, sweet aroma and flavor. They are good in casseroles, in soups (put some in your next pot of minestrone), as part of a grain stuffing, in pilafs, as the base for salads, and even sprinkled on them. They pair naturally with rice. The berries usually need to presoak to soften the outer layers, but that step can be skipped in the slow cooker. The timing will vary somewhat, depending on the age of the berries. You can also use this recipe to cook farro, an ancient grain enjoying a revival. ○ *Makes about 3 cups; serves 4 to 6*

COOKER: Medium round
SETTING AND COOK TIME: HIGH for 3½ to 4½ hours

1 cup wheat berries
4 cups water

1. Put the wheat berries in a dry skillet over medium-high heat and toast, stirring constantly, until the grains pop and deepen in color, about 4 minutes. This step is optional, but many cooks like this toasted flavor a bit better than that of the raw grain.

2. Transfer the wheat berries to the slow cooker and add the water. Cover and cook on HIGH until tender, 3½ to 4½ hours.

3. Drain well and serve immediately or let cool before storing in the refrigerator, where it will keep, covered, for 3 days.

Wild Rice–Almond Casserole

Wild rice should have a smoky-rich, nutty flavor. Remember when inspecting the rice that the darker the rice, the stronger the flavor. It has only its hull removed, not the bran, so the cooking water will always be dark because of the rich bran layer. During cooking, you want a grain that swells and splits slightly down the side to show a gray-white interior. If it splits and curls like a butterfly, it is overcooked and you need to adjust your timing for future batches. Some recipes call for cooking wild rice in large amounts of water, then draining it off; we never do that since the water is nutrient rich. ○ *Serves 6*

COOKER: Medium round
SETTING AND COOK TIME: LOW for 4½ to 6 hours

2 cups wild rice
1 cup slivered almonds
1 to 2 shallots, to your taste, finely chopped
½ cup finely chopped celery
8 ounces fresh mushrooms, chopped or sliced
6 cups vegetable broth
Salt and freshly ground black pepper to taste

1. Rinse the rice under cold running water until the water runs clear, then drain.

2. Combine all the ingredients except the salt and pepper in the slow cooker; stir to combine. Cover and cook on LOW until the kernels are open and tender, but not mushy, 4½ to 6 hours. Do not remove the lid before the rice has cooked at least 4 hours.

3. Season with salt and pepper, and serve immediately.

Not-from-the-Slow Cooker Accompaniments

While the slow cooker is bubbling away all day, usually all the cook has to do is plan a salad or vegetable and a starchy, grain-based side dish to accompany the one-pot meal. Here are a few of our very favorite starchy side dishes, from potatoes and rice to couscous, noodle pancakes, and tiny pasta, all made using conventional methods, usually in the oven or on the stove top. We have also included fritters and pancakes to give that extra little touch to your delicious, hearty, old-fashioned one-pot meals. Finally, to cleanse the palate, we offer a mixed green salad.

Baked Rice

 This is an easy and convenient alternative to stove-top rice.
○ *Serves 6 to 8*

3¾ cups water, vegetable broth, beef broth, or chicken broth
1 tablespoons olive oil, sesame oil, or walnut oil
2 cups long-grain white rice
½ to ¾ teaspoon salt, depending on how salty your broth is

1. Preheat the oven to 350°F. Grease a 2½-quart baking dish with olive oil or coat with nonstick cooking spray. Cut a piece of parchment paper the size of the dish, grease, and set aside.

2. Combine the water, oil, rice, and salt in the prepared dish; set the piece of parchment on top of the rice, oiled side down. Cover tightly with a lid or aluminum foil. Bake until all the water is absorbed and rice grains are separate, about 40 minutes. Fluff with a fork before serving.

Lemon Rice

Lemon rice is Beth's mom's perfect basic rice for serving with all types of poultry or vegetable dishes. It is excellent for parties. ◦ *Serves 6*

3 cups water or chicken broth
1½ cups long-grain white or basmati rice, rinsed until the water runs clear
Pinch of salt
6 tablespoons (¾ stick) unsalted butter
1 clove garlic, peeled
Juice and grated zest of 1 lemon
2 tablespoons minced fresh flat-leaf parsley

1. Bring the water to a boil in a large heavy saucepan. Add the rice, salt, and 1 tablespoon of the butter and place the clove of garlic on top. Reduce the heat to the lowest setting. Cover tightly and simmer until all the liquid is absorbed, 20 to 25 minutes.

2. Remove from the heat and let stand for 10 minutes, covered. Stir in the remaining 5 tablespoons of butter, the lemon juice and zest, and parsley. Serve immediately.

Rice Pilaf

Properly made, pilaf is one of the most appealing ways to prepare rice as a side dish. This recipe is the best. Serve with any stew or pot roast. ◦ *Serves 8*

¼ cup (½ stick) unsalted butter
2 medium-size shallots, minced
2 cups long-grain white rice
4 cups boiling water or chicken broth
Pinch of salt

1. In a large, heavy saucepan, melt the butter over medium heat. Add the shallots and rice and cook, stirring, until the shallots are translucent and the rice is coated evenly. Add the boiling liquid and salt. Reduce the heat to the lowest setting, cover tightly, and simmer until all the liquid is absorbed, 20 to 30 minutes.

2. Remove the pilaf from the heat and let stand for 10 minutes, covered; then serve.

Mexican Rice

 exican rice is good with everything from roasts to chili. You can even eat it alone with some cheese on top. ○ *Serves 6*

2 tablespoons olive oil
2 white boiling onions, minced
1 clove garlic, minced
2 cups long-grain white rice
3¾ cups boiling water or chicken broth
Pinch of salt
1 medium-size ripe tomato, peeled, seeded, and chopped
⅓ cup chopped canned roasted green chiles or frozen peas

1. In a large, heavy saucepan, heat the olive oil over medium heat. Add the onions, garlic, and rice and cook, stirring, until the onions are translucent and the rice is evenly coated, about 5 to 8 minutes. Add the boiling water, salt, tomato, and chiles, reduce the heat to the lowest setting, cover tightly, and simmer until all the liquid is absorbed, 25 to 30 minutes.

2. Remove the rice from the heat and let stand for 10 minutes, covered; then serve.

Barley Pilaf

This recipe is for those days when you want something different than rice or noodles as a side dish. For a bit of crunch, stir in ¼ cup of chopped toasted walnuts before serving, and drizzle with walnut oil. ○ *Serves 6*

2 tablespoons unsalted butter
1 large shallot, minced

¾ cup pearl barley
1¾ cups vegetable or chicken broth
Pinch of salt

1. In a medium-size, heavy saucepan, melt the butter over medium heat. Add the shallot and barley and cook, stirring, until the shallot is translucent and the barley is coated evenly, about 5 minutes. Add the broth and salt and bring to a boil.

2. Reduce the heat to the lowest setting, cover tightly, and simmer until all the liquid is absorbed and the barley is tender but still slightly chewy (not mushy), 35 to 40 minutes. Serve immediately.

Couscous with Chickpeas and Parsley

his is a basic couscous, enhanced with the addition of beans to make for a more substantial grain dish. It's one of our favorites. ○ *Serves 4*

1½ cups water, vegetable broth, or chicken broth
2 tablespoons unsalted butter
¼ teaspoon salt
½ teaspoon hot pepper sauce, such as Tabasco
1½ cups couscous
One 15-ounce can chickpeas (garbanzo beans), rinsed and drained
2 tablespoons chopped fresh flat-leaf parsley

1. Bring the water, butter, salt, and hot pepper sauce to a rolling boil in a medium-size saucepan. Pour in the couscous and chickpeas.

2. Remove the mixture from the heat, cover, and let stand until all the liquid is absorbed, 10 to 15 minutes. Add the parsley and fluff the couscous with a fork. Serve immediately.

Herbed Tiny Pasta

erve as an accompaniment under all manner of meat stews and vegetables, even chili. ○ *Makes 6 servings*

Pinch of salt
1¼ pounds tiny pasta shells or bows
3 tablespoons olive oil
2 tablespoons unsalted butter
Salt and freshly ground black pepper to taste
2 to 3 tablespoons chopped fresh herbs of your choice, such as chives, parsley, basil, or marjoram

1. Bring a large pot full of water to a boil, add the salt, then add the pasta and cook until tender but still firm to the bite. Drain in a colander.

2. Transfer the pasta to a medium-size bowl; drizzle with the oil, add the butter, and toss to coat. Season with salt and pepper and sprinkle with the herbs. Serve immediately.

Noodles with Poppy Seeds

A nod to the wonderful cuisine of Hungary, noodles with poppy seeds are great alongside chicken and other poultry dishes. Keep your poppy seeds in the freezer to retain their freshness. ○ *Serves 4 to 6*

12 ounces fettuccine
½ cup (1 stick) unsalted butter
1 to 3 tablespoons poppy seeds, to your taste

1. Cook the fettuccine according to the package directions in large pot of boiling salted water until just tender; pour into a colander and drain well.

2. In the same pot used to cook the pasta, melt the butter over medium heat, then cook the poppy seeds, stirring, for 1 minute to heat through. Return the hot drained pasta to the pan and toss gently to evenly distribute the poppy seeds. Serve immediately.

Oven-Roasted Potatoes

While we have tasty potato recipes made in the slow cooker elsewhere in this book, if your cooker is bubbling away with a nice stew or roast and you want to serve it with potatoes, these can be prepared quickly in the oven.
o *Serves 6*

1½ pounds small red or white potatoes, halved or quartered
¼ cup olive oil
1 teaspoon salt
Freshly ground black pepper to taste
1 to 2 tablespoons chopped fresh herbs, such as thyme, savory, marjoram, or rosemary, to your
   taste

Preheat the oven to 450°F. On a sheet pan or in a shallow gratin dish, toss the potatoes with the oil, salt, pepper, and herbs. Roast until browned, about 30 minutes, turning over with a metal spatula once or twice during the roasting for even browning. Serve hot.

Mashed Potato Casserole

This make-ahead casserole is incredibly good with all manner of meat stews and roasts, such as turkey, and even short ribs. It is a generous recipe that will feed a crowd. o *Serves 8*

5 pounds baking potatoes, such as russet or Idaho, peeled and quartered
One 8-ounce package cream cheese, cut into chunks and softened
¼ cup (½ stick) unsalted butter, cut into pieces
1 cup sour cream (reduced fat is okay)
½ cup hot whole milk
1 teaspoon salt
¼ teaspoon white pepper

1. Preheat the oven to 375°F. Butter a 9 x 13-inch baking dish or shallow ceramic casserole.

2. In a large saucepan, cover the potatoes with salted cold water by 1 inch, bring to a boil, reduce the heat to medium, and simmer until tender, about 20 minutes. Drain and return the potatoes to the pan. While still warm, add the cream cheese and butter, and whip with a handheld electric mixer on low speed; be careful not to overbeat. Beat in the sour cream, milk, salt, and pepper.

3. Transfer the potatoes to the prepared baking dish and bake until the top is pale golden, 30 to 40 minutes. Serve hot.

Note: The casserole can be assembled up to 24 hours ahead, covered with plastic wrap, and refrigerated. Add about 20 minutes to the baking time.

Potato Pancakes

We have always had a fondness for crispy homemade potato pancakes, or latkes, the ultimate in elegant country food and also a traditional dish during the Jewish holiday of Chanukah. The russet's high starch content makes for a pancake that cooks up crisply and does not fall apart as you flip it over. The baking powder lightens the pancakes a bit. Serve these with brisket or pot roast for a satisfying dinner. ○ *Makes 2 to 3 dozen; serves 8 to 10*

> 4 large russet potatoes (3 to 3½ pounds)
> 1 medium-size yellow onion
> 3 large eggs, lightly beaten
> ½ teaspoon baking powder (optional)
> ⅓ cup all-purpose flour or matzoh meal
> Salt and freshly ground black pepper to taste
> ¼ cup olive or canola oil, or more as needed

1. Peel and coarsely grate the potatoes and the onion by hand or in a food processor. Place them in a tea towel and wring out the excess moisture. Transfer to a large bowl, add the eggs, baking powder, if using, and flour, and season with salt and pepper. Stir until well combined.

2. Heat the oil in a large, heavy skillet over medium-high heat. With an oversized spoon, drop the batter into the pan and flatten the pancakes slightly with the back of the spoon. Fry until crisp and golden brown on both sides, turning once, 3 to 5 minutes total. Drain on paper towels and serve immediately.

Corn Fritter Cakes

C orn fritter cakes are a good accompaniment to meatloaf, pork, chicken, or sausage. These have a pronounced corn flavor and a nice texture that comes from the large proportion of fresh vegetables in the batter. Serve with a tablespoon of sour cream and a drizzle of hot pepper jelly or crock gravy. ○ *Makes 16 to 20 fritters; serves 6 to 8*

1¼ cups all-purpose flour

¼ cup medium-grind yellow cornmeal, preferably stone-ground

2 teaspoons baking powder

½ teaspoon salt

Pinch of white pepper

⅔ cup whole milk

2 large eggs

3 tablespoons unsalted butter, melted

2 tablespoons minced red or green bell pepper

5 ears fresh yellow or white corn, kernels cut off the cob; or 2½ cups frozen corn, thawed

¼ to ½ cup olive oil, as needed

1. Combine the flour, cornmeal, baking powder, salt, and pepper in a large bowl. Make a well in the center and add the milk, eggs, and melted butter, stirring just until combined. Fold in the bell pepper and corn with a rubber spatula. Do not overmix; the batter will have small lumps.

2. Heat 2 tablespoons of the oil in a griddle or heavy skillet over medium heat. Using a ¼-cup measure or large spoon for each fritter cake, pour the batter onto the griddle. Cook until crispy; the edges should be dark brown and dry and the bottoms golden brown, about 2 minutes. Turn once, cooking the other side until golden, about 1 minute. Drain on a double layer of paper towels. Continue frying the fritter cakes, using 2 tablespoons of oil for each batch. Serve immediately or keep warm in a preheated 250°F oven until ready to serve.

Savory Wild Rice Pancakes

Wild rice pancakes have an appealing flavor and texture that are hard to resist. They are perfect with pot roasts and chicken dishes. These are among the best, most toothsome preparations of wild rice, so don't skip by them; make them every chance you get. The recipe is from Beth's book *The Best Quick Breads* (Harvard Common Press, 2000). ◦ *Makes 16 to 20 pancakes; serves 4 to 6*

¼ cup (½ stick) unsalted butter
1 medium-size shallot, minced
1 cup all-purpose flour
1 tablespoon baking powder
½ teaspoon salt
3 large eggs
1 cup whole milk
1½ cups cooked and cooled wild rice

1. Melt the butter in a medium-size skillet over medium heat, add the shallot, and cook, stirring, until tender. Set aside.

2. Combine the flour, baking powder, and salt in a medium-size bowl with a whisk or in a food processor. Add the shallots, eggs, and milk and beat or process just until smooth. The batter will be thin, but thicker than crêpe batter. Stir in the wild rice.

3. Heat a griddle or heavy skillet over medium heat until a drop of water skates over the surface, then lightly grease with butter or oil. Using ⅛ cup measure for each pancake, pour the batter onto the griddle. Cook until bubbles form on the surface, the edges are dry, and the bottoms are golden brown, about 2 minutes. Turn once, cooking the other side until golden, about 1 minute more. Serve immediately or keep warm in a preheated 250°F oven until ready to serve.

Noodle Pancakes

Either use leftover egg noodles or cook up a fresh batch for making these wonderful pancakes, excellent with brisket and pot roasts. ◦ *Makes about 18 pancakes; serves 4*

8 ounces fine egg noodles

2 tablespoons unsalted butter

1 small white onion, minced

2 large eggs, lightly beaten

Salt and freshly ground black pepper to taste

¼ cup olive or canola oil

1. Cook the noodles according to the package directions until *al dente,* "firm to the bite," and drain well.

2. In a small skillet, melt the butter over medium heat, then add the onion and cook, stirring, until transparent. Combine the drained noodles and onion in a medium-size bowl, add the eggs, season with salt and pepper, and stir to blend well.

3. Heat the oil in a large, heavy skillet over medium heat. With an oversized spoon, drop the noodle mixture by the spoonful into the pan and flatten slightly with the back of the spoon to form thin pancakes. Fry until crisp and golden brown, then turn over to cook the other side, 3 to 5 minutes total. Drain on paper towels and serve immediately.

Mixed Green Salad
à la Vincent Schiavelli

Vincent Schiavelli wrote the most wonderful first cookbook, *Papa Andrea's Sicilian Table* (Citadel Press, 1993). In it he records his grandfather's recipes, including instructions on how to make a great simple green salad. He remarks that "a salad is more art than science, and not difficult to master." It is a wonderful accompaniment to your braise or stew, or as its own course to serve after. If you use one of the premixed bitter lettuce combos that are available now at many supermarkets and farmers markets, combine it with at least half as much regular green leaf lettuce to balance the sweet and bitter and make the salad most enjoyable. One pound of lettuce will feed four people a heaping two-cup serving each. This is an adaptation of Vincent's *insalata mista,* mixed green salad.

Any mixture *a la momento* of sweet and bitter salad greens, such as butter or romaine lettuce, red leaf lettuce, cos lettuce, iceberg, radicchio, watercress, fennel, endive, baby spinach, màche, or arugula, washed, well dried, and torn by hand into pieces (not cut, which will discolor the leaves)

Fine sea salt to taste

Red or white wine vinegar, such as Zinfandel vinegar, Cabernet vinegar, Champagne vinegar, black fig vinegar, or a good organic cider vinegar

Olive oil, extra-virgin, virgin, or light, as your palate and purse dictate

Thinly sliced red onion, grated or sliced beets, lightly cooked green beans, grated carrot, sliced tomatoes, avocado dipped in lemon juice, edible flower petals (such as nasturtiums), baby zucchini slices, sliced mushrooms, sprouts, olives, and cucumber (optional), as desired

Freshly ground black or white pepper to taste

Put the lettuces in a large bowl. Sprinkle lightly with the salt to open the lettuce to receive the vinegar; a few pinches are all that are needed even for a large salad. Toss with your hands or tongs. Sprinkle with the vinegar until the aroma rises gently from the bowl. Toss again. Drizzle with the olive oil, about three times as much oil as the vinegar. Toss again. Keep a light hand; you can always add more. Toss in any other ingredients, such as mushrooms and cucumbers, or arrange on top. Grind some black or white pepper over the top and serve. Never add too much of anything, "you don't want a vinegary or oily salad, but ingredients enhanced by the dressing," says Vincent. If you use lemon juice instead of the vinegar, use equal parts of juice and oil.

The Beauty of Greens

We give serving suggestions with many of our recipes. Most of the time, since the meal is an all-in-one-pot, all that is needed is a bit of bread or a nice green salad. Well, it is easy to get into a rut and make the same salad and the same dressing all the time.

Finding new recipes for salad dressings has got to be one of the most elusive projects in the food world; you have to notice one in a food magazine or have a great one at someone's house. So here is something extra: a few excellent salads and a list of our favorite tried-and-true vinaigrettes and dressings to pour over your simple pile of greens. Beth originally compiled this list as a gift for her catering clients who loved all the different vinaigrettes and dressings she served. They last 5 to 7 days in the refrigerator in a covered container.

Vinaigrettes are a combination of oil and vinegar. To make a vinaigrette, place your vinegar and any other flavor ingredients in a small bowl. In a slow, steady stream, add the oil and use a wire whisk to beat until the mixture is combined. Use immediately, let stand up to 2 hours, or refrigerate up to a week. You can also mix vinaigrettes with an immersion blender, a food processor, or just simply shake it in a screw-top jar. While vinaigrettes let the greens be the stars of the salad, dressings, including the four here, demand to be noticed. They are best with simple greens—any of the lettuces or spinach. A dressing usually comes together in a minute or two; most are just whisked together in a bowl.

Everyday Mustard Vinaigrette

Good on all kinds of lettuces, spinach, and steamed broccoli and asparagus.
○ Makes ½ cup

2 tablespoons white or red wine vinegar or cider vinegar
½ to 1 teaspoon Dijon or coarse-grained mustard, to your taste
⅓ cup olive oil
Salt and freshly ground black or white pepper to taste

Balsamic Vinaigrette

If you use white balsamic vinegar, use a white wine vinegar or Champagne vinegar.
○ Makes about 1 cup

2 tablespoons balsamic vinegar
2 tablespoons red wine vinegar
1 shallot, minced
⅔ cup olive oil
Salt and freshly ground black pepper to taste

Raspberry Vinaigrette

Good on a salad with fruit, such as oranges and red onion, berries, and avocado.
○ Makes ¾ cup

¼ cup raspberry vinegar
1 teaspoon Dijon mustard
½ cup walnut or another nut oil
Salt and freshly ground black or white pepper to taste

Sherry Vinaigrette

Good on all sorts of seasonal greens. ○ Makes 1 cup

¼ cup aged sherry wine vinegar

¾ cup olive oil

Salt and freshly ground black or white pepper to taste

Tiny pinch of crumbled saffron threads (optional)

Put all the ingredients in a bowl and whisk to combine.

Sesame Soy Vinaigrette

Great on seasonal greens. ○ Makes about ½ cup

3 tablespoons rice vinegar

1½ teaspoons honey

2 teaspoons soy sauce

2 tablespoons toasted sesame oil

¼ cup vegetable oil or cold pressed sesame oil

Salt and freshly ground black pepper to taste

2 teaspoons sesame seeds, toasted in a dry skillet over medium heat until fragrant

Put all the ingredients in a bowl and whisk to combine.

Roquefort Blue Cheese Dressing

Creamy, rich, and delicious, this never goes out of style. ○ Makes about 2 cups

1½ cups mayonnaise (can be a mayonnaise substitute or nonfat)

⅓ cup buttermilk

⅓ cup sour cream (can be low fat)

2 tablespoons fresh lemon juice

½ teaspoon Worcestershire sauce

Pinch of salt, or to taste

A few grinds of black pepper

5 ounces Roquefort bleu cheese, coarsely crumbled (1 cup)

Put all the ingredients, except the cheese, in a bowl and whisk to combine. Stir in the cheese.

Honeyed French Dressing

Good on bean salads, cold green beans, and tossed seasonal greens. ○ Makes 1¼ cup

5 tablespoons red wine vinegar

2 tablespoons tomato paste

2 tablespoons honey

1 clove garlic, pressed

Dash of hot pepper sauce, such as Tabasco

¾ cup olive oil

Salt and freshly ground black pepper to taste

Put all the ingredients in a bowl and whisk to combine.

Green Goddess Dressing

Good on crunchy cold greens, such as romaine. ○ Makes about 2 cups

1 cup sour cream (can be low fat)

1 cup mayonnaise (can be a mayonnaise substitute or nonfat)

1 tablespoon fresh lemon juice

1 tablespoon white wine vinegar or white balsamic vinegar

1 tablespoon anchovy paste (from a tube)

1 tablespoon minced fresh flat-leaf parsley

1 shallot, minced

A few grinds of black pepper

Put all the ingredients in a bowl and whisk to combine or blend in a small food processor.

Light Caesar Dressing

Excellent with cold romaine lettuce, croutons, and shredded Parmesan cheese.
○ Makes about 1 cup

⅔ cups light sour cream

3 to 5 anchovy fillets, to your taste, oil patted off with a paper towel

2 tablespoons fresh lemon juice

1 tablespoon minced shallot

1 to 2 cloves garlic, to your taste, pressed

1 teaspoon Worcestershire sauce

½ teaspoon freshly ground black pepper

Combine all the ingredients in a food processor or blender and process until smooth.

The New-Fashioned Bean Pot

When we think of our favorite slow cooker recipes, what comes to mind pretty much looks like a hill of beans and legumes. The slow cooker, whose invention was inspired by the electric bean pot, is the most efficient way to cook dried beans and legumes, no matter what type you choose—mottled, black, red, or white. Minimal evaporation occurs during the cooking, just like in the old potbelly-shaped, brown-and-cream clay bean pot that went in the oven or was buried in the embers of a fire.

The term "bean" refers to not only regular beans, but also legumes and peas, known as pulses. A legume is technically an edible seed inside a pod. There is a vast variety from which to choose, each with its own size, appearance, and texture. Beans are usually cooked in their dried form, but during summer months, you may also come across fresh ones—always called fresh shell beans—especially at your farmers market. Fresh beans will always cook much faster than dried beans and need no soaking. Fully mature beans and legumes are never eaten raw because they are completely indigestible.

Once you embrace the world of beans, you will be amazed at the vast variety available—old favorites such as pinto beans, black-eyed peas, and black beans, as well as newly available heirlooms such as cranberry beans, chestnut-flavored Christmas limas, and yellow eyes. In this chapter, we have tried to provide you with a wide range of recipes so you can experiment.

Beans have a reputation of being hard to cook. We demystify that and give simple directions for the best slow cooker beans. The cooking time depends on the size of beans, how long they have been presoaked, and their age. (The older the beans, the more water and time they need to rehydrate; if your beans are *really* old, more than two years, replace them.) As one of our testers wrote: "Cook until tender, anywhere from 4 to 8 hours on HIGH, depending on your slow cooker and the phase of the moon. If you're going to be out of the house, put the slow cooker on LOW and make sure you've got an extra 2 inches of liquid in it. Cook 8 to 10 hours, bringing it to HIGH whenever you get back to the house."

We have included tips for cooking and soaking beans, as well as an easy reference chart with cooking times. You will have to eyeball your own particular crock full of beans for the correct doneness, but our guide will get you close to the mark. The rule of thumb is to have three times the amount of liquid as there are beans, which translates to 2 to 3 inches of liquid above the beans. You can always use more water—3 quarts to a pound of beans is not unusual—then drain later. We also like to add acidic ingredients—such as tomatoes, vinegar, and lemon juice—towards the end of the cooking time, to avoid toughening the beans. Always be sure to add the salt when the beans are almost done; if you add it in the beginning, the beans will never get tender. Your bean mantra is "soak, simmer, then flavor."

Store cooked beans in their liquor. Keep your stash for up to 3 days in the refrigerator, ready to rinse and use in salads, or freeze them in small amounts, to be added to your salads, as a side dish, or in slow cooker soups and stews at a moment's notice. Beans frozen in 1-cup increments can be defrosted quickly in the microwave or even added, frozen, to a bubbling pot of soup.

While this chapter is devoted to dishes made predominantly with beans, recipes with beans as an added ingredient can be found throughout this book (don't miss our chili chapter or the bean stews in the vegetable chapter). While there are many recipes for beans made from scratch, we also have included many recipes utilizing canned beans for convenience. But for plain eating, hearty beans fresh from the pot, with their earthy aroma filling the kitchen after hours of cooking, are a soul-satisfying meal. Our favorite way to eat freshly cooked beans of all types is a soup bowl full, simply drizzled with a fruity olive oil, walnut oil, or sesame oil, a squeeze of fresh lemon, and a sprinkling of sea salt and freshly ground black pepper—with hunks of fresh bread or fresh flour tortillas on the side to sop up all the thick juices in the bottom of the bowl. Where's the spoon?

How Many Dried Beans are Equivalent to a 15-Ounce Can?

Beans are famously economical: One cup of dried beans cooked with 3 to 4 cups of water, depending on the type of bean cooked, will yield about 3 cups of cooked beans. So, for an amount equivalent to a 15- or 16-ounce can of beans, which contains about 1¾ cups of beans, cook ¾ cup of dried beans. One pound of dried beans, about 2⅓ cups, will yield 6 to 7 cups of cooked beans.

Tips for Cooking Dried Beans in the Slow Cooker

While researching this section, we cooked dozens of pots of beans. We tried presoaking and not presoaking. We cooked on LOW and on HIGH. We used different sizes and shapes of slow cookers. Here's what we think are the best practices for slow-cooking beans:

1. *Do* presoak dried beans before cooking them in the slow cooker. (The exceptions are the same as for stove-top bean cookery: lentils and split peas.) While it is possible to slow-cook unsoaked beans, we found that cooking times are much more predictable if the beans have been soaked beforehand. Soak them in cold water for 6 hours or overnight, or use the quick-soak method: Bring the beans to a boil on the stove in a large pot with plenty of water and continue boiling for 2 minutes. Cover the pot, remove from the heat, and let stand for

1 hour. Drain the beans and cook them as indicated in the particular recipe, or follow our chart below.

2. Cook beans on HIGH. We found that beans cook more evenly on the HIGH heat setting of a slow cooker.

3. Use either a medium-size or large slow cooker, and make sure it is large enough so that there is plenty of room for the beans to bubble without spilling over. Most small slow cookers don't have a HIGH setting, so we don't recommend them for cooking beans. In addition, they are too small for anything greater than ½ cup of dried beans. We found that the shape of a slow cooker doesn't matter. Round and oval cookers performed equally well.

4. For 1 cup of presoaked beans, use 4 cups of water or broth. For 2 cups of presoaked beans, use 6 cups of water or broth. Cooking times will vary some-

•• Slow Cooker Bean Cooking Times ••

The cooking times suggested below are based on 1 to 2 cups of beans or legumes with at least 3 inches of water to cover. Beans can also be cooked in broth or vegetable stock, which tastes especially nice if the beans will be eaten as a side dish. The beans should always be completely covered with liquid throughout the entire cooking time. They are done when tender and most of the cooking liquid has been absorbed, although if you are making a dish to eat with a spoon, like Tuscan beans, they can remain soupy. Always check towards the end of the cooking time and add more boiling water if the beans look too dry. If they are to be used in another dish, such as chili, soup, or vegetable stew, cook them until *al dente* rather than totally soft.

The following chart tells approximately how long to cook various kinds of dried beans on HIGH in the slow cooker. Each cup of dried bean will swell to about 3 cups when cooked. These times are meant to be used as guidelines because variables such as hard or soft water, the mineral composition of the soil where the beans were grown, and the age of the beans can affect cooking times. Hard water will lengthen the cooking time. Remember that beans and legumes always take slightly longer to cook at higher altitudes. All beans, except split peas and the various kinds of lentils, should be presoaked (see page 183 for details), which rehydrates them, making for more even cooking, and leaches off some of the compounds that make beans hard to digest (note the foamy water that is poured off).

Presoaked Dried Bean	Cooking Time on HIGH
Anasazi	3 hours
Black beans (turtle beans)	3 hours

what based on the moisture level of the beans and the amount, so be sure to check 30 minutes to 1 hour or so before the time is up in case you need to add some boiling water. The liquid level should never drop below the level of the beans; keep it at least ½ inch above for good measure. The ultimate doneness test? Bite into one.

5. Do not add salt until *after* the beans are cooked; salt added at the beginning toughens them and they will not absorb water properly during the cooking process.

6. You can store your cooked beans in their liquor (flavored cooking water) and serve them as a soup, or drain in a colander or scoop out the beans with a slotted spoon. If you find the crock too heavy to lift to drain them in the colander, the slotted spoon works perfectly.

Presoaked Dried Bean	Cooking Time on HIGH
Black-eyed peas	3½ hours
Cannellini beans	3 hours
Chickpeas (garbanzo beans)	3½ to 4 hours
Fava beans	2½ hours
Flageolets	3½ to 4 hours
Great Northern beans	2½ hours
Kidney beans	3 hours
Lentils, brown	1½ hours (firm-tender) for salads, 2 hours (completely tender) for soup
Lentils, green (du Puy)	2 hours
Lentils, red	1½ hours
Lima beans	2½ hours for baby or small 2 hours for large
Navy beans	2½ to 3 hours
Pink beans (pinquito), small	3½ hours
Pinto beans	3 hours
Red beans, small	2½ hours
Soybeans	4 hours
Split peas, green or yellow	2½ hours
White beans, small	3 hours

Slow Cooker Pot of Beans

Beans are the kind of good-to-eat and good-for-you food that doesn't get much publicity. They're not flashy, and the dried onces are one of the best bargains in the supermarket, in terms of both money and nutrition. If you have ever nervously timed beans in a hissing pressure cooker or laboriously scraped burned beans from a pot that got too hot on the bottom, we've got a little secret to tell you: The slow cooker is the way to go. Unlike the pressure cooker, you don't need to-the-minute timing. Unlike the stove top, there is almost no risk of burning your beans, as long as you follow our simple directions. Refer to our Slow Cooker Bean Cooking Times chart (pages 184–185) so as not to overcook the beans, which can get mushy. Yellow split peas and chickpeas are the exception; they remain soft and shapely no matter how long they are cooked. ○ *Serves 6 to 8*

COOKER: Large round or oval
SETTING AND COOK TIME: HIGH, see Slow Cooker Bean Cooking Times chart, pages 184–185, for timing

One 1-pound package dried beans of your choice
10 cups water
1 bouquet garni: 4 sprigs fresh flat-leaf parsley, 1 bay leaf, 1 or 2 sprigs fresh thyme,
    1 sprig fresh tarragon, 10 black peppercorns, and 1 clove peeled garlic,
    wrapped up in cheesecloth and tied with kitchen twine (optional)
Fine sea salt to taste

1. Put the beans in a colander and rinse under running water; pick over for damaged beans and small stones. Transfer to the slow cooker (it must be large enough so that there is plenty of room for them to bubble without spilling over) and cover with 3 inches of cold water. Soak for 6 to 12 hours and drain.

2. Add the 10 cups of water and bouquet garni, if using, to the beans in the cooker. Cover and cook on HIGH. The beans need to be covered with liquid at all times to cook properly. They will transform the water into a liquid, called bean liquor, that is similar in color to whatever bean you are cooking, When done, the beans will be tender and hold their shape, rather than fall apart. Leave whole or gently mash a portion of the beans in the pot, which will thicken them nicely.

3. Serve immediately in soup bowls, topped with a sprinkling of sea salt and grated cheese, if desired. Or let stand in the cooker for 1 hour, uncovered, then transfer the beans, with their liquor, to a covered storage container and refrigerate or freeze. Or drain and use in another recipe.

Single-Serving Slow Cooker Beans: Soak a handful of beans before going to bed, then make your lunch early in the morning and eat in the afternoon. In a small or medium slow cooker, combine ½ cup of presoaked beans and 3 cups of water, or 1 cup of beans and 4½ cups of water. Refer to the Slow Cooker Bean Cooking Times chart on pages 184–185 for the exact time, depending on what type of bean you are cooking. Cover and cook on HIGH as directed above. It will be the same for a small pot of beans as for a large pot.

Basic Savory Beans

This is the recipe to make for a slightly more complex flavored pot of beans than our Slow Cooker Pot of Beans. The best beans for this recipe are kidneys, navy, small white beans, cranberry beans, small red beans, pintos, appaloosa, Jacob's cattle, raquels, pinquitos, black-eyed peas, and yellow eyes. We also use mixed beans packaged for bean soup. ● *Serves 6 to 8*

COOKER: Large round or oval
SETTING AND COOK TIME: HIGH, see Slow Cooker Bean Cooking Times chart, pages 184–185, for timing

One 1-pound package dried beans of your choice
1 medium-size yellow onion, chopped
1 clove garlic, chopped or left whole
½ bay leaf
1 teaspoon dried oregano, marjoram, or savory
Pinch of ground cumin
Pinch of ground coriander
3 to 4 cups water, as needed
3 to 4 cups chicken broth, as needed
Fine sea salt and freshly ground black pepper to taste

1. Put the beans in a colander and rinse under cold running water; pick over for damaged beans or small stones. Transfer to the slow cooker (it must be large enough so that there is plenty of room for the beans to bubble without spilling over) and cover by 3 inches with cold water. Soak for 6 to 12 hours and drain.

2. Add the onion, garlic, herbs, and spices to the beans in the cooker and enough of the water and broth to cover them by 3 inches. Cover and cook on HIGH. The beans need to be covered with liquid at all times to cook properly. They will transform the water and broth into a liquid, called bean liquor, similar in color to whatever bean you are cooking. When done, they will be tender and hold their shape, rather than fall apart. Season with salt and pepper. Leave whole or gently mash a portion of the beans in the pot, which will thicken them nicely.

3. Serve immediately. Or let stand in the cooker 1 hour, uncovered, then transfer with their liquor to a covered storage container to refrigerate or freeze. Or drain and use in another recipe.

•• Converting Regular Bean Recipe Cooking Times •• into Slow Cooker Cooking Times

While many recipes from other sources designate a LOW cook time to cook plain beans, we found that almost every bean we tested cooked best on HIGH. Our recipes give directions for the temperature that gives the best results, but you have some flexibility here. You can have the beans on HIGH while you are home, then switch to LOW if you have to leave the house, and the beans, unattended. When you are making a baked bean recipe, we recommend cooking the dried beans initially on HIGH, then after the flavoring ingredients are added, switching to LOW for the extended time. We never rush Boston Baked Beans (page 194); that long, long cooking time is what makes the dish so special. We include this time chart for your convenience, since we used it a lot for reference while creating these bean recipes.

If a Recipe Reads	Slow Cooker Time on LOW	Slow Cooker Time on HIGH
15 minutes	2 to 2½ hours	1 to 1½ hours
30 minutes	3 to 4 hours	2 to 2½ hours
45 minutes	5 to 6 hours	3 to 3½ hours
1 hour	6 to 8 hours	4 to 4½ hours
1½ hours	9 to 10 hours	5 to 5½ hours
2 hours	10 to 12 hours	6 to 6½ hours
3 hours	14 to 18 hours	7 to 7½ hours

Slow Cooker Pinto Beans

A pot of beans simmering slowly on the back of the stove is an integral part of Spanish, Mexican, and Southwestern cooking. It is pure comfort food and every friend we have from a Latin American country talks lyrically about mom's pot of beans, always available and eaten with the family in the kitchen. Traditionally they are cooked in an earthenware bean pot called an *olla,* and the slow cooker mimics their lovely, slow-cooked quality. You can use pink beans, black beans, or anasazi beans in place of the pintos. This recipe is adapted from California food writer Jacquie Higuera McMahan. We soak the beans, but seasoned cooks swear they need no presoaking, so you be the judge. ✺ *Serves 6*

COOKER: Large round
SETTING AND COOK TIME: HIGH for 3 to 4½ hours

One 1-pound package dried pinto beans
9 cups water
2 dried New Mexican, California, or ancho chiles
3 cloves garlic, peeled
1 small yellow or white onion, chopped
2 to 3 teaspoons fine sea salt, to your taste

1. Put the beans in a colander and rinse under cold running water; pick over for damaged beans and small stones. Transfer to the slow cooker and cover by 3 inches with cold water. Soak for 6 to 12 hours and drain.

2. Add the 9 cups of water, the chiles, garlic, and onion. Cover and cook on HIGH for 3 to 4½ hours. Towards the end of the cooking time, season with the salt and remove the chiles. The beans need to be covered with liquid at all times to cook properly; add boiling water if the level falls too low. When done, they will be tender and hold their shape, rather than fall apart. Leave whole or gently mash a portion of the beans in the pot, which will thicken them nicely.

3. Use them to make mashed frijoles, or serve the beans in soup bowls or as a side dish, topped with grated cheddar or Monterey Jack cheese, if desired. To store the beans, let stand in the cooker for 1 hour, uncovered. Then transfer with their liquor to a covered storage container and refrigerate or freeze.

Frijoles

Eat these mashed beans fresh as is, or sauté them the next day for *refritos,* or refried beans. You will need a cast-iron skillet (10- to 12-inch is perfect) or another nice, heavy skillet, and some leaf lard. This is the highest grade of lard, made from the fat around the kidneys of a pig, and actually has less choles-terol than butter. ○ *Serves 6*

2 to 3 tablespoons canola oil, olive oil, or leaf lard
1 recipe Slow Cooker Pinto Beans (page 189), cooked and cooled
Finely shredded Monterey Jack, crumbled *coteja*, or freshly grated
    Parmesan cheese for serving refried beans

1. Heat 1 to 2 tablespoons of the oil in a large skillet. Ladle in a cup of the beans and about ¼ cup of their liquid. Simmer over medium to medium-high heat to evaporate the liquid, mashing the beans with the back of an oversized metal spoon. When really thick, add another cup of beans and more liquid, cooking and mashing again. Continue until you have mashed all of the beans with at least half of the cooking liquid (reserve the excess so you can add some if the beans are too thick).

2. Reduce the heat to low and simmer the beans until thick, but not as thick as re-fried beans, about 20 minutes. Serve immediately or, for refried beans, let cool to room temperature and refrigerate, covered. The beans will thicken as they cool.

3. To make refried beans, heat 1 tablespoon of oil in a clean heavy skillet and add 2 cups cold pinto beans. Cook until they sizzle around the edges. Sprinkle with cheese and serve.

Frijoles Charros

Charros were the elegant horsemen of Mexico, but later the term described the Mexican cowboys who settled and worked in Texas. These are the cow-boy beans of the American Southwest, which would be simmering all day in an earthenware *olla* on the back of the stove for dinner or over the open fire out on the range. Depending on the age of your beans, you may need to add a bit more boiling water during cooking. Serve with white rice and cornbread. ○ *Serves 6*

COOKER: Large round
SETTING AND COOK TIME: HIGH for 3½ to 5 hours; add salt, oregano, cumin, and cilantro during last hour

One 1-pound package dried pinto beans
11 cups water
2 jalapeños, stems removed
6 to 8 ounces cooked chorizo (Mexican sausage), chopped
4 strips bacon, chopped
5 cloves garlic, chopped
1 small yellow or white onion, chopped
2 to 3 teaspoons salt, to your taste
½ teaspoon dried oregano
½ teaspoon ground cumin
¼ cup fresh cilantro leaves, chopped

FOR SERVING:
Freshly grated cheddar cheese, such as longhorn
Fresh tomato and onion salsa

1. Put the beans in a colander and rinse under cold running water; pick over for damaged beans and small stones. Transfer to the slow cooker and cover by 3 inches with cold water. Let soak for 6 to 12 hours and drain.

2. Add the 11 cups of water, jalapeños, chorizo, bacon, garlic, and onion. Cover and cook on HIGH for 3½ to 5 hours. The beans need to be covered with liquid at all times to cook properly. When done, they will be tender and hold their shape, rather than fall apart.

3. Towards the end of the cooking time, season with the salt and remove the chiles. Add the oregano, cumin, and cilantro leaves. Let the beans simmer 1 hour more, uncovered, which will thicken them nicely.

4. Serve the beans immediately in soup bowls, topped with grated cheddar and fresh tomato and onion salsa. Or let cool in the cooker 1 hour, uncovered. Then transfer with their liquor to a covered storage container to refrigerate or freeze.

Cheater's Refried Beans

 Okay, so we are talking real convenience here, but these are great with sausages or alongside enchiladas. ◦ *Serves 4 to 6*

COOKER: Small round
SETTING AND COOK TIME: LOW for 2 to 4 hours

One 16-ounce can refried pinto or refried black beans
1¼ cups rinsed and drained canned or slow-cooked whole pinto or black beans
2 to 3 tablespoons unsalted butter, olive oil, canola oil, chicken fat, or bacon drippings

1. Put the refried beans, whole beans, and butter in the slow cooker; stir with a wooden spoon to combine a bit.

2. Cover and cook on LOW until hot, 2 to 4 hours. Stir and serve immediately under poached eggs, sprinkled with *queso fresco* or soft goat cheese, or alongside an enchilada and some rice.

Italian White Beans with Pancetta

This kind of recipe typifies the ingenuity of simple country cooking. Beans are cooked with some bacon, vegetables, a sprig of herb, and broth, then served topped with goat cheese and olives. This makes a delicious main or side dish. ◦ *Serves 4*

COOKER: Medium round
SETTING AND COOK TIME: HIGH for 3½ to 4½ hours

1 heaping cup dried cannellini beans
A few slices of pancetta or prosciutto, chopped
¼ cup olive oil
3 shallots, halved

1 medium-size carrot, quartered

2 ribs celery, halved

1 bay leaf

Sprig of fresh thyme or savory

One 15-ounce can chicken broth

Fine sea salt and freshly ground black pepper to taste

4 ounces fresh goat cheese, such as Chabis or Montrachet, crumbled

½ cup sliced pitted black olives, or your choice, drained

1. Put the beans in a colander and rinse under cold running water; pick over for damaged beans and small stones. Transfer to the slow cooker and cover by 3 inches with cold water. Soak for 6 to 12 hours, drain, and add back to the cooker.

2. In a medium-size skillet over medium-high heat, cook the pancetta in the olive oil, stirring, for 8 minutes. Add the shallots, carrot, and celery; cook, stirring, until just softened. Transfer the mixture to the beans in the cooker along with the bay leaf and herb sprig. Add the broth and enough water to cover the beans by 2 inches. Cover and cook on HIGH for 3½ to 4½ hours. The beans need to be covered with liquid at all times to cook properly. Towards the end of cooking, season with salt and pepper. When done, the beans will be tender and hold their shape, rather than fall apart. Remove the bay leaf and herb sprig and discard.

3. Serve the beans in soup bowls, topped with the crumbled goat cheese and sliced olives.

Tuscan Beans with Herbs

T he traditional terra-cotta bean pot, called a *fagioliera,* cooks beans gently so that they retain their beautiful shape even when totally tender. These beans are a great side dish to fish and meats, served drizzled with extra virgin olive oil, or used day old in soups and stews. This is adapted from a recipe by Faith Willinger, an inspired writer on the food of Italy. ☉ *Serves 6*

COOKER: Large round
SETTING AND COOK TIME: HIGH for 2½ to 3½ hours

2½ cups dried white beans, such as great northern or navy

2 sprigs fresh sage

1 bay leaf

1 head garlic, left whole and unpeeled

10 cups water

1 tablespoon coarse sea salt, or to taste

A few grinds of black pepper

Extra virgin olive oil for serving

1. Put the beans in a colander and rinse under cold running water; pick over for damaged beans and small stones. Transfer to the slow cooker and cover by 3 inches with cold water. Soak for 6 to 12 hours and drain.

2. Add the sage, bay leaf, garlic, and 10 cups of water. Cover and cook on HIGH for 2½ to 3½ hours. The beans need to be covered with liquid at all times to cook properly. When done, they will be tender and hold their shape, rather than fall apart. Towards the end of the cooking time, add the sea salt and remove the bay leaf and head of garlic (you can squeeze the cooked garlic back into the beans if you like or discard).

3. Let the beans cool in the cooker for 1 hour, uncovered, then drain off all but ½ cup of the liquid. Serve, seasoned with more salt and several grinds of black pepper, and drizzled with olive oil. Or transfer the beans and their liquor to a covered storage container and refrigerate for up to 7 days.

Boston Baked Beans

S traight from Beantown, here is the original: no tomatoes or garlic in sight. The molasses and salt pork are essential to the flavor. This recipe, right down to the submerged whole onion, has the exact same ingredients as those recorded by Abigail Adams of Massachusetts, wife of one president and mother to another, in her own handwritten cookbook from the late 1700s. No work was done on Sundays, so the ritual of weekly bean baking in the outdoor beehive oven began on Friday night. Saturday night it was baked beans and brown bread for supper; for Sunday breakfast, leftover beans with codfish cakes and green tomato relish. You will be cooking the beans a full 10 to 12 hours, so you may decide to let them cook overnight. The dash of baking soda helps minimize the beans' gassy qualities. These are the beans to mash cold and pile on whole wheat bread. ○ *Serves 6 to 8*

COOKER: Medium or large round
SETTINGS AND COOK TIMES: HIGH for 1½ hours to precook the beans, then HIGH to bring to a boil and LOW for 10 to 12 hours

1 pound dried small white navy or pea beans
½ teaspoon baking soda
One 8-ounce piece salt pork
½ cup dark molasses
½ cup firmly packed light or dark brown sugar
1½ teaspoons dry mustard
1½ teaspoons salt
¼ teaspoon freshly ground black pepper
1 medium-size white onion, peeled, left whole, and scored with a crisscross
    through the root end
6 cups boiling water

1. Rinse the beans in a colander under cold running water and pick over for damaged beans and small stones. Transfer to the slow cooker. Cover with cold water by 2 inches, soak overnight, and drain.

2. Cover the beans with fresh water by 3 inches. Add the baking soda, cover, and cook on HIGH until still undercooked, about 1½ hours. Drain.

3. Meanwhile, simmer the salt pork in boiling water for 10 minutes to remove excess salt; drain and rinse under cold running water. Pat dry and dice.

4. Combine the drained beans, salt pork, molasses, brown sugar, mustard, salt, and pepper in the cooker; stir to mix well. Push the onion into the center of the beans and add the boiling water; it will cover everything by ½ inch. Cover and cook on HIGH to bring to a boil, then reduce the heat to LOW and cook until the beans are soft, thick, and bubbling, 10 to 12 hours. Do not stir, but you can add more boiling water to keep the beans moist if you need to. Traditionally, the beans are cooked with the cover off for the last 30 minutes to thicken them to the desired consistency.

Maple Pork and Beans

This is the Vermont version of Boston baked beans, with the molasses omitted and luscious maple syrup added instead. This recipe is adapted from a little known cookbook, *Cooking from a Country Farmhouse* by Susan Wyler (HarperPerennial, 1993). You want grade B maple syrup if you can get it because it is a bit more intensely maple in flavor, but any real maple syrup will do. Serve with one of our steamed brown breads, pages 449–454. ◦ *Serves 6 to 8*

COOKER: Medium or large round
SETTING AND COOK TIME: LOW for 10 to 12 hours; salt pork rind needs to be removed at 4 to 6 hours

1 pound dried small white navy beans
One 12-ounce piece meaty salt pork
2 medium-size white onions, chopped
¾ cup ketchup
½ cup pure maple syrup, preferably grade B
⅓ cup firmly packed dark brown sugar
1 tablespoon Dijon mustard
¼ teaspoon cayenne pepper
3 cloves
2 cups boiling water, or as needed to cover

1. Rinse the beans in a colander under cold running water; pick over for damaged beans and small stones. Transfer to the slow cooker and cover with cold water by 2 inches. Soak 6 to 12 hours and drain.

2. Cut the rind off the salt pork in one piece with about ½ inch of fat attached; reserve. Cut the salt pork into strips 1½ inches long and ½ inch wide and thick. Simmer the salt pork strips in boiling water for 5 minutes to remove excess salt; drain and rinse under cold running water.

3. Add the salt pork, onions, ketchup, maple syrup, brown sugar, mustard, cayenne, and cloves to the beans in the cooker; stir to mix well. Add the boiling water to cover. Lay the reserved piece of salt pork rind on the top, cover, and cook on LOW for 4 to 6 hours.

4. Remove the rind, cover, and continue to cook the beans on LOW until the beans are soft, thick, and bubbling, another 6 hours.

Vegetarian Baked Beans

S ince baked beans are so wonderful made in the slow cooker, we included this great version of Boston-style baked beans, probably made in Shaker communities. You will be cooking the beans a full 10 to 12 hours, so plan accordingly. The navy bean is a small white oval bean so named because it has been a staple in the U.S. Navy for generations. These are so good; try them even if you have no vegetarians around. ● *Serves 6 to 8*

COOKER: Medium or large round

SETTINGS AND COOK TIMES: HIGH for 1½ hours to precook the
　　beans and then for a short time to bring the ingredients to a boil, then
　　LOW for 10 to 12 hours

1 pound dried white navy beans

¼ cup ketchup

¼ cup pure maple syrup, preferably B grade

¼ cup molasses

1¼ teaspoons dried summer or winter savory, or 2½ teaspoons chopped fresh

1 teaspoon baking soda

1 teaspoon salt

¼ teaspoon freshly ground black pepper

1 medium-size white onion, peeled, left whole, scored with an X at the root end,
　　and studded with 4 cloves

Boiling water to cover

½ cup (1 stick) butter or margarine, cut into pieces

1. Rinse the beans in a colander under cold running water; pick over for damaged beans and small stones. Transfer to the slow cooker. Cover with cold water by 2 inches, soak overnight, and drain.

2. Cover the beans with fresh water by 3 inches. Cover and cook on HIGH for 1½ hours, until still undercooked. Drain.

3. Return the beans to the cooker and add the ketchup, maple syrup, molasses, savory, baking soda, salt, and pepper; stir to mix well. Press the whole onion down into the center of the beans. Add boiling water to cover by ½ inch; stir gently. Cover and cook on HIGH to bring to a boil, then reduce the heat to LOW and cook until the beans are soft, thick, and bubbling, 10 to 12 hours.

4. Remove the onion and stir in the butter until melted. Taste for seasoning and serve hot.

Vegetarian Frijoles Negros

Black beans, also known as turtle beans, are the cornerstone of Central and South American soul food, just as pinto beans are in Mexican cooking. Once a specialty item, we notice they are readily available in every supermarket. They have an appealing, rather addictive, flavor and are easy to digest. If you like a smoky edge to your black beans, add 1 or 2 canned chipotle chiles. We like to float a few tablespoons of olive oil on top of the cooked the beans when serving. You can use these beans refried or pureéd as a dip because they are nice and thick. ◦ *Serves 4*

COOKER: Large round
SETTING AND COOK TIME: HIGH for 4 to 6 hours

One 1-pound package black turtle beans
1 medium-size yellow onion, finely chopped
1 medium-size green or red bell pepper, seeded and finely chopped
1 or 2 jalapeños, seeded and minced
½ teaspoon ground cumin
1 bay leaf
½ cup canned tomato sauce or salsa
8 cups water
1 tablespoon red wine vinegar
Salt to taste
Crumbled goat cheese (optional) for serving

1. Put the beans in a colander and rinse under cold running water; pick over for damaged beans and small stones. Transfer to the slow cooker. Cover with cold water by 3 inches, soak for 6 to 12 hours, and drain.

2. Add the onion, bell pepper, jalapeño, cumin, bay leaf, tomato sauce, and 8 cups of water. Cover and cook on HIGH for 4 to 6 hours. Check at 3 hours to gauge doneness. The beans need to be covered with liquid at all times to cook properly. When done, they will be tender and hold their shape, rather than fall apart. At the end of the cooking time, you will have plenty of liquid left over in the cooker. Remove the bay leaf, add the vinegar, and season with salt. Serve hot, sprinkled with goat cheese, if desired.

Stewed Black Beans

Be sure to use lots of water when cooking black beans if you want a medium consistency. They tend to be thick like a soup otherwise (which we love as well). Serve with lots of plain yogurt and salsa on top. ○ *Serves 4 to 6*

COOKER: Large round
SETTING AND COOK TIME: HIGH for 4 to 6 hours

One 1-pound package black turtle beans
1 medium-size yellow or white onion, finely chopped
1 medium-size carrot, coarsely grated
2 cloves garlic, chopped or left whole
½ teaspoon ground cumin or pure New Mexican chile powder
½ bay leaf or 1 sprig fresh summer or winter savory
Pinch of dried marjoram
4 to 6 cups water, depending on desired consistency
4 to 6 cups chicken or vegetable broth, depending on desired consistency
2 tablespoons white miso
Salt and freshly ground black pepper to taste
Hot sauce, such as Tabasco, to taste

1. Put the beans in a colander and rinse under cold running water; pick over for damaged beans and small stones. Transfer to the slow cooker. Cover with cold water by 3 inches, soak for 6 to 12 hours, and drain.

2. Add the onion, carrot, garlic, cumin, bay leaf, marjoram, and equal amounts of the water and broth. Cover and cook on HIGH for 4 to 6 hours. The beans need to be covered with liquid at all times to cook properly. When done, they will be nice and tender, yet hold their shape. At the end of the cooking time, you will have plenty of liquid left with the cooked beans.

3. Discard the bay leaf or herb sprig. Swirl in the miso and stir until dissolved. Season the beans with salt, pepper, and hot sauce and serve.

Mexican Black Beans with Pork

T his bean and pork stew is made with canned black beans, allowing you to skip the presoaking and cooking stages. It makes a great, simple meal when served with salad and focaccia or oversized flour tortillas with butter. ○

Serves 4 to 6

COOKER: Medium or large round
SETTING AND COOK TIME: LOW for 8 to 9 hours

1 pound boneless pork loin, trimmed of any fat and cut into 1-inch cubes
1 teaspoon chili powder
1 teaspoon ground coriander
Salt to taste
1 medium-size yellow onion, chopped
1 garlic clove, minced
Two 15-ounce cans black beans, rinsed and drained
One 16-ounce can stewed tomatoes, coarsely chopped, with their juice
2 cups water
Freshly ground black pepper to taste

FOR SERVING:
Hot cooked white rice
¼ cup chopped fresh cilantro

1. Toss the pork with the chili powder, coriander, and salt until coated evenly. Heat a large ungreased skillet over medium-high heat, then lightly brown the pork with the onion and garlic, stirring.

2. Transfer the pork mixture to the slow cooker, stir in the beans, tomatoes with their juice, and water, season with pepper, cover, and cook on LOW for 8 to 9 hours.

3. Serve the beans and pork ladled over steamed white rice and garnished with cilantro.

Orange Black Beans with Cumin

H ere is a fabulous recipe loosely adapted from one of our favorite cookbooks, *The Stanford University Healthy Heart Cookbook* (Chronicle Books, 1997). Canned black beans are incredibly versatile and, since they are also easy to digest, should be a regular part of every bean lover's diet. ◦ *Serves 2 to 4*

COOKER: Medium round
SETTING AND COOK TIME: HIGH for about 1½ hours

Two 15-ounce cans black beans, rinsed and drained
2 tablespoons firmly packed light or dark brown sugar
1 medium-size shallot, minced
1 rib celery, minced
½ cup orange juice
½ cup chicken broth
½ teaspoon ground cumin
Pinch of ground cinnamon or cardamom
Salt and freshly ground black pepper to taste

FOR SERVING:
Hot cooked white rice
¼ cup chopped fresh cilantro leaves
½ cup chopped fresh tomatoes

1. Combine the beans, brown sugar, shallot, celery, orange juice, broth, cumin, and cinnamon in the slow cooker. Cover and cook on HIGH for about 1½ hours.

2. Season with salt and pepper and serve hot ladled over rice, and garnished with the cilantro and tomatoes.

Slow Cooker Chickpeas

C hickpeas, also known as garbanzo beans, show up in cuisines from the Mediterranean to India. They are very hard beans, so presoaking is important, and they must be cooked on HIGH in the slow cooker. Chickpeas are the essential ingredient in hummus, the chickpea purée that is standard fare in the Middle East. Freshly cooked chickpeas are fabulous in lettuce salads with grated carrot and tomato wedges, and added to soups. They are also wonderful with lamb or chicken in one of our stews. ○ *Serves 6*

COOKER: Large round
SETTING AND COOK TIME: HIGH for 3½ to 6 hours

One 1-pound package dried chickpeas
9 cups water
2 teaspoons fine sea salt, or to taste

1. Put the chickpeas in a colander and rinse under cold running water; pick over for damaged beans and small stones. Transfer to the slow cooker. Cover with cold water by 3 inches, soak for 6 to 12 hours, and drain.

2. Add the 9 cups water. Cover and cook on HIGH for 3½ to 6 hours. Check at 3½ hours to gauge doneness. Towards the end of the cooking time, season with the salt. The chickpeas need to be covered with liquid at all times to cook properly. When done, they will be tender and hold their shape, rather than fall apart. Cut a bean in half with a knife to check.

3. Let the chickpeas stand in the cooker for 1 hour, uncovered. Then transfer with their liquor to a covered storage container to refrigerate or freeze, or drain them and use in another recipe.

Chickpeas with Chard

T here is a book called *Wake Up and Cook,* compiled by Tricycle Press (Riverhead Books, 1997), with an assemblage of writings and poems by Zen Buddhists, who consider good food as much a part of their spiritual path as contemplative practice. In it is a section by composer John Cage, who adheres to a simple diet of brown rice and all sorts of dried beans. He cooks the beans, then adds a flavoring agent and a salty element, such as soy sauce, at the end. In the same spirit, here is a recipe by Darra Goldstein, culinary authority and editor of the journal *Gastronomica.* It is an ever-so-good way to make chickpeas with lots of greens into a simple, satisfying main dish. ☉ *Serves 2 to 3*

COOKER: Medium round

SETTING AND COOK TIME: HIGH for 4½ to 5 hours; sautéed onions, chard, tomato paste, and seasonings added at 3 to 3½ hours

½ cup dried chickpeas

1 bunch Swiss chard (1½ pounds), rinsed, stems discarded, leaves coarsely chopped; or
    1½ pounds spinach, rinsed, tough steams removed, and large leaves chopped

2 cups water

¼ cup olive oil

2 small white onions, finely chopped

2 tablespoons tomato paste

½ teaspoon fine sea salt, to taste

Pinch of cayenne pepper or pure New Mexican chile powder

Few grinds of black pepper

1. Place the chickpeas in a colander and rinse under cold running water; pick over for damaged beans and small stones. Transfer to the slow cooker (it must be large enough so that there is plenty of room for the chickpeas to bubble without spilling over). Cover with 3 inches of cold water and soak 6 to 12 hours.

2. If using Swiss chard, blanch the chopped leaves in boiling water for 3 minutes.

3. Drain the chickpeas, add the 2 cups water, cover, and cook on HIGH until just tender, 3 to 3½ hours. The chickpeas need to be covered with liquid at all times to cook properly.

4. In a small skillet over medium-high heat, heat the olive oil, then cook the onions, stirring, until almost golden and browned around the edges, about 8 minutes.

5. When the chickpeas are tender, add the onions and oil, the wilted chard (dripping with water is fine) or raw spinach, tomato paste, salt, cayenne, and black pepper. Cover and continue to cook on HIGH for another 1½ hours. Serve hot.

• • Marinated Chickpea Salad • •

This salad, made with freshly cooked chickpeas, is simply wonderful. You can add extra ingredients if you like—leftover cooked green beans, grated carrot, sliced black olives, tomatoes—but it is really good as is. It takes almost no time to assemble and is satisfying. ○ Serves 4

3 tablespoons red wine vinegar, cider vinegar, or fresh lemon juice
¼ cup olive oil
2 heaping cups cooked Slow Cooker Chickpeas (page 202), drained if necessary
1 medium-size shallot, minced; or ½ small red onion, finely chopped
3 tablespoons chopped fresh flat-leaf parsley
Dash of salt and freshly ground black pepper

In a medium-size bowl, whisk together the vinegar and oil. Add the chickpeas, shallot, and parsley; toss to combine. Season with salt and pepper. Marinate at room temperature for 30 minutes before serving or refrigerate for up to 24 hours. Serve cold or at room temperature.

Crock-Baked Soybeans

With all the positive attention soy foods have been getting lately, you would think that soybeans would be on everyone's table. Though soymilk, toasted soy nuts, tofu, and the fresh soybeans known as edamame do turn up in the kitchens of the health-conscious with great regularity, soybeans in their most basic form do not. We think it's because people don't know how to cook soybeans. And we think that's a shame, because soybeans are nice beans to get to know! They are cute little yellow ovals and have a mildly nutty flavor. Even when cooked until tender they hold their shape better than most other beans. And like all beans, they absorb flavors of added ingredients beautifully. The toasted sesame oil included here gives the beans a hint of smoky richness without adding much fat. ○ *Serves 4 to 5*

COOKER: Medium or large round
SETTINGS AND COOK TIMES: HIGH for 4 hours, then LOW for 5 to 6 hours

1 cup dried soybeans
4 cups water, or to cover
½ medium-size yellow onion, sliced into half-moons
¼ cup firmly packed light or dark brown sugar
¼ cup molasses
1 teaspoon salt
½ teaspoon dry mustard
2 tablespoons toasted or black sesame oil

1. Rinse the beans in a colander under cold running water; pick over for damaged beans and small stones. Transfer to the slow cooker. Cover with cold water by 2 inches, soak 6 to 12 hours, and drain.

2. Cover with the 4 cups water. Cover and cook on HIGH until tender, about 4 hours. The beans need to be covered with liquid at all times to cook properly.

3. Drain the cooked beans and return them to the cooker. Add the onion, brown sugar, molasses, salt, mustard, and sesame oil; stir to combine. Cover and cook on LOW for 5 to 6 hours, until the soybeans are flavorful but still moist and the onion is soft. Stir gently so as not to mash the beans and serve hot.

Southwestern Bean Pot

While this recipe calls for some of the wonderful heirloom and exotic beans now grown in the Southwest, it will work with any bean, especially black-eyed peas. Beth loves using the ham bone after a feast of honey-baked ham. Serve this over a mound of soft polenta with a side of sautéed Swiss chard. The Christmas lima is a lovely red-and-white-speckled bean. ● *Serves 8*

COOKER: Medium or large round
SETTING AND COOK TIME: HIGH for 5 to 6 hours; salsa added at 3½ hours

One 1-pound package dried Christmas lima, cranberry, pinto, or anasazi beans
7 cups water
1 large yellow onion, chopped
One 12-ounce ham hock or leftover meaty ham bone
One 8-ounce can or jar green chile salsa, tomato sauce, or stewed tomatoes
1 teaspoon salt, or to taste

1. Put the beans in a colander and rinse under cold running water; pick over for damaged beans and small stones. Transfer to the slow cooker. Cover with 3 inches of cold water; soak for 6 to 12 hours, and drain.

2. Add the 7 cups of water, onion, and ham hock. Cover and cook on HIGH for 3½ hours, then stir in the salsa.

3. Cover and continue to cook on HIGH for another 1½ to 2½ hours. The beans should be covered with liquid at all times to cook properly, but the mixture should be thick. When done, the beans will be tender and hold their shape, rather than fall apart. Remove the ham hock or bone and pick off the meat. Return the meat to the crock and stir to combine. Season with the salt and serve.

Slow Cooker Lentils

T his recipe calls for brown lentils, also known as European lentils. Some-times they are tinged with some green, but usually they are an earthy brown. We also like the French gray-green lentils du Puy, which are a tad smaller than regular brown lentils and are excellent in salads because of their ability to hold their shape after cooking. Do not use this recipe to cook red lentils (also known as Egyptian lentils), which are best for soups and dal since they break down into a smooth purée quickly. Here we wanted firm lentils that would hold their shape when added later to soups, stews, or salads dressed with vinaigrette. For a quick side dish, drain the lentils, then add them to a hot skillet and heat with some oil, bacon fat, or butter. Or mash them and serve with a drizzle of olive oil or a pat of butter. ❍ *Serves 10 to 12*

COOKER: Medium round
SETTING AND COOK TIME: HIGH for 2 to 3 hours

1 pound dried brown lentils or French green lentils du Puy
7 cups water, as needed
Salt (optional) to taste

1. Put the lentils in a colander and rinse under cold running water; pick over for damaged lentils and small stones. Transfer to the slow cooker. Add enough of the water to cover by 3 inches. Cover and cook on HIGH until they reach the desired tenderness. If you want undercooked lentils for adding to soups, cook for about 2 hours; if you want tender lentils for a salad, cook for about 3 hours. If you continue to cook any longer, they will begin to break down and get a bit mushy, as in a lentil soup. For storage in the freezer, the firmer lentils are best.

2. Season the lentils with salt, if desired. Remove from the cooker and let cool to room temperature. If the beans have a lot of liquid, drain some of it off. Use imme-diately in a recipe or refrigerate, covered, for 3 to 4 days. Or drain the lentils com-pletely, rinse, then freeze in 1-cup batches in freezer bags (lay them flat) for up to 2 months. Frozen lentils are great for adding to soups and stews.

Lentils with Ham and Rosemary

This recipe is from a *Cooking Light* magazine article on slow cookers published some years back and now posted on the Internet. This savory combination of ham and lentils garnered a four-star rating from users, which really caught our attention. Use any type of ham: leftover honey baked ham from a picnic or holiday meal, a 1-pound ham steak from the meat department, or thick slices of Black Forest ham from a deli. ○ *Serves 8*

COOKER: Medium or large round
SETTING AND COOK TIME: HIGH for 2½ to 3 hours

2 medium-size yellow onions, chopped
2 cups diced cooked ham (see above)
1 cup diced carrot or parsnip
1 cup chopped celery
2 cloves garlic, chopped
¾ teaspoon dried rosemary, crushed
¾ teaspoon rubbed sage
¼ teaspoon freshly ground black pepper
1 bay leaf
1 pound dried brown lentils, picked over and rinsed
One 14.5-ounce can beef broth
5 cups water, or as needed to cover everything by 3 inches
Chopped fresh flat-leaf parsley for serving (optional)

1. Combine all the ingredients in the slow cooker, except the parsley. Cover and cook on HIGH until the lentils are tender, 2½ to 3 hours. Add boiling water if you want soupier lentils.

2. Discard the bay leaf. Garnish with parsley, if desired, before serving.

Old-Fashioned "One-Pot" Bean Dinner

The original recipe for this dish, which still graces many an American heartland buffet table, appeared in one of the early Rival cookbooks that accompanied the first cookers. This casserole is very rich, so it needs very few side dishes; we like coleslaw, garlic bread, and a tossed green salad. The comment that came with this recipe said, "Makes a big hit . . . especially with the men."

○ *Serves 10*

COOKER: Large round or oval
SETTING AND COOK TIME: LOW for 6 to 9 hours

8 ounces to 1 pound lean ground beef
½ pound sliced bacon or turkey bacon, cut into 2-inch pieces
1 medium-size yellow onion, finely chopped
Two 31-ounce cans pork and beans
One 16-ounce can red kidney beans, rinsed and drained
One 15.5-ounce can butter lima beans, drained
1½ cups ketchup
¼ cup firmly packed light or dark brown sugar
1 tablespoon liquid smoke flavoring (optional)
3 tablespoons cider vinegar

1. In a medium-size skillet, cook the ground beef over medium-high heat until browned; drain off the fat and transfer the meat to the slow cooker. In the same skillet, cook the bacon and onion over medium heat, stirring, until limp, about 6 to 8 minutes. The bacon should be slightly undercooked; drain off the fat. Transfer the mixture to the cooker, add the remaining ingredients, and stir to combine.

2. Cover and cook on LOW until hot and bubbly, 6 to 9 hours.

Vegetarian Cholent

C holent is a classic hearty stew of European Jewish origin, usually made with beef brisket. The word *cholent* comes from the Old French *chald,* which means "warm." Since religious law prohibits the lighting of a fire on the Sabbath, this dish was originally cooked overnight in the diminishing heat of the local baker's wood-burning oven, to be served at noon the next day. It is a long-cooking dish featuring dried lima beans and barley, and it is still prepared to this day in observant homes (KitchenAid even makes an oven with a special, extra-slow Shabbat setting) and traditionally eaten after synagogue on Saturday. It is perfectly suited for the convenience of the slow cooker. This recipe is adapted from one of our favorite books, *Out of Our Kitchen Closets,* published by the Congregation Sha'ar Zahav of San Francisco (1987). It feeds a group nicely. Serve this with challah, steamed green beans, and a mixed vegetable and greens salad dressed with a vinaigrette. ○ *Serves about 16*

COOKER: Large round or oval
SETTINGS AND COOK TIMES: HIGH for 1 hour, then LOW for 12 to 16 hours

1 cup dried lima beans
1 cup dried red kidney beans
1 cup dried pinto beans
1 cup dried brown lentils
¾ cup olive oil
1 large white onion, sliced ½ inch thick
1 cup pearl barley
1 package Manischewitz lima bean and barley dry soup mix
2 tablespoons sesame seeds
1¼ teaspoons cumin seeds
1 teaspoon paprika
4 ribs celery, chopped
2 cloves garlic, minced
4 vegetable bouillon cubes, crushed
16 small white or red new potatoes, scrubbed (if your potatoes are medium-size, use half the amount and peel and quarter them)

Cold water or vegetable broth (omit the bouillon cubes if using broth)

1 tablespoon fine sea salt, or to taste

Freshly ground black pepper to taste

1. Put the lima, kidney, and pinto beans in a colander and rinse under cold running water; pick over for damaged beans and small stones. Transfer to the slow cooker. Cover with cold water by 3 inches, soak for 6 to 12 hours, and drain. Pick over and rinse the lentils.

2. Heat 3 tablespoons of the oil in a medium-size skillet over medium heat and cook the onion, stirring, until softened, about 5 minutes.

3. Add the lentils, the sautéed onion, the remaining 9 tablespoons of oil, the barley, dry soup mix, sesame seeds, cumin seeds, paprika, celery, garlic, and crushed bouillon cubes to the beans in the cooker; stir to combine. Lay the potatoes over the top, pressing them into the beans. Cover completely with the fresh cold water or broth, leaving about 1 inch of headroom at the top. Cover and cook on HIGH for 1 hour.

4. Turn the cooker to LOW and cook for 12 to 16 hours.

5. Before serving, season with the salt and pepper and serve in shallow soup bowls.

Beans and Sausage

With all the wonderful lean and spicy sausages out today, we need plenty of good recipes to make use of them. Sausages have been the cornerstone of one-pot dishes for centuries (it's hard to imagine a gumbo or cassoulet without sausage) because they are a convenient way to preserve meat. Beyond beef and pork, there are now sausages made from veal, turkey, and chicken. You can get sausages fresh (which need to be completely cooked before adding to a slow cooker recipe), smoked, or fully cooked. Substitute any canned beans you like; just use a combination of two types. The great northern bean, easily found canned, is mild and pairs nicely with other more assertive beans. Serve this with a nice loaf of fresh bread and butter, and a little green salad. ○ *Serves 4 to 6*

1 pound fresh sausage, such as turkey Italian sausage; or 1 pound smoked or fully cooked
   sausage, such as bratwurst, chicken apple sausage, or kielbasa

¼ cup water (if using fresh sausage)

2 tablespoons olive oil

2 small bell peppers, any color, seeded and cut into strips

1 medium-size yellow onion, chopped

1 garlic clove, minced

One 15-ounce can white beans, such as great northern, butter beans, or cannellini, rinsed and
   drained

One 15-ounce can red beans, such as small red or kidney beans, rinsed and drained

One 14.5-ounce can diced tomatoes, with their juice

¼ cup dry red wine

Salt and freshly ground black pepper to taste

1. In an ungreased skillet over medium heat, lightly brown the sausage. If the sausage is smoked or fully cooked, slice and set aside. If fresh, add the water, cover, and cook until completely cooked through, 8 to 10 minutes. Uncover and cook for a few minutes more. Let cool and slice.

2. Wipe out the skillet and warm the oil over medium heat. Add the peppers, onion, and garlic; cook, stirring, until just tender. Transfer to the slow cooker and add the sausage, beans, tomatoes and their juice, and wine. Cover and cook on HIGH for 3 to 4 hours, or LOW for 6 to 8 hours. Near the end of the cooking time, check the consistency and cook with the lid off to thicken, if desired. Season with salt and pepper and serve.

The Wonderful World of Chili

Sounds amazing, but the thick and spicy meat stew called *chili con carne,* or "chile with meat," is as American as apple pie. It is a traditional homespun dish that displays the creativity and originality of cooks born and bred in the borderland desert of the United States and northern Mexico. Chili smacks of the colorful, fiery, nutritious, festive, and addictive qualities that characterize neighboring Mexican cuisine, but it is not a Mexican food.

Chili, spelled with an "i" at the end, not an "e" (tipping off the reader that it is about chili the dish not a chile pepper), is a wildly popular dish all over the country. It is also one of the premier reasons to own a slow cooker. The first dish most cooks make in their new cookers is chili. It is great party fare, as well as a simple dinner or lunch for the kids.

Chili is something of an obsession to those who belong to the Chili Appreciation Society or the International Chili Society. Their members are passionate purists and they make the rules when it comes to the criteria of what makes chili a chili: Is the chili full of beans and what kind? Which cut of meat—brisket or chuck? Ground meat or hunks? Should the heat come from the chili powder or ground chiles, or both? Olive oil or lard or bacon drippings? Tomatoes or no tomatoes? Masa harina, cornmeal, or neither? Beer, water, or tequila?

Chili is characterized by a flavor and color combination of spicy-hot red chile powder and Southwestern herbs, such as oregano and cumin, and even accents of cinnamon and cloves. While chili has a reputation for inducing uncontrollable perspiration, lip burning, runny noses, and tears, you can most certainly make a mild chili in which all the individual, subtle flavors are discernible.

Chili stews are made with or without beans. While all sorts of beans show up in chilies today, the traditional bean is the pinto, also called the *frijol* bean or Mexican red bean, a faintly streaked, reddish-brown and pink bean grown in the Southwest. The pinto (a Spanish word that means "painted") is a variety of the *Phaseolus vulgaris* species, which includes kidney beans, pink beans, and navy beans, also used to make chili. Today's chili makers do not limit themselves, though; there are chilies made with black turtle beans (an incredibly popular bean for vegetarian chilies), great northerns (a favorite in white chilies), black-eyed peas, Anasazi beans, cannellini (white kidneys), dappled black-and-white appaloosas, giant pintos, and the mottled brown-and-cream Jacob's cattle beans. In any of our recipes, you can substitute one of these more exotic Ameri-

Red Chile Powder

Many chili recipes specify the blend called chili powder; in addition, we often call for red chile powder, which is the ground powder of a single type of dried chile. Red chile powder is a standard in old Southwest pioneer and hacienda kitchens, used for flavoring everything from soups, sauces, and frijoles to chorizo, tamales, and gravy. The chiles are grown in California and New Mexico and usually the package of chile powder will indicate where it was grown, for example, Hatch, Chimayo, San Juan Pueblo.

We were introduced to Dixon chile powder by our Southwest cooking expert, Jacquie Higuera McMahan. Dixon is called the Rolls Royce of ground chiles for its incomparable flavor. Use chile powder, referred to as "the salt of the Southwest," for sprinkling over potatoes, in meatloaf, stews, rubs, red chile sauce, rice, and, of course, in your homemade chilies.

We particularly like ancho chile powder, the most beloved dried chile of Mexico, for its lovely sweetness. It is often used in combination with other dried chiles to mellow their sharpness. Ancho is readily available in the Hispanic section of your supermarket.

Chipotle powder is relatively new to the marketplace and a welcome and convenient addition to the chile pantry. It is an easy way to add the distinctly spicy, smoky heat of chipotle peppers to many kinds of food. Use it with discretion, though—it really packs a punch. Cayenne pepper is a chile powder too, one that many cooks have on their spice racks already. It is so hot, though, that it tends to be used in very small quantities to contribute heat, not flavor, to chili stews.

The best way to obtain California or New Mexican chile powders is by mail order. You can order Dixon or Chimayo chile powders from the Chile Shop, 109 E. Water Street, Santa Fe, NM 87501 (505-983-6080; www.thechileshop.com). We keep it in a spring-top glass jar, right on the counter for quick access. You can also put it in the freezer if it will take you a while to use it up.

can-grown varieties to vary the flavor of your chili. Mixing two or three different varieties is also popular, especially in vegetarian versions.

Beef and/or pork are the standard meats in most recipes, but sometimes different types of sausages or crumbled sausage meat and salt pork appear. Chicken and turkey, the basis for white chili, are really popular with modern palates. Some recipes, from as far away as Morocco, call for simply lamb, water, chiles, and spices. The Navajo eat their chili with lamb, red chiles, and hominy.

How should you thicken a chili? Use dry masa harina, the cornmeal used for making tortillas (keep some in the freezer just for thickening your chilies); it is the traditional way, and adds a wonderful flavor. Start with 2 tablespoons mixed with ¼ cup of cold water to make a slurry. It will be thin; make sure there are no lumps. Pour the slurry into the hot chili and stir. Cook on LOW for about 20 minutes, or HIGH for 10 minutes; the chili will thicken slightly. If you want it even thicker, repeat. If your chili is too thick, just add more liquid and cook a bit longer to heat the stew. Remember that if your chili is too saucy, you can serve it Cincinnati style–over spaghetti.

We have assembled a variety of chilies to appeal to all types of cooks and diners. We have ones prepared with chicken and turkey, as well as ones made with ground beef and steak. We have a few vegetarian bean chilies that are every bit as good as their meat-filled siblings. All chilies can be made a day or two ahead; they just get better as they sit.

While most chilies are offered with warm fresh corn or flour tortillas, they can be served with biscuits, sopapillas (little fried bread triangles), and, of course, all manner of cornbreads, corn sticks, and cornmeal muffins. Chili and foods made with cornmeal are a natural pairing (consider that tamale pie is simply a thick chili baked with cornmeal mush on top). A hunk of homemade whole wheat bread, crusty French bread, or a fluffy shepherd's bread certainly goes well with chili, too.

Annie Oakley Chili Cook-Off Rules

1. **Restrain from snuff dipping while leaning over the chili pots.**
2. **Avoid playing tricks on other contestants, and absolutely no rubber snakes or plastic spiders in the cooking area.**
3. **When the winners are announced, there will be no pinching, biting, or jostling.**

·· All Manner of Chiles ··

Julie was brought up in New Mexico, so she has a "sixth sense" about chiles. Beth, on the other hand, was raised in New Jersey and, as a result, she is constantly referring to lists to figure out which chile is best with what and how hot they are.

A few simple axioms: Fresh chiles tend to be milder, dried chiles stronger. Fresh chiles taste more pronounced than canned. Rehydrate dried chiles to develop their flavor; they will not rehydrate properly in salted water or stock. Every chile has a different level of heat and a slightly different flavor. In general, the smaller the pepper, the hotter; the more pointed the shape, the hotter. Big chiles are safe; little ones are dangerous to the uninitiated. Much of the heat is in the membranes and seeds, not the meat. You can cool any pepper by removing the seeds and soaking it in a solution of water and salt or vinegar (1 tablespoon of either to 2 cups of water). Don't rub your eyes while working with chiles, and do wear those wonderful plastic gloves they use in delis (ask for a few pair and keep them in the napkin drawer for just this purpose). Here is a quick overview of the chiles we use throughout the book.

Anaheim: These are available fresh and are also marketed as California green chiles and *chiles verdes.* They are the chiles in the cans labeled "roasted green chiles" and are mild to medium on the heat index.

Banana chile: Yellow to red in color, these fresh chiles, also called Hungarian wax chiles, range from mild to medium-hot.

Chile de árbol: Only available dried, these little pointed red chiles are found in cellophane bags in the Hispanic section of the supermarket. They are a type of cayenne and are extremely hot!

Chipotle: These dried and smoked ripe jalapeños are sold canned, packed in adobo sauce, as well as dried and ground into a powder. They have an unmistakable smoky, complex flavor and are also quite hot; add them to a dish with care.

Jalapeño: Two inches long, bright dark green, and moderately hot, these are now a very widely used pepper, especially in salsas. Fresh jalapeños are sold canned and *en escabeche* (marinated), which are milder than fresh. If you end up with a big batch of fresh jalapeños, blanch them for 5 minutes in boiling water, drain on paper towels, let cool, and store whole in plastic freezer bags in the freezer.

New Mexico: When fresh, these chiles are green, and they are sold under such variety names as Big Jims, Sandias, and 6-s. They are like Anaheims, but with more heat and flavor. When sold dried (usually only in the Southwest), either whole (usually fashioned into ristras or garlands) or as a powder, they are red and used to make oxblood-red chile sauces.

Poblano: Sold fresh, these are smaller, heart shaped, and more rounded than Anaheims, and they have a tough skin. Use just like bell peppers for stuffing (although they are not as firm) and for rajas (chile strips). The poblano is often confused with the pasilla, which has really thin flesh and dries into the *chile negro.* When dried, the poblano is called an *ancho.*

Serrano and habanero: Smaller and lots hotter than jalapeños, both of these peppers, sold fresh, are an acquired taste, so don't use them unless you really know your crowd. The serrano looks like a little jalapeño and the habanero is like a little golden lantern, though it can also be green in color.

Really Old-Fashioned Chili with Salsa Cruda

This is a very mild gringo chili, the classic chili con carne with beans. We like to plop some fresh salsa on top as well. Some chili lovers stir in a cup of chopped olives at the end of cooking. You can serve this mild chili, mixed with cooked macaroni, to children. Serve with corn muffins or corn sticks. ● *Serves 8 to 10*

COOKER: Medium round or oval
SETTING AND COOK TIME: LOW for 8 to 9 hours; salt added during last hour

2 pounds ground sirloin
2 medium-size yellow onions, chopped
1 medium-size green, yellow, or red bell pepper, seeded and chopped
3 cloves garlic, minced
Two 15-ounce cans red kidney beans, rinsed and drained
Two 14.75-ounce cans diced tomatoes, with their juice
One 8-ounce can tomato sauce
1½ cups beef broth, chicken broth, or water
2 tablespoons chili powder or mild chile powder, such as
    California or ancho, or to taste
½ teaspoon dried oregano
½ teaspoon ground cumin
Salt to taste

SALSA CRUDA:
3 to 4 large ripe tomatoes, finely diced
1 small red onion, finely diced
1 jalapeño, seeded and minced
⅓ cup chopped fresh cilantro
Juice of 1 lime
Garlic powder to taste
Salt to taste

FOR SERVING:
Shredded sharp cheddar cheese
Sliced avocado

1. In a very large skillet over medium-high heat, cook the ground sirloin, onion, bell pepper, and garlic until the meat is no longer pink, breaking up any clumps;

drain off the fat. Transfer to the slow cooker and add the kidney beans, tomatoes, tomato sauce, broth, chili powder, oregano, and cumin, and stir to combine. Cover and cook on LOW for 8 to 9 hours, stirring occasionally, if possible. The last hour, season with salt. The longer you let the chili simmer, the better it gets, up to a point, of course.

2. To make the salsa cruda, combine all the ingredients in a bowl and refrigerate until serving. If you must make it the night before, add the cilantro and lime juice at the last minute.

3. Serve the chili in bowls topped with salsa, cheese, and avocado slices.

1-2-3-4 Chili with Beef and Beans

H ere is another beef-and-bean chili, this time with pinto beans, beer, and green chiles. *Crema Mexicana* is more liquidy than American sour cream, and the flavor is smoother. Serve this with cornbread or whole wheat tortillas. ○

Serves 6 to 8

COOKER: Medium round or oval
SETTING AND COOK TIME: LOW for 8 to 9 hours, or HIGH for 4 to 5 hours; salt added during last hour

1½ **pounds lean ground chuck or sirloin**
1 **large yellow onion, chopped**
2 **cloves garlic, minced**
One 15-ounce can pinto beans, rinsed and drained
Two 14.5-ounce cans diced tomatoes with green chiles, such as Rotel, with their juice
One 6-ounce can tomato paste
One 7-ounce can diced roasted green chiles
¾ **cup Mexican beer (not dark)**
2 **teaspoons chili powder**
1½ **teaspoons pure ancho chile powder**
1 **teaspoon ground cumin**
1 **teaspoon dried oregano, savory, or marjoram**
Salt to taste

FOR SERVING:

Shredded sharp cheddar cheese

Sour cream or *crema Mexicana*

Chopped fresh tomatoes

Chopped green onions

Chopped fresh cilantro

Warm cornbread or whole wheat tortillas

1. In a large skillet over medium-high heat, cook the ground beef, onion, and garlic until the meat is no longer pink, breaking up any clumps; drain off the fat. Transfer to the slow cooker, and add the pinto beans, tomatoes, tomato paste, chiles, beer, chili powder, ancho powder, cumin, and oregano, and stir to combine. Cover and cook on LOW for 8 to 9 hours, stirring occasionally, if possible, or on HIGH for 4 to 5 hours. The last hour, season with salt. The longer you let the chili simmer, the better it gets, up to a point, of course.

2. Serve the chili in bowls with plenty of toppings and warm cornbread or whole wheat tortillas.

Senator Barry Goldwater's Arizona Chili

T he idea of a chili cook-off in the U.S. Senate is comforting and reassuring, since it means the people making the laws of the country are not only being properly fed, but understand the laws of chili-mania and humor. The senator declared chili the official food of the United States, embodying "the robust and indomitable American spirit." This is a very simple chili compared to the other ones in this collection—sort of just the basics. Serve with cornbread with honey and butter. ○ *Serves 4 to 6*

COOKER: Medium round or oval

SETTINGS AND COOK TIMES: HIGH for 2 to 2½ hours, then LOW for 8 to 9 hours; salt added during last hour

1 pound dried pinto beans, picked over, soaked overnight in cold water to cover, and drained

3 cloves garlic, peeled

1 pound coarse-ground lean beef

2 medium-size yellow onions, chopped

One 6-ounce can tomato paste

3 tablespoons chili powder

1 tablespoon ground cumin

2 teaspoons salt, or to taste

FOR SERVING:

Shredded sharp cheddar cheese

Chopped fresh tomatoes

Chopped green onions

Warm cornbread or saltine crackers

1. Place the drained beans and whole garlic cloves in the slow cooker and add enough water to cover by 3 inches. Cover and cook on HIGH until tender but not mushy, 2 to 2½ hours. Drain and discard the garlic. The beans can be prepared up to this point and refrigerated overnight.

2. In a large skillet over medium-high heat, cook the ground beef and onions until the meat is no longer pink, breaking up any clumps; drain off the fat. Transfer to the cooker, and add the partially cooked pinto beans, the tomato paste, chili powder, and cumin, and add enough water to cover. Stir to combine. Cover and cook on LOW for 8 to 9 hours, stirring occasionally, if possible. During the last hour, season with salt.

3. Serve the chili in bowls with plenty of toppings and warm cornbread.

Salsa Chili with Cilantro Cream

When you use jarred salsa, it is like adding thick seasoned tomato sauce. There are many types of salsa out there now, including ones that contain corn and black beans. You can choose medium, mild, or hot salsa, as your palate dictates. This makes a small batch of thick chili, which can cook in one of the smaller cookers, such as a 2½ quart, with no problem. Or double or triple the recipe, as desired, and use a large cooker. There is no precooking of ingredients, but you can brown the meat first if you like. ● *Serves 4*

COOKER: Small or medium round or oval

SETTING AND COOK TIME: LOW for 7 to 8 hours; bell pepper and pinto beans
added at 5 to 6 hours

1 pound boneless beef chuck, tri tip (a triangular sirloin cut), or
round steak, trimmed of excess fat and cut into bite-size pieces
1 large yellow onion, chopped
2 cloves garlic, finely chopped
1 tablespoon chili powder
2 teaspoons ground cumin
Two 16-ounce jars thick-and-chunky salsa, mild or hot
One 14.5-ounce can diced tomatoes, with their juice
1 medium-size red or green bell pepper, seeded and chopped
One 15-ounce can pinto beans, rinsed and drained
Salt to taste

CILANTRO CREAM:
⅔ cup sour cream
¼ cup minced fresh cilantro
2 tablespoons fresh lime juice

Warm cornbread for serving

1. Put the meat, onion, garlic, chili powder, cumin, salsa, and tomatoes in the slow cooker and stir to combine. Cover and cook on LOW for 5 to 6 hours.

2. Add the bell pepper and pinto beans, season with salt, and continue to cook on LOW for another 2 hours. The longer you let it simmer, the better it gets, within reason, of course.

3. To make the cilantro cream, combine all the ingredients in a small bowl, and stir until well combined. Cover and chill until serving. Serve the chili in bowls with a dollop of the cilantro cream and cornbread.

Chili Californio

Here is another no-bean chili with stew meat. You make your own tomato sauce first, then add the browned meats. Serve it with Julie's Skillet Cornbread (page 236). ○ *Serves 8 to 10*

COOKER: Large round or oval

SETTINGS AND COOK TIMES: HIGH to start, then LOW for 8 to 10 hours

2 medium-size yellow onions, finely chopped

2 ribs celery, chopped

2 cloves garlic, minced

½ teaspoon salt

One 14.5-ounce can diced tomatoes, with their juice; or

    4 medium-size ripe tomatoes, peeled, seeded, and chopped

3 tablespoons tomato paste

3 tablespoons olive oil, lard, or bacon drippings

1 medium-size red or green bell pepper, seeded and chopped

2 pounds beef round steak, trimmed of excess fat and cut into ½-inch cubes

1 pound pork shoulder, trimmed of excess fat and cut into ½-inch cubes

1 tablespoon all-purpose flour or whole wheat pastry flour

¼ cup chili powder

1 tablespoon light or dark brown sugar

1 tablespoon cider vinegar or red wine vinegar

2 teaspoons pure New Mexico or California chile powder

2 teaspoons dried oregano

1 bay leaf

1 jalapeño (optional)

1 cup water

1 cup pitted ripe California black olives, drained and chopped

1 cup shredded Monterey Jack cheese

FOR SERVING:

Chopped red onions

Chopped fresh cilantro

1. Combine half of the onions, the celery, garlic, salt, tomatoes, and tomato paste in the slow cooker. Cover and cook on HIGH while you prepare the remaining ingredients.

2. In a large skillet over medium-high heat, heat 2 tablespoons of the oil, then cook the remaining onions and the bell pepper, stirring, until softened, 6 to 8 minutes. Remove from the heat.

3. If you like, using a handheld immersion blender, partially purée the tomato sauce in the cooker, then add the sauéed vegetables and continue cooking on HIGH.

4. In the skillet you just used, brown the beef and pork cubes on all sides in the remaining 1 tablespoon of oil, sprinkling the meat with the flour. (You will need to do this in batches.) Add the cubes of meat to the cooker. Add the chili powder, brown sugar, vinegar, chile powder, oregano, bay leaf, whole jalapeño, if using, and water and stir to combine. Cover and cook on LOW for 8 to 10 hours.

5. Taste for salt and remove the bay leaf and whole jalapeño. Stir in the olives and cheese. Serve the chili in bowls with a soup spoon and sprinkle with onions and cilantro.

White Chili

Developed for the mellower palates of the 1990s, white chili includes chicken, green chiles, and white beans in place of the more robust red beans, tomatoes, red chile powder, and beef. Don't leave this chili on for hours after cooking, or the chicken will dry out. ● *Serves 6 to 8*

COOKER: Medium or large round or oval

SETTINGS AND COOK TIMES: HIGH for 2 to 2½ hours, then LOW for 6 to 6½ hours; zucchini, corn, and salt added during last hour

1 pound dried great northern beans, picked over, soaked overnight
    in cold water to cover, and drained
8 cups chicken broth
2 cloves garlic, minced
2 medium-size yellow onions, chopped
3 tablespoons olive oil
3 boneless, skinless chicken breast halves, any fat removed, and cut in half
1 medium-size jalapeño, seeded and minced
Two 4-ounce cans chopped roasted green chiles
1½ teaspoons dried oregano
1½ teaspoons ground cumin
¼ teaspoon ground cloves
¼ to ½ teaspoon cayenne pepper or pure New Mexico chile powder, to your taste
2 medium-size zucchini (optional), thinly sliced into rounds

1 cup canned, fresh, or frozen corn kernels (optional)

1½ teaspoons salt, or to taste

FOR SERVING:

3 cups shredded Monterey Jack cheese

½ cup minced fresh cilantro

1. Put the drained beans, 6 cups of the broth, the garlic, and half the onions in the slow cooker. Cover and cook on HIGH until the beans are tender but not mushy, 2 to 2½ hours. Add some boiling water to keep them covered, if necessary; the beans will be soupy. The beans can be prepared up to this point and refrigerated overnight.

2. Heat 2 tablespoons of the olive oil in a large skillet over medium-high heat; cook the remaining onion until tender. Add the chicken, jalapeño, and remaining tablespoon of oil and cook until the chicken is no longer pink on the outside, 5 to 6 minutes; transfer everything to the cooker. Add the roasted chiles, oregano, cumin, cloves, cayenne, and remaining 2 cups of broth; stir to combine. Cover and cook on LOW for 6 to 6½ hours, stirring occasionally, if possible. During the last hour, add the zucchini, corn, and salt.

3. Remove the chicken from cooker, shred with a fork, and return to the cooker. To thicken the chili, mash some of beans against the side of the pot with the back of a large spoon. Serve the chili in bowls with the cheese on top, garnished with cilantro.

Turkey Thigh and Hominy Chili

T his is a *Sunset* magazine recipe adapted from the *Best of Sunset* collection of 2001. As far as we are concerned, there can never be too many recipes utilizing the delicious dark meat of turkey thighs. If you can find canned golden tomatoes, do use them; they are delicious, and give a totally different look to the chili than when you use red tomatoes. ◦ *Serves 6*

COOKER: Medium or large round or oval

SETTING AND COOK TIME: LOW for 6 to 8 hours

1 medium-size yellow onion, chopped

1 medium-size red bell pepper, seeded and chopped

1 jalapeño, seeded and minced

2 ribs celery, chopped

3 cloves garlic, minced

1 cup chicken broth

1 tablespoon chili powder

1½ teaspoons ground cumin

½ teaspoon pure ancho chile powder

1½ teaspoons dried oregano

3 pounds turkey thighs (about 3), skin and excess fat removed and rinsed

One 15-ounce can golden or white hominy, rinsed and drained

Two 15-ounce cans chopped golden tomatoes, drained; or
   one 28-ounce can chopped plum tomatoes, drained

Salt to taste

FOR SERVING:
Shredded Monterey Jack cheese
Sliced ripe California black olives
Minced red onion
Chopped fresh cilantro

1. Combine the onion, bell pepper, jalapeño, celery, garlic, broth, chili powder, cumin, ancho powder, and oregano in the slow cooker. Arrange the turkey thighs on top and pour the hominy and tomatoes over them. Cover and cook on LOW until the turkey meat pulls away easily from the bone, 6 to 7 hours.

2. Remove the turkey from the cooker and shred the meat, discarding the bones; return the meat to the chili. Season with salt. Serve the chili in shallow bowls with the toppings.

Vegetarian Chili sin Carne

H ere is a wonderful, fast, meatless chili—all of the flavor comes from the beans and the mild, yet still robust, seasonings. It is a favorite recipe from Marian Burros, adapted to the slow cooker, with some bulgur wheat added to bulk up the sauce. We use canned beans, so you can pop this one together early in the morning for a special lunch. The tofu topping adds even more nutrition. We like to mix different kinds of beans, such as black and pintos, or black-eyed peas and pintos, or kidneys, pintos, and black beans. Serve this over hot brown rice and accompany with warm cornbread and a big green salad. Fresh saltine crackers are good, too. ○ *Serves 4*

COOKER: Medium or large round or oval
SETTINGS AND COOK TIMES: HIGH for 1 hour, then LOW for 4 to 6 hours;
   salt added during last hour

⅓ **cup bulgur wheat**
⅔ **cup boiling water (or replace some of the water with**
   juice drained off the tomatoes)
2 tablespoons olive oil
2 medium-size yellow onions, chopped
1 medium-size green, yellow, or red bell pepper, seeded and chopped
2 to 3 cloves garlic, to your taste, minced
One 28-ounce can diced tomatoes, drained
One 15-ounce can tomato purée
Two 15-ounce cans red kidney or pinto beans, rinsed and drained
2 tablespoons chopped canned jalapeño
2 tablespoons chili powder or pure New Mexican chile powder, or to taste
1½ tablespoons ground cumin
2 tablespoons light or dark brown sugar
2 teaspoons dried oregano or marjoram
½ teaspoon ground coriander
¼ teaspoon ground cloves
Pinch of ground allspice
Salt to taste

FOR SERVING:
Shredded Monterey Jack cheese
Sliced ripe California black olives
Sliced avocado
Extra-firm tofu, rinsed, blotted dry, and cut into cubes
Chopped fresh cilantro

1. Put the bulgur in the slow cooker and add the boiling water; let stand for 15 minutes.

2. Heat the olive oil in a large skillet over medium-high heat and cook the onions, bell pepper, and garlic, stirring, until softened, 5 to 10 minutes. Transfer the mixture to the cooker. Add the drained tomatoes, tomato purée, beans, jalapeño, chili powder, cumin, brown sugar, oregano, coriander, cloves, and allspice and stir to combine. Cover and cook on HIGH for 1 hour.

3. Turn the cooker to LOW and cook for 4 to 6 hours. During the last hour, season with salt.

4. Serve the chili in bowls topped with cheese, olives, avocado slices, tofu, and lots of cilantro.

Vegetarian Black Bean Chili

R ich, dark, flavorful vegetarian black bean chili is easy to make and a delight to devour. We were introduced to this version at Green's Restaurant in Fort Mason on the docks in San Francisco in the 1980s. You could buy it to go at the bakery and sit outside on the edge of the docks overlooking the bay to eat it with some fresh Tassajara Bakery whole wheat bread. It is still a daily offering, and one of the best chilies ever concocted. ● *Serves 4*

COOKER: Large round or oval

SETTINGS AND COOK TIMES: HIGH for 2½ to 3 hours, then LOW for 8 to 9 hours; tomatoes and salt added during last 1 to 2 hours

1 pound dried black turtle beans, picked over and soaked overnight
    in cold water to cover
1 bay leaf
1½ tablespoons chili powder or a combination of pure New Mexican
    chile powder and ancho chile powder
1 tablespoon cumin seeds
2 teaspoons paprika
½ teaspoon cayenne pepper
1 teaspoon dried marjoram or oregano
3 tablespoons olive oil
1 medium-size yellow onion, finely chopped

1 medium-size green bell pepper, seeded and finely chopped

4 cloves garlic, chopped

1 tablespoon chopped canned chipotle chile in adobo sauce

One 14-ounce can chopped tomatoes, with their juice, or

    4 large ripe tomatoes, peeled, seeded, and chopped

1 teaspoon salt, or to taste

½ cup chopped fresh cilantro

FOR SERVING:

Shredded Muenster cheese

Sour cream

6 sprigs fresh cilantro (optional)

1. Drain the beans, put them in the slow cooker, add the bay leaf and chili powder, and cover with 3 inches of water. Cover and cook on HIGH until tender but not mushy, 2½ to 3 hours. The beans can be prepared up to this point and refrigerated overnight.

2. Heat a large cast-iron, or other heavy metal skillet. Add the cumin seeds, paprika, cayenne, and marjoram and shake the pan to lightly toast, about 2 minutes, until the seeds are a shade or two darker. Pour into a mortar and grind into a coarse powder with a pestle.

3. Heat the oil in the skillet and cook the onion, bell pepper, and garlic, stirring, until softened, about 5 minutes. Transfer to the cooker along with the chipotles; stir to combine. Cover and cook on LOW for 8 to 9 hours.

4. Stir in the tomatoes and salt. Cover and cook another 1 to 2 hours.

5. Stir in the cilantro and serve in bowls: Put a layer of cheese on the bottom of each bowl, add the beans, top with sour cream and then with a sprig of cilantro, if you like.

Easiest Black Bean and Brown Rice Chili

Julie created the first version of this chili years ago, when she was writing a kids cooking column for the *San Jose Mercury News*. There are no onions to chop, nothing to saute, and it is indeed easy enough for kids to make. The big surprise is the complexly flavored result, thanks in large part to the canned chipotle chile. These chiles are smoked, dried, and sold reconstited, canned in adobo sauce. They are fiery hot. Canned chipotles keep for a long time in the refrigerator or freezer, so don't hesitate to buy a can for this recipe.

This chili is now a favorite of kids and adults alike. There is one cautionary tale associated with it: One time a friend made a quadruple batch for a large party (be sure to use a large cooker if you multiply this recipe). But she misread the part about the chipotle, adding half a *can* of chiles to each batch instead of half of *one* chile. Later, we rescued the party leftovers by blending them with a few batches of chili that we'd made without any chile at all. In addition to its other virtues, this chili freezes well. ● *Serves 4*

COOKER: Medium round
SETTING AND COOK TIME: LOW for 6 to 8 hours

Two 15-ounce cans black beans
One 14.5- to 16-ounce can crushed or chopped tomatoes with their liquid
½ cup brown rice
1 teaspoon onion powder
⅛ teaspoon garlic powder
¼ teaspoon ground cumin
½ teaspoon dried oregano
½ to 1 whole canned chipotle chile, to your taste, cut into small pieces
Plain yogurt or warm flour tortillas for serving

1. Pour the beans and their liquid and the tomatoes and their liquid into the slow cooker. Add the brown rice, onion powder, garlic powder, cumin, oregano, and chipotle; stir to combine. Cover and cook on LOW for 6 to 8 hours.

2. Serve the chili in bowls, topped with a spoonful of yogurt, or wrap some in a warm tortilla.

Lucky Chili

I t is a tradition of home chef and caterer Nancyjo Riekse, of Auburn, California, to make a pot of spicy beans of some sort for friends the first week of the New Year to bring them luck and prosperity. This is one of the favorites, made with coffee. Cooking it slowly in the cooker makes this chili very rich. Nancyjo serves Lucky Chili with her homemade flour tortillas, which she makes with herbs worked into the dough. Serve with toppings or spoon it over rice. ○ *Serves 6 to 8*

COOKER: Large round or oval
SETTING AND COOK TIME: LOW for 8 to 12 hours; cilantro and salt added during last hour

2 cups freshly brewed coffee
2 cups vegetable broth
Two 28-ounce cans crushed tomatoes, with their juice
1 medium-size yellow onion, diced
4 garlic cloves, chopped
Four 15-ounce cans black beans, rinsed and drained; or 6 to 8 cups cooked black beans,
    depending on how thick you want it
¼ cup firmly packed light or dark brown sugar
2 tablespoons chili powder, or more to taste
1 tablespoon ground cumin
3 to 4 cloves, to your taste
⅓ cup chopped fresh cilantro
Salt to taste

FOR SERVING:
Chunky mango and tomato salsa
Cubed avocado
Sour cream
Shredded Monterey Jack or cheddar cheese

1. Combine all the ingredients in the slow cooker, except the cilantro and salt. Cover and cook on LOW for 8 to 12 hours, stirring occasionally, if possible. During the last hour, stir in the cilantro and season with salt. The longer you let it simmer, the better it gets, within reason, of course.

2. Serve the chili in bowls with toppings.

Lentil Chili

(T)his is a spicy chili that includes a generous quantity of vegetables, and lentils instead of beans. It is made without tomatoes, giving the chili a totally different taste. ○ *Serves 4 to 6*

COOKER: Medium round or oval
SETTING AND COOK TIME: LOW for 6 to 8 hours;
   olive oil and salt added during last hour

1 medium-size yellow onion, diced
1 medium-size red bell pepper, seeded and chopped
1 jalapeño, seeded and finely chopped
2 ribs celery, chopped
1 medium-size carrot, chopped
3 cloves garlic, minced
2 tablespoons light or dark brown sugar
2 tablespoons chili powder
1 tablespoon ground cumin
½ teaspoon cayenne pepper or 1 teaspoon pure New Mexico chile powder
2 teaspoons dried oregano
1 teaspoon dried thyme
1 teaspoon dry mustard
2½ cups dried brown lentils, rinsed and picked over
8 cups chicken broth
3 tablespoons olive oil
Salt to taste

FOR SERVING:
Sour cream or *crema Mexicana*
Chopped fresh tomatoes
Chopped green onions (white part and some of the green)
Chopped fresh cilantro

1. Combine all the ingredients in the slow cooker, except the olive oil and salt. Cover and cook on LOW, stirring occasionally, if possible, until the lentils are soft, 6 to 8 hours. During the last hour, add the olive oil and season with salt.

2. Serve the chili in bowls with toppings. You can also spoon it over brown rice.

North Indian Chili

This is the same template we use for a Southwestern American, tomato-based chili, but it is flavored with Indian spices and mellowed with some evaporated milk at the end. *Rajmah,* or red kidney beans, are very popular in the western area of Delhi and the Punjab, also known as the Indian heartland. You can use whole cumin seeds and coriander seeds if you like, and grind them by hand with your mortar and pestle. Serve over steamed basmati rice. ○ *Serves 4 to 6*

COOKER: Medium round or oval
SETTING AND COOK TIME: LOW for 5½ to 6½ hours;
    evaporated milk added during last 30 minutes

2 tablespoons olive oil

2 medium-size red onions, chopped

3 cloves garlic, minced

2 tablespoons grated fresh ginger

1 to 2 canned jalapeños *en escabeche,* to your taste, chopped

2 teaspoons ground coriander

1¼ teaspoons ground cumin

½ teaspoon cayenne pepper

¼ teaspoon turmeric

One 14.5-ounce can diced tomatoes, with their juice

3 tablespoons tomato paste

1 cup water

Three 15-ounce cans red kidney beans, rinsed and drained

½ teaspoon salt, or to taste

½ cup evaporated milk or heavy cream

FOR SERVING:
Chopped red onion
Chopped fresh cilantro
Plain yogurt
Warm chapatis

1. Heat the olive oil in a large skillet over medium-high heat, then cook the onions, stirring, until softened, about 5 minutes. Add the garlic, ginger, jalapeños, and spices, and cook, stirring, until the onions are browned. Transfer to the slow cooker, add the tomatoes with their juice, tomato paste, water, and kidney beans, and stir to combine. Cover and cook on LOW for 5 to 6 hours.

2. Stir in the salt and evaporated milk, cover, and continue to cook on LOW for another 30 minutes.

3. Serve the chili in bowls with the toppings and warm chapatis, if you can find them.

Chili, Olive, and Cheese Casserole

B eth's friend Gina DeLeone-Dodd said about this chili, "This is the best chili casserole I have ever had!" Gina's casserole is a true short cut because it includes canned chili—sort of a scandal for true chili heads. You just open the cans, dump 'em into the crock, stir it up, cover, and it all cooks into a sort of dense soufflé, dubbed chili goo at the local kindergarten. Adds Gina, "I serve it with sour cream, chopped onions, and more grated cheese if I'm feeling spunky, but it is great just plain." Kids will love this. Put it on after breakfast in time for a hot lunch. We add 1 to 2 chopped canned jalapeños *en escabeche* for an X-rated adult version. ● *Serves 4 to 6*

COOKER: Large round
SETTING AND COOK TIME: LOW for 4 to 5 hours

Two 40-ounce cans chili (vegetarian, fat-free, regular with beef, or a combination), or four to six
    15-ounce cans
One 15-ounce can pitted ripe California black olives, drained and sliced
One 12- to 15-ounce can red enchilada sauce, regular or hot
2 cups shredded medium or sharp cheddar cheese
Half of a 14-ounce bag tortilla chips, coarsely crushed
A few dashes of hot pepper sauce, such as Tabasco, or your favorite hot pepper sauce, or to taste

1. Put the chili, olives, enchilada sauce, cheese, and half the tortilla chips in the slow cooker and stir to combine. Cover and cook on LOW until bubbly hot and the cheese is melted, 4 to 5 hours.

2. At the end, stir in the remaining tortilla chips and season with hot sauce.

Chili or beans and cornbread are a traditional pairing, probably stemming from the old Western chuck wagon and Mexican rancho cooking popular from California to Texas. And there are lots of pan cornbreads, corn sticks, and muffins from which to choose. Homemade cornbreads are a real house specialty, and since they are quick breads, they are made in a flash in your oven while your chili or beans slow-cook. When Beth worked at St. Michael's Alley, in Palo Alto, California, there was always a request for fresh cornmeal muffins with chiles and cheese on the day the chef made his spicy chili. Here are some recipes for cornbreads, muffins, and corn sticks to serve with your myriad chilies. If you're in a hurry, go ahead and make cornbread from a mix, such as Dromedary or Jiffy. As our friend Jacquie McMahan taught us, for an 8.5-ounce package of cornbread mix, use ½ cup evaporated milk (it acts like cream in the batter), 1 large egg, and 1 tablespoon of melted butter in place of the ingredients suggested on the package. All cornbreads freeze well, but they really taste best hot from the oven.

Old-Fashioned Buttermilk Cornbread ○ Serves 12; makes one 9 x 13-inch pan

Here is a cornbread that is not sweet, yet still moist and full of flavor. We make it with many variations, one just as perfect as the next, and yet so different in flavor. But the plain cornbread is every bit as good. Beth loves the variation with whole canned hominy added.

2 cups fine-grind yellow cornmeal, preferably stone-ground

2 cups unbleached all-purpose flour or whole wheat pastry flour

⅓ cup firmly packed light brown sugar

2 tablespoons baking powder

1¼ teaspoons salt

4 large eggs

2¼ cups buttermilk

½ cup (1 stick) unsalted butter, melted

1. Preheat the oven to 400°F (reduce the heat to 375°F if using a Pyrex dish). Grease a 9 x 13-inch baking dish.

2. Whisk or sift the cornmeal, flour, brown sugar, baking powder, and salt in a large bowl.

3. In a small bowl, whisk together the eggs and buttermilk. Add to the dry ingredients and pour the melted butter over the top of the batter. Stir until all the ingredients are moistened yet thoroughly blended, but take care not to overmix. Add any extra ingredients, such as bacon or pecans, at this time (see Variations on next page).

4. Pour the batter into the prepared pan. Bake until golden around the edges and a cake tester inserted into the center comes out clean, 35 to 40 minutes. Let stand for 10 minutes before cutting into thick squares.

Old-Fashioned Buttermilk Cornbread with Bacon: In a medium-size skillet over medium-high heat, cook 1 cup of diced smoked bacon until crisp. Drain on paper towels and add to the batter. Bake as directed.

Old-Fashioned Buttermilk Cornbread with Hominy: Add 1½ cups of rinsed and drained canned hominy to the batter. Bake as directed.

Old-Fashioned Buttermilk Cornbread with Nuts: Toast 1 cup of pecans, walnuts, or hazelnuts on a baking sheet in a 350°F oven for 8 to 10 minutes; cool and coarsely chop. Add to the batter and bake as directed.

Old-Fashioned Buttermilk Cornbread with Black Olives: Add 1 cup of chopped pitted ripe California black olives to the batter (drain first on a layer of paper towels). Bake as directed.

Old-Fashioned Buttermilk Cornbread with Apples and Sausage: Add 1½ cups coarsely chopped tart cooking apples (about 2 whole) and 1 diced fully cooked smoked chicken-apple sausage to the batter. Bake as directed.

Julie's Skillet Cornbread o Serves 8

There is something special about baking cornbread in a cast-iron iron skillet. Yes, the dark, hot surface makes for an extra-crisp, extra-browned crust, but there is also the visual pleasure of seeing the tender cornbread nestled in the rustic pan. It always elicits ooohs and aaahs from the diners when we take the heavy pan out of the oven. This simple yet delicious recipe fits perfectly in a 12-inch cast-iron skillet. It is a breeze to stir together; you can have it on the table about half an hour after thinking, "Mmmmm, cornbread sounds good."

1½ **cups fine-grind yellow or white cornmeal, preferably stone-ground**
1½ **cups unbleached all-purpose flour**
⅓ **cup sugar**
1½ **tablespoons baking powder**
¾ **teaspoon salt**
½ **cup mild vegetable oil or canola oil**
2 **large eggs**
1½ **cups milk**

1. Preheat the oven to 400°F. Coat a 12-inch cast-iron skillet with nonstick cooking spray.

2. Sift together the cornmeal, flour, sugar, baking powder, and salt.

3. In a small bowl, whisk together the oil, eggs, and milk. Add to the dry ingredients, stirring until just mixed; the batter will be slightly lumpy.

4. Pour the batter into the prepared skillet and bake until golden brown and the bread springs back when touched lightly in the center, 25 to 30 minutes. Cool 5 minutes. Cut into wedges and serve.

Note: If you have a 10-inch skillet, use 1 cup of cornmeal, 1 cup of flour, ¼ cup of sugar, 1 tablespoon of baking powder, ½ teaspoon of salt, ⅓ cup of oil, 1 large egg, and 1 cup of milk. The recipe will serve 6.

Chile, Corn, and Cheese Muffins • Makes 12 muffins

This fantastic muffin recipe is from Chef Kip McClerin, who made them at La Casa Sena restaurant in Santa Fe in the 1990s. They are soft and rich, and we love them so much that we make them whenever possible.

1 cup frozen white corn kernels, thawed
1 cup coarsely shredded mild cheddar cheese
1 cup coarsely shredded Monterey Jack cheese
1 cup unbleached all-purpose flour, plus extra as needed
1¼ cups fine- or medium-grind yellow cornmeal, preferably stone-ground
2 teaspoons baking powder
½ teaspoon salt
½ cup (1 stick) unsalted butter or margarine, softened
¾ cup sugar
4 large eggs
½ cup milk
One 4-ounce can canned diced roasted green chiles, drained

1. Preheat the oven to 375°F. Grease the 12 cups of a standard muffin tin.

2. In a medium-size bowl, combine the corn, cheeses, flour, cornmeal, baking powder, and salt.

3. With an electric mixer, cream the butter and sugar together in large bowl until fluffy. Add the eggs, milk, and chiles, beating until well blended. Add the corn-flour mixture to the butter mixture. Beat well to make a thick, creamy batter that falls off the spoon in clumps. Add an additional 2 to 4 tablespoons of flour if the batter is still too loose.

4. Spoon the batter into the prepared muffin tin, filling each cup level with the top. Bake until golden and the tops are dry and springy to the touch, 20 to 25 minutes. A cake tester

will come out clean when inserted into the center. Let cool in the pan for 5 minutes before removing to cool on a rack. Serve warm. Store any leftovers in the refrigerator.

Fresh Double Corn Sticks ○ Makes 18 corn sticks or muffins

A basket of these corn sticks is sure to delight at any meal. Enjoy them with egg dishes for breakfast, a soup or salad at lunch, or a chicken dinner. They absolutely melt in your mouth. If you don't have a corn stick pan, you can make the batter into muffins.

1 cup unbleached all-purpose flour

1 cup fine- or medium-grind yellow cornmeal, preferably stone-ground

3 tablespoons sugar

2½ teaspoons baking powder

1 teaspoon red pepper flakes

¼ teaspoon salt

⅔ cup buttermilk

⅔ cup heavy cream

6 tablespoons (¾ stick) unsalted butter, melted

2 large eggs, separated

1½ cups fresh yellow or white corn kernels, or frozen baby corn, thawed

1. Preheat the oven to 425°F. Grease a corn stick pan with solid vegetable shortening (you will be making about 18 corn sticks, so use a second pan or plan to reuse one pan).

2. In a large bowl, whisk together the flour, cornmeal, sugar, baking powder, red pepper flakes, and salt.

3. In a large 4-cup measuring cup, combine the buttermilk, cream, melted butter, and egg yolks, then add to the dry ingredients, stirring with a large rubber spatula until just combined. Stir in the corn.

4. Using an electric mixer, beat the egg whites in a medium-size bowl until they form soft peaks that hold their own shape. With the spatula, fold the whites into the batter until there are no more streaks.

5. Spoon the batter into the prepared corn stick pan molds so that the batter is even with the top of the pan. Bake until golden around the edges, firm to the touch, and a cake tester inserted into the center comes out clean, 12 to 18 minutes. Unmold immediately and serve hot. The corn sticks can be frozen in plastic freezer bags for up to 1 month, then reheated before serving.

Savory Sauces, Pizza, and Pasta Casseroles

Sauces are the cornerstones of so many cuisines and they can make a plain dish something special. They are flavor enhancements and are often the primary focus of a dish, especially where pasta is concerned. The modern cook is able to whip up dishes with an international flair just by knowing a few good sauces.

We have found that, in the slow cooker, sauces that do not need a thickener or reduction, or the variable heat of a stove top, work beauti-

fully. The classic Mexican- and Italian-style sauces are especially nice made on their own in the crock, since they require long, slow cooking. You can make a reduction in the slow cooker by using the HIGH heat setting and leaving the lid off, but it will be a slower process than if attempted on the stove top. Slow cooker stews and braises tend to make their own sauces. For tips on the best way to thicken those sauces, see page 19.

A note on other classic sauces, such as béchamel, and the delicate emulsion sauces, such as hollandaise and béarnaise: After you have made your sauces on the stove top, you can use a slow cooker on the WARM setting in place of a double boiler to hold your sauce for about 2 hours before serving. Please do not use the LOW setting, which is too high for just warming and can curdle eggs.

Homemade pizza sauce is so easy and makes the pie that comes out of your oven taste extraordinary. We tell you how to make the dough, too. As for pasta, you can't make just any kind in the slow cooker. The recipes must be carefully constructed so that the pasta cooks through without turning to mush. We came up with some pasta casseroles that work beautifully and are perfect for buffet suppers on chilly evenings.

P.S.: You'll find barbecue sauces in the Ribs and Wings chapter on pages 387 to 402.

Salsa Mexicana

S *alsa fresca,* uncooked salsa, is nice, but sometimes we want one with the texture of jarred salsa so that it can be used for either dipping chips or as a sauce for poached eggs, vegetables, and casseroles. When you purée the sauce, you can leave it a bit chunky. The restaurants in the Yucatan Peninsula of Mexico, where Beth visited, would put out bowls of still-hot cooked salsa on the tables at the beginning of lunch. ○ *Makes about 3 cups*

COOKER: Medium round
SETTING AND COOK TIME: LOW for 5 to 6 hours

3 tablespoons olive oil
1 large yellow banana chile or 2 serrano chiles roasted (see Note on page 117),
     peeled, seeded, and chopped
2 small white onions, chopped
2 cloves garlic, chopped
One 28-ounce can tomato purée
2 tablespoons tomato paste
1½ cups chicken broth
2 tablespoons chopped fresh cilantro
1 tablespoon chili powder, or to taste
½ teaspoon ground cumin
½ teaspoon dried Mexican oregano or marjoram
Salt to taste

1. In a medium-size skillet over medium heat, heat the oil, then cook the chiles, onions, and garlic, stirring, until softened, about 5 minutes. Transfer to the slow cooker and add the tomato purée and paste, broth, cilantro, chili powder, cumin, and oregano. Stir to combine, then cover and simmer on LOW for 5 to 6 hours.

2. Use a handheld immersion blender to partially purée the sauce right in the insert or transfer to a blender to purée. Season with salt. The sauce will keep, refrigerated, for 5 to 7 days and frozen for up to a month.

Marinara Sauce

Marinara sauce is a quick red sauce in the family of Italian tomato sauces. Some use butter as their base, but this one uses olive oil, though you can make it half-and-half if you like. The sauce has a pure, clean taste and can be made with either canned or fresh tomatoes, as the season dictates. This is also nice with canned golden tomatoes if you happen to find them on your supermarket shelf. Serve this over angel hair pasta, gemelli twists, radiatore, or fusilli, accompanied by crusty bread and a salad of Belgian endive dressed with olive oil and white balsamic vinegar in a vinaigrette. ○ *Makes about 5 cups; serves 6 to 8*

COOKER: Medium round or oval
SETTING AND COOK TIME: LOW for 4 to 5 hours

⅓ cup olive oil, or half olive oil and half unsalted butter
1 medium-size yellow onion, finely chopped
1 clove garlic, minced
Two 28-ounce cans whole plum tomatoes, with their juice, or 3 pounds
    ripe plum tomatoes, seeds squeezed out and cut into chunks
3 ounces (half of a 6-ounce can) tomato paste
Pinch of sugar
Salt and freshly ground black pepper to taste

1. Over medium heat in a medium-size skillet, heat 3 tablespoons of the oil, then cook the onion and garlic, stirring, until softened, about 5 minutes.

2. Transfer to the slow cooker, add the remaining olive oil, the tomatoes, tomato paste, and sugar and stir to combine. Cover and cook on LOW for 4 to 5 hours.

3. Season the sauce with salt and pepper. If using canned tomatoes, use a handheld immersion blender to purée the sauce right in the insert; if using fresh, purée with the fine disk of a food mill to remove the tomato skins. If not serving the sauce with hot pasta immediately, return it to the cooker, where it will stay warm on LOW for a few hours. The sauce will keep, refrigerated, for up to a week or frozen for 2 months.

Fresh Tomato Sauce

T his is a very special sauce, the one to make with the end-of-summer bounty from the garden or farmers market. Choose the sweetest, most flavorful tomatoes. Any variety will do. We like to combine red tomatoes with yellow or orange ones for a beautiful, multicolored effect. If your tomatoes are really good, you might want to leave out the herbs and enjoy the pure tomato flavor on its own. This recipe makes enough for 1 pound of pasta—rotini squiggles, penne tubes, farfalle butterfly bowties, conchiglie shells, ravioli, or angel hair. To double or triple the recipe, use a large slow cooker. ● *Makes about 2 to 3 cups; serves 4 to 6*

COOKER: Medium round or oval
SETTING AND COOK TIME: LOW for 2 to 3 hours

2 pounds ripe tomatoes, peeled, seeded, and cored
2 tablespoons unsalted butter
¾ cup chopped onion
1 clove garlic, minced
1 teaspoon salt, or to taste
1 tablespoon chopped fresh basil, or 2 teaspoons chopped fresh flat-leaf parsley,
    or 1½ tablespoons chopped mixed herbs, such as basil, thyme, parsley, marjoram,
    and oregano in any combination (optional)
Large pinch of sugar (optional)

1. Chop the tomatoes coarsely. Do this by hand; a food processor will chop them too small. You want pieces about ¾ to 1 inch thick. Transfer the tomatoes to the slow cooker.

2. Melt the butter over medium heat in a medium-size skillet. Add the onion and garlic and cook, stirring a few times, until softened but not browned, about 5 minutes. Scrape into the slow cooker. Add the 1 teaspoon of salt and stir well. Cover and cook on LOW for 2 to 3 hours.

3. At the end of the cooking time, stir in the herbs, if you are using them. Cover and cook for 5 to 10 minutes longer. Taste for salt and add the sugar, if desired.

Chunky Tomato Basil Sauce

T his is basically a punched-up marinara sauce left chunky and oh, so good, on cooked pasta. This recipe can be doubled if you want to freeze some, but make it in a larger cooker. If you are not a garlic lover, just leave it out. Try this on fettuccine or rotini and serve with crusty bread and a salad of arugula, grated carrots, and garbanzo beans. ○ *Makes about 5 cups; serves 4 to 6*

COOKER: Medium round or oval
SETTINGS AND COOK TIMES: HIGH for 2 to 2½ hours, then LOW for 30 minutes; salt, pepper, remaining basil, and parsley added during last 30 minutes

2 tablespoons unsalted butter
2 tablespoons olive oil
1 medium-size yellow onion, finely chopped
1 to 2 cloves garlic, to your taste, minced
Two 28-ounce cans whole plum tomatoes, drained (if packed in purée, don't drain) and coarsely chopped

2 tablespoons dry red or white wine

Pinch of sugar

¼ cup shredded fresh basil

Pinch of dried thyme or oregano

Salt and freshly ground black pepper to taste

2 tablespoons chopped fresh flat-leaf parsley

1. In a medium-size skillet over medium heat, melt the butter in the olive oil. Cook the onion, stirring, until softened, about 5 minutes. Add the garlic and cook, stirring, for 2 minutes.

2. Transfer to the slow cooker. Add the tomatoes, wine, sugar, 2 tablespoons of the basil, and the thyme and stir to combine. Cover and simmer on HIGH for 2 to 2½ hours.

3. Season the sauce with salt and pepper and stir in the remaining 2 tablespoons of basil and the parsley. Cover and cook on LOW for 20 to 30 minutes longer. Serve the sauce hot. It will keep, refrigerated, up to a week and frozen for 2 months.

Red Clam Sauce: This is known in Italy as *linguine alle vongole.* The raw clams are cooked in the tomato sauce, flavoring it with their juice. You can also substitute whole mushrooms for the clams if a vegetarian dish is called for. Add 3 dozen scrubbed small clams in their shells to the hot tomato sauce in the slow cooker, preferably oval, on HIGH heat. Cover and cook for 5 to 10 minutes. Check to see if all the clams are open; if not, cover and cook a few minutes longer. (Discard any that do not open.) Serve immediately over hot pasta, preferably linguine, and garnish with chopped fresh flat-leaf parsley. No cheese, please; traditionally seafood pastas are served without cheese.

Italian Mushroom and Eggplant Sauce

With its meaty texture, eggplant makes a wonderful vegetarian pasta sauce, which pairs well with ziti. You can use regular globe eggplants, white eggplant, or Japanese eggplants interchangeably. ● *Makes about 3 cups; serves 4 to 6*

COOKER: Medium round or oval

SETTING AND COOK TIME: LOW for 7 to 8 hours, or HIGH for 3½ to 4 hours; parsley, salt, and pepper added during last hour

1 medium-size eggplant, cut in half lengthwise, sprinkled with salt,
   drained on paper towels 30 minutes, and rinsed

3 cloves garlic

¼ cup olive oil

1 medium-size yellow onion, finely chopped

One 28-ounce can whole plum tomatoes, with their juice, crushed; or
   one 28-ounce can crushed tomatoes

One 6-ounce can tomato paste

12 ounces fresh mushrooms, sliced

3 tablespoons dry red wine

1½ teaspoons dried or 1 tablespoon chopped fresh oregano or marjoram

3 tablespoons minced fresh flat-leaf parsley

Salt and freshly ground black pepper to taste

1. Preheat the oven to 400°F. Arrange the eggplant and garlic cloves on an oiled baking sheet. Brush with olive oil and bake until tender, about 20 minutes. Let cool, then remove the skin from the eggplant and coarsely chop the pulp; smash the garlic to squeeze the cloves out of their skins.

2. Heat the oil in a medium-size skillet over medium heat. Cook the onion, stirring a few times, until softened, about 5 minutes.

3. Transfer the onion mixture, roasted eggplant, and smashed garlic to the slow cooker. Add the tomatoes, tomato paste, mushrooms, wine, and oregano and stir to combine. Cover and cook on LOW for 7 to 8 hours, or on HIGH for 3½ to 4 hours. Add the parsley and season with salt and pepper during the last hour. The sauce will hold on LOW for a few hours. It will keep, refrigerated, for 3 to 5 days.

Classic Italian Meat Sauce

T his very traditional sauce, containing no herbs or garlic, is wonderful with cheese-filled ravioli or your favorite pasta shape. It makes enough sauce for 3 pounds of ravioli or 2 pounds of pasta, such as spaghetti. If you want less, just cut the recipe in half. ○ *Makes 8 to 9 cups; serves 12*

COOKER: Medium round or oval
SETTING AND COOK TIME: LOW for 6 to 8 hours

½ **cup olive oil**
2 medium-size yellow onions, chopped
2 medium-size carrots, finely chopped
2 stalks celery, finely chopped
1 pound lean ground beef
Salt and freshly ground black pepper to taste
1½ **cups dry red wine, such as Chianti**
Two 28-ounce cans whole plum tomatoes, with their juice; or 2 pounds
fresh ripe plum tomatoes, peeled, seeded, and cut into chunks
One 6-ounce can tomato paste
½ **cup beef broth**

1. Heat the oil in a large skillet over medium heat. Cook the onions, carrots, and celery, stirring occasionally, until just browned, 10 to 15 minutes. Add the beef and cook until no longer pink; season with salt and pepper.

2. Transfer to the slow cooker. Add the wine to the pan over high heat and cook, scraping up any browned bits stuck to the bottom, until it reduces to half its volume. Pour into the crock and add the tomatoes, tomato paste, and broth. Cover and cook on LOW for 6 to 8 hours. Serve the sauce hot. It will keep in the refrigerator up to 4 days and in the freezer for a month.

Meatballs in Tomato-Wine Sauce

Hearty yet tender meatballs in a robust tomato sauce are perfect with pasta. There's always spaghetti, but we especially like them with penne or another chunky pasta shape. Leftover meatballs make super knife-and-fork sandwiches. Just ladle them over a crusty Italian roll that you've warmed and split open. If you like a chunky tomato sauce, use diced tomatoes; for a smoother sauce, use tomato purée. This recipe makes enough for 1 pound of pasta. ○ *Serves 6*

COOKER: Medium or large round or oval
SETTINGS AND COOK TIMES: HIGH to start, then LOW for 5 to 6 hours

SAUCE:
2 tablespoons olive oil
1 large yellow onion, finely chopped
2 to 3 cloves garlic, to your taste, minced
¾ cup dry red wine
One 28-ounce can diced tomatoes, with their juice; or one 28-ounce can tomato purée
One 6-ounce can tomato paste
1 teaspoon salt
½ teaspoon freshly ground black pepper
1 teaspoon dried basil or 1 tablespoon minced fresh basil
1 teaspoon dried oregano or 1 tablespoon minced fresh oregano
¼ teaspoon ground allspice
1 bay leaf
2 tablespoons minced fresh flat-leaf parsley, or more to taste

MEATBALLS:
1½ pounds lean ground beef
1 cup plain dry bread crumbs
2 large eggs
3 tablespoons freshly grated Parmesan cheese
1 teaspoon salt
¼ teaspoon freshly ground black pepper
¼ teaspoon dried basil or ¾ teaspoon minced fresh basil

¼ teaspoon dried oregano or ¾ teaspoon minced fresh oregano
¼ cup minced fresh flat-leaf parsley
Dash of ground allspice
1½ tablespoons olive oil
¼ cup dry red wine

1. To prepare the sauce, heat the olive oil in a large nonstick skillet over medium-high heat. Add the onion and garlic and cook, stirring a few times, until softened but not browned, about 5 minutes. Add the wine, bring to a boil, and continue boiling for 1 to 2 minutes, scraping up any browned bits stuck to the bottom of the pan.

2. Transfer to the slow cooker. Add the tomatoes, tomato paste, salt, pepper, basil, oregano, parsley, allspice, and bay leaf and stir to combine. Cover and cook on HIGH while you prepare the meatballs.

3. To prepare the meatballs, put the ground beef in a large bowl, breaking it up a bit with your fingers or a large fork. Add the bread crumbs, eggs, Parmesan, salt, pepper, basil, oregano, parsley, and allspice. Gently but thoroughly blend the ingredients, using your hands or a large fork. Be careful not to compact the meat, which will make your meatballs tough. Gently shape the mixture into 12 meatballs, each a bit bigger than a golf ball.

4. Heat the olive oil in a large nonstick skillet over medium-high heat. Add the meatballs and brown on all sides, turning carefully, 6 to 10 minutes total. Using a slotted spoon, transfer them to the sauce. Pour off any fat from the skillet, return to the stove, and add the wine. Cook over high heat for 2 or 3 minutes, scraping up any browned bits stuck to the pan. Pour over the meatballs. If the meatballs are not covered by tomato sauce, carefully spoon some sauce over them. Cover and cook on LOW for 5 to 6 hours. Remove the bay leaf and serve the meatballs and sauce over pasta.

Slow Cooker Pizza Sauce

Pizza sauce is different than pasta sauce. It is smooth, deep brick red, and very thick, so that it can be spread over the pizza dough. The secret to a sauce with the right density is the amount of tomato paste. We also like to use dried herbs here. We got this recipe online from Rachael at her recipe message group RKGRecipes@yahoo.com. The sauce cooks for at least 10 hours, so be prepared to make it the day before and set it to cook overnight, or start it very early in the morning for an evening pizza party. This is a winner. Rachael notes "this is very inexpensive to make; you can make up enough for two VERY large pizzas for pennies." Store the leftover sauce in the freezer, where it will keep for up to a month. ○ *Makes about 6 cups, enough to cover four 14-inch pizzas*

COOKER: Medium round or oval
SETTING AND COOK TIME: LOW for 10 to 14 hours

Two 12-ounce cans tomato paste
One 16-ounce can tomato sauce
3 tablespoons olive oil
2 to 4 cloves garlic, to your taste, crushed
2 tablespoons dried oregano
1 tablespoon dried basil
2 to 4 tablespoons minced fresh flat-leaf parsley, to your taste
1 to 2 tablespoons sugar, to your taste
¼ cup water, or as needed
3 tablespoons freshly grated Parmesan, Romano, or Asiago cheese
Salt and freshly ground black pepper to taste

1. Place the tomato paste and sauce, oil, garlic, herbs, and 1 tablespoon of the sugar in the slow cooker. Add just enough water to smooth out the sauce. Cover and cook on LOW for 10 to 14 hours, stirring occasionally if you can, until thickened.

2. Taste for sugar, adding more if necessary, then stir in the cheese. Season with salt and pepper. Let the sauce cool to room temperature before using. It will keep, refrigerated, up to 4 days.

The bread machine is perfect for mixing and raising homemade pizza dough. It is easy and the dough turns out perfectly! After the dough has risen, you remove it from the bread pan, shape it by hand, and top as desired. Then bake it in your kitchen oven. If you're going to be making pizza regularly, invest in a ceramic pizza stone; it helps to distribute even, strong heat in the home oven. A very hot oven is the key to producing a crisp crust with a chewy inside. If the oven temperature is too low, you will get a tough crust. Use a "power pan," a metal pizza pan with Swiss cheese–sized holes in it; it is the best pan for making pizza on a stone. Be sure to use unbleached all-purpose flour; it is easier to roll out because it contains less gluten-forming proteins than bread flour. You can use all or just a portion of the dough because it can be conveniently refrigerated overnight or frozen for up to 3 months. To use refrigerated dough, let it rest for 20 minutes at room temperature before rolling it out. Let frozen dough defrost overnight in the refrigerator.

These recipes have been adapted from Beth's book *The Bread Lover's Bread Machine Cookbook* (Harvard Common Press, 2000). They make 1½ pounds of dough, enough for two thin 12- to 14-inch rounds, one ¼-inch-thick round or deep-dish crust, four 8-inch crusts, six individual minicrusts, or one crust to fit into an 11 x 17-inch rectangular baking sheet.

Pizza Dough Master Recipe

1⅓ cups water
¼ cup extra virgin olive oil
3½ cups unbleached all-purpose flour
1 tablespoon sugar
1½ teaspoons salt
2 teaspoons bread machine or instant yeast

1. Combine all the ingredients in the pan according to the manufacturer's instructions. Program for the DOUGH or PIZZA DOUGH cycle and press Start. When it's ready the dough will be soft.

2. Pick up with step 4 of Timeline for Making and Baking Pizza on page 253.

Rachael's Pizza Dough with Cheese and Garlic

The addition of cheese and fresh garlic makes a very savory and aromatic dough. We added a bit more water to make a slightly softer dough.

1¼ cups warm water

3 to 4 tablespoons extra virgin olive oil

3½ cups unbleached all-purpose flour

¼ cup freshly grated Pecorino Romano or Parmesan cheese

1 to 2 cloves garlic, to your taste, minced

¾ teaspoon salt

2 teaspoons bread machine or instant yeast

Beth's Semolina Pizza Dough

Be sure to get the fine semolina durum flour used for making pasta, not the coarse grind, such as farina. A favorite Italian ingredient, semolina is a very high protein flour ground from durum wheat, which adds a lot of chewiness to the dough.

1½ cups water

3 tablespoons extra virgin olive oil

3⅓ cups unbleached all-purpose flour

⅔ cup semolina pasta flour (also called durum flour)

1 tablespoon sugar

2 teaspoons salt

2 teaspoons bread machine or instant yeast

Whole Wheat Pizza Dough

Whole wheat adds a grainy texture and extra-nutty flavor to this crust.

1⅓ cups water

¼ cup extra virgin olive oil

2¾ cups unbleached all-purpose flour

¾ cup whole wheat flour

1 teaspoon salt

2 teaspoons bread machine yeast

Timeline for Making and Baking Pizza

Here are the steps for making a homemade pizza:

1. Prepare your pizza sauce. Prepare your dough of choice on the PIZZA DOUGH or DOUGH cycle of your bread machine. All recipes can also be made by hand or using a heavy-duty mixer fitted with a dough hook or a food processor fitted with the dough blade.

2. Prep the cheese and/or extra toppings. You can cook or roast your own vegetables, or use precooked canned or frozen ones, such as artichoke hearts, olives, and sun-dried tomatoes. Use only precooked meats or seafood on your pizzas; never use them raw. Set aside the cheese and toppings at room temperature or refrigerate if they will sit for more than 15 minutes or so.

3. Preheat the oven to 450° to 500°F for at least 30 minutes, with a baking stone or pizza tiles set on the center or lowest rack, if you have them.

4. After the rising cycle ends, at the beep, immediately remove the pizza dough and place on a work surface lightly sprinkled with yellow cornmeal, semolina, or rice flour. Divide into the desired number of portions or leave whole. With a rolling pin or pressing with your fingers and the heels of your hands, roll out the dough from the center outward, rotating the dough as you roll or press to get an even circle. Lift up the dough and pull to get the desired size. Place the dough on a cornmeal- or semolina-sprinkled pizza pan, pressing a ½-inch rim around the crust. For a thin crust, proceed directly to the next step. For a thick crust, cover the crust with a clean tea towel and let rise at room temperature until puffy and doubled in bulk, 30 to 40 minutes, before topping and baking.

5. Spread with sauce almost to the rim with a large rubber spatula, sprinkle with some cheese, and arrange any other toppings on top. Finish with a bit more melting cheese. Fresh cheeses that melt well are best for pizza, such as mozzarella, Gorgonzola, provolone, Monterey Jack, fontina, Brie, feta, and fresh goat cheese. Top with an herb, if using, then drizzle with olive oil. Feel free to vary proportions to suit your palate, just don't overload the pizza. You want a bit of each flavor in every bite, so distribute everything evenly.

6. Immediately place the assembled pizza in its pan directly on the stone in the oven and bake until the crust is brown and crisp, 12 to 15 minutes (5 to 8 minutes longer for a thick crust). Check the underside of the crust by lifting with a metal spatula to be sure it is browned enough. With heavy oven mitts, transfer the pizza to a cutting board and slide off the pan. Cut into wedges with a pizza wheel, kitchen shears, or a serrated knife. Eat it hot!

Pizza Margherita · Makes one 14-inch pizza

1 recipe pizza dough of your choice (pages 251–252), rolled out

About 1½ cups Slow Cooker Pizza Sauce (page 250)

8 ounces mozzarella cheese, thinly sliced

10 large fresh basil leaves, thinly sliced into ribbons

Olive oil for drizzling

Spread the dough with the tomato sauce, leaving a ½-inch border. Lay the mozzarella over the top. Sprinkle with the basil and drizzle with olive oil. Bake as instructed on page 253.

Black Olive Pizza · Makes one 14-inch pizza

1 recipe pizza dough of you choice (pages 251–252), rolled out

About 1½ cups Slow Cooker Pizza Sauce (page 250)

6 ounces mozzarella cheese, thinly sliced

1½ cups shredded fontina cheese

1½ cups chopped black olives of your choice

Dried oregano or marjoram

Olive oil for drizzling

Spread the dough with the tomato sauce, leaving a ½-inch border. Lay the mozzarella over the top, then sprinkle evenly with the fontina. Top with the olives. Sprinkle with oregano and drizzle with olive oil. Bake as instructed on page 253.

Pepperoni Pizza · Makes one 14-inch pizza

1 recipe pizza dough of your choice (pages 251–252), rolled out

About 1½ cups Slow Cooker Pizza Sauce (page 250)

4 ounces pepperoni sausage, peeled and thinly sliced

6 ounces mozzarella cheese, thinly sliced

1 cup shredded provolone cheese

4 ounces fresh mushrooms, sliced

1 green bell pepper, seeded and cut crosswise into rings

Olive oil for drizzling

Spread the dough with the tomato sauce, leaving a ½-inch border. Dot with the pepperoni slices. Lay the mozzarella over the top, then sprinkle evenly with the provolone. Top with the mushrooms and the green pepper rings. Drizzle with olive oil. Bake as instructed on page 253.

Mediterranean Pizza with Feta and Red Onion ● Makes one 14-inch pizza

1 recipe pizza dough of your choice (pages 251–252), rolled out

About 1½ cups Slow Cooker Pizza Sauce (page 250)

6 ounces mozzarella cheese, thinly sliced

1 cup crumbled feta cheese

½ cup pitted black olives of your choice, drained and chopped or sliced

A few thin slices of red onion, separated into rings

Olive oil for drizzling

Spread the dough with the tomato sauce, leaving a ½-inch border. Lay the mozzarella over the top. Sprinkle evenly with the feta. Scatter the olives over the top and scatter some red onion rings all over. Drizzle with olive oil. Bake as instructed on page 253.

Pizza Vegetariana ● Makes one 14-inch pizza

1 recipe pizza dough of your choice (pages 251–252), rolled out

About 1½ cups Slow Cooker Pizza Sauce (page 250)

4 ounces mozzarella cheese, thinly sliced

2 medium-size zucchini, thinly sliced

1 or 2 red bell peppers, roasted (see Note on page 117), peeled, seeded, and cut into strips; or roasted eggplant slices

One 10-ounce package frozen artichoke hearts, defrosted

2 plum tomatoes, cut into wedges

1 cup broccoli florets, cooked in salted boiling water until just tender and drained

1 cup cauliflower florets, cooked in salted boiling water until just tender and drained

½ to ¾ cup freshly grated Parmesan or Asiago cheese, to your taste

Olive oil for drizzling

This is best made in a pizza pan with a 1-inch rim, since it has a heavy topping. Spread the dough with the tomato sauce, leaving a ½-inch border. Lay the mozzarella over the top. Top with layers of the zucchini, peppers or eggplant, artichoke hearts, tomato wedges, broccoli, and cauliflower. Sprinkle with the Parmesan and drizzle with olive oil. Bake as instructed on page 253.

Macaroni and Cheese

Move over boxed mac and cheese; this version is just as simple and a whole lot tastier. The recipe is adapted from the food section of the *San Diego Tribune*. Pasta in the slow cooker is a bit of a challenge since there must be enough liquid to cook the pasta, but not so much that it will get mushy. We love this recipe because it is the old-fashioned mac and cheese, without a heavy white sauce to make first. The combination of the evaporated milk and egg replaces the flour as the thickener; canned milk does not curdle as fresh milk–based sauces sometimes do. Kids love the macaroni shape, so resist substituting any other shape of pasta. Please note that the pasta goes into the cooker *uncooked*. This recipe can be doubled and cooked in the large cooker. ○ *Serves 4*

COOKER: Medium round
SETTING AND COOK TIME: LOW for 3½ to 4 hours

1½ cups skim or low-fat milk

One 15-ounce can evaporated skim milk

1 large egg, beaten

¼ teaspoon salt

Large pinch of freshly ground black pepper

1½ cups shredded medium or sharp cheddar cheese, such as Oregon Tillamook, Vermont
   colby, or Wisconsin longhorn

8 ounces elbow macaroni (about 2 cups)

2 tablespoons freshly grated or shredded Parmesan cheese

1. Coat the slow cooker with nonstick cooking spray. Combine the low-fat and evaporated milks, egg, salt, and pepper in the cooker and whisk until smooth. Add the cheese and macaroni; gently stir with a rubber spatula to coat evenly with the milk and cheese mixture. Sprinkle the Parmesan on the top.

2. Cover and cook on LOW until the custard is set in the center and the pasta is tender, 3½ to 4 hours. Do not cook more than 4 hours, as the sides will dry out and burn.

Macaroni and Italian Cheese: For the cheddar, substitute a combination of 1 cup of shredded fontina (4 ounces) and ½ cup of diced or shredded mozzarella (2 ounces).

Macaroni and Swiss Cheese: Substitute an equal amount of shredded Gruyère or Emmenthaler cheese for the cheddar.

Macaroni and Blue Cheese: Add ½ cup of crumbled Gorgonzola (2 ounces), Stilton, Roquefort, or American blue cheese to the cheddar and macaroni.

Easy Cheesy Ravioli Casserole

R avioli tossed with jarred sauce is certainly not difficult to make on the stove, but sometimes it is more convenient to do all of the preparation ahead so you can serve up a steaming hot, tomato-y plateful of tender pasta pillows right from your slow cooker. This is also a great trick when you will be serving a meal over an extended period of time, say at a buffet, or when family members are arriving home at different times after a busy day. Do take care when selecting both the sauce and the ravioli. The sauce should be a brand and type you really enjoy, but on the plain side. We have found that some of the sauces with large flecks of herbs or lots of garlic or onion powder do not hold up well in the slow cooker. The ravioli should be medium-sized; the super-large ones tend to fall apart upon serving. If you purchase refrigerated ravioli, freeze them yourself before using them in this recipe. ○ *Serves 8 to 10*

COOKER: Large round
SETTING AND COOK TIME: HIGH for 2½ to 3½ hours, or LOW for 5 to 6 hours

1 tablespoon olive oil
1 medium-size yellow onion, chopped
2 cloves garlic, minced
Two 26- to 28-ounce jars tomato-based pasta sauce of your choice
¾ cup dry red wine
One 8-ounce can tomato sauce
1 to 2 teaspoons dried basil or Italian herb blend, or 1 to 2 tablespoons chopped fresh basil
    (optional)
Two 25-ounce packages frozen ravioli of your choice (do not defrost)
2 cups shredded mozzarella cheese
½ cup freshly grated or shredded Parmesan cheese

1. Coat the slow cooker with nonstick cooking spray.

2. In a large, deep skillet or Dutch oven, heat the oil over medium-high heat. Add the onion and cook, stirring a few times, until softened, about 5 minutes. Add the garlic and cook for 1 minute more; don't allow it to burn. Add the pasta sauce, wine, and tomato sauce. Bring to a boil, reduce the heat to a simmer, and cook, stirring occasionally, for 3 to 5 minutes more. Taste the sauce. If desired, add the basil.

3. Pour 2 cups of the tomato sauce into the cooker. Add one package of the frozen ravioli, then sprinkle with half of the mozzarella and 2 tablespoons of the Parmesan. Add 2 more cups of the sauce, the last package of ravioli, the remaining mozzarella, and 2 tablespoons of the Parmesan. Cover with the remaining tomato sauce.

4. Cover and cook on HIGH for 2½ to 3½ hours, or LOW for 5 to 6 hours. The casserole is done when a ravioli from the center of the casserole is hot throughout. Sprinkle with the remaining ¼ cup of Parmesan, cover, and let cook 10 minutes more.

Creamy Penne with Mushroom and Tuna Sauce

T his casserole is an old-time favorite and one kids like. You can double the amount of cream cheese if you do not want to use any fresh goat cheese, but the goat cheese adds a nice flavor and the cream cheese makes it milder. We love the cornflake crumb topping. ○ *Serves 4*

COOKER: Medium round
SETTING AND COOK TIME: HIGH for 1½ to 2 hours, or LOW for 4 hours

2 tablespoons unsalted butter
2 medium-size shallots, chopped
8 ounces fresh mushrooms, quartered
2 tablespoons all-purpose flour
1 cup chicken broth

One 13-ounce can evaporated milk

One 3-ounce package cream cheese, crumbled

3 ounces goat cheese, crumbled

One 6.5-ounce can solid white albacore tuna, drained well and flaked

1 heaping cup frozen petite peas

Salt and freshly ground black pepper to taste

8 ounces penne

TOPPING:

½ cup crushed cornflakes

1½ tablespoons unsalted butter, melted

1 cup shredded cheddar cheese

1. In a medium-size skillet over medium heat, melt the butter, then cook the shallots and mushrooms until softened, about 5 minutes. Sprinkle with the flour and cook for 30 seconds. Add the broth and milk. Bring to a boil, stirring to avoid clumping, until thickened into a thin white sauce. Add the cheeses and stir until melted. Add the tuna and peas and stir to combine. Season lightly with salt and pepper.

2. Meanwhile cook the penne in boiling water until *al dente,* firm to the bite. Take care not to overcook; you want the pasta undercooked. Drain and add to the tuna sauce and stir to coat evenly.

3. Coat the slow cooker with nonstick cooking spray. Pour the pasta mixture into the cooker.

4. To make the topping, combine the cornflake crumbs and butter in a small bowl; work together with your fingers to coat evenly. Add the cheddar, working it into crumbs, and sprinkle over top of the pasta. Cover and cook on HIGH until hot and bubbly, 1½ to 2 hours, or on LOW about 4 hours. The pasta will be soft, but not mushy. Serve immediately.

Rigatoni and Sausage

T his easy recipe was created by personal home chef Nancyjo Riekse. "The pasta and sauce cook up slightly dry as a casserole in the cooker," she said. "Just like kids like it." ○ *Serves 6*

COOKER: Medium round
SETTING AND COOK TIME: LOW for 3½ to 4 hours; needs to be stirred halfway through

1 pound sweet Italian turkey sausages, casings removed and crumbled
One 26- to 28-ounce jar tomato pasta sauce
1 pound rigatoni, uncooked
Freshly grated or shredded Parmesan cheese for serving

1. Coat the slow cooker with nonstick cooking spray.

2. In a medium-size skillet over medium-high heat, brown the sausage.

3. While the sausage is cooking, pour the pasta sauce into the cooker. Fill the empty jar with water and pour it into the cooker. Add the rigatoni and cooked sausage; gently stir with a rubber spatula to combine well. Cover and cook on LOW until the pasta is tender, 3½ to 4 hours. Stir once halfway through cooking. Do not cook more than 4 hours because the sides will dry out and burn. Serve immediately sprinkled with Parmesan cheese.

Poultry, Game Birds, and Rabbit

From a homey enchilada casserole to elegant party fare such as Poussin Paprikash, the slow cooker is a great way to cook chicken, turkey, Cornish hen, rabbit, and duck. We admit we didn't always see it that way! In fact, we made all of the classic mistakes when we began to experiment with poultry in our slow cookers. We cooked it too long, ruining the flavor and turning the texture to sawdust. We didn't take the time to brown chicken pieces and ended up with un-

appetizingly pale poultry. We used too much liquid and drowned it. But we finally learned, and these recipes are the happy result.

There are exceptions to every rule, including the guidelines that follow here, but in general, this is what we found in slow cooking dozens of poultry dishes: Unless you are making soup, broth, or a poached dish, use very little liquid—much less liquid than in stove-top or oven cooking. Generally speaking ½ to ¾ cup is enough.

For soup, broth, or poached chicken, you will want to cover the poultry with liquid if possible, just as you would on the stove. If you are cooking chicken parts, it is usually worth the extra step of sautéing them on the stove top first to improve the final dish's color and flavor. Cooking chicken parts with the skin on, and removing it for serving, if desired, will often keep the chicken from drying out. If you are cooking whole chickens or ducks, an oval cooker is preferable, because it will cradle a whole bird nicely, but you can still get delicious results in a round cooker. We use plenty of boneless breasts and thighs;

they cook on HIGH for a short time and are a great weekday slow cooker meal. Chicken wings are also stellar in the slow cooker; check out our recipes in the Ribs and Wings chapter on page 387.

Chicken is grouped by class, size, quality (a USDA inspection evaluation), and age, which will tell you how to cook the bird. Young birds are the most tender and suitable for all sorts of slow cooker dishes, either in parts or whole. Young chickens include *broilers* (7 to 9 weeks old), *fryers* (9 to 12 weeks old), *roasters* (10 to 20 weeks old), *poussins* (very young chickens under 6 weeks old), and *capons* (desexed male, 16 to 20 weeks old). *Game hens* (4 to 5 weeks old) are a cross between a Plymouth Rock hen and a Cornish gamecock and are fun for entertaining. Older chickens are labeled *stewing hen, hen,* or *mature chicken* and are over 10 months old. These older birds are really good for braising and stews since they have lots of connective tissue, which moist heat will break down; they are also very economical. Figure on about 8 ounces of meat bone-in, per serving, and 4 to 6 ounces per serving boneless, or less if you are serving other meats.

Turkeys are available in parts, such as drumsticks, wings, and thighs, ground, and bone-in and boneless breast roasts, all of which are good for slow cooking. The exception is a whole turkey, which is too large to fit in the cooker and is best prepared by traditional means. Count on 1 pound of meat per person bone-in, and 4 to 6 ounces per person boneless, or less if you are serving other meats.

Commercial farm-raised game and game birds are available now throughout the year in supermarkets and butcher shops, not just from seasonal hunting in fields and forest—opening new frontiers for home cooks. Duck, squab, and quail are usually sold frozen. Pheasant is usually available fresh September to February, but it is also available frozen year-round. Butcher shops are the best places to shop for game. All, except ducks, are only sold whole, so for many recipes you will need to have the butcher cut them into pieces if you do not want to do it yourself. While the flavor of farm-raised game birds is a bit more robust than that of chicken and turkey, it is much tamer than the birds' leaner wild counterparts. Some game is gently aged to tenderize it (though not to the degree of days of old, when game was hung in a shed until "high" or slightly rotten). Since most tame game is still very lean, it normally needs some fat to cook, but in the slow cooker, the moist braising process eliminates the barding and basting normally associated with cooking game.

Rabbit has virtually fatless lean meat and is raised with no steroids or hormones, making it a healthful alternative to chicken. It has mild-flavored white meat and in all respects can be handled like chicken. It does beautifully in the slow cooker. Older rabbits must be braised or stewed; they are just too tough otherwise. Small fryers are about 3 pounds and roasters are 4 pounds and up. We usually have the butcher cut the rabbit into 6 or 8 pieces for easy handling in the crock—the loin, legs, ribs, and back or saddle. Please note that cooking wild rabbit is a bit different than cooking with domesticated; wear rubber gloves when handling because of harmful bacteria, which will die when cooked. Domestic rabbits are so tasty and convenient that, unless you have a tradition of hunting in your family, there is no need to fuss with wild cousins.

All commercially raised ducks in America are descended from the wild North American mallard and the muscovy of South America. Today's domestic ducks are bred with a nice layer of fat, a large breast, and tasty and succulent flesh, much subtler than the flavor of wild duck.

•• Slow Cooker Poultry Pointers ••

It is important to cook with poultry that has been handled and stored properly. Fresh poultry needs to be stored in the refrigerator until preparation time and cooked within 1 to 2 days of purchase, or else frozen, to minimize bacterial growth. Before cooking, rinse thoroughly with cold water and pat dry. Either load the slow cooker immediately with the raw poultry, or precook as directed in the recipe and put the poultry in the cooker immediately after browning. Since the slow cooker takes a while to reach a safe bacteria killing temperature, unless your are prebrowning, the poultry needs to go directly from the refrigerator to the cooker, and the cooker must be turned on quickly. Please note the danger zone for bacterial growth in poultry is between 40°F and 140°F. The slow cooker takes 3 to 4 hours on the LOW setting to get the contents up to a safe food temperature of 140°F to 165°F; it will then increase to over 200°F by 6 hours. The same temperatures will be reached in half the amount of time on the HIGH setting. We recommend not lifting the lid the first 3 to 4 hours to allow the heat to come to the proper cooking temperature as fast as possible.

Never use room-temperature poultry; it will reach the correct temperature as the slow cooker heats up. Unless a recipe specifically calls for it, never put still-frozen poultry in the slow cooker, since it will take longer to reach a safe cooking temperature.

Small poultry pieces cook more efficiently than large pieces or a whole bird. Boneless pieces, such as breast and thighs, cook fastest; bone-in pieces take longer. Please add time, 1 to 2 hours, if you are substituting bone-in poultry when boneless is called for in a recipe.

Domestic ducks are disease resistant and are raised without use of antibiotics. We limited our recipes to boneless duck breasts for a quick and delicious way to cook duck in the slow cooker. A boneless half breast weighs about 4 to 5 ounces.

The largest breast of all game birds is on the pheasant. Once upon a time, the brilliantly plumed bird was served in America more often than chicken. The ring-necked pheasant, one of dozens of species of the bird, is the most available, and is farmed in California and Pennsylvania. The meat is lean, delicate, and pale pink. Growth hormones and steriods are not used. A pheasant weighs 2 to 3 pounds and serves 2 people.

Poultry should be cooked throughout but still be juicy and the juices should run clear. When properly cooked there will be no trace of pink when the meat is pierced with a fork at the thickest point. Poultry is done when the internal temperature reaches about 180°F on an instant-read thermometer, an invaluable tool when cooking meat in the slow cooker.

Thaw frozen poultry in the refrigerator in its original wrapping with a plate underneath to catch any dripping; it is important that the bird remain cold while thawing. Estimate 24 hours thawing time in the refrigerator per 5 pounds; parts will thaw in half a day. Refrigerate cooked poultry within 2 hours of cooking; never let it come to room temperature before refrigerating it. The "sell by" stamp date is 7 days after the bird was processed and is the cutoff date for sale. Refrigerated, the bird will still be good. If you have any doubt, ask the butcher how fresh the bird is and by when it should be cooked. Never buy frozen poultry that has frozen liquid in the package, an indication that it was frozen after sitting out for a while or was refrozen. Poultry will keep frozen for 9 to 10 months maximum.

Because raw poultry may carry harmful organisms or bacteria, take care when handling it. Wash the poultry thoroughly and dry it before working. Wash your hands, work surfaces, and utensils with hot soapy water before and after handling. Poultry is always cooked completely through, never rare like beef and lamb, since the organisms can permeate the flesh. In red meat, the organisms exist only on the surface. Slow cooking is an excellent method to thoroughly cook poultry of all types.

If you want a thick, richly flavored sauce to serve with your poultry dishes, you will often find yourself reducing the cooking liquid on the stove, and perhaps thickening it, before serving. This takes only a few minutes and is well worth the time.

Basic Poached Chicken Breasts

This recipe takes advantage of the large bags of boneless, skinless chicken breasts that are available in the freezer section of your supermarket or large discount warehouse. Leave the chicken in the bag and defrost it overnight in the refrigerator before loading it into the cooker. This recipe couldn't be more simple and practical for your daily cooking. ○ *Makes 7 pounds cooked breasts*

COOKER: Large round or oval
SETTING AND COOK TIME: LOW for 6 to 8 hours

About 7 pounds boneless, skinless chicken breasts, rinsed in cold water
One 14.5-ounce can chicken broth

1. Put the chicken in the slow cooker and pour over the broth. Cover and cook on LOW for 6 to 8 hours.

2. Shred a few breasts immediately for burritos or fajitas. Or let cool, shred, and portion into quart-size plastic freezer bags to use in casseroles, chicken pot pie, pasta, stir-fries, pizza, or in a chicken salad. The chicken will keep, frozen, for 3 months.

Chicken Sour Cream Enchilada Casserole

Several years ago, Julie visited a California expat living in London and asked what she could bring from the States. Monterey Jack cheese for enchiladas, please, came the answer! And it's true: mild, creamy white Monterey Jack melts beautifully and tempers the heat of the chile sauce, making for delightful enchiladas and enchilada casseroles, too! For the chicken, use our recipe for Basic Poached Chicken Breasts (above) or, for simplicity's sake, broil 1 pound boneless, skinless chicken breasts until lightly browned on top and cooked through, about 15 minutes (cut into the thickest part of a piece to check). If you are really in a hurry, buy a rotisserie chicken at the deli counter. There is no need to season the chicken before adding it to the casserole. If you can't find green chile enchilada sauce in a can (we like Las Palmas brand), purchase green chile salsa instead. ○ *Serves 8*

COOKER: Medium or large round or oval
SETTING AND COOK TIME: HIGH for 2 hours, or LOW for 4 hours

1 tablespoon vegetable oil
1 large yellow onion, chopped
One 24- to 32-ounce can green chile enchilada sauce
1 dozen soft corn tortillas, each one cut into 4 strips
2½ to 3 cups cooked boneless, skinless chicken, cut into ¾ -inch pieces
4 cups finely shredded Monterey Jack cheese
2 cups sour cream (reduced fat is okay)

1. In a large skillet, heat the oil over medium-high heat, then add the onion and cook, stirring, until softened, about 5 minutes. Set aside.

2. Pour about ½ cup of the enchilada sauce into the slow cooker; tilt to spread it around. In layers add one-quarter of the tortilla strips, one-quarter of the remaining sauce, one-third of the sautéed onion, one-third of the chicken, and one-quarter of the cheese. Repeat the layers two more times, ending with the cheese. Finish the casserole with the remaining tortilla strips, sauce, and cheese.

3. Spoon the sour cream over the surface of the casserole in big dollops. Use a spatula or the back of a large spoon to gently spread it all around without disturbing the layers. Cover and cook on HIGH for 2 hours, or on LOW for 4 to 5 hours.

4. To serve, use a long-handled spoon to reach down through all of the layers for each serving. Make sure each diner gets some of the sour cream.

"Quick" Teriyaki Chicken

Of course, this title is a play on words. If you really want quick teriyaki chicken, you should make it on the stove. If you want "quick" teriyaki chicken, make it with boneless, skinless chicken pieces in your slow cooker. (If you want even slower teriyaki chicken, make it with bone-in chicken thighs, drumsticks, or wings; see page 275.) Julie learned several teriyaki tricks incorporated here from Atsuko Ishii, a California friend from Tokyo. Atsuko likes to use the domestically produced Hakusan sake for cooking. Mirin is a sweet Japanese cooking wine. Atsuko cautions you to be sure to read labels so that you buy genuine mirin, not the so-called imitation mirin that is also sold. The difference in flavor is dramatic. Low-sodium soy sauce works fine in this recipe. Be sure to buy naturally brewed soy sauce (sometimes called fermented). Serve this with steamed medium-grain rice. ○ *Serves 4*

COOKER: Medium or large round or oval
SETTING AND COOK TIME: HIGH for 2 hours for breasts, 3 hours for thighs

4 boneless, skinless chicken breast halves, or 6 boneless, skinless chicken thighs
¼ cup sake
2 tablespoons mirin
4 teaspoons soy sauce
1 teaspoon light or dark brown sugar

1. Coat a cast-iron skillet or another heavy skillet with nonstick cooking spray, then spray it a second time. (For this recipe, it is best to avoid a pan with a nonstick coating.). Heat the skillet over high heat. When it is very hot, add the chicken in one single layer, with the smooth side (formerly the skin side) down. If necessary, do this in batches. Allow the chicken to cook until it is a deep golden brown, 2 to 4 minutes. Turn and brown the other side. Transfer to the slow cooker, smooth side up.

2. Return the skillet to the stove, lower the heat to medium, and add the sake, mirin, soy sauce, and brown sugar. Cook, scraping up any browned bits stuck to the pan. Pour the liquid over the chicken. Cover and cook on HIGH for 2 hours for breasts, 3 hours for thighs.

Pollo Colorado (Chicken in Red Chile Sauce)

H ere's a quickie chicken variation of *chile colorado*. This version makes use of individually frozen boneless, skinless chicken breasts, which are such a popular freezer item. (*Chile colorado* is the simple red chile sauce of the Southwest; *colorado* is Spanish for "red.") The chicken goes in straight from the freezer, no browning required. You can enjoy this on its own as a stew or as the basis of fabulous enchiladas, burritos, or tacos. ○ *Serves 4 to 5*

COOKER: Medium or large round or oval
SETTING AND COOK TIME: LOW for 5 to 7 hours

2 medium-size yellow onions, peeled
2 medium-size red bell peppers, seeded
3 large or 4 medium-size individually frozen boneless, skinless
    chicken breast halves (do not thaw)
One 28-ounce can Las Palmas red chile sauce (sometimes labeled
    "enchilada sauce"), hot, medium, or mild, as desired; or 3 to 4 cups
    Red Chile Sauce (below)

1. If you are going to eat *pollo colorado* as a stew, chop the onions and peppers into ¾-inch pieces. If you are going to use it as an enchilada, burrito or taco filling, slice the onions and peppers. Put the vegetables in the cooker, tossing to mix well. Arrange the frozen chicken breast halves on top of the vegetables and pour over the chile sauce. Cover and cook on LOW until the chicken is tender, 5 to 7 hours.

2. Transfer the chicken to a cutting board. Cut it into chunks if you are making a stew; slice or shred it if you are going to be filling tortillas. Return the chicken to the cooker and stir to coat with the sauce and mix with the vegetables. It will keep, refrigerated, for about 4 days.

Red Chile Sauce

This is the real thing—no tomatoes (for Salsa Mexicana, with tomatoes, see page 241). It's the basic red sauce of New Mexico, where chiles are proudly grown and consumed in great quantities. A building block of countless dishes, it is used by the

spoonful as a condiment or by the cup in everything from *huevos rancheros* to enchiladas. It keeps well in the refrigerator. Be sure to buy pure ground red chile, which is usually found in plastic pouches in the Mexican food section, not chili powder, which is sold with the spices. If you can't find ground chile in your area, look for the large whole, dried red New Mexico chile pods. Wash them, cut them open, discard the stems, remove the seeds and veins (unless you want really hot chile sauce), let the pods dry completely, then grind them very finely in the blender.
○ *Makes about 4 cups*

¼ cup vegetable oil

2 cloves garlic, pressed or very finely minced

¼ cup all-purpose flour

1 cup pure ground chile powder, mild, medium, or hot, to your taste

4 cups water

Salt to taste

In a large skillet or a Dutch oven, heat the oil over medium-high heat. Add the garlic and cook, stirring, for 1 or 2 minutes; do not let the garlic brown. Stir in the flour. Reduce the heat to medium and add the chile powder; chile burns very easily, so keep stirring. Stir in the water. Raise the heat to medium-high and let the sauce come to a simmer. Season with salt. The sauce is ready to use as is, but if you want a thicker sauce, let it simmer for 10 to 15 minutes more. It will keep, refrigerated, for a week or frozen for up to 3 months.

Orange Hoisin Chicken

I f you like Chinese food, you are probably familiar with hoisin sauce, even if you didn't know what it was called. Sweet, savory, and thick like molasses, it's often used in marinades and barbecue sauces as well as on its own. Here it's a part of the sauce in which you cook and serve lean chicken breasts. We like this with plenty of brown rice to catch the extra sauce. Adding the chicken frozen slows down the cooking somewhat, but this is still a relatively quick dish.

○ *Serves 4 to 6*

COOKER: Medium or large round or oval
SETTING AND COOK TIME: LOW for 5 to 6 hours

2 tablespoons frozen orange juice concentrate, thawed
¼ cup honey
2 tablespoons soy sauce
2 tablespoons hoisin sauce
3 slices peeled fresh ginger, about ¼ inch thick
3 cloves garlic, minced or pressed
1 tablespoon sesame oil
6 individually frozen boneless, skinless chicken breast halves (do not thaw)
2 teaspoons cornstarch
2 teaspoons cold water
1 tablespoon sesame seeds (optional), toasted in a dry skillet over medium heat until fragrant

1. In a zippered-top plastic bag, combine the orange juice concentrate, honey, soy sauce, hoisin sauce, ginger, garlic, and sesame oil. One at a time, put the chicken pieces in the bag, seal, and gently shake to coat with the sauce. Transfer the coated chicken to the slow cooker, then pour the remaining sauce over the chicken. Cover and cook on LOW until the chicken is tender and cooked through, 5 to 6 hours.

2. Transfer the chicken to a warm platter. Strain the sauce through a fine-mesh strainer into a small saucepan. In a cup or small bowl, stir together the cornstarch and cold water. Bring the sauce to a boil over high heat, add the slurry, and cook, stirring a few times, until thickened, 1 or 2 minutes. Pour some of the sauce over the chicken and pass the rest on the side. If desired, sprinkle the sesame seeds over the top.

Salsa Chicken

This recipe makes use of basic pantry items for a quick dinner that is astoundingly good. There is a wealth of fabulous jarred salsas on the market today. You can get a plain salsa or one with black beans and corn in it. Serve this with all the fixings—warm flour tortillas, shredded lettuce, avocado slices, chopped tomatoes, sour cream, shredded sharp Longhorn cheddar, lime wedges—or, more simply, over steamed long-grain white rice with crumbled goat cheese or shredded cheddar cheese on top. ○ *Serves 6 to 8*

COOKER: Medium or large round or oval

SETTING AND COOK TIME: HIGH for 3 to 3½ hours; cumin, chile powder, and lime juice added during last 15 minutes

6 boneless, skinless chicken breast halves (about 2 pounds), trimmed of fat

1½ cups thick prepared salsa of your choice, medium or hot

1 teaspoon ground cumin

Pinch of pure ground red chile powder

3 tablespoons fresh lime juice

1. Coat the slow cooker with nonstick cooking spray and arrange the chicken in it. Pour the salsa over the chicken. Cover and cook on HIGH until the chicken is tender and cooked through, 3 to 3½ hours. The chicken will make some of its own juice, thinning out the salsa a bit.

2. Stir in the cumin, chile powder, and lime juice, cover, and cook for another 15 minutes before serving.

Chicken with Beer

This hearty dish began the evening at one of the tasting dinner parties Julie held with Batia Rabec—a skilled slow cooker cook who loves to entertain. Try it with mashed potatoes. Choose a light-colored beer that you like to drink; the dark beers are too strongly flavored. *Herbes de Provence* is a blend that usually includes lavender along with other, more common, herbs such as thyme.

○ *Serves 4*

COOKER: Medium or large round or oval
SETTING AND COOK TIME: HIGH for 3 to 4 hours;
    baked in the oven 20 minutes to finish

About ¾ cup all-purpose flour
4 boneless chicken breast halves, with skin on
2 tablespoons unsalted butter
½ cup beer
1 teaspoon salt
⅛ teaspoon freshly ground black pepper
¼ teaspoon dried *herbes de Provence*
2 bay leaves, broken in half

1. Put the flour on a shallow plate or a pie plate. One piece at a time, dredge the chicken in the flour, coating both sides and shaking off any excess.

2. Melt the butter in a large skillet over medium-high heat. When it foams, add the chicken, skin side down, and cook until deep golden brown on both sides, 5 to 7 minutes per side. Transfer the chicken to the slow cooker. Add the beer to the skillet and bring it to a boil, scraping up any browned bits stuck to the pan. Pour over the chicken. Sprinkle with the salt, pepper, and *herbes de Provence*. Tuck the bay leaves in among the chicken pieces. Cover and cook on HIGH for 3 to 4 hours.

3. Preheat the oven to 400°F. With a slotted spoon, transfer the chicken to a shallow baking dish. Discard the bay leaves. Pour any liquid remaining in the cooker over the chicken. Bake, uncovered, until lightly browned, about 20 minutes. Serve immediately.

Caribbean Jerked Chicken

erk sauce has gone from being a national specialty of Jamaica to something you can order in many American restaurants. Of course, the first time you hear the name "jerk sauce," it is hard to take it seriously in a culinary sense, but it has a long and beloved history. The sauce was cooked by Jamaican slaves, who found their freedom after escaping from the sugar plantations on the island. One of their classic dishes was pork seasoned with a rub of local spices and hot chiles, cooked over an open fire until completely dried out, which preserved the meat. These spices can be used to season chicken or beef, as well as pork. When cooked in the slow cooker, the jerked meat is moist and succulent. Serve this with long-grain white rice, minced green onion, and papaya slices. ○ *Serves 4*

COOKER: Medium or large round or oval
SETTING AND COOK TIME: LOW for 5 to 6 hours

½ cup sliced green onions (white part and some of the green; about 12)
2 tablespoons grated fresh ginger
1½ teaspoons ground allspice
½ teaspoon ground cinnamon
1 tablespoon olive oil
3 jalapeños, seeded and coarsely chopped
1 teaspoon freshly ground black pepper
½ teaspoon salt
Pinch of red pepper flakes
1 to 2 cloves garlic, to your taste, pressed
2 tablespoons firmly packed dark brown sugar
1 tablespoon cider vinegar
1 tablespoon orange juice
2 teaspoons Worcestershire sauce
4 bone-in chicken thighs, with skin on, and 4 drumsticks

1. In a food processor, combine the green onions, ginger, allspice, cinnamon, oil, jalapeños, black pepper, salt, red pepper flakes, and garlic and process until very finely chopped, almost smooth. Stir in the brown sugar, vinegar, orange juice, and

Worcestershire to form a paste. Using a brush, apply the jerk sauce so it completely coats the chicken; use up all of the sauce.

2. Put a wire rack in the slow cooker. Place the chicken on the rack. Cover and cook on LOW until the chicken is tender and cooked through, 5 to 6 hours. Serve immediately.

Teriyaki Chicken Thighs

The sauce for this delicious, mahogany-colored chicken is based on a recipe from Julie's friend Atsuko Ishii, who is originally from Tokyo. It includes two kinds of Japanese rice wine, sake, and mirin. While sake is used for drinking as well as cooking, mirin is a cooking wine. Mirin is sweeter than sake and has a warm, honey-gold color. When you shop for mirin, be sure to buy the real thing; imitation mirin is packed in similar bottles and it is not as good. Atsuko likes Hakusan sake and Takhara mirin, both of which are brewed in California. **o**

Serves 6

COOKER: Medium or large round or oval
SETTING AND COOK TIME: HIGH for 5½ to 6 hours; lid is removed during last hour

12 bone-in chicken thighs
1 tablespoon vegetable oil
½ cup sake
¼ cup mirin
2 tablespoons soy sauce
2 teaspoons light or dark brown sugar

1. Remove the skin from the thighs. Trim away and discard any large pieces of fat. Heat the oil in a large, heavy skillet over high heat. A cast-iron skillet is ideal. When hot, add the chicken in a single layer, in batches, without crowding, smooth side (formerly the skin side) down. Cook until deep golden brown on both sides, 3 to 4 minutes per side. As they brown, transfer the thighs to the slow cooker. Pour off any fat from the skillet. Add the sake, mirin, soy sauce, and brown sugar to the skillet, bring to a boil, and cook, scraping up any browned bits stuck to the pan. Pour over the chicken. Cover and cook on HIGH until the chicken is cooked through and beginning to brown, 4½ to 5 hours.

2. Use a spoon or turkey baster to pour some of the sauce over the chicken. Leave the lid off and cook 1 hour more on HIGH, until the chicken has browned and the sauce has reduced by about half.

3. Place the chicken on a platter and pour the sauce remaining in the cooker over it.

Chicken Cacciatore

C *acciatore* is Italian for "hunter's stew." Although this is probably one of the Western world's most famous chicken dishes, it was originally made with rabbit, and this recipe works well with cut-up rabbit pieces. It is from Beth's sister, Amy, who considers cacciatore her favorite dinner. Serve it with steamed white rice or hot cooked fettuccine and a Caesar salad. ○ *Serves 4*

COOKER: Medium or large round or oval
SETTING AND COOK TIME: HIGH for 2½ to 3 hours, or LOW for 6 to 7 hours

One 16-ounce jar Italian marinara sauce, such as tomato-basil,
   or about 2 cups homemade marinara sauce (page 242)
1 medium-size yellow onion, cut in half and sliced into half-moons
1 to 3 cloves garlic, to your taste, minced
1 medium-size green bell pepper, seeded and cut into 1½-inch chunks
4 boneless, skinless chicken thighs and 4 chicken drumsticks, skin removed
6 ounces fresh mushrooms, quartered
2 tablespoons all-purpose flour or instant flour, such as Wondra (optional)
2 tablespoons water (optional)
2 tablespoons dry white wine (optional)

1. Layer half of the tomato sauce and all of the onion, garlic, bell pepper, and chicken in the slow cooker. Sprinkle the mushrooms on top and cover with the remaining tomato sauce. Cover and cook until the chicken is tender and cooked through, 2½ to 3 hours on HIGH, or 6 to 7 hours on LOW. The chicken will add some of its own juices to the dish.

2. Transfer the chicken to a warm platter. If you wish a thicker sauce, in a small bowl, whisk together the flour, water, and wine until smooth. Stir into the sauce in the cooker, turn the cooker to HIGH, cover, and cook until thickened, 10 to 15 minutes. Pour the sauce and vegetables over the chicken and serve.

Moroccan Chicken Thighs with Chickpeas and Cumin

T his is a tagine, or stew with Moroccan flavors. We kept this one less spicy, traditionally speaking, although you can add ¼ teaspoon of cayenne if you like. Serve this with a salad with sliced fresh oranges and radishes. ○ *Serves 4*

COOKER: Medium or large round or oval
SETTING AND COOK TIME: LOW for 6 to 7 hours

Two 16-ounce cans chickpeas (garbanzo beans), rinsed and drained
One 15-ounce can whole plum tomatoes, drained and cut into 1-inch cubes
1 large red bell pepper, seeded and cut into 1-inch squares
1 medium-size red onion, chopped
¼ cup golden raisins
2 tablespoons tomato paste
2 tablespoons water
1½ teaspoons ground cumin
Pinch of paprika
4 boneless, skinless chicken thighs, cut into 1-inch cubes
2 tablespoons creamy peanut butter, almond butter, or cashew butter

FOR SERVING:
Hot cooked couscous or brown rice
3 tablespoons chopped fresh cilantro

1. Put the chickpeas, tomatoes, bell pepper, onion, raisins, tomato paste, water, cumin, and paprika in the slow cooker; stir well. Scatter the chicken on top. Cover and cook on LOW until the chicken is tender and cooked through, 6 to 7 hours.

2. Stir in the nut butter. Serve hot over the couscous, garnished with the cilantro.

Chicken with Onions and Cheese

his chicken dish is rich and hearty, perfect after a day of skiing in the winter or hiking in the fall. Serve it with a crisp green salad. The large quantity of onions reduces into a mass of creamy sweetness in the slow cooker. This is not a dietetic dish, but if you wish, you may cut some of the fat by removing the chicken skin before adding the cheese. Thanks go to Batia Rabec for this recipe. o

Serves 4 to 6

COOKER: Medium or large round
SETTING AND COOK TIME: HIGH for 4½ to 5 hours;
   broiled for a few minutes at the end to melt the cheese

About ¾ cup all-purpose flour
6 bone-in chicken thighs, with skin on
2 tablespoons unsalted butter
2 cups sliced yellow onions
1 teaspoon salt, or more to taste
⅛ teaspoon freshly ground black pepper, or more to taste
½ cup dry white wine
6 slices Muenster cheese (5 or 6 ounces) ¼ inch thick,
   cut into approximate shape of chicken pieces

1. Put the flour on a shallow plate or a pie plate. One piece at a time, dredge the chicken in the flour, coating both sides and shaking off any excess.

2. Melt the butter in a large skillet over medium-high heat. When it foams, add the chicken, skin side down, and cook until deep golden brown on both sides, 5 to 7 minutes per side. Transfer to a plate. Add the onions to the pan and cook, stirring, until softened but not browned, about 5 minutes.

3. Using a slotted spoon, make a bed of the onions in the slow cooker. Place the chicken on top, skin side up. Season with the salt and pepper, and pour over the wine. Cover and cook on HIGH until the chicken is tender and cooked through, 4½ to 5 hours.

4. Meanwhile, preheat the broiler. Transfer the chicken to a plate. Use a slotted spoon to transfer the onions to a shallow baking dish large enough to hold the chicken in a single layer. Spread them out as evenly as possible. Taste the sauce remaining in the cooker for salt and pepper. Arrange the chicken on top of the onions and pour the sauce over it. Top each piece of chicken with a slice of cheese. Broil about 4 inches from the heating element until the cheese is melted. Serve hot.

Chicken with Golden Raisins

Here's another dish from slow-cooker genius Batia Rabec. It demonstrates something Batia figured out a while ago: dried fruit is a perfect match for the slow cooker. Its concentrated flavor can stand up to long cooking, and during the process it softens and soaks up flavor, as well as some excess liquid from the sauce. Fresh fruit, on the other hand, usually falls apart, contributes more water, and makes for a thinner sauce. Batia and Julie tried making this with fresh grapes and it wasn't nearly as good as when made with raisins! This is elegant, as is Batia's cooking style, but it is really an easy, one-step recipe. ❍ *Serves 4 to 6*

COOKER: Medium or large round
SETTINGS AND COOK TIMES: LOW for 4 hours, then HIGH for 1 hour

About ¾ cup all-purpose flour
6 bone-in or boneless chicken thighs, with skin on
2 tablespoons unsalted butter
½ cup full-bodied dry red wine, such as Cabernet Sauvignon
1 teaspoon salt, or more to taste
⅛ teaspoon freshly ground black pepper, or more to taste
¼ cup heavy cream
¼ cup golden raisins

1. Place the flour on a shallow plate or a pie plate. One piece at a time, dredge the chicken in the flour, coating both sides and shaking off any excess.

2. Melt the butter in a large skillet over medium-high heat. When it foams, add the chicken, skin side down, and cook until deep golden brown on both sides, 5 to 7 minutes per side. Transfer the chicken to the slow cooker. Add the wine to the pan, bring to a boil, and cook, scraping up any browned bits stuck to the pan. Pour over

the chicken and season with the with the salt and pepper. Cover and cook on LOW for 4 hours.

3. Stir in the cream and the raisins. Cover, turn the cooker to HIGH, and cook until the chicken is tender and cooked through, another hour.

4. Serve the chicken hot, with the raisins and sauce.

Orange and Honey Chicken Drumsticks

When you want to nosh on something larger than a chicken wing, go for the drumsticks. The tapioca is used as a thickening agent for the sauce.

○ *Serves 4 to 6*

COOKER: Medium or large round or oval
SETTING AND COOK TIME: HIGH for 2 to 2½ hours

12 drumsticks
One 6-ounce can frozen orange juice concentrate, thawed
¼ cup honey
2 tablespoons quick-cooking tapioca
One 4-ounce can chopped roasted green chiles
¼ teaspoon salt
1 medium-size shallot, minced

Arrange the chicken in the slow cooker. Combine the remaining ingredients in a medium-size bowl, whisk to blend, and pour over the chicken. Cover and cook on HIGH for 2 to 2½ hours. Serve hot.

•• Slow Cooker Poached Eggs ••

Poached eggs are so nice on toast and so easy to produce in the slow cooker. Use the freshest eggs for the best flavor. An oval cooker is best, if you have one, because you can cook a larger number of eggs at one time. You will need one Pyrex or ovenproof custard cup for each egg. Use as many as you like, as long as they fit in the cooker in one layer. It is okay to put the custard cups directly on the bottom of the cooker since the heat comes from around the sides instead of just the bottom, as in a saucepan.

COOKER: Medium or large oval
SETTING AND COOK TIME: HIGH for about 30 to 45 minutes; eggs added during last 12 to 15 minutes

1 to 2 fresh eggs per person

1. Pour about ½ inch of tap water, as hot as possible, into the slow cooker. Cover and cook on HIGH for 20 to 30 minutes.

2. Coat the custard cups, one for each egg, with cooking spray. Break 1 egg into each cup. Place the cups in the cooker in a single layer. Cover and cook on HIGH for 12 to 15 minutes if you like your yolks runny. You can test them by pressing each egg yolk gently with a spoon. When the white is firm but the yolk is still soft, they are done.

3. If you need to keep one batch of eggs warm while cooking more, ease them out of the cups with the edge of a spoon and place them in a bowl of very warm salted water while you poach the rest of the eggs. Drain the reserved eggs on a clean tea towel before serving.

Eggs Benedict • Serves 6

Eggs Benedict is the quintessential brunch dish—rich, creamy, and just a bit out of the ordinary.

3 English muffins, fork-split to make 6 halves, or 6 oversized biscuits, split
6 slices Canadian bacon, grilled or pan-fried for a few minutes, or smoked turkey
6 Slow Cooker Poached Eggs
2 to 2½ cups hollandaise sauce (page 413)

Toast the English muffins or warm the biscuits in the oven. Arrange one on each serving plate. Cover each with a slice of Canadian bacon, then a poached egg. Pour over some hollandaise and serve immediately while still hot.

Basic Poached Whole Chicken

C ooking a whole chicken in the slow cooker, unattended, is a convenient, way to obtain moist, tender meat for a variety of dishes—comforting casseroles, elegant composed salads, spicy burritos, and tacos. Your bonus is about a cup of very concentrated drippings. You can refrigerate them, skim off the fat, and add the drippings to your final dish to enhance the flavor.

Unlike a roasted chicken made in the oven, slow-cooker-cooked chicken will not have a crisp skin. Don't fret about this: just remove the skin and discard it. Do this after cooking so that the skin can protect the chicken flesh and keep it moist while it's in the crock. We've often seen chicken cooked this way referred to as roasted, but we feel that is misleading. We prefer to call it poached, even though you do not add any liquid to the cooker. ● *Serves 4 to 6*

COOKER: Medium or large oval
SETTING AND COOK TIME: LOW for 6 to 7 hours

One 3- to 4-pound broiler/fryer
¾ to 1 teaspoon salt
½ teaspoon freshly ground black pepper

1. Wash and dry the chicken thoroughly. Reserve the giblets and neck for another use. Cut off any lumps of fat. Season the chicken inside and out with salt and pepper. Place in the slow cooker, breast side up. Cover and cook on LOW until an instant-read thermometer inserted into the thickest part of the thigh registers 180°F, 6 to 7 hours.

2. Transfer the chicken to a platter. Pour the liquid from the cooker into a separate container and refrigerate; then skim off the fat after it congeals. Or pour the cooking juices into a gravy separator and then into a container and refrigerate if not using. When the chicken is cool enough to handle, remove the skin and cut or shred the meat from the carcass. Refrigerate the meat if not using it immediately.

Mexican-Style Lime and Cilantro Whole Chicken

L ime and cilantro add some sparkle to plain chicken. Here the chicken cavity is stuffed with lime halves and the whole bird is crock-poached. Serve for dinner with rice and beans, or pick the meat off the bones and make soft tacos (see box, page 284). ● *Serves 4 to 6*

COOKER: Medium or large oval
SETTING AND COOK TIME: LOW for 6 to 7 hours

One 3- to 4-pound broiler/fryer
¾ to 1 teaspoon salt
½ teaspoon freshly ground black pepper
Juice of 1 small or ½ large lime
½ cup fresh cilantro sprigs
2 cloves garlic, peeled

1. Wash and dry the chicken thoroughly. Reserve the giblets and neck for another use. Cut off any lumps of fat. Season the chicken inside and out with salt and pepper. Place in the cooker, breast side up. Squeeze the juice of the lime over the chicken and put the rind, cilantro sprigs, and garlic into the cavity. Cover and cook on LOW until an instant-read thermometer inserted into the thickest part of the thigh registers 180°F, 6 to 7 hours.

2. Transfer the chicken to a platter. Pour the liquid from the cooker into a separate container and refrigerate; then skim off the fat after it congeals. Or pour the cooking juices into a gravy separator and then into a container and refrigerate if not using. When the chicken is cool enough to handle, remove the skin, and cut or shred the meat from the carcass. Refrigerate the meat if not using it immediately.

•• Soft Tacos ••

Here's an easy way to turn your crock-poached bird into fun-to-eat soft tacos. Let your family and friends customize their own tacos. ○ Serves 6

1 tablespoon oil or nonstick cooking spray

1 large onion, cut in half and sliced into half moons

½ teaspoon dried oregano

¼ cup dry white wine

Shredded meat and defatted drippings from Mexican-Style Lime and
Cilantro Whole Chicken (page 283)

¾ cup prepared salsa, mild or hot

Salt and freshly ground black pepper to taste

TO SERVE:
Warm flour tortillas
Finely shredded Monterey Jack cheese
Chopped fresh tomatoes
Shredded lettuce
Fresh cilantro sprigs
Lime wedges

1. Heat the oil in a large skillet or coat the skillet thoroughly with nonstick cooking spray and heat over medium-high heat. Add the onion and cook, stirring, until softened, about 5 minutes. Add the oregano and continue to stir 1 to 2 minutes longer. Add the wine and stir until it has almost boiled off. Add the chicken, shredding any large pieces with your fingers. When the chicken is hot, stir in about one-third of the drippings, allowing them to sizzle, and reduce again until syrupy. Add about half of the remaining drippings and allow to reduce until syrupy. Add the salsa and the remaining drippings. When the liquid comes to a boil, cover and allow to simmer for about 10 minutes.

2. Season the chicken mixture with salt and pepper. If it is too wet to suit your taste, increase the heat and cook, uncovered, for a few moments.

3. Serve the chicken wrapped in warm flour tortillas, folded soft taco–style or wrapped burrito-style, with the toppings of your choice: shredded cheese, lettuce, tomato, cilantro, and a squeeze of lime juice.

Slow Cooker Lemon Chicken with Potatoes and Mushrooms

We adapted this recipe for a whole crock-poached chicken from one that originally appeared in the *Los Angeles Times*. It was then featured in Kim Boatman's "Home Plates" column, in our *San Jose Mercury News* Food and Wine section, which is where we encountered it. We like to serve this in soup plates, as a sort of knife-and-fork stew/soup hybrid. If you have a large cooker, you will have room for a larger number of potatoes. Put them on top of everything else so they steam until tender. Cook this dish on LOW if you must be gone all day, but we think the flavor is significantly better when it's cooked on HIGH for a shorter period of time. ○ *Serves 6*

COOKER: Medium oval or large round or oval
SETTING AND COOK TIME: HIGH for 3½ to 4½ hours

One 3- to 4-pound broiler/fryer
2 cubes chicken bouillon
½ large lemon or 1 small lemon
¼ teaspoon paprika
3 tablespoons minced fresh flat-leaf parsley
2 medium-size or 1 large onion, cut into wedges
2 cloves garlic, chopped
2 tablespoons soy sauce
¼ teaspoon salt
⅛ teaspoon freshly ground black pepper
6 to 12 small Yellow Finn or Yukon Gold potatoes, unpeeled
6 ounces fresh mushrooms, sliced ½-inch thick

1. Rinse and dry the chicken thoroughly. Reserve the giblets and neck for another use. Cut off any lumps of fat. Put one bouillon cube inside the cavity. Squeeze the lemon, reserving the juice. Put the lemon rinds in the cavity. Put the chicken in the slow cooker, breast side up, and sprinkle with the paprika and parsley. Distribute the onion wedges and garlic around the chicken. Pour over the soy sauce and lemon juice and season with the salt and pepper. Crumble the remaining bouillon cube, and sprinkle that over the chicken as well. Top with the potatoes and mushrooms. Cover and cook on HIGH until an instant-read thermometer inserted into the thickest part of the thigh registers 180°F, 3½ to 4½ hours.

2. To serve, discard the lemon halves and portion the potatoes, mushrooms, onions, and chicken into shallow bowls or soup plates, discarding the skin and bones. Spoon some of the liquid over each serving.

Red-Cooked Chicken

R ed cooking is a Chinese method of poaching or braising meats, eggs, or vegetables in a spiced mixture of soy sauce, rice wine, and water. The delicious liquid is saved, refrigerated, and re-used for subsequent red-cooked dishes, gaining complexity and flavor with each use. We first learned about red-cooked chicken from Sharon Noguchi, a colleague and friend of Julie's who enthusiastically described the ease of the method and the terrific results. We wasted no time in adapting red cooking to the slow cooker, and we must say, it's a perfect match. Recipes for the red-cooking liquid vary greatly, both in the proportion of soy sauce to water and in the spices and other flavorings. You can adjust both the soy and the seasonings to your own taste. See the recipe for Red-Cooked Rump Roast on page 323. ● *Serves 4 to 6*

COOKER: Medium or large, oval preferred
SETTING AND COOK TIME: HIGH for about 2 hours; chicken is turned at 1 hour

One 3- to 4-pound broiler/fryer

RED-COOKING LIQUID:
1½ cups water
1 cup soy sauce
¼ cup rice wine or dry sherry
2 tablespoons sugar
2 green onions (white and green parts), roughly chopped
Two ½-inch slices ginger, lightly crushed
1 whole star anise (see Note)

1 stick cinnamon
1 clove garlic, lightly crushed
1 strip (about 3 inches) orange zest, removed with a vegetable peeler

1. Wash the chicken and dry thoroughly. Remove the giblets and discard or reserve for another use. Cut off any lumps of fat. If you have time, place the chicken on a plate and refrigerate it uncovered for a couple of hours. The drier the chicken is, the more color it will absorb from the sauce.

2. Combine the red-cooking liquid ingredients in the crock and stir to dissolve the sugar. Add the chicken and turn to coat it with liquid. Leave it breast side up. Cover and cook on HIGH for 1 hour.

3. Carefully turn the chicken over, breast side down, using a sturdy wooden spoon inserted in the cavity and a rubber spatula to help you guide the chicken; take care to avoid splashing. Cover and cook on HIGH until an instant-read thermometer inserted into the thickest part of the thigh registers 180°F, about 1 hour more.

4. Remove the chicken from the cooker. If you wish to serve it cold, refrigerate, uncovered, until chilled before cutting it up. To serve the chicken warm, put it on a cutting board and allow it to cool a bit. Then carve the chicken Western style, or if you have a heavy cleaver, chop it into 2-inch pieces. Arrange the chicken on a platter and drizzle a few tablespoons of the cooking liquid over it.

5. Allow the cooking liquid to cool a bit, then pour it through a strainer into a heavy glass jar. Discard any solids. Refrigerate the liquid, but do not cap the jar until the liquid has cooled completely. It will keep in the refrigerator for a week to 10 days. For longer storage between uses, freeze it. Thaw before cooking with it. To reuse the red-cooking liquid, discard the solidified fat at the top. Pour the liquid into the cooker, add a fresh chicken, and proceed as directed in the recipe. After every third or fourth use, refresh the liquid by adding ½ cup of soy sauce and half of the seasonings.

Note: If you can't find the star-shaped whole star anise pods in the Asian foods section or on the spice aisle of your supermarket, check the Latin American foods section, where they may be labeled *anis estrella*. Or try an Asian or Latin American market.

Chinese Poached Chicken

se this for Chinese chicken salad or with vegetables in stir-fries. Star anise is sold with Latin American as well as Asian ingredients. Look for *anis estrella.* ● *Serves 4 to 6*

COOKER: Medium or large oval
SETTING AND COOK TIME: LOW for 6 to 7 hours

One 3- to 4-pound broiler/fryer
1 bunch green onions (white and green parts), trimmed
2 cloves garlic, bruised
5 coin-sized slices ginger, peeled and bruised with the side of a large knife
½ cup fresh cilantro sprigs
1 whole star anise
¼ cup light soy sauce
3 tablespoons dry vermouth
¼ cup water

1. Wash and dry the chicken thoroughly. Reserve the giblets and neck for another use. Cut off any lumps of fat. Put the green onions, garlic, ginger, cilantro, and anise in the cavity. Put the chicken in the slow cooker, breast side up. Combine the soy sauce, vermouth, and water in a small bowl and pour over the chicken. Cover and cook on LOW until an instant-read thermometer inserted in the thickest part of the thigh registers 180°F, 6 to 7 hours.

2. Transfer the chicken to a platter. Pour the liquid from the cooker into a separate container and refrigerate; then skim off the fat after it congeals. Or pour the cooking juices into a gravy separator and then into a container and refrigerate if not using. When the chicken is cool enough to handle, remove the skin, and cut or shred the meat from the carcass. Refrigerate the meat if not using it immediately.

Chinese Sweet-and-Sour Chicken with Sesame Seeds

erve this delicious chicken dish, courtesy of a Foster Farms brand chicken package wrapper, with steamed long-grain white rice. ○ *Serves 4 to 6*

COOKER: Medium or large oval
SETTING AND COOK TIME: HIGH for 3½ to 4½ hours

One 3- to 4-pound broiler/fryer
⅓ cup soy sauce
⅓ cup firmly packed light brown sugar
¼ cup water
¼ cup dry sherry or apple juice
1 tablespoon ketchup
½ teaspoon red pepper flakes
2 green onions, trimmed and halved
1 clove garlic, pressed
2 tablespoons cornstarch
1 tablespoon water
2 tablespoons sesame seeds, lightly toasted in a dry skillet
    over medium heat until fragrant

1. Wash and dry the chicken thoroughly. Reserve the giblets and neck for another use. Cut off any lumps of fat. Put the chicken in the cooker, breast side up. Combine the soy sauce, brown sugar, water, sherry, ketchup, red pepper flakes, green onions, and garlic in a small bowl; pour over the chicken. Cover and cook on HIGH until an instant-read thermometer inserted in the thickest part of the thigh registers 180°F, 3½ to 4½ hours.

2. Transfer the chicken to a platter. Remove and discard the green onions. Combine the cornstarch with the water and stir the slurry into the sauce. Cook on HIGH, stirring constantly, until thickened. Spoon the sauce over the chicken, sprinkle with the sesame seeds, and serve.

Chicken Curry

With our love of the slow cooker and ethnic cuisines, we were inspired to cook this fabulous curry. You may skip the step of browning the chicken if you wish and just layer it in the cooker raw. If you like your curry creamy, add 1 cup of whole-milk or low-fat yogurt (don't use nonfat) with the peas during the last half hour of cooking. Serve this over steamed basmati rice. ○ *Serves 4 to 6*

COOKER: Medium or large round or oval
SETTINGS AND COOK TIMES: HIGH for 1 hour,
   then LOW for 4 to 4½ hours; peas added during last 30 minutes

2 to 3 pounds mixed boneless chicken breast halves and thighs,
   breast halves each cut into 2 pieces
3 tablespoons sesame or olive oil
3 medium-size onions, chopped
2 cloves garlic, pressed; or 2 jalapeño chiles, seeded and chopped
1½ teaspoons ground coriander
1 teaspoon turmeric
1 teaspoon ground cumin
1 tablespoon chopped fresh ginger
2 teaspoons paprika
½ teaspoon red pepper flakes
½ teaspoon brown mustard seeds
One 28-ounce can crushed tomatoes
Juice of ½ lemon
1 head cauliflower, broken into small florets, and stems discarded
1 cup frozen petite peas, thawed; or 2 to 3 cups fresh baby spinach
Salt to taste

1. Cut chicken thighs into large or small pieces, removing the skin (leave the skin on the breast pieces). Coat the slow cooker with nonstick cooking spray. Heat the oil in a large skillet over medium-high heat and brown the chicken on all sides; transfer to a plate. Add the onions to the pan and cook, stirring a few times, until softened, about 5 minutes. Add the garlic or chiles, coriander, turmeric, cumin, ginger, paprika, red pepper flakes, and mustard seeds and cook gently for 2 minutes, stirring constantly. Add the tomatoes and lemon juice and mix well. Purée half of the tomato-onion mixture in a blender or food processor or in the pan with a handheld immersion blender.

2. In layers add to the cooker one-third of the chicken (dark meat first) and one-quarter of the sauce, and sprinkle with one-third of the cauliflower. Repeat the layers two more times, and finish with the remainder of the sauce. Cover and cook on HIGH for 1 hour.

3. Turn the cooker to LOW and cook for 4 to 4½ hours.

4. During the last 30 minutes, toss in some peas or a few handfuls of fresh baby spinach, season with the salt, cover, and cook until tender. To cook a bit faster, switch to HIGH heat.

Cornish Game Hens with Mango Tomato Salsa Fresca

A Cornish game hen is like a small plump chicken. Here we use a basic recipe for crock-roasting and serve the game hens with a refreshing raw salsa, great for summer dining. Please use this recipe for plain game hens, served simply without any sauce at all; they are delicious with a sprinkling of any dried herb blend. ○ *Serves 3 to 6*

COOKER: Large oval
SETTING AND COOK TIME: HIGH for 3 to 5 hours

3 tablespoons olive oil
3 Cornish game hens, rinsed and blotted dry
1 teaspoon salt
½ teaspoon freshly ground black pepper
½ teaspoon seasoned salt-free herb blend, such as Mrs. Dash or McCormick,
    or an Italian herb blend
3 cloves garlic, cut in half
1½ tablespoons cold unsalted butter, cut into pieces

MANGO-TOMATO SALSA FRESCA:

4 medium-size ripe tomatoes, finely chopped

1 or 2 large ripe mangoes, peeled, pitted, and chopped

3 green onions (white part and some of the green), chopped

¼ cup coarsely chopped fresh cilantro

2 tablespoons chopped fresh flat-leaf parsley

2 to 3 teaspoons chopped jalapeño, to your taste, seeded and minced

Juice of 1 lime

¼ teaspoon salt

1. Grease the slow cooker with some of the olive oil. Split each game hen; to do so, place the bird, breast side up, on a cutting surface. Holding the bird with one hand and using kitchen shears with the other, cut the breast in half, starting from the neck end. Turn the bird over and cut down both sides of the backbone, as close to it as possible, leaving 2 halves; discard the backbone or use for soup stock. Season the halves on both sides with the salt, pepper, and the herb blend. Tuck a piece of garlic in the cavity of each half of a game hen. Drizzle with a bit of olive oil. Arrange the hens side by side (it's okay if they touch), cut side down, in the cooker. Dot with the butter. Cover and cook on HIGH until the meat is tender when pierced with the tip of a knife, the juices run clear, and an instant-read thermometer inserted in the thickest part of the thigh registers 180°F, 3 to 4 hours.

2. Meanwhile, prepare the salsa: Combine all the ingredients in a small bowl and refrigerate for several hours so the flavors blend. Serve the salsa with the hens.

Cornish Game Hens with *Herbes de Provence*: Instead of the herb blend, sprinkle the hens with 3 tablespoons dried *herbes de Provence*.

Poussin Paprikash

Chicken paprikash is authentically Hungarian to the bone, a national dish consisting of moist chicken in a beguilingly rosy sauce. It is served in every home and restaurant. Every time Beth asks her Hungarian relatives for a familial recipe (none of them are written down), she has to endure a vigorous lecture on how there is only one way to make the best this or that traditional dish, when of course there are a bevy of recipes out there, varying from cook to cook. It is far easier to consult Beth's favorite Hungarian cookbook by Susan Derecskey (*The Hungarian Cookbook,* Harper and Row, 1972) for guidance and the final word. Here the *paprikás* is made with poussin, which is baby chicken, but you can substitute boneless chicken breasts just as easily. Be sure to use Hungarian paprika. While there are many grades, the main ones are sweet and hot; you want sweet for a paprikash. Some food writers call for several tablespoons of paprika for a recipe that is otherwise similar to ours; with the slow cooker we think it best to use less paprika since the cooker will concentrate the spice. Serve with Noodles with Poppy Seeds (page 170), plain buttered egg noodles, spätzle dumplings (the traditional side dish), or rice, if you must. It is also customary to accompany with a simple sliced cucumber salad with vinegar dressing; it cuts the richness of the meal. ○ *Serves 2 to 4*

COOKER: Medium round or oval
SETTING AND COOK TIME: HIGH for 2½ to 3 hours, then LOW for 10 minutes

3 tablespoons unsalted butter
Two 1-pound poussins, halved (see Note); or 4 boneless chicken breast halves, with skin on
2 medium-size to large shallots, chopped
2 to 3 teaspoons sweet Hungarian paprika, to your taste
½ cup chicken broth
½ medium-size green bell pepper, seeded and cut into ½-inch-wide strips
1 whole canned plum tomato, drained on paper towels and finely chopped
½ cup sour cream, at room temperature if possible
4 teaspoons all-purpose flour
Salt and freshly ground black pepper to taste

1. Melt the butter in a large skillet over medium-high heat. When it foams, add the poussin halves, skin side down, and cook until just colored on both sides, not brown or crisp, about 5 minutes per side; you may have to do this in batches. Transfer the poussin to the slow cooker. Add the shallots to the skillet and cook, stirring, until softened, about 5 minutes. Add the paprika and cook, stirring, about 1 minute. Add the broth and cook, scraping up any browned bits stuck to the pan. Pour the broth over the poussin; it will come halfway up the sides. Sprinkle the bell pepper and tomato pieces over the top. Cover and cook on HIGH until the poussins are tender and cooked through, 2½ to 3 hours. They will add some of their own juices to the broth.

2. Whisk together the sour cream and flour in a small bowl. Remove a few tablespoons of the cooking liquid and stir carefully into the sour cream.

3. Transfer the poussins to a warm platter. Leave the cooker on HIGH, add the sour cream to the liquid, and whisk until smooth. Cook for a few minutes until hot and thickened. Season with salt and pepper. Return the poussins to the cooker, nestling them in the sauce, turn the cooker to LOW, and cook for 10 minutes. Serve directly out of the vessel.

4. Place the poussin halves and the noodles or dumplings side by side on the plate, spoon some of the sauce over all, then pass the rest.

Note: To cut a poussin in half, holding the bird with one hand and using kitchen shears with the other, cut the breast in half, starting from the neck end. Turn the bird over and cut down both sides of the backbone, as close to it as possible, leaving 2 halves; discard the backbone or use for soup stock.

Bunny's Turkey Breast

T urkey lovers will rejoice at this excellent *dindonneau braisé,* young turkey cooked in a braising stock. To quote Brillat-Savarin, the famous French chef and chronicler of all his gustatory experiences, "turkey is delightful to look at, titillating to smell, and delicious to taste." We heartily agree. ○ *Serves 4 to 6*

COOKER: Medium or large round or oval
SETTING AND COOK TIME: HIGH for 3 to 3½ hours

1 large yellow onion, cut in half and sliced into half-moons
One 2½- to 3-pound bone-in turkey breast half, rinsed and patted dry
¼ cup water
1 to 2 tablespoons olive oil or unsalted butter, cut into pieces
1 to 2 tablespoons mixed chopped fresh herbs, such as basil, marjoram,
    thyme, oregano, parsley, and a bit of rosemary

One 1.8-ounce package turkey gravy mix (optional)
Dinner rolls, homemade or from the baker, for serving

1. Coat the slow cooker with olive oil or butter-flavor nonstick cooking spray. Arrange the onion slices in the cooker. Place the turkey breast, skin side up, on the onions; pour in the water. Drizzle with the oil or dot with butter and sprinkle with the herbs. Cover and cook on HIGH for 3 to 3½ hours. Don't peek before the minimum time has passed. The turkey is done when an instant-read meat thermometer inserted in the thickest part of the breast registers 170° to 180°F. The breast will not be browned, but oh-so-moist.

2. When the turkey is cooked, transfer it to a platter, cover with aluminum foil, and let stand for 10 minutes before carving. There will be a lot of liquid in the crock from the meat.

3. Strain the cooking liquids through a cheesecloth-lined colander set over a bowl and press to squeeze the juice from the onions. If you like, pour the broth into a small saucepan, bring to a boil, and add the packaged turkey gravy mix. Or you can just serve the liquid as is. Serve the hot gravy or jus and sliced turkey with dinner rolls.

Apricot Honey-Glazed Turkey

T his sweet and tangy turkey is a treat and is lower in fat than many dark-meat turkey dishes because the skin is removed before cooking. Skinning a turkey leg requires a bit of finesse and dry hands. Use a small, sharp knife to loosen the skin from around the meaty end of the drumstick. Pull back the skin over the knobby end of the bone, effectively turning the skin inside out, almost like a sock. Cut off the skin as close to the bony knob as possible. We figure on one turkey part per person here, but if the legs or thighs are large, you may wish to carve the meat off the bones, in which case this should serve 6. ○ *Serves 4*

COOKER: Medium or large, oval preferred
SETTING AND COOK TIME: HIGH for 3 to 3½ hours

4 turkey legs or thighs, skinned (see headnote page 295)

1 teaspoon paprika

1 teaspoon salt

¼ teaspoon freshly ground black pepper

½ teaspoon dried rosemary, crushed, or 1½ tablespoons chopped fresh rosemary

½ teaspoon dried thyme, or 1½ tablespoons chopped fresh thyme

¼ cup apricot jam

2 tablespoons honey

1 tablespoon fresh lemon juice

1 tablespoon barbecue sauce

1 tablespoon soy sauce

1 teaspoon cornstarch

1 teaspoon cold water

1. Wash the turkey and pat dry. In a small bowl, combine the paprika, salt, pepper, rosemary, and thyme. Rub all over the turkey legs. Set aside for 15 minutes or refrigerate, covered, for 2 to 3 hours.

2. Coat the slow cooker with nonstick cooking spray. Put the turkey in the cooker. In a small bowl, combine the jam, honey, lemon juice, barbecue sauce, and soy sauce. Pour over the turkey; stir if necessary to coat the turkey. Cover and cook on HIGH until the turkey is tender, 3 to 3½ hours.

3. Preheat the oven to 375°F. Transfer the turkey to a baking dish, tent with aluminum foil, and keep warm in the oven while you finish the sauce.

4. Pour the sauce from the cooker into a small saucepan. Combine the cornstarch and cold water in a small bowl, stirring to remove any lumps. Bring the sauce to a boil and continue boiling for 2 to 3 minutes to reduce the sauce and concentrate the flavors. Add the slurry and cook for 2 or 3 minutes more, until thickened.

5. Remove the turkey from the oven, pour the glaze over the turkey, and serve.

Braised Herbed Turkey Legs

T urkey legs take beautifully to the gentle heat of the slow cooker, becoming tender and savory. Use a mixture of fresh herbs, depending on what is available in your garden or market. If you include rosemary in the mix, use a light hand so it doesn't overpower the other flavors. ◉ *Serves 4 to 6*

COOKER: Medium or large, oval preferred
SETTING AND COOK TIME: HIGH for 2 to 3 hours

1½ tablespoons olive oil
1½ tablespoons unsalted butter
4 turkey legs
1 cup chopped onion
½ cup sliced carrots (½ inch thick)
⅓ cup sliced celery (½ inch thick)
2 cloves garlic, chopped
½ cup dry white wine
3 to 4 tablespoons mixed chopped fresh herbs, such as basil, marjoram, thyme,
    oregano, parsley, and a bit of rosemary, plus more (optional) for garnish
¾ teaspoon salt
¼ teaspoon freshly ground black pepper
2 tablespoons heavy cream or 1 tablespoon unsalted butter (optional)
Rice, couscous, or mashed potatoes for serving

1. In a large, heavy skillet, heat the oil and butter together over medium-high heat. Brown the turkey legs all over, 4 to 6 minutes total. As they brown, transfer the turkey legs to the slow cooker. Add the onion, carrots, celery, and garlic to the skillet and cook, stirring, until softened a bit, about 5 minutes. Add the wine and bring to a boil, scraping up any browned bits stuck to the pan. When the wine has reduced a bit, 2 to 3 minutes more, stir in the herbs and cook for 30 seconds.

2. Scrape the mixture into the cooker, distributing it as well as possible over and around the turkey legs. Season with the salt and pepper. Cover and cook on HIGH until the turkey is tender, 2 to 3 hours.

3. Preheat the oven to 375°F. Transfer the turkey to a baking dish, tent with aluminum foil, and keep warm in the oven while you finish the sauce.

4. Pour the sauce through a fine-mesh strainer into a small saucepan, bring to a boil, and continue boiling for 4 to 5 minutes to reduce the sauce and concentrate the flavors. If desired, stir in the cream or butter until the cream is hot or the butter just melts.

5. Serve the turkey, on or off the bone, with the vegetable and herb sauce, over rice, fluffy couscous, or mashed potatoes. Garnish with fresh herbs if desired.

Mexican Turkey

T urkey thighs work beautifully in the slow cooker. The meat is a bit tougher than chicken, so it holds up nicely in the slow cooker environment, emerging moist beyond belief. Shred the meat and roll it up in tortillas for a great lunch. ○ *Serves 6 to 8*

COOKER: Medium or large round or oval
SETTING AND COOK TIME: HIGH for 3 to 3½ hours

2 pounds turkey thighs, skinned
One 8-ounce can tomato sauce
One 4-ounce can chopped roasted green chiles, with their juice
2 medium-size or 3 small white onions, chopped
2 tablespoons Worcestershire sauce
2 tablespoons chili powder
Pinch of ground cumin
1 clove garlic, crushed

TO SERVE:
8 large flour tortillas, at room temperature
¾ cup shredded cheddar cheese
⅔ cup sour cream
Diced fresh tomatoes
Shredded iceberg lettuce

1. Put the turkey thighs in the slow cooker. Add the tomato sauce, chiles, onions, Worcestershire, chili powder, cumin, and garlic and stir to coat the thighs with the mixture. Cover and cook on HIGH until the turkey is tender, 3 to 3½ hours.

2. Remove the turkey from the cooker and, once it cools a bit, pick the meat off the bones. Shred the meat, return it to the cooker, and stir to combine well with the sauce. Spoon the meat and sauce onto a tortilla and roll up. Top with cheese, sour cream, tomatoes, and lettuce. Repeat with the remaining tortillas and toppings and serve immediately.

M's Turkey Taco Salad

B eth's friend M makes this taco salad for lunch for her coworkers every so often. In return, the diners pay a few dollars, which is donated to their charity of choice for that week. The slow cooker makes delicious hot taco meat. M uses vine-ripened tomatoes, either salad or plum, and a thick commercial jarred salsa, such as Pace Picante. She likes to use a medium hot salsa for cooking, but a mild one for serving as a topping. To save time, you can cook the meat sauce on HIGH for about 1½ to 2 hours. Serve with warm buttered flour tortillas. ◦ *Serves 6*

COOKER: Medium round
SETTING AND COOK TIME: LOW for 4 to 6 hours

MEAT SAUCE:
1½ pounds ground dark turkey meat
One 16-ounce jar tomato salsa

SALAD:
1 medium firm-ripe avocado
6 cups thick shredded or chopped iceberg or romaine lettuce
3 cups corn chips
One 15-ounce can pinto beans, rinsed, drained, and
    heated in a saucepan or microwave
1½ cups shredded cheddar cheese
One 16-ounce jar tomato salsa
2 medium-size ripe tomatoes, coarsely chopped
1 cup cold sour cream, stirred
One 4-ounce can sliced ripe California black olives, drained

1. Coat the slow cooker with nonstick cooking spray. To make the meat sauce, put the ground turkey and salsa in the cooker. Cover and cook on LOW until cooked thoroughly, 4 to 6 hours. Stir the sauce.

2. To make the salad, slice the avocado and put all the salad components in separate containers. On each individual plate layer some lettuce, a handful of corn chips, some of the hot meat, a spoonful or two of hot pinto beans, shredded cheese, some salsa, diced tomatoes, sour cream, avocado, and olives.

Turkey Shiitake Meat Loaf

This is one low-fat meat loaf that doesn't taste it. It's moist and packed with flavor. Yes, you can use fresh shiitakes instead of the dried ones, but we prefer the dried because of their more pronounced taste. Be sure to buy ground turkey that does not include skin. We like to use half breast meat, half thigh and leg meat because the breast meat alone is too dry. This is best made in an oval cooker for a traditionally shaped loaf. ○ *Serves 6 to 8*

COOKER: Medium or large, oval preferred
SETTING AND COOK TIME: LOW for 7 to 9 hours;
    tomato sauce added during last 30 minutes

6 large or 12 small dried shiitake mushrooms
1½ pounds ground turkey (a mixture of light and dark meat is best)
3 slices whole wheat sandwich bread
1 large yellow onion, quartered
2 cloves garlic, peeled
2 tablespoons chopped fresh flat-leaf parsley
1 tablespoon dried basil, or ¼ cup chopped fresh basil
1 teaspoon dried oregano or 1 tablespoon chopped fresh oregano
1 teaspoon salt
¼ teaspoon freshly ground black pepper
½ cup freshly grated Parmesan cheese
One 15-ounce can tomato sauce

1. Soften the mushrooms by soaking them in boiling water to cover for 1 hour. Or use the microwave: Cover the bowl of mushrooms and water tightly with plastic wrap and microwave 5 minutes on HIGH. Allow to cool before proceeding. Squeeze the liquid from the mushrooms, reserving the liquid. Cut off the tough stems, and chop the caps roughly. Slowly pour the mushroom soaking liquid into a measuring cup, being careful to leave any grit behind in the bowl.

2. Put the ground turkey in a large bowl.

3. Tear the bread slices into quarters or eighths, put in a food processor, and pulse until reduced to crumbs. Transfer to the bowl with the turkey. (Alternately, tear the bread into 1-inch pieces, place in a bowl, and pour over ¼ cup of the mushroom soaking liquid. Add to the turkey.)

4. In the food processor, combine the onion, garlic, parsley, and shiitakes and pulse until finely chopped, but do not let them turn to mush. Transfer to the bowl with the turkey and add the basil, oregano, salt, pepper, cheese, and 1 cup of the tomato sauce. Add ¼ cup of the mushroom soaking liquid if you have not used it to soak the bread, and discard the rest of the liquid. Using your hands or a large fork, mix the ingredients gently but thoroughly, being careful not to compact the meat.

5. Make an aluminum foil "cradle" that will help you easily remove the meat loaf from the cooker when it is done: Tear off a sheet of foil about 24 inches long. Place along the edge of the counter, and tear in half lengthwise. Fold each piece in half lengthwise, then in half again. Place the strips in the cooker in a cross shape, centering them. The edges of the strips will hang over the edge of the cooker. Place the meat mixture on top of the strips and shape into an oval or round loaf, depending on the shape of your cooker, by pressing it gently, evening out the top, and shaping it to fit your cooker. Bend the foil strips toward the meat loaf so they will not prevent the cover of the cooker from closing properly. Cover and cook on LOW until an instant-read thermometer inserted in the center of the loaf registers at least 180°F, 7 to 9 hours.

6. About 30 minutes before the end of the cooking time, bend the foil strips out of the way and pour the remaining tomato sauce over the meat loaf. Cover and continue to cook on LOW for another 30 minutes.

7. To serve, lift the meat loaf onto a cutting board or serving platter, using the foil "handles." Slide out and discard the strips. Slice the meat loaf and serve hot or cold.

Kubis Rolls

While stuffed cabbage rolls with a wide variety of fillings are classic in Slavic cooking, this recipe is a little bit different. It is made with kale. Beth's friend Judy Milano inherited this dish from her Italian grandmother; it is a real family favorite. With her own creativity and culinary flair, Judy has adapted the recipe for a slow cooker casserole. We love kale, with its relatively mild flavor. You want the spruce-green, large-leaved curly kale, not the cream and violet–colored flowering or ornamental kale sometimes found in the produce aisle. After blanching, it retains its color perfectly and it loves to be braised. Judy has no idea where the name "kubis" came from, or even how it is spelled, but the Polish word for cabbage is *kapusta* and the Latin word for kale is *caulis* (pronounced KOOL-is), so kubis is most likely to be an adulterated version of one of those words that has been simplified over the years. Serve this with boiled or mashed potatoes. ○ *Serves 6*

COOKER: Medium or large round
SETTING AND COOK TIME: LOW for 8 to 10 hours

2 to 4 bunches kale or green Swiss chard (you need about 16 big leaves)
1½ pounds ground dark turkey meat; meat loaf mix of beef, pork,
   and veal; or all ground beef
1 cup raw long-grain white or converted rice
1 medium-size onion, finely chopped
3 tablespoons minced fresh flat-leaf parsley
2 cloves garlic, pressed
1 teaspoon salt, or to taste
1 teaspoon dried Italian herb seasoning
½ teaspoon lemon pepper or ground white pepper
One 28-ounce can tomato sauce (Italian-style is nice)
Two 6-ounce cans tomato paste
1 cup water
4 strips bacon

1. Set a large bowl of cold water on the counter; place a few ice cubes in it if you like. Lay out a clean kitchen towel on the counter. Bring a large pot of water to a boil. Salt the water and blanch the kale or chard leaves until tender and wilted, but not soft enough to tear when handled, about 1 minute. Remove by the stem end with tongs, plunge into the cold water to cool, then place on the towel and pat gently with paper towels to dry. Continue to blanch the leaves in batches. Trim off the tough stem and center vein with a paring knife (some people just pound it with a mallet to soften).

2. Put the ground meat, rice, onion, parsley, garlic, and all seasonings in a large bowl. Using your hands or a large spoon, mix gently but thoroughly, being careful not to compact the meat.

3. To fill, lay one leaf flat, underside up, and center a nice heaping tablespoon of the filling (or up to about 3 tablespoons, depending on the size of the leaf) at the base of the stem end. The filling should be a long oval shape. Fold the bottom of the leaf over the filling, then fold in the two sides and continue rolling until the filling is completely encased; you will have a few layers of kale and a neat package. Some cooks tie each stuffed leaf with kitchen twine, but if you arrange them seam side down, they will be fine. Make about 16 rolls.

4. Coat the slow cooker with nonstick cooking spray. Place the kubis rolls side by side in the cooker in layers; depending on the size of your cooker, you will have 3 to 4 layers.

5. Whisk together the tomato sauce, tomato paste, and water until smooth. Pour over the kubis rolls; add more water so the liquid just covers the rolls or use some of the water in which you blanched the kale. Lay the bacon over the top. If you have some extra leaves, you can lay them over the bacon; this is optional, but it is a nice way to use up extra leaves. Cover and cook on LOW until the leaves are tender and the filling is firm and cooked through (you will have to test one by cutting in half), 8 to 10 hours.

6. Serve 2 or 3 rolls per person. This dish is even tastier served the next day; let cool in the cooker on the counter, cover, and refrigerate overnight. The next day, bring the crock close to room temperature on the counter, then set into the slow cooker base and heat on LOW until hot.

Southwest Turkey Sausage
and Hominy Stew

With the advent of so many artisan sausage companies, we are delighted at the array of sausages made from meats other than pork, such as turkey and duck. This is an easy and delightful stew made with hominy, turkey sausage, plenty of peppers, a touch of chili powder, and a hint of tequila. It is sure to become a favorite. ● *Serves 4*

COOKER: Medium round or oval
SETTING AND COOK TIME: LOW for 5 to 7 hours

1¼ cups prepared salsa, medium or hot
1 cup coarsely chopped red bell pepper (1-inch pieces)
1 cup coarsely chopped yellow bell pepper (1-inch pieces)
One 10-ounce box frozen yellow or white corn kernels, thawed
1 tablespoon chili powder
One 15.5-ounce can white or golden hominy, rinsed and drained
One 12-ounce package smoked turkey sausages, cut into ½-inch-thick rounds
2 tablespoons tequila

FOR SERVING:
3 cups hot cooked long-grain white or brown rice
½ cup crushed tortilla chips, baked or regular
1 medium-large ripe mango (10 to 14 ounces), peeled and sliced off the pit
⅓ cup chopped fresh cilantro
¼ cup chopped green onions (white part and some of the green)
¾ cup sour cream (reduced fat or nonfat are okay)

1. Combine the salsa, bell peppers, corn, chili powder, hominy, sausage pieces, and tequila in the slow cooker. Cover and cook on LOW for 5 to 7 hours.

2. To serve, divide the rice among 4 bowls; top each serving with the stew, some crushed chips, mango slices, cilantro, green onions, and a big dollop of sour cream.

Duck Breasts with Port Wine Sauce

I t's probably easiest to make this with boneless duck breasts, which we buy frozen in vacuum packages. Or use duck legs or the pieces of a duck that you have disjointed yourself. If you are nervous about flaming the port, you may skip that part. Just add the port to the duck in the skillet, bring it to a boil, and cook for a minute or two before transfering the duck to the cooker. If you are going to flame the port, be sure to use a skillet that does *not* have a nonstick coating; cast iron or stainless steel work well. This recipe is another gem from Julie's friend Batia Rabec. ○ *Serves 4*

COOKER: Medium oval or large round or oval
SETTING AND COOK TIME: LOW for 6 to 7 hours

2 tablespoons unsalted butter
4 boneless duck breast halves, with skin (about 1½ pounds total)
⅓ cup port wine
Grated zest of 1 orange
1 teaspoon salt
⅛ teaspoon freshly ground black pepper
2 tablespoons cornstarch
¼ cup milk (low fat is okay)

1. Melt the butter in a large skillet (not a nonstick one) over medium-high heat. When it foams, add the duck, skin side down, and cook until deep golden brown on both sides, 2 to 3 minutes per side. Add the port and bring to a boil. Being careful of long sleeves and dangling hair, touch a long lit match to the liquid in the pan and turn off the heat. The liquid will catch fire and burn for about 30 seconds, then the flames will die out. With a slotted spoon, transfer the duck to the slow cooker. Return the liquid in the pan to a boil and cook briefly, scraping up any browned bits stuck to the pan. Pour over the duck, then sprinkle with the orange zest, salt, and pepper. Cover and cook on LOW for 6 to 7 hours.

2. Preheat the oven to 375°F. With a slotted spoon, transfer the duck to a shallow baking dish. Tent with aluminum foil and keep warm in the oven while you finish the sauce.

3. Skim and discard as much fat as possible from the liquid in the cooker, then pour into a small saucepan. In a small bowl, stir the cornstarch into the milk to make a smooth slurry. Bring the sauce to a boil, add the slurry, and cook, stirring, until it thickens, 3 to 4 minutes. Taste for salt and pepper. Serve the duck with the sauce.

Braised Quail

Quail are a real gourmet treat. They were the main course in the film *Babette's Feast,* peering out of puff pastry. They are often confused with partridge (they are called that in the South), another very small bird, but unlike partridge, quail like to walk in groups called coveys instead of flying. Quail are farm raised these days and are available frozen; they will vary in size from 4 to 8 ounces with all their bones, so check your cooking time in the slow cooker so as not to drastically overcook. The white flesh is amazingly firm, succulent, and tasty. Here we braise quail whole and serve them on bread so that the juices are soaked up nicely. If you are using a baguette, you will need 3 slices per person, but if you use a larger loaf, 1 or 2 slices are enough. You can also serve the quail on a bed of cooked lentils, or even a nice black bean chili with a salsa (they are very good with beans). It is proper etiquette to nibble the legs and thighs with your fingers because they are diminutive in relation to a dinner knife. If perchance you end up with leftovers, serve them cold on a bed of lettuce, surrounded with orange, avocado, or tomato slices. Drizzle the salad with a sherry vinaigrette and accompany with a hunk of cornbread fresh from the oven. ○ *Serves 3 to 4*

COOKER: Medium oval or large round or oval
SETTING AND COOK TIME: HIGH for 1¾ to 2¼ hours; mushrooms added at 1 hour

1 medium-size onion, cut in half and sliced into half moons
6 to 8 quail, rinsed and patted dry
Salt and ground white pepper to taste
6 tablespoons (¾ stick) unsalted butter
2 tablespoons all-purpose flour

1 cup dry white wine

1¼ cups chicken broth

2 bay leaves

6 ounces fresh mushrooms, thinly sliced

CROUTONS:

4 to 6 tablespoons (½ to ¾ stick) unsalted butter

9 to 12 rounds French bread

2 to 3 tablespoons minced fresh chives for garnish

1. Put the onion in the slow cooker to make a bed of sorts for the birds.

2. Season the quail with salt and pepper. Melt the butter in a large skillet over medium-high heat and brown the quail on all sides. Transfer to the cooker; they can be arranged side by side or stacked. Sprinkle the flour into the pan, blending well with the pan juices, and cook for 1 or 2 minutes. Add the wine and broth, stir well, and bring to a boil, scraping up any browned bits in the pan. Pour the pan juices over the quail. Add the bay leaves. Cover and cook on HIGH for 1 hour.

3. Add the mushrooms, cover, and cook until the meat is tender, another 45 minutes to 1¼ hours.

4. Discard the bay leaves and taste for salt and pepper.

5. To make the croutons, in a large skillet over medium heat, melt the butter, then brown the bread rounds on both sides until golden.

6. To serve, put 3 pieces of warm bread on each warm dinner plate. Arrange the quail, 2 per person, on top, and pour over the mushrooms and juices. Sprinkle with the chives.

Pheasant in a Crock

W hen Beth was catering she served a lot of pheasant. There was a great pheasant farm up the hill from Los Gatos, California, and while waiting for her order to be filled, she got to wander around the yards watching the ring-necked birds roam pecking the ground for insects. This recipe is adapted from a British one called pheasant in a brick. The pheasant is cooked in an unglazed earthenware clay pot that looks like a miniature metal drum turned sideways with a spout on the end. It was originally designed for slow-cooking chicken. This bird is bathed in orange juice and wrapped in bacon, herbs, and garlic. It is delicious and mighty simple. ○ *Serves 2*

COOKER: Medium round or oval
SETTING AND COOK TIME: HIGH for 3½ to 4½ hours

3 to 4 sprigs fresh thyme
3 sprigs fresh parsley
2 cloves garlic, one crushed, the other sliced
One 2- to 3-pound pheasant, rinsed and patted dry
Salt and freshly ground black pepper to taste
1 large orange
4 strips smoky bacon or pepper bacon
1 tablespoon olive oil
¼ cup chicken broth

1. Put the thyme, parsley, and crushed garlic inside the pheasant. Tuck the garlic slices between the legs and body. Season the pheasant with salt and pepper. Remove the zest from the orange in long, thick, curly strips and lay them over the breast. Wrap the breast with the bacon and put the pheasant in the slow cooker. Halve the orange and squeeze the juice all over the bird. Put one of the squeezed orange halves in the cavity. Drizzle the pheasant with the olive oil and broth. Cover and cook on HIGH until the meat is tender and an instant-read meat thermometer inserted in the thigh registers 180°F, 3½ to 5 hours.

2. Serve the pheasant on a platter, with the juices poured over.

Rabbit Hunter's Style

This dish is pure old European. Cut the rabbit into 8 portions: 2 front legs; the saddle or back, cut into 2 portions; the 2 back legs; and the 2 ribs. This recipe, often referred to by its French name, *lapin sauté chasseur*, is adapted from one served at the German restaurant Kasteel Franssen in Oak Harbor on Whitbey Island in Washington Sound. Serve it over rice or alongside steamed new potatoes. ○ *Serves 2 to 3*

COOKER: Medium or large round or oval
SETTING AND COOK TIME: HIGH for 3½ to 5 hours; mushrooms added at 2 hours

One 2½- to 3-pound rabbit, cut into 8 pieces, rinsed, and patted dry
Salt and freshly ground black pepper to taste
4 strips bacon
4 shallots, chopped
3 cloves garlic, minced
2 tablespoons all-purpose or whole wheat pastry flour
½ cup dry white wine
One 8-ounce can tomato sauce
½ cup water
1 teaspoon chopped fresh thyme
1 teaspoon minced fresh basil
1½ cups sliced fresh mushrooms, such as plain white button mushrooms or wild mushrooms, or
   a combination
¼ cup chopped fresh flat-leaf parsley

1. Season the rabbit liberally with salt and pepper. In a large skillet, cook the bacon over medium-high heat until crisp. Transfer to paper towels to drain, then crumble and set aside. Add the rabbit to the hot bacon fat and brown on all sides. Transfer to the slow cooker. Add the shallots and garlic to the pan and cook, stirring, for 2 minutes. Sprinkle with the flour, then add the wine and cook, scraping up any browned bits stuck to the pan. Add the tomato sauce, water, thyme, and basil and bring to a boil. Pour over the rabbit. Cover and cook on HIGH for 2 hours.

2. Add the mushrooms, cover, and continue to cook on HIGH until the rabbit is very tender and falling off the bone, another 1½ to 3 hours. Taste for salt and pepper. Serve garnished with the parsley and crumbled bacon.

Beef, Veal, and Venison

Beef is the king of the slow cooker: it is versatile and delicious. While for other cooking methods most cooks look for the leanest, most expensive cuts for their convenience and the fabulous flavor, what you want for your slow cooker are the tougher cuts. These are the meats that are perfect for the slow cooker, which will turn them into fall-apart tender meals.

The tougher cuts, the ones with the greatest muscle density, are perfect for making braises, stews, and pot roasts in the slow cooker. These cuts come from the parts of the animal that do the most work—the neck, shoulders (chuck), foreleg area (brisket), hind section (round steak), and undersides (flank and plate areas). These tougher cuts—the brisket, chuck roasts, and short ribs—are usually the best buys at the meat market. Many cooks prefer to cut their own stew meat from a large roast; we wish to encourage that practice. It is not only economical, but also will give you the best meat for stewing. Quite often packaged stew meat is cut from a section like the top round, which looks nice but cooks up dry and tough.

While cuts taken from the muscular part of a steer start out tough, long moist cooking produces tender, luscious, deeply flavored dishes. This is because the muscles are interwoven with connective tissue, which dissolves over long cooking, producing a silky, fork-tender meat.

When choosing a cut of beef, look for slightly moist meat with a light cherry red to red-brown hue, a clean smell, tight grain, marbled intramuscular fat (flecks of fat throughout the meat), and white external fat. Check the expiration date before buying packaged meat and always store beef in the refrigerator. You want to look for USDA Choice grade meats because they are the juiciest and most flavorful. But often the lower grade, Select, which is a lot leaner than Choice, is also fine for stewing and braising. Shop at a reliable supermarket or small butcher shop and do not hesitate to ask questions; fine cooks value the advice of a knowledgeable meat cutter or butcher.

The following are the traditional cuts to use for braising. They are the best for pot roasts and for cutting up as stew meat.

Chuck roast, often sold as a flat hunk, cooks up moist and tender, never tough and stringy. Pick out one that is appropriate for the shape and size of your slow cooker. This is the cut to use for cutting your own stew meat. *Flank steak* is also excellent, rolled and tied, for a pot roast. Or you can use *beef cheeks* or *shin meat.*

The *brisket* is always boneless. It can be bought whole at 10 to 15 pounds, but is usually sold cut into the brisket *first cut, center cut,* and *point cut.* The point is a fattier section but is excellent braised. Brisket is marinated in spices to make corned beef.

The *bottom round,* a solid hunk of muscle, is also boneless. It is the meat used in the classic Swiss steak and sauerbraten and is marinated to compensate for the lack of fat. While some people love a pot roast from the bottom round, most prefer the chuck. Bottom round is also good for stew meat. *Braciole,* thin pieces cut from the top or bottom round, are also used for braising as a roulade or as beef rolls called paupiettes.

Oxtails are one of our favorite meats in the slow cooker. It is the tail portion of cattle cut into hunks. It is a humble meat not often cooked today, but once you try it, we think you'll love it. Oxtails contain lots of collagen, which melts into gelatin as it dissolves, resulting in loads of flavor and a silky texture. *Beef shanks,* not commonly sold in this country, are great for braising and cutting up for stew meat. The shank is also an excellent choice for making stock. Try throwing a slice in the bean pot or in a soup for added flavor.

Veal is meat from a four-month-old calf. Some cuts contain lots of collagen and make superior, tender braises. While veal is not especially popular in the United States, Europeans embrace it and have a multitude of recipes for it. You can choose formula-fed veal (sold under the brand name Provimi), which is pale pink, or grass-fed veal, which is from animals that are allowed to roam and graze; this meat is ruddier in color and more flavorful. Veal takes to all sorts of spices, vegetables, and aromatic braising liquids because of its delicate taste. It is the leanest of all meats. *Veal breast, shoulder roasts, veal cheeks,* and *blade roasts* are really good for cutting up into stew meat, and they are the most economical cuts. One of the great French stew classics is *blanquette de veau,* veal stew cooked in a rich cream sauce.

As always, be aware of keeping all food

The Best Slow Cooker Cuts of Beef

Chuck blade roast or chuck 7-bone roast

Boneless chuck roast

Chuck arm steak

Chuck mock tender

Shoulder pot roast

Flatiron roast

Brisket or corned beef

Top round steak

Bottom round steak

Swiss steak (bottom round)

Short ribs

Crosscut beef shanks and shin

Braciole

Oxtails

Beef cheeks

The Best Slow Cooker Cuts of Veal

Bone-in blade roast

Veal shoulder roast

Chuck shoulder clod roast

Veal breast

Veal cheeks

Veal shanks

Braising, or slow-cooking in liquid, is the easiest way to tenderize meat and bring out its luscious flavors. A braise is not the same as a stew; a braise refers to a large cut of meat while a stew is meat that is cut up into small pieces. A braise uses a small amount of liquid and a stew is submerged in plenty of savory liquid. In a braise, the cooking liquid ends up as sauce. Here's what we learned about braises and stews made in the slow cooker.

If you are making a stew, first put hard veggies such as potatoes and carrots into the cooker. Then brown uniform-sized pieces of meat in a heavy Dutch oven or skillet in uncrowded batches, adding the meat to the slow cooker crock as you finish browning. Then brown onions and any other vegetables called for in the recipe. Transfer them to the crock, add the cooking liquid to the skillet, and deglaze the pan, which means scraping up all the delicious browned bits from the bottom of the pan. Deglazing gives the juices and cooking liquids a deep color and rich taste. Bring the liquid to a boil, then pour it over the meat, cover, and start the slow cooker. Because the slow cooker insert is earthenware, you don't need to worry about any acidic ingredients, such as tomatoes or wine, reacting with it.

In general, if you want the flavor of the meat to penetrate the liquid and don't care about texture (if you are making stock or soup, for instance), start with cold water and cook on LOW. If you want to keep some of the flavor in the meat and still have a somewhat firm texture to eat along with the liquid, start with cold water but cook on HIGH for 1 hour before switching to LOW; this speeds up the cooking process. If you want the optimum texture and as much flavor as possible to stay in the meat, pat the meat dry with paper towels and brown it in a skillet over high heat, then load it into the slow cooker with hot liquid. The searing process, important in traditional braises, caramelizes the surface, adding considerable flavor. Meat stews should always be cooked at a low simmer, never at a boil, to fully develop their character and flavor, a process that is perfectly performed in the slow cooker. The collagen, the tough, stringy substance in the connective tissue, converts to gelatin. That is why your sauce shimmers and your meat becomes tender.

How do you know your braise or stew is done? The meat will pull away from the bone, if there is one, and you should be able to pierce or cut the meat with a fork. For tips on degreasing the cooking liquid, see page 17.

Beef stews and braises taste great made a day or two in advance and reheated. They keep for up to 3 days in the refrigerator and can be frozen for up to 3 months.

preparation surfaces clean and free from bacterial contamination by washing your hands, counters, cutting boards, and knives with warm soapy water. *E. coli* is the pathogen most commonly associated with beef. It lives on the surface of the meat, but proper preparation habits will insure no cross-contamination, and the heat from cooking will kill any existing bacteria. Never eat raw meat, and freeze any meat stored longer than three days. Thaw all meat in the refrigerator or microwave, not at room temperature.

Our Best Pot Roast with Roots

This simple, old-fashioned pot roast is sublimely delicious: meltingly tender meat, with a rich-tasting sauce. Take the time to dice the vegetables finely (¼ to ½ inch on a side), brown the meat well, and bring the water to a full boil before adding it to the crockery insert. Each of these steps plays a part in the dish's final goodness. Look for a thick pot roast. If it is too big to lay flat in your cooker, cut it in half and stack the pieces one atop the other. If you cook the pot roast for the full amount of time, it may be too tender to slice. Just serve it in luscious chunks—they will be fork-tender—with broad egg noodles, corkscrew pasta, or mashed potatoes to soak up the juices. ● *Serves 4 to 6*

COOKER: Medium oval or large round or oval
SETTING AND COOK TIME: LOW for 8 to 9 hours

2 tablespoons olive oil, or more as needed
½ cup finely diced carrot
½ cup finely diced celery, including some leaves
½ cup finely diced turnip
½ cup finely diced onion
One 3-pound boneless chuck roast, trimmed of as much fat as possible and blotted dry
½ teaspoon salt
¼ teaspoon freshly ground black pepper
½ cup dry red wine
¾ cup water

1. In a large, heavy skillet, heat 1 tablespoon of the oil over medium-high heat. Add the carrot, celery, turnip, and onion, and cook, stirring a few times, until softened, about 5 minutes. Transfer to the slow cooker.

2. Heat the remaining 1 tablespoon of oil in the skillet over medium-high heat. Add the pot roast and brown well on the first side. This will take 2 or 3 minutes if the pan is really hot, a bit longer if not. If the meat is very lean or your pan does not have a nonstick finish, add a bit more oil before turning with tongs to allow the second side to brown. Season it with the salt and pepper and place in the cooker on top of the vegetables. Pour the wine into the skillet and bring to a boil, scraping up any browned bits stuck to the pan. When the wine has reduced to a syrupy consistency, in 1 or 2 minutes, pour it over the meat. Add the water to the skillet and allow to come to a full boil. Pour over the meat, cover, and cook on LOW for 8 to 9 hours.

3. To serve, transfer the meat to a cutting board, scraping any clinging vegetable bits back into the cooker. Pour the vegetables and liquid through a mesh strainer set over a bowl. Use the back of a spoon to press hard on the vegetables, extracting as much liquid as possible; discard the vegetables. Allow this liquid, or gravy, to settle for a few moments so that the fat rises to the surface. Skim off as much of it as possible from the gravy. Slice the pot roast against the grain. Serve it with the gravy.

Lazy Day Braised Pot Roast

T his is lazy because there is no browning, no fussing. Just load up the cooker and later in the day thicken the flavorful juices collected in the crock. This recipe has much more liquid than the others, and that is the basis for your gravy. The meat stays moist and tender, just the way we like our pot roast. It is just as good the next day. ○ *Serves 6 to 8*

COOKER: Medium oval or large round or oval
SETTING AND COOK TIME: LOW for 6 to 8 hours

One 4-pound boneless chuck roast, trimmed of as much fat as possible and blotted dry
½ teaspoon salt
¼ teaspoon freshly ground black pepper
4 large carrots, cut into 3-inch lengths

4 large potatoes, peeled and quartered

1 large yellow onion, quartered

2 bay leaves

3 cups water

½ cup cider vinegar

3 tablespoons unsalted butter, softened

3 tablespoons all-purpose flour

1. Put the roast in the slow cooker and sprinkle with the salt and pepper. Add the carrots, potatoes, onion, and bay leaves. Pour the water and vinegar over the meat and vegetables. Cover and cook on LOW for 6 to 8 hours.

2. Transfer the meat and vegetables to a heated platter and cover with aluminum foil. Turn the cooker to HIGH. You will have about 3 full cups of liquid. In a small bowl, mash together the butter with the flour to make a *beurre manié* (see page 20). Add to the hot liquid in the cooker and stir with a whisk until melted and the liquid thickens. Ladle some over the meat and vegetables and serve the remainder in a bowl.

Skye's Braised Pot Roast with Vegetables

S kye Stewart is our marketing and publicity director at The Harvard Common Press. Here is her recipe for pot roast with lots of nice chunks of vegetables, an adaptation of Favorite Pot Roast from *Mable Hoffman's Crockery Cookery* (HPBooks, 1995), with a few of Skye's personal tweaks, deletions, and additions (the parsnips). When she doesn't use the parsnips, she doubles the carrots, but we love the combination. We also like the use of a meat rub and no searing, so the meat is flavorful despite a minimum of work getting the crock loaded up and cooking. Skye makes this in a large slow cooker (a 7-quart). The servings are generous, so there will be delicious leftovers. ○ *Serves 6 to 8*

COOKER: Medium oval or large round
SETTING AND COOK TIME: LOW for 8 to 9 hours

1 teaspoon salt

¼ to ½ teaspoon freshly ground black pepper, to your taste

¼ teaspoon paprika

3 to 3½ pounds boneless chuck roast, trimmed of as much fat as possible and blotted dry

1 rib celery, coarsely chopped

1 large onion, cut into wedges

2 to 3 carrots, cut into 1-inch-thick coins

2 to 3 parsnips, peeled and cut into 1-inch-thick coins

4 starchy potatoes, peeled or not, each cut into 8 pieces

1 cup beef broth

1. Combine the salt, pepper, and paprika. Rub all sides of the roast with the spice mix. Put the vegetables in the slow cooker with the potatoes as the top layer. Put the meat on top of the potatoes. Pour the broth over the vegetables and meat.

2. Cover and cook on LOW for 8 to 9 hours. Serve the meat and vegetables right out of the cooker and ladle the hot juices over all.

Braised Beef Brisket

W hether we were standing in line at the post office or were at a cooking group, when we got around to asking "What is your favorite dish to make in the slow cooker?" the answer was often a piece of beef with a package of dried onion soup mix combined in the crock and cooked all day. "Oh, it is just outrageously delicious after a long day driving kids from the soccer field to basketball tournaments," we were told. We shrugged snobbishly and went on collecting myriad other recipes, all made from scratch, but that simple beef recipe kept popping up. Well, once we found it in *The Complete Meat Cookbook* by Bruce Aidells and Denis Kelly (Houghton Mifflin, 1998), we felt we had permission from the high priests to include it here. This is everybody's mom's recipe from the 1950s edition of *The Joy of Cooking*, which took advantage of the host of new packaged commercial foods designed to save time in the kitchen. Use the brisket, as we do here, or short ribs or a pot roast. It makes great leftovers. ❍ *Serves 8 to 10*

COOKER: Medium oval or large round or oval

SETTING AND COOK TIME: LOW for 6 to 9 hours

One 4- to 5-pound brisket or boneless chuck roast, trimmed of
    as much fat as possible and blotted dry

3 medium-size yellow onions, cut in half and thinly sliced into half moons

2 ribs celery, chopped

1 cup prepared chili sauce

One 12-ounce bottle beer (not dark)

½ cup water

1 package dried onion soup mix

1 teaspoon salt

¼ teaspoon freshly ground black pepper

1. Put the roast in the slow cooker. If the meat is too big to lie flat in your cooker, cut it in half and stack the pieces one atop the other. Add the sliced onions and the celery.

2. In a medium-size bowl, combine the chili sauce, beer, water, onion soup mix, salt, and pepper; pour it over the meat and vegetables. Cover and cook on LOW for 6 to 9 hours.

3. Skim off as much fat as possible from the sauce, slice the meat, and serve with the sauce.

Tangy Tomato Brisket

B risket is a stringy chunk of beef, cut from the cow's chest area. It is often turned into corned beef or barbecued beef Texas style, but it's also popular as a pot roast, especially among American Jews. Every published or photocopied synagogue cookbook has at least one recipe for a braised brisket. The flavors of the braising liquid range from the savory (broth, beer, or tomato juice) to the super sweet (Coca-Cola!). A constant is sliced onions, usually lots of them. When we began to experiment with briskets in the slow cooker, we faced the problem of too much liquid. Our solution was to concoct a sort of braising paste, based on tomato paste, rather than a braising liquid. As the meat releases its juices, the super-flavorful paste thins out into a lovely sauce, reminiscent of a barbecue sauce. If you want an abundance of sauce (perhaps to make knife-and-fork sandwiches), double the braising paste. ○ *Serves 6 to 8*

COOKER: Medium oval or large round or oval
SETTING AND COOK TIME: LOW for 5 to 7 hours

3 ounces tomato paste (half of a 6-ounce can)
¼ cup firmly packed light brown sugar
2 tablespoons cider vinegar
½ teaspoon Worcestershire sauce
⅛ teaspoon dry mustard
2 to 3 large cloves garlic, pressed
One 3- to 4-pound brisket, trimmed of as much fat as possible and blotted dry
Salt and freshly ground black pepper to taste
Paprika to taste
1 tablespoon oil of your choice
2 large or 3 small yellow onions, cut in half and thinly sliced into half-moons

1. In a small bowl, stir together the tomato paste, brown sugar, vinegar, Worcestershire, mustard, and garlic.

2. If the meat is too big to lie flat in your slow cooker, cut it in half. Season the meat generously with salt, pepper, and paprika.

3. In a large, heavy skillet, preferably one without a nonstick coating, heat the oil over high heat. When hot, brown the brisket very well, about 3 minutes per side. Transfer to a plate. Add the onions to the pan and cook, stirring a few times, until browned or even a bit blackened on the edges, 5 to 7 minutes.

4. Put half the onions in the cooker. (If you have cut your brisket into 2 pieces, place one-third of the onions in the cooker.) Smear the tomato paste mixture thickly on both sides of the brisket and place in the cooker, with the fattier side facing up. Top with the remaining onions. (If you have cut your brisket into 2 pieces, place one-third of the onions between the two pieces of brisket , and the remaining onions on top of the second piece.) Pour any meat juices from the plate over the brisket. Cover and cook on LOW until the brisket is tender when pierced with a fork, 5 to 7 hours.

5. Transfer to a cutting board and cut on the diagonal, against the grain, into thin slices. Pour the sauce into a bowl and allow to settle so that you can skim the fat. Serve the meat with the sauce and sliced onions.

Chopped Beef Sandwiches: Overcook the brisket slightly, 7 to 8 hours in all; it will be practically falling apart when you try to lift if from the sauce. Chop any large pieces of beef that remain, then use two forks to pull the meat apart into small pieces. Pile the meat and sauce onto warmed buns and serve hot.

Corned Beef and Cabbage

Once on a road trip on St. Patrick's Day, Beth stopped in a small brewery in Hopland, California. To the side of the old standup bar serving Red Tail Ale was a small restaurant. All the food was homemade in a kitchen the size of a large broom closet. The specialty that day was corned beef (spiced by the chef) and cabbage, steamed potatoes and carrots, homemade bread, and, for dessert, grasshopper pie in a chocolate cookie crust. The meal was memorable and she has been recreating it ever since. Corned beef is one of the most popular slow cooker dishes. ● *Serves 8*

COOKER: Medium or large round or oval
SETTINGS AND COOK TIMES: LOW for 9 to 11 hours for the meat,
   then HIGH for about 30 minutes for the cabbage

6 medium-size red potatoes, quartered
4 medium-size carrots, cut into 2-inch chunks on the diagonal
1 medium-size yellow onion, cut into 6 wedges
One 3- to 4-pound corned beef brisket with seasoning packet, rinsed
3 cloves
½ teaspoon black peppercorns
2 teaspoons firmly packed dark brown sugar
One 12-ounce can beer, strong or mild flavored
1 medium-size head white cabbage, cut into 8 wedges, each secured with
   kitchen twine so it doesn't fall apart in the cooker
½ cup Dijon mustard for serving

1. Put the potatoes, carrots, and onion in the slow cooker. Lay the corned beef on top of the vegetables and sprinkle with the seasonings from packet, the cloves, peppercorns, and brown sugar. If the meat is too big to lie flat in your cooker, cut it in half and stack the pieces one atop the other. Add the beer and enough water to just cover the brisket. Cover and cook on LOW for 9 to 11 hours.

2. Remove the corned beef and place in a serving casserole. Arrange the vegetables around the beef; cover with aluminum foil to keep warm.

3. Put the cabbage in the cooker with the cooking liquid and turn the setting to HIGH. Cover and cook until crisp-tender, 20 to 30 minutes.

4. Serve the beef, sliced across the grain, with the mustard, vegetables, and cabbage. Pass the juices from the crock in a bowl.

Corned Beef with Molasses-Bourbon Glaze

The slow cooker is perfect for corned beef. Here you give the meat some extra corning with your own blend of spices and glaze it in the oven for 15 minutes with a tasty sweet coating. Serve this with roasted potatoes and carrots instead of the usual cabbage accompaniment. ○ *Serves 6 to 8*

COOKER: Medium oval or large round or oval
SETTING AND COOK TIME: LOW for 9 to 11 hours; baked in the oven for 15 minutes to finish

One 3- to 4-pound corned beef brisket with seasoning packet, rinsed
2 bay leaves
8 black peppercorns
2 allspice berries
1 small cinnamon stick
1 teaspoon yellow mustard seeds
2 dried chiles de árbol

GLAZE:
1 cup firmly packed dark brown sugar
1 tablespoon dry mustard or Dijon mustard
¼ cup light molasses
⅓ cup bourbon

1. Put the corned beef in the slow cooker. If the meat is too big to lie flat in your cooker, cut it in half and stack the pieces one atop the other. Add water to just cover the brisket. Add the bay leaves, peppercorns, allspice, cinnamon, mustard seeds, and chiles. Cover and cook on LOW for 9 to 11 hours.

2. Meanwhile, make the glaze by mixing together the brown sugar, mustard, molasses, and bourbon in a medium-size bowl. Cover and refrigerate until needed.

3. When the brisket is tender, preheat the oven to 375°F. Line a large rimmed baking sheet with aluminum foil and coat with oil. Lift the brisket out of its cooking liquid and transfer to the baking sheet. Spoon the glaze over the beef to coat the entire surface on both sides. Bake, basting with any leftover glaze, for 15 minutes to set the glaze.

Red-Cooked Rump Roast

Red-cooked rump roast was a delicious surprise. The red-cooking liquid subtly flavors the entire roast, adding a gentle note of soy sauce and spice. Despite the long cooking time, the effect is not at all overpowering. This roast is delicious hot or at room temperature and it makes unbelievably wonderful cold sandwiches the next day. Try the sliced meat on crusty French rolls, with a smear or mayonnaise and a few rings of mild onion. For more details about red-cooking, see the recipe for Red-Cooked Chicken on page 286. You will need enough red-cooking liquid to cover the meat by at least two-thirds. ○ *Serves 8 to 10*

COOKER: Medium or large, oval preferred
SETTINGS AND COOK TIMES: HIGH for 30 minutes to 1 hour, then
   LOW for 7 to 8 hours; roast is turned at 4 hours on LOW

About 3 cups red-cooking liquid, fresh (see page 286) or reserved from previous uses
One 3-pound rump roast, blotted dry

1. Pour the red-cooking liquid into the slow cooker. Cover and cook on HIGH for 30 minutes to 1 hour.

2. Put the roast in the cooker and turn to coat both sides with liquid. It is okay if the liquid covers the roast completely. Cover, turn the heat to LOW, and cook for 4 hours.

3. Turn over the roast, cover, and continue to cook on LOW for 3 to 4 hours more.

4. Lift the roast out of the cooking liquid and place on a cutting board. Allow to cool a bit, then carve into thin slices (about ¼ inch thick) and serve with a few spoonfuls of the cooking liquid drizzled over it. Or, if you wish to serve it cold, refrigerate until chilled before slicing.

5. Allow the remaining cooking liquid to cool a bit, then pour it through a strainer into a heavy glass jar. Discard any solids. Refrigerate the liquid, but do not cap the jar until the liquid has cooled completely. It will keep in the refrigerator for a week to 10 days and in the freezer for up to 3 months. Thaw it before using. To reuse the red-cooking liquid, remove and discard the solidified fat on top. Pour the liquid into the slow cooker crock, and proceed as directed in the recipe with fresh meat. After every third or fourth use, refresh the liquid by adding ½ cup of soy sauce and half of the seasonings.

Crocked Beef Fajitas

T here are never enough recipes for flank steak, in our opinion. It is one of the tastiest, yet trickiest, cuts of beef to cook anywhere but outside on the grill. This is so simple, it is scary, because it is so good. Fajitas are eaten as a make-your-own-mini-burrito or soft taco. Unlike with other recipes, you don't have to marinate the meat first, since that is automatically taken care of as the meat slow-cooks. ○ *Serves 6*

COOKER: Medium round or oval
SETTING AND COOK TIME: LOW for 6 to 8 hours

¾ cup prepared chunky salsa, such as a fire-roasted one
1 tablespoon tomato paste
1 tablespoon olive oil
1 clove garlic, minced
3 tablespoons fresh lime juice
1 teaspoon freshly ground black pepper
½ teaspoon salt

One 1½-pound flank steak, trimmed of excess fat and silver skin

1 large white onion, cut in half and thinly sliced into half-moons

3 red bell peppers, seeded and cut into ¼-inch-wide strips

TO SERVE:

Warm flour tortillas (the small ones, not the *grandes* for burritos)

1 cup guacamole

1 cup chopped plum tomatoes

½ bunch fresh cilantro, chopped

1. In a small bowl, combine salsa, tomato paste, olive oil, garlic, lime juice, pepper, and salt. Lay the flank steak in the slow cooker and pour the mixture over it, making sure to coat all exposed surfaces well. Lay the onion and bell peppers on top. Cover and cook on LOW for 6 to 8 hours, until the meat is tender.

2. Remove the steak and vegetables from the juice and transfer to a serving platter. Cover with aluminum foil and let stand 10 minutes. Cut the meat across the grain into ½-inch-thick slices. Serve it heaped over warm tortillas, with the peppers and onions on top. Garnish with a dab of guacamole, the some chopped tomatoes, and the cilantro on top.

Swiss Steak

S wiss steak is not from Switzerland. Rather it is a favorite German dish that has been a fixture of American heartland cooking for more than a century. Thick beefsteak is tenderized by pounding it or "swissing" (hence the name of the dish), a technique reserved for formidable cuts of meat. Then the meat is braised with onions, tomatoes, mushrooms, and celery in a pot with a tight-fitting lid, usually over a low open fire, on the stove top, or in the oven. But the slow cooker does the job even better. The meat is cut into serving-size pieces, rather than left whole, and is accompanied with mashed potatoes, buttered egg noodles, or sautéed red cabbage. ❍ *Serves 6*

COOKER: Medium or large round or oval

SETTING AND COOK TIME: LOW for 9 to 10 hours

One 3-pound top round steak, 1 inch thick, edges trimmed,
    cut into 4- to 5-inch square pieces, and blotted dry
1 clove garlic, pressed
2 to 3 tablespoons Worcestershire sauce, to your taste
½ cup all-purpose flour
1 teaspoon dried thyme
½ teaspoon paprika
½ teaspoon salt
½ teaspoon freshly ground black pepper
2 to 4 tablespoons light olive oil
1 medium-size yellow onion, chopped
½ cup chopped carrots
½ cup thinly sliced celery
8 ounces fresh mushrooms, sliced
1 cup prepared chili sauce
1 cup vegetable broth

1. Rub each piece of meat with the garlic and Worcestershire. In a zippered-top plastic bag or bowl, combine the flour, thyme, paprika, salt, and black pepper. Toss the meat in the mixture until evenly coated. With a mallet, pound into both sides of the steak as much of the seasoned flour as the steak will hold. (You can do this in the plastic bag if you are careful.)

2. In a large skillet over medium-high heat, warm 1 tablespoon of the oil until very hot. Add half the meat and brown on all sides, 4 to 5 minutes. Transfer to the slow cooker. Repeat with the remaining meat, adding oil as needed. Add the onion to the skillet and cook, scraping up any browned bits stuck to the pan, until slightly softened, about 3 minutes. Transfer to the cooker. Toss the carrots and celery together in a small bowl and add them to the slow cooker along with the mushrooms, chili sauce, and broth, making sure the meat is nestled into the sauce mixture. Cover and cook on LOW until the meat is tender enough to cut with a fork, 9 to 10 hours.

3. At the end of cooking, taste for salt and pepper. Serve hot with the pan juices.

Mom's Beef Stew

Fancy is fine, but sometimes it's just too much. Here is the most basic beef stew you can imagine—beef, carrots, potatoes, onions, mushrooms, and peas in a gravy with a hint of tomato flavor—and, of course, it's the one we make the most. If you are cooking for a crowd, you can double the recipe, but leave out the potatoes, which take up a lot of room in the slow cooker. Then serve it over rice, noodles, or mashed potatoes that you have cooked separately. ◦ *Serves 6 to 8*

COOKER: Medium or large round or oval

SETTINGS AND COOK TIMES: LOW for 8 to 9 hours, then HIGH for about 15 minutes; or HIGH for 4¼ to 5¼ hours; peas added during last 15 minutes

8 to 12 small, flavorful boiling potatoes (1 to 1½ pounds total), such as Yellow Finn, Butterball, or Yukon Gold (for a large cooker, use the larger quantity)

4 large carrots, cut into 1 to 1½-inch lengths, really thick pieces halved lengthwise

½ cup all-purpose flour

½ teaspoon paprika

½ teaspoon salt

⅛ teaspoon freshly ground black pepper

2 to 2½ pounds boneless beef chuck, trimmed of any excess fat, cut into 1½-inch chunks, and blotted dry

1 to 2 tablespoons olive oil, as needed

1 large onion, or 2 small onions, cut into a total of 6 or 8 wedges

1 large rib celery, outer strings removed with a knife or vegetable peeler, and sliced ½ inch thick

6 to 8 medium-size fresh mushrooms, cut in half

2 cups beef broth

¼ cup tomato paste

1 tablespoon soy sauce

1 tablespoon red wine vinegar

½ teaspoon sugar

Pinch of ground cloves

Salt and freshly ground black pepper (optional) to taste

1 small bay leaf

2 sprigs fresh flat-leaf parsley

One 10-ounce package frozen peas, thawed

1. Place the potatoes in the slow cooker. Top with the carrots.

2. In a zippered-top plastic bag or a bowl, combine the flour, paprika, salt, and pepper. Toss the beef in the mixture, shaking off any excess, and transfer to a plate. Repeat with the remaining meat.

3. In a large skillet, heat 1 tablespoon of the oil over medium-high heat. Add some of the meat, being careful not to crowd the skillet. Allow to brown on the first side before gently stirring and turning so the pieces can brown all over. As the pieces are browned, use a slotted spoon to transfer to the cooker. Repeat with the remaining meat, adding more oil to the skillet if necessary.

4. When all of the meat has been browned, add the onion, celery, and mushrooms to the cooker and stir gently to distribute them throughout the meat, trying not to disturb the potatoes and carrots on the bottom layer.

5. In a bowl or 4-cup glass measure, stir together the broth, tomato paste, soy sauce, vinegar, sugar, and cloves. Pour into the cooker. If the broth is unseasoned, season with salt and pepper. Tuck the bay leaf and parsley sprigs into the stew. Cover and cook on LOW for 8 to 9 hours, or cook on HIGH for 4 to 5 hours.

6. Discard the parsley and bay leaf. Stir in the peas, cover, and cook on HIGH until the peas are hot, 10 to 15 minutes. Serve the stew hot, on plates or in shallow bowls.

Beef Ragoût

H ere is another wonderful beef stew. For the red wine, use a Chianti or Zinfandel for character. Be sure to brown the meat for the best flavor. We love this one with spaetzle dumplings, steamed white rice, or buttered egg noodles.

○ *Serves 4 to 5*

COOKER: Medium or large round or oval
SETTINGS AND COOK TIMES: LOW for 6 to 7 hours, then HIGH for 45 minutes; salt, pepper, zucchini, and mushrooms added during last 45 minutes

2 tablespoons olive oil
2 pounds lean beef stew meat or beef cross rib roast, trimmed of fat, cut into 1½-inch chunks, and blotted dry

2 medium-size onions, coarsely chopped

2 large tomatoes, peeled, seeded, and chopped, or
  one 14.5-ounce can diced tomatoes with their juice

1 cup dry red wine

1 cup baby carrots

2 cloves garlic, minced

2 tablespoons quick-cooking tapioca

1 teaspoon dried Italian herb seasoning

½ teaspoon salt

¼ teaspoon freshly ground black pepper

2 medium-size zucchini, ends trimmed, cut in half lengthwise and
  sliced crosswise into ¼-inch-thick half-moons

8 ounces fresh mushrooms, thickly sliced

1. In a large skillet over medium-high heat, warm 1 tablespoon of the oil until very hot. Add half of the beef and brown on all sides, 3 to 4 minutes total. Transfer to the slow cooker. Add the remaining 1 tablespoon of oil and brown the remaining beef.

2. Add the onions to the skillet and brown slightly over medium-high heat. Add the tomatoes and wine and bring to a boil, scraping up any browned bits stuck to the pan; pour into the cooker. Add the carrots, garlic, tapioca, and Italian herbs to the cooker. Cover and cook on LOW for 6 to 7 hours.

3. Add the salt, pepper, zucchini, and mushrooms, cover, turn the cooker to HIGH, and cook for about 45 minutes, until the meat, mushrooms, and zucchini are tender. Serve in shallow bowls or on rimmed dinner plates.

Hungarian Beef Stew with Paprika and Marjoram

T he Hungarians are masters of this country stew, traditionally made in a *bogrács,* or cauldron, over an open fire. The slow cooker is a perfect medium: a heavy cooking vessel and slow, low temperature. It is a stew that cannot be rushed, and the taste will tell you just how wonderful this old-fashioned meal-in-a-bowl is. It is thinner than a regular stew, thickened with potatoes and often served with egg noodles stirred in at the end, although this is optional for American palates. You can vary the dish by adding shredded cabbage or a combination of carrots, kohlrabi, and green beans, cut into 1-inch pieces, and added halfway through cooking. The paprika can be sweet or hot, so long as it is imported Hungarian paprika. Beth loves this method of cooking the garlic; it is put on a toothpick and discarded after cooking. Hearty braised goulash needs only crusty bread and a nice white wine. Goulash is traditionally served from the cooking pot at the table. This recipe is adapted from Susan Derecskey, one of Beth's copyeditors and the author of *The Hungarian Cookbook* (Harper and Row, 1972), one of Beth's favorites. ◦ *Serves 4*

COOKER: Medium round or oval
SETTING AND COOK TIME: LOW for 7 to 8 hours

3 tablespoons olive oil, another cooking oil, or lard

1½ pounds lean beef stew meat, trimmed of fat, cut into 1½-inch chunks, and blotted dry

1 medium-size onion, coarsely chopped

1 medium-size green bell pepper, seeded and cut into ½-inch-wide strips

1 teaspoon paprika

2½ cups beef broth

1½ cups water

Large pinch of dried marjoram

¼ teaspoon caraway seeds, crushed well in a mortar with a pestle,
    or pulsed in a mini–food processor

¾ cup tomato purée

2 cloves garlic, peeled and stuck on toothpicks

Salt to taste

1. In a large skillet over medium-high heat, warm 1½ tablespoons of the oil until very hot. Add the beef and brown on all sides, 3 to 4 minutes total.

2. Put the meat in the slow cooker.

3. Add the onion and bell pepper to the skillet, add the remaining 1½ tablespoons of oil, and brown slightly over medium-high heat, stirring a few times, about 5 minutes. Add the paprika and stir a bit. Add the broth and water and bring to a boil, scraping up any browned bits stuck to the pan; pour into the cooker. Add the marjoram, caraway, and tomato purée. Nestle the garlic into the stew. The meat should be covered with the cooking liquid. Cover and cook on LOW until the meat is tender, 7 to 8 hours.

4. Remove the garlic and discard. Taste for salt and serve.

Estofado

(E) *stofado* is a Southwestern beef stew. Beth makes this all the time with whatever salsa is in the refrigerator, whether it be from a jar or freshly made. Use a good red wine vinegar, such as a Zinfandel or Cabernet vinegar. You might want to bake up a batch of Cheese Biscuits (page 333) to go along with this as well. ○ *Serves 4*

COOKER: Medium or large round
SETTING AND COOK TIME: LOW for 6 to 8 hours

2 pounds beef stew meat, such as boneless chuck, trimmed of any excess fat,
    cut into 1- to 1½-inch chunks, and blotted dry
Salt and freshly ground black pepper to taste
2 tablespoons all-purpose or whole wheat pastry flour
3 tablespoons olive oil
1 large yellow onion, finely chopped
1 cup smooth or chunky tomato salsa, homemade (page 241) or prepared
3 tablespoons red wine vinegar
Pinch of dried oregano or marjoram
¼ cup water
⅓ cup dry red wine
2 tablespoons chopped fresh flat-leaf parsley

1. In a zippered-top plastic bag or a bowl, toss the beef, in batches, with the salt, pepper, and flour.

2. In a large skillet over medium-high heat, warm 1½ tablespoons of the oil until very hot. Add the onion and cook, stirring, until softened, about 5 minutes, then transfer to the crock. Add half the beef to the skillet and brown on all sides, 3 to 4 minutes total. Transfer to the slow cooker. Brown the remaining beef in the oil and add to the cooker. Add the salsa, vinegar, oregano, and water to the cooker and stir to evenly distribute.

3. Pour the wine into the skillet and place over medium heat. Stir constantly, scraping up any browned bits stuck to the pan; it will reduce a bit. Pour into the cooker and stir. Cover and cook on LOW for 6 to 8 hours.

4. Season with salt and pepper and stir in the parsley. If the *estofado* is too thin for you, use a *beurre manié* (page 20) to thicken it a bit. Serve with rice.

• • Homemade Biscuits • •

One of the best quick-and-easy breads to make to serve with your stews are biscuits. These come together quickly and bake in a flash. Remember the secret to good biscuits is to work the dough as little as possible and keep it moist by adding very little flour while cutting out the biscuits. ○ Makes about 1 dozen biscuits

2 cups unbleached all-purpose flour or whole wheat pastry flour,
   plus 2 tablespoons for sprinkling
2 tablespoons yellow cornmeal for sprinkling
2 teaspoons baking powder
¼ teaspoon baking soda
¼ teaspoon salt
6 tablespoons (¾ stick) cold unsalted butter, margarine,
   or solid vegetable shortening, cut into pieces
1 large egg
¾ cup cold buttermilk

1. Preheat the oven to 425°F. Line a baking sheet with parchment paper and sprinkle it with the 2 tablespoons flour and then the cornmeal.

2. In a large bowl, whisk together the 2 cups of flour, baking powder, baking soda, and salt. Cut the butter into the dry ingredients with a pastry blender, 2 knives, or your finger-tips, or process briefly in a food processor. The mixture should resemble coarse crumbs, with no large chunks of butter. If the butter gets very soft at this point, refrigerate the mixture for 20 minutes to rechill. Add the egg and buttermilk, stirring just to moisten all the ingredients. The dough will be moist and a bit sticky.

3. Turn out the dough onto a lightly floured work surface and pat it out into a rectangle about ¾ inch thick. Take care not to add too much flour at this point or the biscuits will be tough. Cut with a floured 2½-inch biscuit cutter or glass, pushing straight down without twisting. Dip the cutter into flour before cutting each biscuit to avoid sticking. Cut the biscuits as close together as possible for a minimum of scraps. Pack together and reroll the scraps to cut out additional biscuits.

4. Place the biscuits ½ inch apart on the baking sheet. Bake immediately in the preheated oven until golden brown, 15 to 18 minutes. Serve hot.

Cheese Biscuits o Makes about 1 dozen biscuits

After catering a party or dinner there is always lots of cheese left over, and what to do? Make some wonderful biscuits with the Brie or Gouda.

2 cups unbleached all-purpose flour plus 2 tablespoons for sprinkling

1 tablespoon sesame seeds for sprinkling

1 tablespoon baking powder

¼ teaspoon salt

5 tablespoons cold unsalted butter, margarine, or solid vegetable shortening, cut into pieces

¾ cup cold buttermilk

4 ounces Brie (most of the rind removed), Gouda, smoked mozzarella,
  or Monterey Jack cheese, cut into ½-inch cubes

1. Preheat the oven to 450°F. Line a baking sheet with parchment paper and sprinkle with the 2 tablespoons of flour, then with the sesame seeds.

2. In a medium-size bowl, whisk together the 2 cups of flour, baking powder, and salt. Cut the butter into the dry ingredients with a pastry blender, 2 knives, or your fingertips, or process briefly in a food processor. The mixture should resemble coarse crumbs, with no large chunks of butter. If the butter gets very soft at this point, refrigerate the mixture for 20 minutes to rechill. Add the buttermilk, stirring just to moisten all the ingredients. Fold in the Brie cubes. The dough will be moist and a bit sticky.

3. Turn out the dough onto a lightly floured work surface and pat it out into a rectangle about ¾ inch thick. Take care not to add too much flour at this point or the biscuits will be tough. Cut with a floured 2½-inch biscuit cutter or glass, pushing straight down without twisting. Dip the cutter into flour before cutting each biscuit to avoid sticking. Cut as close together as possible for a minimum of scraps. Pack together and reroll the scraps to cut out additional biscuits.

4. Place the biscuits ½ inch apart on the baking sheet. Bake immediately in the preheated oven until golden brown, 10 to 14 minutes. Serve hot.

Japanese-Style Beef Curry Rice

Mildly spiced curried stews served over rice are extremely popular in Japan. The classic version consists of beef, onions, potatoes, and carrots in a flour-thickened sauce. Thanks to shelf-stable pouches of prepared curries and packaged curry sauce mixes, curry rice is a quick and kid-friendly lunch or dinner in countless Japanese homes, as well as school and company cafeterias. Here's a version you can make at home. If you don't like a thick background to your beef stew, just skip the thickening step, reduce the amount of curry powder to 2 teaspoons, and omit the water. Add the curry powder to the onions when you are sautéing. For authentic flavor, look for a Japanese brand of curry powder in your Asian market. Definitely serve your beef curry over steamed Japanese-style rice, which would be a short- or medium-grain white rice. ○ *Serves 4*

COOKER: Medium or large round or oval

SETTINGS AND COOK TIMES: LOW for 6 to 7 hours, then HIGH for about 30 minutes; flour, peas, and curry powder added during last 30 minutes

3 medium-size baking potatoes, peeled and cut into 1-inch chunks

3 to 4 medium-size carrots, cut into ½-inch-thick rounds or half-moons

¼ cup vegetable oil

1 pound beef stew meat, such as boneless chuck, trimmed of fat, cut into 1-inch cubes, and blotted dry

1 medium-size onion, chopped

1 clove garlic, minced

1 teaspoon salt

½ teaspoon freshly ground black pepper

2 cups beef broth

2 cups water

3 tablespoons all-purpose flour

1 tablespoon curry powder

1 cup frozen peas (optional), thawed

Hot short- or medium-grain cooked white rice for serving

1. Put the potatoes in the slow cooker. Layer the carrots on top.

2. In a large nonstick skillet over medium heat, heat 1 tablespoon of the oil. Add the beef and brown on all sides. You may have to do this in batches. Transfer the meat to the cooker. Heat another tablespoon of the oil in the skillet, add the onion and garlic, and cook, stirring a few times, until softened, about 5 minutes. Add the salt and pepper and cook 2 to 3 minutes more. Transfer to the cooker. Pour the broth into the skillet, bring to a boil, and scrape up any browned bits stuck to the pan. Pour into the cooker and add the water. Cover and cook on LOW until the meat is tender and the vegetables cooked through, 6 to 7 hours.

3. In a small skillet or saucepan, heat the remaining 2 tablespoons of oil over medium-high heat. Add the flour and cook, stirring, until it begins to brown, about 5 minutes. Add the curry powder and stir about 1 minute more. Remove from the heat. Turn the cooker to HIGH. Scoop out ½ cup of the liquid from the cooker, add it to the flour mixture, and stir until no lumps remain. A little bit at a time, stir the flour mixture into the stew, working carefully so as not to break up the potatoes and the carrots. Stir in the frozen peas if using. Cover the slow cooker and continue to cook on HIGH until the sauce is thickened and the peas are hot, 20 to 30 minutes. Put the rice in bowls and serve the curry on top.

Beef in Guinness

B eef in Guinness is a good English-style recipe, which comes from our Brit friend Susie Dymoke, who loves her aged 4-quart Rival slow cooker. A self-taught cook, Susie had the honor of working with Michel Roux at the Waterside Inn at Bray, which was awarded three Michelin stars, and cooking for members of the royal household before becoming director of the culinary program of Sur La Table, in Los Gatos, California, for its first two and a half years.

Guinness stout, a bittersweet combination of hops and roasted barley, contributes to the flavor of this stew, a simplified cousin of the Flemish *carbonnade au boeuf,* so don't substitute another brew. Beer is an excellent braising liquid when the tenderness of the meat is in doubt. You want the dark beer rather than Pilsner-style American beer, which is more bitter. This American rendition calls for a chuck roast that you cube yourself, rather than regular stew meat, but

British cooks look for shin beef, which has a lot of connective tissue and gives a velvety texture to the stew. Serve with mashed potatoes or buttered egg noodles.

● *Serves 6*

COOKER: Medium or large round or oval
SETTING AND COOK TIME: LOW for 8 to 9 hours

One 2½-pound 7-bone chuck roast, trimmed of excess fat,
    cut into 1½-inch chunks, and blotted dry
3 to 4 tablespoons all-purpose flour
1 teaspoon salt
¼ teaspoon freshly ground black pepper
¼ cup olive oil
3 medium-size yellow onions, roughly chopped
One 14.9-ounce can or bottle Guinness stout
1 pound baby carrots
3 medium-size turnips, peeled and diced
1 medium-size (1-pound) eggplant, peeled or not, diced
8 ounces fresh mushrooms, sliced
2 cloves garlic, finely chopped
Zest of ½ large orange, cut into strips
1 bouquet garni: 3 or 4 sprigs fresh flat-leaf parsley, 3 or 4 sprigs fresh thyme,
    ⅓ fresh California bay leaf or 1 whole dried Turkish one, one 2-inch piece of celery,
    tied together in a cheesecloth sqaure

1. In a zippered-top plastic bag or a bowl, toss the meat, in batches, with the flour, salt, and pepper, shaking off the excess. In a large skillet over medium-high heat, warm 2 tablespoons of the oil until very hot. Add half the meat and cook until browned on all sides, 4 to 5 minutes total. Transfer to the crock. Repeat with the remaining oil and meat. Transfer to the slow cooker.

2. Add the onions to the skillet and cook, scraping up any browned bits stuck to the pan, until softened slightly, about 3 minutes; transfer to the cooker. Pour in the beer, and in layers add the carrots, turnips, eggplant, mushrooms, and garlic on top of the meat. Nestle the orange zest and bouquet garni into the center of the meat and vegetables. Cover and cook on LOW until the meat is tender enough to cut with a fork, 8 to 9 hours.

3. Remove the bouquet garni, then taste for salt and pepper, and serve.

Braised Beef in Espresso

T he addition of coffee to a beef stew may look new and innovative, but it is one of the oldest methods of enriching a sauce. You can use freshly brewed strong coffee or instant espresso powder dissolved in boiling water. Try topping this stew with dumplings if you like (see page 143). ○ *Serves 6*

COOKER: Medium or large round or oval
SETTING AND COOK TIME: LOW for 7 to 8 hours

3 pounds beef stew meat, such as boneless chuck, trimmed of fat,
    cut into 1½-inch chunks, and blotted dry
2 tablespoons all-purpose flour
Pinch of salt
Pinch of freshly ground black pepper
3 tablespoons olive oil
2 medium-size onions, chopped
3 carrots, cut diagonally into 2-inch chunks
4 new red or white potatoes, diced
6 small turnips, peeled and quartered
1 cup strong coffee
½ teaspoon dried thyme
½ cup dry red wine

1. In a zippered-top plastic bag or a bowl, toss the beef with the flour, salt, and pepper, shaking off the excess. In a large skillet over medium-high heat, warm 1½ tablespoons of the oil until very hot. Add half the beef and brown on all sides, about 5 minutes. Transfer to the slow cooker. Repeat with the remaining oil and beef.

2. Add the onions to the skillet and cook, stirring, until softened, about 5 minutes. Transfer to the cooker and add the carrots, potatoes, and turnips. Add the coffee and thyme to the cooker. Pour the wine into the skillet and bring to a boil over medium heat, stirring constantly and scraping up any browned bits stuck to the pan. Pour into the cooker and stir. Cover and cook on LOW until the meat is tender, 7 to 8 hours. Taste for salt and pepper, and serve.

Sloppy Joes

S loppy Joes are a perennial lunch and suppertime American favorite—and not just among kids! We've had turkey Joes and tofu Joes, but we like the sandwiches made with good ol' hamburger best. For a sloppier, knife-and-fork version, add 1 cup of tomato sauce to the beef mixture before slow cooking. You can double this recipe using the same size cooker. ○ *Serves 4*

COOKER: Medium round or oval
SETTING AND COOK TIME: LOW for 6 to 7 hours

1 pound lean ground beef

1 medium-size onion, finely chopped

½ large red bell pepper, seeded and finely chopped

1 large rib celery, finely chopped

1 clove garlic, minced

One 6-ounce can tomato paste

2 tablespoons cider vinegar, or more as needed

2 tablespoons firmly packed light or dark brown sugar, or more as needed

1 teaspoon paprika

½ teaspoon dry mustard

¾ teaspoon salt

½ teaspoon chili powder, or to taste

¼ teaspoon freshly ground black pepper, or to taste

1 teaspoon Worcestershire sauce

Dash of hot sauce, such as Tabasco

Dash of cayenne pepper

Hamburger buns or other soft sandwich rolls for serving

1. In a large, nonstick skillet over medium-high heat, cook the beef with the onion, bell pepper, celery, and garlic, stirring to break up the meat. When the meat is cooked through, transfer the meat and vegetables to the slow cooker. Add the remaining Sloppy Joe ingredients and stir to combine well. Cover and cook on LOW for 6 to 7 hours.

2. Taste and add more vinegar or sugar, if desired. Serve the meat mixture spooned into the buns.

California Tamale Pie with Corn and Black Olives

T amale pie is really a casserole that combines the ingredients found in old-fashioned tamales. It takes a fraction of the time of the old-fashioned version and out comes a delicious hot meal. Use fresh corn in the summer and frozen or canned corn in the winter. For a great lunch or dinner, all it needs is a salad and chopped fresh tomatoes, with flan or ice cream for dessert. ○ *Serves 4*

COOKER: Medium round or oval

SETTING AND COOK TIME: HIGH for 3 to 4 hours; cheese and oil added during last 10 minutes

1 pound lean ground beef

2 small white onions, chopped

3 tablespoons pure mild to medium-hot ground chile powder, like ancho or pasilla

¾ cup medium-grind yellow cornmeal

1¼ cups whole milk

2 large eggs, beaten

1 to 2 teaspoons salt, to your taste

Pinch of ground cumin

One 16-ounce can stewed tomatoes, drained and chopped

3 to 4 ears fresh corn, kernels cut off the cob; or 2 cups frozen corn, thawed; or drained canned whole-kernel corn

One 14-ounce can pitted ripe California black olives, drained, and coarsely chopped or halved

1½ cups shredded sharp cheddar cheese, or a combination of cheddar and Monterey Jack cheese

1 to 2 tablespoons olive oil

1. Coat the slow cooker with nonstick cooking spray. Heat a medium-size nonstick skillet over medium heat. Add the beef and onions and cook until the meat is no longer pink and the onion is limp, using a wooden spoon or spatula to break up the meat. Drain the fat from the pan and sprinkle the meat with the chile powder. Cook for 1 minute and transfer the meat and onions to the slow cooker.

2. In a large bowl, whisk together the cornmeal, milk, egg, salt, and cumin with a whisk until smooth. Stir in the tomatoes, corn, and olives, then pour the mixture into the cooker and stir to combine all the ingredients. Cover and cook on HIGH for 3 to 4 hours.

3. Sprinkle the cheese over the top, drizzle with the oil, cover, and continue to cook on HIGH for 10 minutes more to melt the cheese. Serve spooned directly from the crock.

Tex-Mex Enchiladas

H ere is our version of meat enchiladas in a luscious quick red chile sauce, courtesy of our wonderful cooking friend, Jacquie Higuera McMahan. You must make the sauce first, which only takes about 30 minutes, but it can be made a day or two ahead and reheated. ○ *Serves 4 to 5*

COOKER: Medium round or oval
SETTING AND COOK TIME: LOW for 6 to 7 hours

ENCHILADA RED SAUCE:
1 tablespoon olive oil
3 cloves garlic, minced
1 teaspoon dried oregano
½ teaspoon ground cumin
One 28-ounce can red chile purée, preferably Las Palmas brand
2 tablespoons masa harina
⅔ cup water
1 to 2 tablespoons pure New Mexican red chile powder, to your taste
1 tablespoon light or dark brown sugar

1½ pounds lean ground beef
1 medium-size white onion, chopped
½ teaspoon salt
½ teaspoon freshly ground black pepper
6 soft yellow or white corn tortillas
3 to 4 ears fresh corn, kernels cut off the cob; or 2½ cups frozen corn, thawed;
    or drained canned whole-kernel corn

2 cups shredded sharp cheddar cheese, or a combination
    of cheddar and Monterey Jack cheese
Two 2.5-ounce cans sliced ripe California olives, drained

FOR SERVING:
Sour cream
Guacamole

1. To make the sauce, in a medium-size skillet over medium heat, warm the olive oil and cook the garlic, stirring, for a minute; do not brown. Add the herbs and red chile purée, bring to a simmer, and cook for 15 minutes. Whisk together the masa harina and water, then whisk into the sauce; simmer for 10 minutes. Stir in the red chile powder and brown sugar and cook for another 10 minutes.

2. In a medium-size skillet over high heat, cook the ground beef and onion until the meat is no longer pink and the onion is limp, using a wooden spoon or spatula to break up the meat. Add the salt and pepper.

3. Coat the slow cooker with nonstick cooking spray. Place 2 tortillas in the bottom of the cooker. In layers add one-third of the meat, corn, sauce, cheese, and olives. Repeat the layers 2 more times, beginning with the tortillas and ending with the olives. Cover and cook on LOW for 6 to 7 hours.

4. Serve straight out of the cooker and accompany with sour cream and guacamole.

Old-Fashioned Meat Loaf

Many cooks swear the meat loaf that emerges from a slow cooker is better than any that comes out of an oven. Please note the directions include a technique for removing the tender free-form loaf without breaking it. We have included five recipes in this chapter from which to choose. This one is our basic, which most resembles Mom's meat loaf from way back when. ○ *Serves 6*

COOKER: Medium or large round or oval
SETTINGS AND COOK TIMES: HIGH for 1 hour, then LOW for 6 hours;
    ketchup and bell pepper rings added during last 30 minutes

MEAT LOAF:

1½ pounds ground chuck

1 large egg, beaten

1 or 2 slices whole wheat or white sandwich bread

¼ cup minced onion

¼ cup minced green, red, or yellow bell pepper

¼ cup minced celery

2 teaspoons seasoned salt or salt-free herb blend, such as Mrs. Dash or McCormick

¼ teaspoon dried thyme

A few grinds of black pepper

½ cup tomato juice or V-8 vegetable juice

TOPPING:

¾ cup ketchup or prepared chili sauce

4 bell pepper rings, ½ inch thick

1. Combine the ground chuck and egg in a large bowl. Tear the bread slices into quarters or eighths, put in a food processor, and pulse until reduced to about ½ cup of crumbs. Transfer to the bowl. (Alternately, tear the bread into 1-inch pieces, place in a bowl, pour over ¼ cup of the tomato juice, then add the meat.) Add the onion, minced bell pepper, celery, salt, thyme, pepper, and tomato juice. Using your hands or a large fork, mix gently but thoroughly.

2. Make an aluminum foil "cradle" that will help you easily remove the meat loaf from the slow cooker when it is done: Tear off a sheet of foil about 24 inches long. Place along the edge of the counter, and tear in half lengthwise. Fold each piece in half lengthwise, then in half again. Place the strips in the cooker in a cross shape, centering them. The edges of the strips will hang over the edge of the cooker. Place the meat mixture on top of the strips and shape into an oval or round loaf, depending on the shape of your cooker, by pressing it gently, evening out the top, and shaping it to fit your cooker. Bend the foil strips toward the meat loaf so they will not prevent the cover of the cooker from closing properly. Cover and cook on HIGH for 1 hour.

3. Turn the cooker to LOW and cook until an instant-read meat thermometer inserted in the center of the meat loaf registers at least 160° to 165°F, about 6 hours.

4. About 30 minutes before the end of the cooking time, bend the foil strips out of the way, pour the ketchup over the top of the loaf, and arrange the pepper rings decoratively over the meat loaf. Cover and cook for another 30 minutes on LOW.

5. To serve, lift the meat loaf onto a cutting board or serving platter, using the foil "handles." Slide out and discard the foil strips. Slice the meat loaf and serve hot or refrigerate and serve cold the next day.

Classic Meat Loaf

W e love this meat loaf with its classic combination of beef, pork, and veal. Its secret ingredient is oatmeal, which replaces the traditional breadcrumbs. We think you will love it, too. Be sure to serve with lots of ketchup. ○ *Serves 6*

COOKER: Medium or large round or oval
SETTINGS AND COOK TIMES: HIGH for 1 hour, then LOW for 6 hours; ketchup added during last 30 minutes

1 tablespoon olive oil
½ cup minced onion
1¼ pounds ground sirloin
½ pound ground pork
½ pound ground veal
1 large egg (optional), beaten
¾ cup quick-cooking rolled oats
1 cup ketchup
2 tablespoons Worcestershire sauce
1 teaspoon salt
A few grinds of black pepper

1. Heat the oil in a small skillet over medium heat and cook the onion, stirring, until softened, about 5 minutes; let cool.

2. Put the ground meats and egg, if using, in a large bowl. Add the sautéed onion, oats, ½ cup of the ketchup, the Worcestershire, salt, and pepper. Using your hands or a large fork, mix gently but thoroughly, being careful not to compact the meat.

3. Make an aluminum foil "cradle" that will help you easily remove the meat loaf from the slow cooker when it is done: Tear off a sheet of foil about 24 inches long. Place along the edge of the counter, and tear in half lengthwise. Fold each piece in half lengthwise, then in half again. Place the strips in the cooker in a cross shape, centering them. The edges of the strips will hang over the edge of the cooker. Place the meat mixture on top of the strips and shape into an oval or round loaf, depending on the shape of your cooker, by pressing it gently, evening out the top, and shaping it to fit your cooker. Bend the foil strips toward the meat loaf so they will not prevent the cover of the cooker from closing properly. Cover and cook on HIGH for 1 hour.

4. Turn the cooker to LOW and cook until an instant-read meat thermometer inserted in the center of the meat loaf registers at least 160° to 165°F, about 6 hours.

5. Thirty minutes before the end of cooking, bend the strips out of the way and pour the remaining ½ cup of ketchup over the meat loaf. Cover and cook for another 30 minutes on LOW.

6. To serve, lift the meat loaf onto a cutting board or serving platter, using the foil "handles." Slide out and discard the foil strips. Slice the meat loaf and serve hot or refrigerate and serve cold the next day.

Salsa Meat Loaf

his is Beth's basic meat loaf. The salsa keeps it moist, and the oatmeal binds the ingredients together. It takes very little time to assemble, which makes it ideal for a weeknight supper. ○ *Serves 6 to 8*

COOKER: Medium or large round or oval
SETTINGS AND COOK TIMES: HIGH for 1 hour, then LOW for 6 hours;
    salsa topping added during last 30 minutes

2 pounds ground sirloin

1 large egg, beaten

½ cup quick-cooking rolled oats

1½ cups thick prepared tomato salsa of your choice, mild or medium

3 tablespoons minced red onion

2 teaspoons dried marjoram or oregano

1 teaspoon ground cumin

1 teaspoon salt

A few grinds of black pepper

1 tablespoon olive oil

1. Combine the ground beef, egg, oats, and 1 cup of the salsa in a large bowl. Add the onion, marjoram, cumin, salt, and pepper. Using your hands or a large fork, mix gently but thoroughly, being careful not to compact the meat.

2. Make an aluminum foil "cradle" that will help you easily remove the meat loaf from the slow cooker when it is done: Tear off a sheet of foil about 24 inches long. Place along the edge of the counter, and tear in half lengthwise. Fold each piece in half lengthwise, then in half again. Place the strips in the cooker in a cross shape, centering them. The edges of the strips will hang over the edge of the cooker. Place the meat mixture on top of the strips and shape into an oval or round loaf, depending on the shape of your cooker, by pressing it gently, evening out the top, and shaping it to fit your cooker. Bend the foil strips toward the meat loaf so they will not prevent the cover of the cooker from closing properly. Cover and cook on HIGH for 1 hour.

3. Turn the cooker to LOW and cook until an instant-read meat thermometer inserted in the center of the meat loaf registers at least 160° to 165°F, about 6 hours.

4. About 30 minutes before the end of the cooking time, combine the oil with the remaining ½ cup salsa. Bend the foil strips out of the way and pour the salsa mixture over the meat loaf. Cover and cook for another 30 minutes on LOW.

5. To serve, lift the meat loaf onto a cutting board or serving platter, using the foil "handles." Slide out and discard the foil strips. Slice the meat loaf and serve hot or refrigerate and serve cold the next day.

Fresh Chile and Corn Chip Meat Loaf

T he addition of corn chips crushed into crumbs gives this meat loaf a decidedly different flavor—sweet and earthy. It's another simple recipe, and a good way to use up all those corn chips after a party. ◦ *Serves 4 to 6*

COOKER: Medium or large round or oval

SETTINGS AND COOK TIMES: HIGH for 1 hour, then LOW for 5 to 6 hours

1½ pounds lean ground chuck or sirloin

1 cup baked corn chips, crushed or whirled in the food processor to make coarse crumbs

1 small white boiling onion, minced

1 jalapeño, seeded and finely chopped

3 tablespoons finely chopped fresh cilantro

1 teaspoon chili powder

½ teaspoon ground cumin

¼ teaspoon salt

1 large egg, slightly beaten

One 8-ounce can tomato sauce

1. Combine the ground beef, corn chip crumbs, onion, jalapeño, cilantro, chili powder, cumin, salt, egg, and half of the tomato sauce in a large bowl. Using your hands or a large fork, mix gently but thoroughly, being careful not to compact the meat.

2. Make an aluminum foil "cradle" that will help you easily remove the meat loaf from the slow cooker when it is done: Tear a sheet of foil that is about 24 inches long. Place it along the edge of the counter and tear in half the long way. Fold each piece in half lengthwise, then in half again lengthwise. Place the strips in the cooker in a cross shape, centering them. The edges of the strips will hang over the edge of the cooker. Place the meat mixture on top of the strips and shape into an oval or round loaf, depending on the shape of your cooker, by pressing it gently, evening out the top, and shaping it to fit your cooker. Bend the strips toward the meat loaf so they will not prevent the cover from closing properly. Spoon the remaining tomato sauce over the loaf. Cover and cook on HIGH for 1 hour.

3. Turn the cooker to LOW and cook until an instant-read meat thermometer inserted in the center of the meat loaf registers at least 160° to 165°F, 5 to 6 hours.

4. To serve, lift the meat loaf onto a cutting board or serving platter, using the foil "handles." Slide out and discard the foil strips. Slice the meat loaf and serve hot or refrigerate and serve cold the next day.

Meat Loaf on a Bed of Potatoes

 If you are a meat loaf lover, you will enjoy this variation—the meat loaf is placed on top of sliced potatoes, and they cook in the crock at the same time. ○ *Serves 6 to 8*

COOKER: Medium or large round or oval
SETTINGS AND COOK TIMES: HIGH for 1 hour, then LOW for 6 to 7 hours

MEAT LOAF:
2 tablespoons olive oil
3 large russet potatoes, peeled and cut into 1- to 1½-inch cubes
2 pounds ground sirloin
2 large eggs, beaten
¾ cup crushed saltine crackers (saltless tops are okay)
¾ cup ketchup
1 teaspoon salt
A few grinds of black pepper

TOPPING:
¾ cup ketchup
⅓ cup firmly packed light brown sugar
1 teaspoon Dijon mustard

1. Grease the bottom of the slow cooker insert with the olive oil. Add the potatoes, toss lightly to coat, and arrange in a neat bed.

2. Combine the ground beef, eggs, crumbs, ketchup, salt, and pepper in a large bowl. Using your hands or a large fork, mix gently but thoroughly, being careful not to compact the meat. Shape the mixture into an oval or round loaf, depending on the shape of your cooker, and place on top of the layer of potatoes.

3. To make the topping, stir together the ingredients in a small bowl and pour over the meat loaf. Cover and cook on HIGH for 1 hour.

4. Turn the cooker to LOW and cook until an instant-read meat thermometer inserted in the center of the meat loaf registers at least 160° to 165°F, 6 to 7 hours.

5. To serve, lift the meat loaf onto a cutting board or serving platter, using a large spatula. Surround with the potatoes. Slice the meat loaf and serve hot.

Crock Hot Dogs

We agree that there's nothing like a hot dog toasted on the grill, but sometimes it's just not convenient. For those times, the slow cooker can be a real lifesaver, especially if you're serving up wieners to a passel of kids, if you need to keep them hot over a long period of time, or if you will be busy during a party and want people to be able to help themselves. Slow cooker hot dogs get a bit browned and caramelized, which enhances their flavor. We find it a tastier method than simmering them in water. Feel free to multiply this recipe for as many hot dogs as you can fit in your cooker. Use pork, chicken, turkey, or kosher beef hot dogs—whatever you like best. ● *Serves 8*

COOKER: Medium round or oval
SETTING AND COOK TIME: HIGH for 1½ to 2 hours

8 hot dogs (about 1 pound)

1. Put the hot dogs in the slow cooker. Cover and cook on HIGH until hot and slightly browned around the edges, 1½ to 2 hours.

2. Remove with metal tongs and serve hot, in buns, with the fixings.

Classic Veal Stew

his makes a small batch of veal stew with root vegetables. It's Beth's favorite recipe for cut-up veal. Serve it with a green salad and fresh bread.

○ *Serves 2 to 3*

COOKER: Medium round or oval
SETTING AND COOK TIME: LOW for 8 hours; peas added at 6½ hours

1 pound boneless veal stew meat or veal shoulder, trimmed of fat,
    cut into 1½-inch chunks, and blotted dry
¼ cup all-purpose flour
¼ teaspoon salt
¼ teaspoon freshly ground black pepper
3 tablespoons olive oil
1 cup chicken broth
1 medium-size yellow onion, chopped
2 cloves garlic, crushed
1 teaspoon dried thyme or 5 fresh thyme sprigs
½ pound baby carrots or 3 medium-size carrots, sliced
½ pound small red potatoes, cut in half
½ cup frozen petite peas, thawed

1. In a zippered-top plastic bag or a bowl, toss the veal with the flour, salt, and pepper, shaking off the excess. In a large skillet over medium-high heat, heat the oil until very hot. Add the veal and cook until browned on all sides, 4 to 5 minutes total. Transfer to the slow cooker. Add the broth, onion, garlic, thyme, carrots, and potatoes, cover, and cook on LOW for 6½ hours.

2. Stir in the peas, cover, and continue to cook on LOW until the veal is tender enough to cut with a fork, another 1½ hours.

3. Taste for salt and pepper and serve hot.

Veal Stew with Sun-Dried Tomatoes and Rosemary

T his veal stew, from food writer Peggy Fallon, is best made with fresh rosemary, the herb that is found in so many dishes of Italy. Because of its decidedly Italian flavor, we like to serve this saucy stew over soft polenta or buttered egg noodles. ● *Serves 4 to 6*

COOKER: Medium or large round or oval
SETTING AND COOK TIME: HIGH for 5½ to 6 hours

2 pounds boneless veal stew meat, trimmed of fat, cut into 1½-inch chunks, and blotted dry
¼ cup all-purpose flour
1 teaspoon salt
¼ teaspoon freshly ground black pepper
3 tablespoons olive oil
½ cup dry white wine
One 14.5-ounce can low-sodium chicken broth
1 large yellow onion, cut in half and sliced into half moons
8 ounces fresh mushrooms, sliced
4 large cloves garlic, thinly sliced
⅓ cup oil-packed sun-dried tomatoes, drained and cut into thin strips
1 to 1½ teaspoons minced fresh rosemary, or 2 teaspoons dried rosemary, crushed, or to taste
1 teaspoon balsamic vinegar

1. In a zippered-top plastic bag or a bowl, toss the veal, in batches, with the flour, salt, and pepper, shaking off any excess. In a large skillet over medium-high heat, warm 1½ tablespoons of the oil until very hot. Add half the veal and cook until browned on all sides, 4 to 5 minutes total. Transfer to the slow cooker. Repeat with the remaining oil and veal.

2. Add the wine to the skillet, bring to a boil, and cook, scraping up any browned bits stuck to the pan, until the wine has thickened slightly, 1 to 2 minutes. Pour into the cooker. Add the broth, onion, mushrooms, and garlic; stir to evenly distribute. Cover and cook on HIGH until the veal is tender enough to cut with a fork, 5½ to 6 hours.

3. Stir in the tomatoes, rosemary, and vinegar. Taste for seasoning before serving.

Veal Stew Peperonata

Because of the large amounts of bell peppers, this is a more assertive veal stew than most. ● *Serves 4*

COOKER: Large round or oval
SETTING AND COOK TIME: LOW for 7½ to 8 hours;
    herbs added during last 30 minutes to 1 hour of cooking

2 pounds boneless veal stew meat or veal shoulder, trimmed of fat,
    cut into 2-inch chunks, and blotted dry
¼ cup all-purpose flour
½ teaspoon salt
½ teaspoon freshly ground black pepper
3 tablespoons olive oil, or as needed
1 medium-size yellow onion, chopped
1 pound bell peppers, red, green, yellow, orange, or mixed,
    seeded and cut into 1½-inch squares
2 cloves garlic, minced
One 14.5-ounce can imported Italian whole tomatoes, drained and chopped
1 cup water
2 tablespoons chopped fresh flat-leaf parsley
1 tablespoon chopped fresh basil

1. In a zippered-top plastic bag or a bowl, toss the veal, in batches, with the flour, salt, and pepper, shaking off any excess. In a large skillet over medium-high heat, warm 1½ tablespoons of the oil until very hot. Add half the veal and cook until browned on all sides, 4 to 5 minutes total. Transfer to the slow cooker. Repeat with the remaining oil and veal. Add a bit more oil if needed and then add the onion to the skillet and cook, stirring, until softened, about 5 minutes; transfer to the cooker. Add the bell peppers and garlic to the skillet and cook, stirring, for 1 minute, then transfer to the cooker. Add the tomatoes and water to the crock. Cover and cook on LOW for 7 hours.

2. Stir in the parsley and basil, cover, and continue to cook on LOW until the veal is tender enough to cut with a fork, another 30 minutes to 1 hour. Season to taste.

Venison Stew with Bacon and Mushrooms

T his is a lovely, earthy stew. Beth worked for years for a client who loved to hunt every fall and had a freezer full of venison. It became a challenge to figure out all sorts of new home-cooked dishes for the game meat. Finish this off with a nice balsamic vinegar—it makes the difference—and serve with mashed potatoes, steamed white or brown rice, or buttered egg noodles. ○ *Serves 4 to 6*

COOKER: Medium or large round or oval
SETTING AND COOK TIME: LOW for 8 to 9 hours; mushrooms and bacon added at 5 to 6 hours

·· About Venison ··

The bright red meat called venison, the king of game meats and food of kings, has been a culinary staple in European and American diets for centuries. If you have not been blessed with a hunter in the family, venison is now available farm raised and flash-frozen; it is a superior lean meat. Species of deer have been brought to Texas and Wisconsin from exotic locations such as India and Manchuria to complement America's native wild breeds of white-tailed, mule, and black-tailed deer. New Zealand also farm raises venison. You can mail-order from Lucky Star Ranch, and the meat will arrive on dry ice. (To order, call 607-836-4766.)

Venison is a natural meat, with no added hormones or antibiotics, which is important to some cooks. It is a low-fat alternative to beef, pork, chicken, and some fish. Each type of deer will vary in texture and flavor because of age, the geographic area where it is raised, and muscle tone. Farm-raised venison is less gamey tasting and more tender than wild, and will appeal to the most delicate palates. Since it is so lean and most of the muscle meat is tough, venison must be slow-cooked for the best texture.

The tougher cuts—the shoulder, stew meat, hind leg, and round steak—are throwbacks to campfire cooking, and recipes abound for venison made with coffee, chili, hot sauce, Worcestershire sauce, currant jelly, fruit, and lots of herbs and bacon. These cuts are excellent for stew meat. Marinades are a nice touch and boost flavor, but don't marinate venison longer than 4 to 6 hours. Combine some ground venison with your ground beef in chili, and cut up chunks of chuck or round steak for stew or pot pies.

2 pounds venison stew meat, trimmed of fat, tenderized by pounding, cut into 1½-inch chunks, and blotted dry

Salt and freshly ground black pepper to taste

3 strips smoky bacon

2 tablespoons olive oil

1 large yellow onion, cut in half and sliced into half moons

2 carrots, chopped

1 clove garlic, minced

2 tablespoons all-purpose flour

⅔ cup dry red wine or dry sherry

1 bay leaf

½ teaspoon dried thyme or 1 tablespoon chopped fresh thyme

One 10.5-ounce can low-sodium beef broth

12 ounces fresh mushrooms, sliced or quartered

2 tablespoons balsamic vinegar

1. Season the venison with salt and pepper. In a large skillet over medium-high heat, cook the bacon until crisp; transfer to paper towels and crumble. Add the oil to the bacon drippings and brown the meat in batches on all sides, about 10 minutes total. Transfer to the slow cooker as you finish each batch. Add the onion, carrots, and garlic to the skillet and cook, stirring, for 3 to 5 minutes. Sprinkle with the flour, stir, and transfer to the cooker. Add the wine to the skillet, bring to a boil, and cook, scraping up any browned bits stuck to the pan, until the wine has thickened slightly, 1 or 2 minutes. Pour into the cooker. Add the bay leaf, thyme, and broth; stir to evenly distribute. Cover and cook on LOW for 5 to 6 hours.

2. Add the mushrooms and crumbled bacon and stir to combine. Cover and continue to cook on LOW until the venison is tender enough to cut with a fork, another 3 hours.

3. Remove the bay leaf and stir in the vinegar. Taste for salt and pepper and serve hot.

Pork and Lamb

Once a meat with a bad reputation, today's pork has a rich character and flavor and is very lean (295 calories per 4 ounces). No longer fatty and indigestible, pork contains less cholesterol than beef, veal, lamb, or even the dark meat of turkey or chicken. Almost every cuisine in the Eastern and Western Hemispheres calls pork a staple because it yields a lot of good meat.

Pork, especially salted, is featured in many Yankee recipes, such as baked beans, clam chowder, stews, split pea soups, vegetable preparations such as succotash, even apple pies, since lard was used in place of butter in the crust; it was a daily staple for centuries. In braised dishes made in the slow cooker, flavorful salt pork literally melts, or renders, into the dish. *Salt pork* is salt cured, not smoked like *bacon,* and comes from the same area of the pig, the belly. A chunk of salt pork has a large piece of fat with some streaks of meat. When we call for it in a recipe, especially in the bean chapter, please don't skip it or you will diminish the flavor of the dish. *Canadian bacon* is cured and smoked loin of pork; *Irish bacon* includes the loin and some of the belly meat we call bacon here. The belly also contains the spareribs (see our chapter on Ribs and Wings, page 387). The *rib eyes* are in the the loin section above the ribs. The pork *tenderloin,* small and thin, is the long uncut section. It is lean and easy to overcook. Tie 2 tenderloins together to increase their thickness, and take them out of the cooker when an instant-read ther-

mometer inserted into the thickest part registers 145° to 150°F.

The hind leg, or *ham,* is the largest cut on the pig. The back is where the *loin* is located, while the shoulder is divided into the top, which is the *Boston butt* or *shoulder roast,* and the arm, known as the *picnic.* The picnic is oh-so-tasty and is often used to replace Boston butt. A *blade roast* is a thick, bone-in slice cut off the Boston butt and is some of the most delicious meat on the animal. The pork shank is also known as the *hock,* and is used mostly cured. The shoulder is the favorite of Chinese chefs and is good cut up for stew meat. Large chunks of pork stew meat are also cut off the top of a pork roast. When buying pork, look for firm, pale, reddish-pink meat with a fine grain. The fat should always be creamy white.

Pork roasts, spareribs, pork chops, ham, bacon, and sausage all are common ingredients, each with its own flavor and texture, in our recipes. Since the pork is so lean and contains much less collagen tissue than beef, it is important to get the cuts that will cook best in the moist heat of the slow cooker. Overcook pork and it tends to shrink rather than soften. Pork is never cooked rare; it is always cooked completely through to the bone and should register about 160°F on an instant-read meat thermometer. We recommend checking doneness with an instant-read thermometer when cooking any whole pork roasts.

The shoulder, hocks, Boston butt, blade roast, spareribs, and the picnic are the very best cuts for the slow cooker. Pork is quite delicately flavored, so it will take on the flavors of your sauce. It likes the sweet, such as barbecue sauces and dried fruit, and the strong, such as peanut sauce, soy sauce, and ginger.

If you choose to cook a ham in your cooker, be sure to select one that will fit. We found that half hams fit best. You want 6 to 8 ounces per person for a boneless ham and a tad more for bone in. Hams are now sold fully cooked. If you choose to cook one of the artisan country hams, such as Virginia Smithfield hams, which are dry cured, be sure to soak it at least 48 hours since they are heavily salted; follow the instructions that come with the ham. Ham hocks are like miniature hams; cook them with greens, beans, or split peas, or in a soup or stock. After cooking, remove the skin and bones, then chop the meat.

If you use any type of pork sausage, unless you buy it fully cooked, you must brown and cook it before adding it to the slow cooker, or remove the casing and cook the crumbled meat. Partially cook or fully cook bacon as directed in the recipe. Never add raw sausage or bacon to the slow cooker since they may not cook thoroughly.

The Best Slow Cooker Cuts of Pork

Boneless pork shoulder

Pork rib eyes

Pork blade roast

Pork tenderloin roast

Boston pork butt

Picnic or smoked picnic pork

Ham hocks

Salt pork

Smoked slab bacon

Pork loin roast

Pork ribs

The Best Slow Cooker Cuts of Lamb

Lamb shanks

Lamb shoulder

Lamb shoulder blade (or shoulder arm) chops

Leg of lamb, bone-in, semiboneless, or boneless

Lamb butt

Lamb neck

Lamb is the stuff of myth and legend. It is mentioned in the Bible and was used not only for religious purposes, but for food and wool. It is a meat that is found in every cuisine. It marries equally well with the flavors of Moroccan tagines, Indian curry, Southern barbecue, French stews, Greek dolmas and moussaka, and the cooking of the British Isles. Lamb has a sweet nature that goes well with vegetables of all kinds, fresh and dried fruits, mustard, wine, garlic, tomatoes, and nuts.

The term "spring lamb" refers to animals born in the spring; it even has its own dish in France, *navarin primanteur,* spring lamb and vegetable ragoût. The early Christians had a custom of serving a whole roasted lamb for Easter; the practice was continued by French royalty until the 1700s and is still found in Greece and Italy today.

While many cuisines call lamb their staple protein, in the United States it more of a secondary or tertiary choice, after beef. Statistics note the British and French eat approximately five times the amount of lamb as Americans.

Today's lamb is fresh and of high quality year round; the United States now imports a lot of its lamb from Australia and New Zealand. Mutton refers to lamb two years old or older and is not usually sold in the United States—it has a much stronger flavor than lamb and is also tougher. Most lamb on the market is between 6 and 12 months old. USDA Genuine Spring Lamb is 3 to 6 months in age and is really a specialty; it is very tender and we do not call for it in any of our recipes; it is best reserved for other culinary preparations.

The lamb is divided into the shoulders, forelegs, breast, ribs, and loin. The *leg,* which is usually dry roasted, is fine for slow cooking. The best portions for braising are the *shoulder* and tough foreleg, known as the *shank.* There is a lamb *butt* at the top of the leg at the shoulder, but it is a cut only found at a butcher shop. The lamb shoulder, either bone-in or boneless, is cooked as a whole roast, and it is cut into stew meat and chops. *Shoulder chops* are a wonderful braising cut because they are made up of many muscles. If you love lamb stew, do obtain a lamb *neck;* it is really excellent for full- flavored stews, quite similar in its consistency and delicate flavor to oxtail. Leg of lamb is also cut up for stew. We recommend you cut your own stew meat; already cut-up lamb stew meat is usually miscellaneous leftovers. Lamb shanks are one of the most succulent and exciting meats to prepare in the slow cooker; they end up melting off the bone, whereas in the oven they can get a bit tough and dry. When buying lamb, look for a dark reddish meat with a fine grain and fresh smell. If it smells gamey, it is too old.

Both pork and lamb are best used within 2 to 3 days of purchase or else frozen. Defrost in their wrappers or plastic freezer bags, in the refrigerator, for about 24 hours.

Roast Pork with Apples

O f course pork and apples are a natural combination; here they cook together in a quick and easy Sunday dinner. Serve slices of pork with some apples alongside and accompany with mashed potatoes, peas, and a chutney.

○ *Serves 6 to 8*

COOKER: Medium or large round or oval
SETTINGS AND COOK TIMES: HIGH for 1 hour, then LOW for 7 to 8 hours

One 3- to 4-pound boned and tied pork loin roast, trimmed of visible fat,
    and blotted dry
Salt and freshly ground black pepper
6 to 7 tart cooking apples, peeled, cored, and quartered
¼ cup apple juice, fruity white wine, or Champagne
¼ cup firmly packed light brown sugar
1½ teaspoons ground ginger

1. Preheat the broiler. Season the pork roast with salt and pepper and place on a rack in a shallow roasting pan. Brown it on all sides under the broiler or in a skillet over high heat to remove excess fat; drain well.

2. Coat the slow cooker with nonstick cooking spray. Put the apple quarters in the cooker and set the roast on top of them. Combine the apple juice, brown sugar, and ginger in a small bowl and spoon over the roast, rubbing it all over. Cover and cook on HIGH for 1 hour.

3. Reduce the setting to LOW and cook until fork tender, 7 to 8 hours. Transfer the pork to a warm platter and let rest for 10 minutes. Slice and serve warm.

Thai Pork with Peanut Sauce

A eanut sauce is really in demand these days; it turns up on all sorts of pan-Asian menus since it is so basic to Southeast Asian cuisine. This is an adaptation of a *Cooking Light* recipe that was posted on the Internet, where it received a five-star rating from home cooks. It is fine to use a prepared teriyaki sauce with sesame seeds in it. Serve this over hot jasmine rice. ○ *Serves 4*

COOKER: Medium round or oval
SETTING AND COOK TIME: LOW for 8 to 9 hours

One 2-pound boneless pork loin, trimmed of fat and cut into 4 pieces
2 large red bell peppers, seeded and cut into strips
⅓ cup prepared teriyaki sauce
2 tablespoons rice vinegar
1 teaspoon red pepper flakes
2 cloves garlic, minced
¼ cup creamy peanut butter

FOR SERVING:
½ cup chopped green onions (white part and some of the green)
¼ cup chopped dry-roasted peanuts
2 limes, cut to make 8 to 12 wedges

1. Coat the slow cooker with nonstick cooking spray. Put the pork, bell peppers, teriyaki sauce, rice vinegar, red pepper flakes, and garlic in the cooker. Cover and cook on LOW until the pork is fork-tender, 8 to 9 hours.

2. Remove the pork from the cooker and coarsely chop. Add the peanut butter to the liquid in cooker; stir well to dissolve the peanut butter and blend with the liquid to make the sauce. Return the pork to the sauce and toss to coat the meat evenly.

3. Serve in shallow bowls over hot jasmine rice, and sprinkle each serving with some of the green onions and peanuts. Pass the lime wedges.

Pork Tenderloin and Sauerkraut

T his recipe, from Beth's friend Bunny Dimmel, calls for a lean pork tender-loin instead of one of the richer cuts of pork. It is important to get fresh sauerkraut, which comes in a bag (or in bulk in the refrigerated deli section), rather than canned or in a jar. It just tastes that much better, and also protects the lean meat and keeps it moist. ○ *Serves 6*

COOKER: Medium or large round or oval
SETTING AND COOK TIME: LOW for 8 to 10 hours

2 tablespoons olive oil
2 pounds pork tenderloin, trimmed of silver skin and fat, and blotted dry
4 small yellow onions, quartered
6 cloves garlic, minced
6 medium-size red potatoes, cut in half
8 grinds of black pepper
One 1-pound bag fresh sauerkraut, rinsed

1. In a large skillet over medium-high heat, warm the oil until very hot. Add the meat and cook until browned on all sides, 4 to 5 minutes total. Transfer to the slow cooker. Tuck the onions around the tenderloin, then sprinkle with the garlic and top with the potato halves. Sprinkle with the pepper, and cover with the sauer-kraut. Cover and cook on LOW until the pork is fork-tender, 8 to 10 hours.

2. Transfer the pork and vegetables to a platter. Slice the tenderloin into thick portions, and arrange on dinner plates, surrounded with some of each vegetable and some sauerkraut.

Pork Tenderloin Braised
in Milk with Fresh Herbs

Beth's friend Leslie Mansfield is a cookbook writer based in the Napa Valley, where she and her husband also have a small wine-making venture. This is a recipe she included in her book *The Lewis and Clark Cookbook* (Celestial Arts, 2002), a compilation of recipes for modern cooks based on historic ones. It is so popular that Leslie travels to different parts of the country, from Cincinnati to Arkansas, hosting restaurant dinners with recipes made from the book.

This dish adapts perfectly to the slow cooker. It is unusual because regular milk products curdle in the crock. Well, that is exactly what you want in this recipe; the milk thickens to make the most delectable sauce for the pork. ● *Serves 6*

COOKER: Medium or large round or oval
SETTING AND COOK TIME: LOW for 5 to 6½ hours

¼ cup olive oil
2½ pounds pork tenderloin, trimmed of fat and silver skin and blotted dry
1 tablespoon minced fresh oregano
1 tablespoon minced fresh tarragon
2 teaspoons minced fresh rosemary
1¾ teaspoons salt
8 grinds of black pepper
2 to 2¼ cups hot whole milk

1. In a large skillet over medium-high heat, warm the oil until very hot. Add the meat and cook until browned on all sides, 4 to 5 minutes total. Transfer to the slow cooker. Sprinkle with the herbs, salt, and pepper. Add the milk; it should come halfway up the sides of the pork. Cover and cook on LOW until the pork is fork-tender, 5 to 6½ hours.

2. Transfer the pork to a warm platter and let rest for 10 minutes. Cut the roast into ½-inch-thick slices and spoon over the creamy, thick sauce.

Mahogany Glazed Pork

T he jam, soy sauce, and garlic combination is one that is used over and over as a glaze for pork and chicken. The mixture cooks up dark red and gives the outer part of the meat a succulent, sweet quality. ● *Serves 6 to 8*

COOKER: Large round or oval
SETTING AND COOK TIME: LOW for 8 to 10 hours

⅓ **cup soy sauce**
½ **cup orange marmalade**
1 to 2 cloves garlic, to your taste, pressed
1 to 1½ teaspoons red pepper flakes, to your taste
3 tablespoons ketchup
One 3½-pound boneless Boston pork butt, cut into large pieces, or
  3½ pounds country-style pork spareribs
8 ounces sugar snap peas
½ **cup julienned red bell pepper**

1. Coat the slow cooker with nonstick cooking spray.

2. Combine the soy sauce, marmalade, garlic, red pepper flakes, and ketchup in a small bowl and mix until smooth; brush over both sides of the meat. Arrange the pork butt or ribs in the cooker. (If you have a round cooker, stack the ribs.) Pour over any extra sauce. Cover and cook on LOW until fork-tender and the meat starts to separate from the bone, 8 to 10 hours.

3. Stir in the sugar snap peas and bell pepper; cover and let stand a few minutes to warm. Serve immediately.

Southern Barbecued Pork on a Bun

T his is one delicious way to cook a pork roast. You slice or shred the meat and pile it on fresh rolls with more barbecue sauce on top, or shred the meat, pop it back in the crock with the sauce, and let your diners construct their own sandwiches. Serve with coleslaw and pickles. The meat needs overnight marination, so plan accordingly. ○ *Serves 8*

COOKER: Medium oval or large round or oval
SETTING AND COOK TIME: LOW for 8 to 10 hours

1 cup ketchup
1 cup prepared chili sauce
¼ cup Dijon mustard
3 tablespoons cider vinegar
3 tablespoons Worcestershire sauce
2 tablespoons honey
1 tablespoon soy sauce
½ teaspoon red pepper flakes
4 cloves garlic, minced
One 3-pound boneless Boston pork butt, trimmed of excess fat
¾ cup water
8 kaiser rolls, split

FOR SERVING:
Baked beans
Coleslaw
Pickles

1. In a medium-size saucepan combine ketchup, chili sauce, mustard, vinegar, Worcestershire, honey, soy sauce, red pepper flakes, and garlic. Bring to a boil over medium-high heat, then reduce the heat to medium-low and simmer for 5 minutes, uncovered. Let cool to room temperature.

2. Put the pork butt in a large zippered-top plastic bag. Pour the barbecue sauce over the pork, seal, and marinate at least 8 hours or overnight in the refrigerator, turning the bag over a few times if possible.

3. Remove the pork butt from the marinade and put in the slow cooker. Pour the marinade into a small bowl, add the water, and mix well. Pour over the roast. Cover and cook on LOW until the meat is fork-tender, 8 to 10 hours.

4. Transfer the pork to a platter, tent with aluminum foil, and let stand for 10 to 15 minutes before carving into thin slices. Put a few slices on the bottom half of each Kaiser bun, spoon over some of the barbecue sauce, top with the other half of the bun, and enjoy. Accompany with baked beans, coleslaw, pickles, and napkins.

Pork Chops with Tomato Sauce and Mushrooms

W hile regular loin pork chops are too lean to be really good in the slow cooker, the extra-thick chops with the bone left in work beautifully. Here they are nestled in an Italian-style tomato sauce. Serve with steamed rice or a pasta that will catch the sauce, such as penne. ○ *Serves 4*

COOKER: Medium oval or large round or oval
SETTING AND COOK TIME: LOW for 6 to 8 hours

4 thick bone-in pork loin chops, at least 1 inch thick, blotted dry
8 ounces mushrooms, sliced
1 medium-size yellow onion, chopped
1 large red or yellow bell pepper, seeded and cut into rings or strips
1 clove garlic, minced
Two 8-ounce cans tomato sauce
2 tablespoons balsamic vinegar
2 tablespoons minced fresh flat-leaf parsley
½ teaspoon dried oregano
½ teaspoon dried basil
Pinch of salt
2 tablespoons cornstarch
¼ cup cold water

1. In a large, heavy skillet over medium-high heat, brown the pork chops on both sides.

2. In the slow cooker, combine the mushrooms, onion, bell pepper, and garlic. Nestle the pork chops on top.

3. In a medium-size bowl, combine the tomato sauce, vinegar, parsley, oregano, basil, and salt. Pour over the pork chops. Cover and cook on LOW until the meat is tender, 6 to 8 hours.

4. Transfer the pork to a platter and tent with aluminum foil to keep warm. Transfer the tomato sauce to a medium-size saucepan. In a small bowl, whisk together the cornstarch and water until smooth, and stir the slurry into the sauce.

Bring to a boil over medium heat, stirring, until slightly thickened, about 2 minutes. Serve the sauce over the pork chops.

Oscar's Chile Verde

his is the *chile verde* you make to shred for burritos and casseroles. If you want to make this more of a stew, after shredding the meat add a bunch of cooked, sliced fresh carrots and potatoes along with 2 cups of chicken or turkey broth. ○ *Serves 6*

COOKER: Large round or oval
SETTING AND COOK TIME: LOW for 7 to 9 hours

2 large yellow onions, diced
2 large yellow bell peppers, seeded and chopped
3 jalapeños, seeded and chopped
3½ to 4 pounds pork rib-eye steaks (4 to 5)
Pinch of ground cumin
About 2 cups water, or to cover
1 teaspoon salt, or to taste
Freshly ground black pepper to taste

1. Coat the slow cooker with nonstick cooking spray or oil and layer the onions, bell peppers, jalapeños, and the rib-eye steaks. Sprinkle with the cumin and add enough water just to cover the ingredients. Cover and cook on LOW until the pork shreds easily when pressed with a spoon, 7 to 9 hours.

2. Remove the rib eyes, pull the meat off the bone, and shred; discard the bones. Season the pork with the salt and black pepper, and serve with warm corn or flour tortillas.

Pork Stew in Cider

This recipe, a favorite, comes from Susie Dymoke, who was running the Sur La Table cooking school in Los Gatos when she and Beth first met, then became a manager at La Cucina Mugnaini, makers of exquisite outdoor ovens. Susie now is a wood-fire cooking expert, who teaches classes around the country. Since she rarely measures ingredients for this stew, we were pleased when she did so for our sake. Although the water chestnuts are optional, they add a nice, crunchy texture. The cider is an important ingredient. The alcoholic stuff is best, so look for a good brand, such as Dry Blackthorn. As Susie says, "Slow-cook all day and enjoy!" ○ *Serves 6*

COOKER: Medium round or oval
SETTINGS AND COOK TIMES: HIGH for 20 minutes (optional),
   then LOW for 7 to 9 hours

1 large yellow onion, coarsely chopped
1 large tart cooking apple, such as Granny Smith or pippin, peeled, cored,
   and roughly cut into 1-inch cubes
One 8-ounce can water chestnuts (optional), drained and cut in half
1½ pounds boneless pork shoulder, cut into ½-inch cubes
½ teaspoon salt
7 grinds of black pepper
1½ tablespoons rubbed sage
2 cups dry hard cider
Long-grain rice or egg noodles for serving

1. Coat the slow cooker with nonstick cooking spray. Layer the onion, apple, water chestnuts, and pork in the cooker; sprinkle with the salt, pepper, and sage. Pour the cider over all. Turn to HIGH for 20 minutes, if you have time, to heat through.

2. Cover and cook on LOW for 7 to 9 hours.

3. Serve in shallow soup bowls with long-grain white rice or egg noodles.

Italian Pork Stew

B eth is a contributing writer to a great food magazine called *Cooking Pleasures,* a mail-order-only publication of the Cooking Club of America (888-850-8202). This is a recipe created by food writer/cooking teacher Mary Ellen Evans for the magazine some years ago and an editorial staff favorite. The Italian edge comes from the fennel seed and rosemary, two traditional flavor enhancers in Italian cuisine. Serve this over Polenta (page 156) or pasta. ● *Serves 6*

COOKER: Large round or oval
SETTING AND COOK TIME: LOW for 7 to 9 hours

1 large yellow onion, cut into 8 wedges
2 large red bell peppers, or 1 red and 1 yellow bell pepper,
    seeded and cut into thin strips
2 cloves garlic, minced
3 tablespoons olive oil
2½ pounds boneless pork shoulder, cut into 1½-inch cubes, and blotted dry
One 16-ounce can diced tomatoes (with roasted garlic or other flavoring if desired),
    with their juice
½ cup dry red wine, such as Chianti or Zinfandel
1 teaspoon fennel seeds
½ teaspoon dried orange peel or 2 teaspoons grated orange zest
½ teaspoon dried rosemary, crushed
¼ teaspoon red pepper flakes
¼ teaspoon salt
6 grinds of black pepper
3 tablespoons all-purpose flour
¼ cup water

1. Coat the slow cooker with a nonstick cooking spray. Layer the onion, bell peppers, and garlic in the cooker.

2. In a large skillet over medium-high heat, warm 1½ tablespoons of the oil until very hot. Add half the meat and cook until browned on all sides, 4 to 5 minutes total. Transfer to the cooker. Repeat with the remaining oil and meat. Add the tomatoes and wine to the skillet and bring to a boil, scraping up any browned bits stuck to the pan. Add the fennel, orange peel, rosemary, red pepper flakes, salt, and black pepper. Pour over everything in the cooker. Cover and cook on LOW until the pork is fork tender, 7 to 9 hours.

3. In a small bowl, whisk together the flour and water; whisk the slurry into the hot liquid in the slow cooker, increase the heat to HIGH, and cook, uncovered, until thickened, about 15 minutes.

•• Slow Cooker Cooking by Feel ••

Beth asked her friend Cat Wilson, a psychotherapist, to share her favorite recipes for the slow cooker. Instead of just recipes, Beth was introduced into an entire philosophy of cooking by instinct, based on availability and mood, instead of following a recipe. Many slow cooker aficionados cook by this method, using recipes as templates for improvisation.

"The slow cooker is the working woman's cooking pot," said Cat. "I look into the refrigerator and combine a meat, vegetable, and spice. I mentally sort by flavors based on what is on hand and my experience with different cuisines. So there could be Italian one night and Indian the next.

"The best thing about slow cooking is that it is the most forgiving method of cooking that you will ever find. It may not come out exactly as you intended, but it may even be better than that! The whole point of the slow cooker is that it's for people who aren't cooks. It makes us look like we know what we're doing. And it takes very little time, so those of us who have little time to devote to cooking can make real food that looks and tastes terrific.

"It's also great for doing pork for that pork dish called *carnitas.* I chop the pork across the grain so that it falls apart as it cooks. Then I use regular *carnitas* seasoning from any of the packet mixes because I couldn't make *carnitas* seasoning if I thought about it. The slow cooker makes the best *carnitas* because it makes the meat so tender that it flakes. That is also how I make our taco meat—I use real meat (not hamburger) and cut it so it will fall apart. Then I add the best taco seasoning money can buy. Oh, you can also add onions if your guests aren't picky.

"I make a Polish stew called *bigos;* I got the recipe from my old friend Basia from Poland. Her husband was one of the three leaders of the Polish resistance. She came from a very wealthy family and then married this renegade, much to the dismay of her parents. Basically, *bigos* is a Polish hunter's stew that is made up of all the small bits of different meats; all Polish cookbooks have recipes for it. This recipe is also good when you have odd bits of leftovers—

that's what I usually do. When we come home from dining out, I'll bring home that last little bit of steak. Or if there is a leftover piece of ham, I toss it all in a bag and put it in the freezer until it is full. Then we're ready for *bigos*.

"It really doesn't matter where you start. I get beef, chicken, some kielbasa sausage, turkey and chop them into bite-sized pieces. I get both light and dark cuts of the chicken and turkey for good flavor. My preferences are kielbasa, beef, and chicken. Slice 1 to 2 onions and mix it in. Salt. Fill your pot about three-fourths full. Cover with some nice red wine and nestle one whole fresh plum into the center of it all. That's the magic ingredient. (Don't take the skin off, pit it, or do anything exotic except wash it.) Then you strain and dump in two cans of sauerkraut and stir it well. I just cook it until I get home from work. It varies from day to day. I think it could go for 6, 9, or 12 hours. And maybe a wisp of sherry after it's all cooked. I cook the *bigos* on HIGH; not much of the moisture gets reduced, so you may need to drain off some of the sauerkraut juice at the end.

"*Bigos* tastes much better on the second day because the flavors have had time to mix together. It's one of those 'look in the fridge and see what we've got' meals. It's served with boiled, peeled potatoes and I crunch-steam some carrots to go with it as well. After the *bigos* is cooked down, it is very rich—you can't eat too much because it is so potent and luckily the potatoes make it less rich. But after such a meal, you get a good understanding of the satisfying, substantial quality of eastern European cooking after working all day in the fields.

"The other slow cooker meal I am famous for is jambalaya—the Creole version of hunter's stew. It includes at least some of the following: shrimp, ham, raw fresh oysters, smoked sausage, and chicken. You have to cook the white rice separately and then you ladle this on top when it's done. Again, use any mix of the meats above cut into uniform bite-sized pieces. Add chopped or sliced yellow onion, about 4 or 5 chopped green onions, a couple of stalks of chopped celery with leaves on, and a whole bag of still frozen chopped okra. Also you need 2 or 3 (depending on the size) green, red, or yellow peppers, the sweet kind. You should have proportions of about 50 percent meat and 50 percent veggies, but it really doesn't matter.

"Add salt, paprika, cayenne, a teaspoon of mashed or minced garlic, gumbo filé powder [ground dried sassafras root used as both a flavor and thickening agent], and 1 bay leaf. Add a small can of chopped tomatoes (juice included). Then stir it all up and let it cook for the day. Again, this one tastes really good on the second day. You want it to be wet and saucy enough that it has lots of thick liquid to sit in a bed of rice and be there for the last bite. My cousin is Cajun; he is a cook for the Red Cross through the Southern Baptist Church and has traveled around the world for mass feeding. This is a variation of his recipe. We love the fresh oysters (canned get too mushy, like overcooked liver) and fresh shrimp along with the smoked sausage and chicken. Those are our favorite mixes. A key ingredient is the bell peppers, no matter what color they are. They just add something. With jambalaya, we usually just have salad on the side.

"Here's a great stew: My DiBarney's Red Flannel Stew. DiBarney is my mom's stepdad. When one of the kids was small, he or she couldn't say Daddy Barney, which is what he was called. It came out DiBarney and that's what it remained until his death when he was around 90. He had been in vaudeville until he was 42 and had been all over the world. He was a song and dance man who looked a lot like Maurice Chevalier. He was wonderful, a heart as big as the whole outdoors. When DiBarney died, 2,000 people showed up for the funeral. Most of them were his Eagle Scouts, Boy Scouts, and Cub Scouts and their sons who were Scouts. He also ran the only movie theater in town. I have the tambourine and clappers that he took out of the music box when he had to switch over to talkies.

"This is called Red Flannel Stew because as it cooks, it's supposed to look like your long red flannel underwear boiling on the stove. You can just throw all the raw ingredients in there and go to work and come home and it's dinner!

"Chop up beef into bite-sized cubes. Actually, you chop up everything into bite-sized cubes. Beef, onion, carrots, potatoes (with the peelings on) and add a big old can of tomatoes that you cut into bite-sized hunks. Yummy! Do not add celery. It changes the flavor completely. Do not add peas or string beans. Those are only for minestrone. If you have beef broth or Knorr's beef flavor, use that. And add water. Salt and pepper are all that you add for seasoning. It is wonderful with a big gulp of cold milk and some crackers or fresh bread.

"Sometimes I have made Refrigerator Stew, especially when I cook by country. It's when I clean out the refrigerator and put everything that seems even slightly compatible in the slow cooker. Meat, veggies, everything. Then I cover it with chicken broth or Knorr's broth and water, salt and pepper, wilted veggies, potatoes with the spots cut off, anything goes. I decide what flavor we're in the mood for: French, Italian, Mexican, Chinese, English. Then I use the appropriate seasonings. Toss whatever I've got in the fridge in and add *herbes de Provence,* or basil and oregano, or turmeric, cumin, and chili powder, or Chinese five-spice, or salt and pepper plain. If it's Italian, French, or English, I add noodles; if it's Mexican or Chinese, al add rice (neither of them cooked). Then when I get home, we have the country-appropriate specialty casserole of the day. It's fun and usually is tasty.

"This is food for Pollock painters. As DiBarney used to say, done with a lick and a promise. Dinner is served."

Oscar's Posole

O scar Mariscal was the chef at St. Michael's Alley restaurant when Beth was a pastry chef in the 1970s and '80s. Posole is traditional Mexican fare for Christmas Eve and, of course, for recovering from the festivities on Christmas day. It is a great stew for parties as well. Posole can also be made with chicken. If you like your stew a bit more filling, add a can of rinsed pinto beans. **o** *Serves 6*

COOKER: Medium round or oval
SETTING AND COOK TIME: LOW for 7 to 8 hours;
cilantro, salt, and pepper added during last hour

2 tablespoons olive oil

2 pounds boneless pork shoulder, cut into ½-inch cubes, and blotted dry

1 medium-size yellow onion, chopped

4 to 6 cloves garlic, to your taste, pressed

1 tablespoon chili powder

2 teaspoons dried oregano

½ teaspoon ground cumin

Two 15-ounce cans white hominy, rinsed and drained

One 7-ounce can diced roasted green chiles, with their juice

6 cups chicken broth

¼ cup minced fresh cilantro

½ teaspoon salt, or to taste

Freshly ground black pepper to taste

FOR SERVING:
Shredded iceberg lettuce
Sliced radishes
Chopped green onions (white part and some of the green)
Diced avocado
Toasted pumpkin seeds
Chunky tomato salsa
Chopped fresh cilantro
Lime wedges
Warm flour tortillas

1. In a large skillet over medium-high heat, warm 1 tablespoon of the oil until very hot. Add half the meat and cook until browned on all sides, 4 to 5 minutes total. Transfer to the slow cooker. Repeat with the remaining oil and meat. Add the onion, garlic, chili powder, oregano, cumin, hominy, chiles, and broth and stir to combine. Cover and cook on LOW for 6 to 7 hours.

2. Stir in the cilantro and season with salt and pepper. Cover and continue to cook on LOW for another hour.

3. Serve in shallow soup bowls with your choice of toppings, set out in bowls, and warm flour tortillas.

Navajo Stew

H ere is real home cooking from Four Corners (where New Mexico, Colorado, Utah, and Arizona meet). This is a fast, easy meal. Serve it with French bread, Spanish rice, and a green salad. ● *Serves 4 to 6*

COOKER: Medium or large round or oval
SETTINGS AND COOK TIMES: LOW for 7 to 9 hours, then HIGH for about 20 minutes; chickpeas and chiles added during last 20 minutes

One 2- to 2½-pound Boston pork butt, trimmed of all fat
1 large yellow onion, cut in half and sliced into half moons
Water to cover
One 15-ounce can chickpeas (garbanzo beans), rinsed and drained
One 4-ounce can roasted whole green chiles, drained and cut into ½- to 1-inch-wide strips
Salt and freshly ground black pepper to taste

1. In the morning, put the pork butt and onion slices in the slow cooker and add just enough water to cover. Then cover and cook on LOW until the pork shreds easily when pressed with a spoon, 7 to 9 hours.

2. When ready for dinner, cut the pork butt into cubes or break into uneven pieces. Return to the cooker, add the chickpeas and chiles, turn the cooker to HIGH, and cook until hot, about 20 minutes. Season with salt and pepper. You can thicken the sauce if you like by taking off the lid and cooking for another 15 minutes on HIGH. Serve in bowls.

Sausage and Peppers

One of the best meals ever is a steaming pot of Italian sausages cooked with sweet bell peppers. The dish was originally known in the United States as Frank Sinatra's Sausage and Peppers, and it became a kitchen staple after Dinah Shore put it into her cookbook *Someone's in the Kitchen with Dinah* decades ago (Doubleday, 1971). It is Italian soul food, which we have adapted for the slow cooker. Serve with lots of crusty bread to soak up the juices, or on long hero (aka hoagie or submarine) rolls and eat it like a sandwich, or spoon it over buttered egg noodles. ○ *Serves 4 to 6*

COOKER: Medium or large round or oval
SETTING AND COOK TIME: LOW for 6 to 8 hours

3 large assorted colored bell peppers, such as red, yellow, and orange, seeded and cut into chunks
1 large yellow onion, cut into wedges
3 cloves garlic, peeled
Salt and freshly ground black pepper to taste
1 tablespoon minced fresh thyme
2 tablespoons olive oil
2 pounds assorted sausages, such as hot and sweet Italian and chicken basil
⅓ cup dry red wine

1. Put the peppers in the slow cooker. Add the onion and garlic and toss to combine. Sprinkle with a small amount of salt and pepper and all of the thyme.

2. In a large skillet, heat the olive oil over medium-high heat and brown the sausages all over, 3 to 5 minutes, pricking them with a fork. Place them on top of the vegetables in the cooker. Add the wine to the skillet and bring to a boil, scraping up any browned bits stuck to the pan. Pour into the cooker. Cover and cook on LOW for 6 to 8 hours. Serve the sausage and peppers hot.

Lamb and Cabbage

T his recipe comes as a gift from Beth's friend, talented food stylist, cookbook writer, and food entrepreneur Robert Lambert. Robert's recipes are often out of his Grandma Florrie's recipe box, harkening back to his childhood in rural Michigan. Robert writes of dinner with Grandma in his unpublished work "Journey Home."

"Lamb and cabbage was a family favorite, a boiled dinner more appropriate to spring or fall than summer, though we often had it in summer anyway so those who visited only then could enjoy it too. It was probably conceived as a way to use old and strongly flavored mutton, but is even better with a young leg of spring lamb." ● *Serves 4 to 6*

COOKER: Medium or large round or oval (depending on size of leg of lamb)
SETTINGS AND COOK TIMES: HIGH for 1 hour, then LOW for 4 to 5 hours, then HIGH again for 20 minutes; cabbage added during last 20 minutes

½ **teaspoon allspice berries**
½ **teaspoon black peppercorns**
½ **teaspoon whole cloves**
1 small leg of lamb (about 2 pounds), bone-in or boned and tied
2 cups hot chicken broth (optional)
½ **cup dry white wine (optional)**
¾ **teaspoon to 1 teaspoon salt, to your taste**
1 head cabbage, cored and cut into 8 wedges

1. Put the allspice berries, peppercorns, and cloves in a cheesecloth bag or tea ball and set aside.

2. Put the lamb in the slow cooker. If you are using a round cooker, put the lamb in meaty end down. Add the broth and wine, if using. Add hot water to cover the lamb by an inch. Add the salt, using the lesser amount if you used salted chicken broth. Add the spice ball. Cover and cook on HIGH for 1 hour.

3. Turn the cooker to LOW and cook until the lamb is fork-tender, 4 to 5 hours. About 20 minutes before it is done, preheat the oven to 200°F.

4. Transfer the lamb to a platter, tent with aluminum foil, and place in the oven to keep warm. Put the cabbage wedges in the hot broth remaining in the cooker, cover, and turn the heat to HIGH. Cook until tender, 20 to 30 minutes.

5. Just before cabbage is done, carve the meat. Serve the lamb in shallow bowls with 1 or 2 wedges of cabbage and some of the broth.

Pasta with Lamb Shanks in Beer and Tomato Sauce

T his flavorful dish is positively regal when served over thick, artisan-style pasta. Choose a chunky shape, such as rigatoni or penne, to catch the sauce. We have found the imported brands of dried pasta, such as De Cecco or Barilla, to be well worth searching out, especially when you have gone to the trouble of preparing a topper as delicious as this one. For this recipe, choose a dark beer or ale that is not too bitter. ○ *Serves 4 to 6*

COOKER: Medium or large round or oval
SETTING AND COOK TIME: LOW for 7 to 8 hours

3 tablespoons olive oil

4 lamb shanks (about 5 pounds total), trimmed of fat

2 to 3 ribs celery, to your taste, sliced ⅓ inch thick

2 large carrots, sliced ⅓ inch thick

4 cloves garlic, sliced

1 cup dark beer or ale

¼ cup tomato paste

Two 14.5-ounce cans chopped tomatoes, with their juice

2 tablespoons minced fresh rosemary or 2 teaspoons dried rosemary, crushed

2 teaspoons chopped fresh oregano or ¾ teaspoon dried oregano

1 teaspoon salt, or more to taste

⅛ teaspoon freshly ground black pepper, or more to taste

1 pound thick pasta in a chunky shape

1. In a large skillet, heat the oil over medium-high heat and cook the shanks until golden brown on all sides, 5 to 7 minutes in all. You may have to do this in batches. As they brown, transfer to a plate. Pour off all but about 1 tablespoon of the oil. Add the celery, carrots, and garlic and cook, stirring a few times, until softened, about 5 minutes. Make a bed of the vegetables in the slow cooker and arrange the lamb on top.

2. Add the beer to the skillet and bring to a boil, scraping up any browned bits stuck to the pan. Stir in the tomato paste, chopped tomatoes with their liquid, herbs, salt, and pepper. Bring to a boil, reduce the heat to medium-low, and simmer for about 5 minutes. Pour the sauce over the lamb. Cover and cook on LOW until the lamb is fork-tender, 7 to 8 hours.

3. Preheat the oven to 375°F and bring a large pot of salted water to a boil for the pasta. With a slotted spoon or tongs, transfer the shanks to a shallow baking dish and keep warm in the oven while you cook the pasta and finish the sauce.

4. Strain the sauce, reserving the solids. Remove as much fat as possible from the sauce, and pour it into a small saucepan. Stir in the carrots and celery and bring the sauce to a boil. Reduce the heat to medium-low, and simmer until the sauce thickens a bit, about 10 minutes.

5. Cook the pasta, drain, and arrange on a warm platter, topped with the tomato sauce. Serve each diner pasta and sauce, topped with lamb. Serve hearty eaters an entire lamb shank; for smaller appetites, remove the meat from the bones in large chunks.

Martha's Wine Country Lamb Shanks

T his recipe for lamb shanks has no garlic, no tomatoes, no herbs, nor any fancy ingredients; it is plain old home cooking. Martha, our literary agent, often pours off the collected juice from the shanks and freezes it for inclusion in the next batch. She and her husband live in the midst of a Napa Valley vineyard, so they often cook with wine made from their own grapes, then serve up some more of the same to wash down the stew. Note that this recipe calls for white pepper, not the more pungent black. **o** *Serves 4 to 6*

COOKER: Medium or large round or oval

SETTING AND COOK TIME: LOW for 7 to 8 hours; potatoes and carrots added at 3½ hours

4 lamb shanks (about 5 pounds total), trimmed of fat

½ cup all-purpose flour

3 tablespoons olive oil

1 medium-size yellow onion, chopped

1 cup dry white wine

2 to 3 cups chicken or beef broth, as needed

1 to 1¼ pounds baby new potatoes, left whole

12 ounces baby carrots or thick slices of regular carrots

Salt and white pepper to taste

1. Pierce the lamb shanks a few times with the tip of a knife. On a cutting board or platter, roll the shanks in the flour to completely coat. In a large skillet, heat the oil over medium-high heat and cook the shanks until golden brown on all sides, 5 to 7 minutes in all. You may have to do this in batches. As they brown, transfer the shanks to the slow cooker. Add the onion to the skillet and cook, stirring a few times, until slightly softened, about 3 minutes. Add the wine and bring to a boil, scraping up any browned bits stuck to the pan; pour the onions and wine into the cooker. Add enough of the broth to cover the lamb and season lightly with salt and pepper. Cover and cook on LOW for 3½ hours.

2. Add the potatoes and carrots, cover, and continue to cook on LOW until the lamb is very tender when pierced with a fork and falling off the bone, another 3½ to 4½ hours.

3. Taste for seasoning (Martha likes lots of white pepper). On each dinner plate, place a shank or a portion of one and some potatoes and carrots from the crock, ladling the sauce over all.

Victoria's Lamb Shanks Braised with Garlic, Fresh Rosemary, and White Wine

T his is a homey recipe adapted from the wonderful book *The Pressure Cooker Gourmet* by Victoria Wise (Harvard Common Press, 2003). Yes, you want the full three heads of garlic; they get placed in the crock unpeeled, so there is no culinary anxiety there. The diners can squeeze out the luscious innards as they consume the shanks. Please note this is a smaller recipe than the others for shanks, utilizing only two of them. If you don't want to cut the shanks, have the butcher do it for you. This recipe has a chopped lemon zest garnish that really provides a zing at the end. We also like to chop it finely in the food processor with an equal amount of parsley for a sort of gremolata. Serve this with egg noodles or boiled potatoes. ● *Serves 2 to 3*

COOKER: Medium round or oval
SETTING AND COOK TIME: LOW for 7 to 8 hours

1½ tablespoons olive oil
2 lamb shanks (about 2½ pounds total), trimmed of fat, and each cut crosswise into 3 pieces
¾ cup dry white wine
3 heads garlic, separated into cloves, unpeeled
2 medium-size fresh or canned tomatoes, coarsely chopped
1½ teaspoons chopped fresh rosemary
Salt and freshly ground black pepper to taste
¼ cup chopped lemon zest for garnish

1. In a large skillet, heat the oil over medium-high heat and cook the shanks until golden brown on all sides, about 5 minutes total. As they brown, transfer the shanks to the slow cooker. Add the wine to the skillet and bring to a boil, scraping up any browned bits stuck to the pan. Add the garlic, tomatoes, and rosemary, bring to a boil, and pour over the lamb. Cover and cook on LOW until the lamb is very tender and falling off the bone, 7 to 8 hours.

2. Season with salt and pepper, sprinkle with the lemon zest, and serve from the crock.

Braised Lamb Chops with White Beans

H ere you serve a whole, meaty shoulder lamb chop (which loves the slow braise) with beans and a savory sauce. It is wonderful and economical and loaded with flavor. Feel free to brown your chops in the oil drained from the sun-dried tomatoes for even more flavor. Serve over rice. ○ *Serves 4*

COOKER: Medium oval or large round or oval
SETTING AND COOK TIME: LOW for 5 to 7 hours; beans added halfway through cooking

1 to 2 tablespoons olive oil, as needed
4 shoulder lamb chops
1 medium-size yellow onion, chopped
½ cup chicken broth
½ cup dry white wine
¼ cup chopped oil-packed sun-dried tomatoes, drained
½ teaspoon dried marjoram or thyme
Pinch of ground cumin
One 15-ounce can small white beans, rinsed and drained
Salt and freshly ground black pepper to taste
Hot cooked rice for serving

1. In a large nonstick skillet, heat the oil and brown the lamb on both sides over medium-high heat; transfer to the slow cooker. Add the onion to the skillet and cook for a few minutes until limp; add to the cooker. Add the broth, wine, tomatoes, marjoram, and cumin, cover, and cook on LOW for 2½ to 3½ hours.

2. Add the beans, cover, and continue to cook on LOW until the lamb is very tender, another 2½ to 3½ hours. Season with salt and pepper and serve over rice.

Lamb Goulash au Blanc

With spring lamb coming into the markets and fresh lemons still on the trees in California, this is a great recipe for end-of-winter dining. It is another recipe from Nancyjo Riekse, adapted for the slow cooker from one she has been making for 20 years. If lemon and lamb is a new combination for you, note it is a common pairing in Middle Eastern cuisine. When you see the term *au blanc,* it means that the meat is not browned first. Serve this with buttered wide egg noodles and garnish with grated lemon zest. ● *Serves 4 to 6*

COOKER: Medium or large round or oval
SETTING AND COOK TIME: LOW for 5 to 6 hours

3 tablespoons unsalted butter, softened
1 medium-size yellow onion, chopped
2 pounds fresh spring lamb stew meat, such as shoulder, cut into 1½-inch cubes
1 lemon, seeded and very thinly sliced
1 teaspoon caraway seeds
2 teaspoons dried marjoram
1 clove garlic, peeled
1 cup vegetable broth
Salt and freshly ground black pepper to taste

1. Smear the bottom of the slow cooker with the butter and sprinkle with the onion. Put the lamb in the cooker, and arrange the lemon slices over it.

2. In a mortar, mash together the caraway seeds, marjoram, and garlic with a pestle; stir into the broth. Add the broth to the cooker, cover, and cook on LOW until the lamb is fork-tender, 5 to 6 hours. Season with salt and pepper and serve.

Lamb Curry

C urry" is derived from the Hindi word *kard,* which means both to "cook over a long period of time" and "sauce." So when you see curry in a recipe title, know that the dish is braised like a stew with a variety of spices, including cardamom, a member of the ginger family and a favorite sweet and zesty addition to curries as well as pastries. The pods contain lots of aromatic seeds but are conveniently placed in our spice bag whole or slightly crushed (the shell disintegrates during cooking). Green cardamom pods, picked when immature and dried, and black cardamom pods are available at Indian groceries. A lamb curry such as this, *curry d'agneau,* is one of the classic bistro dishes of France. Thick and aromatic, it's ideal served with long-grain basmati rice. ● *Serves 6*

COOKER: Medium or large round or oval
SETTING AND COOK TIME: LOW for 6 to 8 hours

2 to 4 tablespoons cooking oil

2 medium-size yellow onions, chopped

2 pounds shoulder of lamb, shank, or butt roast, trimmed of visible fat
    and cut into 2-inch cubes

One ½-inch piece fresh ginger, peeled

2 cloves garlic, peeled

2 serrano or jalapeño chiles, seeded

1 cup vegetable or chicken broth

1 tablespoon ground cumin

1 tablespoon ground coriander

½ teaspoon turmeric

1½ tablespoons all-purpose flour

One 14-ounce can unsweetened coconut milk

2 large tart apples, such as Fuji or Granny Smith,
    peeled, cored, and coarsely chopped

5 green cardamom pods

3 black cardamom pods

One 4-inch cinnamon stick

1 bay leaf

4 cloves

1 teaspoon salt, or to taste

½ cup plain yogurt

⅓ cup fruit chutney, processed until smooth in a food processor

FOR SERVING:

Hot cooked basmati rice

½ cup chopped fresh cilantro

1. In a large nonstick skillet, heat half the oil over medium-high heat and brown half the onions and lamb on all sides, about 10 minutes. Remove them to the cooker and brown the remaining onions and lamb. Add to the cooker.

2. Chop the ginger, garlic, and chiles together in a mini–food processor and add a bit of the broth to make a paste. Add this to the skillet along with the cumin, coriander, and turmeric and cook, stirring constantly, for a few minutes. Sprinkle with the flour and add the remaining broth; stir until smooth, then pour into the cooker, and add the coconut milk and apples. Put the cardamom pods, cinnamon stick, bay leaf, and cloves in a cheesecloth bag; nestle into the mixture. Cover and cook on HIGH for 1 hour.

3. Turn the cooker to LOW and cook until the lamb is very tender, 6 to 8 hours.

4. Discard the spice bag and season the curry with the salt. Stir in the yogurt and chutney; let sit, covered, in the cooker for 15 minutes to heat. Serve with basmati rice garnished with the cilantro.

Irish Stew

T he delicious and perennially popular Irish stew, hailing from the green isle of prophets and philosophers, is a classic ragoût in its technique. Just as with stews in France, meat is cut into pieces, browned to caramelize the surface, then cooked in lots of liquid without a thickener. Serve this with Irish soda bread and butter and a pint of cold Guinness for the quintessential pub meal.

o *Serves 6*

COOKER: Medium or large round or oval
SETTINGS AND COOK TIMES: HIGH for 1 hour, then LOW for 6 to 7 hours

1 to 2 tablespoons olive oil, as needed
2 pounds shoulder of lamb, trimmed of fat,
    cut into 1½-inch cubes, and blottted dry
8 new white potatoes, scrubbed and sliced ½ inch thick
8 small white boiling onions, cut in half
One 12-ounce bag baby carrots, or 3 large carrots, cut into thick rounds
4 ribs celery, chopped
2 tablespoons chopped fresh flat-leaf parsley
2½ teaspoons salt-free herb blend, such as Mrs. Dash or McCormick
2 teaspoons dried thyme
1 bay leaf
2 cups water, chicken broth, or vegetable broth
Salt and freshly ground black pepper to taste

1. In a large nonstick skillet, heat 1 tablespoon of the oil over medium-high heat and brown half of the lamb on all sides. Set aside and brown the other half, adding more oil if needed.

2. Layer the potatoes, onions, carrots, and celery in the slow cooker and place the meat on top. Add the parsley, herb blend, thyme, and bay leaf and pour over the water. Cover and cook on HIGH for 1 hour.

3. Turn the cooker to LOW and cook until the lamb and vegetables are very tender, 6 to 7 hours.

4. Season with salt and pepper. If you like your stew thickened, use 1 or 2 tablespoons of *beurre manié* (page 20). Serve the stew straight out of the pot.

Agnello al Forno

A *gnello al forno,* which means "oven-roasted lamb," is a traditional home-cooked dish, especially around Naples. It is layered in a clay casserole and cooked for hours. Although it is often made with goat, the lamb version, usually cut from the shoulder, is most popular. The fresh herbs are a must; don't even consider making this dish with dried. ● *Serves 6*

COOKER: Medium or large round or oval
SETTING AND COOK TIME: LOW for 8 to 10 hours;
   herbs added during last hour of cooking

3 medium-size yellow onions, cut into 8 wedges
2 cloves garlic, minced
2 pounds new white or red potatoes, halved or quartered
2 tablespoons olive oil
2 pounds lamb stew meat, trimmed of some fat,
   cut into 1½-inch chunks, and blotted dry
¼ cup finely chopped fresh flat-leaf parsley
¼ cup finely chopped fresh basil
2 tablespoons finely chopped fresh oregano or savory
8 grinds of black pepper
Salt to taste
2 pounds firm-ripe plum tomatoes, coarsely chopped
2 tablespoons unsalted butter, cut into bits

1. Layer the onions, garlic, and potatoes in the slow cooker.

2. In a large skillet over medium-high heat, warm 1 tablespoon of the oil until very hot. Add half the meat and cook until browned on all sides, 4 to 5 minutes. Transfer to the cooker. Repeat with the remaining oil and meat. Add half of the herbs and all of the pepper to the cooker and season with salt and pepper. Top with the tomatoes and dot with the butter. Cover and cook on LOW until the lamb is fork-tender, 8 to 10 hours.

3. An hour before the end of the cooking time, sprinkle the remaining herbs on top of the meat and vegetables. Serve with rice and a nice green salad.

Ribs and Wings

The slow cooker excels at cooking ribs and chicken wings, favorite summer party foods, and inexpensive dinner fare. Ribs are a bit fatty, so they stay nice and moist during long cooking and they soak up whatever sauce you use to braise them. Slow cooking plus a good marinade/sauce translates into some really tasty, succulent meat. While ribs smoked on a grill or roasted in an oven are chewy, slow-cooked ribs are fall-apart tender. It is a food that can be made with so little fuss, you might buy a slow cooker just to make ribs.

Beef ribs, called *beef short ribs* or *beef chuck short ribs,* depending on the section from which they are cut, come from the 12 ribs that traverse the lower belly area behind the brisket and just below the prime rib. Look for meaty, lean ribs. Often you can find ribs that are cut from the end of the standing rib roast, and these are outrageously good. Short ribs are also referred to as flanken (especially in German cookbooks) and they are cut across the rib bones. English-style ribs are almost boneless. They are cut into individual rectangles with a bit of bone left in, and are usually found in a butcher shop. When purchasing beef ribs, figure a pound per person, and more if you want leftovers.

The pork ribs family includes spareribs, baby back ribs, and country-style ribs. The sweet nature of the pork marries beautifully with a wide range of tangy barbecue sauces and marinades that cook up into succulent, satisfying fare. *Spareribs* are the most popular pork ribs to cook because of their meatiness and wonderful flavor. If you are like most people, when you picture a plate of ribs, spareribs with a fiery tomato barbecue sauce come to mind. Spareribs are cut from the belly area after the bacon is removed. They come in a slab of 2 to 3 pounds with varying amounts of meat and fat attached, enough to feed 2 to 3 diners. Carefully inspect your slab and choose one with plenty of meat relative to the amount of fat. You can cook your slab whole, divide it into one or two sections to stack in your round slow cooker, or divide the slab into portions. We do not precook our ribs in boiling water; the slow cooker does the job perfectly with no fussy preparation. Just load up the cooker and go.

Baby back ribs are a familiar part of upscale American restaurant rib culture, but they are not the meatiest ribs by far. Baby backs are essentially the loin pork chop bones with the boneless meat trimmed off, so what is left is only a small amount of meat. They show up as appetizers because they are very tender and small. A slab only feeds 1 to 2 people, so you will need to fill the slow cooker to the top to feed a group.

Country-style ribs are little loin pork

chops that have been butterflied or split. They are inexpensive with plenty of meat, and are a favorite for braising in the slow cooker.

With all three cuts, buy only USDA 1 graded pork and buy fresh for the best flavor.

Chicken wings are the ultimate fun finger food, perfect for party snacks, picnics, or casual suppers at home because of their size. A chicken wing is made up of three sections, called joints: The first one is the *drumette,* also called a minidrumstick, and that's exactly what it looks like. It's the meatiest part of the wing and has a single center bone. The middle wing joint has two slender bones and a somewhat more modest amount of very flavorful meat. The third joint is the *wing tip;* its best use is in the stockpot, where its bony character will add flavor and body to your chicken soups. If you are baking or frying chicken wings, there is no reason not to cook them whole and let the diners disjoint them. If you are using your slow cooker, however, your cooking space is somewhat limited, so it's really best to disjoint the wings and cook only the first two sections. (Also, whole wings tend to tangle in the slow cooker, which can be frustrating when you are trying to stir them to distribute the seasoning evenly.)

To disjoint a chicken wing, place it on a cutting board. Bend back one of the joints against the board and use a sharp knife to cut right through the joint. When you find just the right spot to cut, your knife will slide through. It won't take you long to get the hang of it. Cut through the other joint in the same manner, then use your knife to trim off any large hanging flaps of skin. Drop the wing tips into a sturdy plastic bag and freeze them for stock.

Thanks to new marketing strategies of the poultry industry, it's now easier than ever to serve chicken wings. At the fresh meat counter, you may be able to find packages of the so-called minidrumsticks. In warehouse stores and large supermarkets, you can buy large bags of frozen first and second wing joints. These are often called *party wings* and are especially convenient because they are frozen individually, which allows you to remove only the quantity you need. There are approximately 10 party wings to a pound. Take out as many as you need and put them in a separate plastic bag. Thaw them in the refrigerator overnight. Or, if you are in a hurry, put them in a plastic bag in a sink full of cold water.

Serve ribs and wings with baked beans, succotash, big green salads, summer bean or vegetable salads, roasted baked potatoes, and corn on the cob. And offer plenty of big paper napkins (and maybe even those paper bibs).

If you don't want to use a commercial barbecue sauce, here are some homemade sauces to concoct in your slow cooker.

Tangy BBQ Sauce • Makes 3 cups

This is just plain ole BBQ sauce, unadulterated and straightforward, and our all-purpose favorite.

COOKER: Medium or large round or oval
SETTING AND COOK TIME: LOW for 5 to 6 hours

⅓ **cup olive oil**
1 large yellow onion, chopped
½ **cup dry red wine or water**
⅓ **cup cider vinegar**
⅓ **cup fresh lemon juice**
¼ **cup firmly packed light or dark brown sugar**
3 tablespoons Worcestershire sauce
1 tablespoon soy sauce
1 tablespoon paprika
1 to 2 teaspoons chili powder, to your taste
2 cups ketchup

1. In a medium-size skillet, heat the oil over medium heat and cook the onion, stirring, until softened, about 5 minutes. Add the wine and vinegar and bring to a boil, scraping up the browned bits sticking to the pan. Transfer to the slow cooker and stir in the remaining ingredients. Cover and cook on LOW for 5 to 6 hours.

2. If the sauce is not thick enough for you, remove the lid, turn the cooker to HIGH, and cook up to 30 minutes, until it reaches the desired consistency. Purée with a handheld immersion blender or transfer to a food processor and process until smooth. Let cool, then transfer to a jar, and store, tightly covered, in the refrigerator up to 2 months.

Blueberry Barbecue Sauce • Makes 4 cups

Beth's sister Meg sent her a cookbook from Whidbey Island in Puget Sound (in Washington State), a place where she often vacations and enjoys incredible locally grown and produced foods. This is a truly unique recipe for a tomato-less barbecue sauce, adapted from that cookbook, claiming Southern roots and a grandmother's touch. Make it in the summer when fresh blueberries are in season, but frozen berries can also be used. The berries will cook down considerably. This recipe also works with blackberries.

COOKER: Medium or large round or oval
SETTING AND COOK TIME: LOW for 6 to 8 hours

1 tablespoon olive oil

1 small yellow onion, diced

2 cloves garlic, smashed

¼ cup Zinfandel wine

⅓ cup cider vinegar

2½ pints fresh or 2½ pounds frozen blueberries (not packed in syrup)

⅓ cup firmly packed light brown sugar

1 tablespoon Worcestershire sauce

Juice of 1 lemon

Large pinch of red pepper flakes

Large pinch of chili powder

Salt and freshly ground black pepper to taste

1. In a small skillet over medium heat, warm the oil and cook the onion and garlic, stirring, until softened, about 5 minutes. Add the wine and vinegar and bring to a boil, scraping up the browned bits sticking to the pan. Transfer to the slow cooker and add the remaining ingredients. Cover and cook on LOW until thick, 6 to 8 hours.

2. If the sauce is not thick enough for you, remove the lid, turn the cooker to HIGH, and cook up to 30 minutes until it reaches the desired consistency. Purée with a handheld immersion blender or transfer to a food processor and process until smooth. Season with salt and pepper. Let cool, then transfer to a jar and store, tightly covered, in the refrigerator up to 2 months.

Honey Barbecue Sauce ○ Makes 5 cups

This is a simple to prepare, on the sweet side, yet still tangy tomato barbecue sauce that will give you plenty of tasty ribs and chicken. You can add more chili powder if you want a spicier sauce.

COOKER: Medium round or oval
SETTING AND COOK TIME: LOW for 5 to 6 hours

Two 8-ounce cans tomato sauce

1 cup ketchup

3 tablespoons tomato paste

2 cloves garlic, smashed; or ¾ teaspoon garlic powder

1 to 2 shallots, to your taste, minced (in a mini–food processor, if possible)

¾ cup honey

¾ cup preserves or jam, such as raspberry, apricot, peach, plum, or orange marmalade

⅔ cup firmly packed light brown sugar

⅓ cup fresh lemon juice

2 tablespoons Worcestershire sauce

2 tablespoons Dijon mustard

1 tablespoon chili powder, or to taste

Large pinch of red pepper flakes

Salt and freshly ground black pepper to taste

1. Put all the ingredients in the slow cooker, except for the salt and pepper; stir to combine. Cover and cook on LOW until thick, 5 to 6 hours.

2. If the sauce is not thick enough for you, remove the lid, turn the cooker to HIGH, and cook for up to 30 minutes until it reaches the desired consistency. Season with salt and pepper. Let cool, then transfer to a jar and store, tightly covered, in the refrigerator up to 2 months.

Barbecue Pork Ribs

Beth's sister Meg has two toddlers and they love ribs, along with their other favorite meal, quesadillas and steamed broccoli. Meg cuts the prepared barbecue sauce with a bit of ketchup to appeal to the younger palate. We think they taste fabulous. ○ *Serves 4 to 6*

COOKER: Large round or oval
SETTING AND COOK TIME: LOW for 8 to 9 hours

2 cups barbecue sauce of your choice, homemade (pages 390–392) or prepared
½ cup ketchup

1 tablespoon Worcestershire sauce

2 tablespoons light or dark brown sugar

4 pounds pork spareribs or baby back ribs, cut into serving pieces of 3 to 4 ribs each,
   or country-style ribs

1. Combine the barbecue sauce, ketchup, Worcestershire, and brown sugar in the slow cooker. Add the ribs, submerging them in the sauce. If you have a round cooker, stack the ribs, with sauce in between. Cover and cook on LOW until tender and the meat starts to separate from the bone, 8 to 9 hours.

2. Transfer the ribs to a platter. If there is extra sauce on the bottom of the cooker, place in a bowl and serve on the side.

Honey Barbecue Pork Ribs

 his glaze is ridiculously simple and splendidly delicious.

○ *Serves 4 to 6*

COOKER: Large round or oval

SETTING AND COOK TIME: LOW for 8 to 9 hours

4 pounds pork spareribs or baby back ribs, cut into serving pieces of 3 to 4 ribs each,
   or country-style ribs

1 yellow onion, sliced

One 16-ounce bottle prepared barbecue sauce, or 2 cups homemade (pages 390–392)

½ cup mild-flavored honey

1. Arrange the ribs and onions in the slow cooker in alternating layers. Combine the barbecue sauce and honey in a medium-size bowl and mix until smooth; spoon over the ribs. If you have a round cooker, spoon the sauce between the layers of ribs and onions. Cover and cook on LOW until tender and the meat starts to separate from the bone, 8 to 9 hours.

2. Transfer the ribs to a platter. If there is extra sauce on the bottom of the cooker, place in a bowl and serve on the side.

Pork Ribs with Molasses Glaze

Molasses is a favorite ingredient in the sweet, sticky glazes that grace ribs from New England to the South. Serve these ribs with potato salad and hot biscuits. ○ *Serves 6 to 8*

COOKER: Large round or oval
SETTING AND COOK TIME: LOW for 8 to 10 hours

½ cup Dijon mustard
½ cup light or dark unsulphured molasses
⅓ cup cider vinegar
⅓ cup firmly packed light or dark brown sugar
1 to 2 teaspoons hot pepper sauce, such as Tabasco, to your taste
Pinch of salt
4 pounds pork spareribs or baby back ribs, cut into serving pieces of 3 to 4
    ribs each, or country-style ribs

1. Combine the mustard, molasses, vinegar, brown sugar, hot pepper sauce, and salt in a medium-size, heavy saucepan and bring to a boil over medium heat; reduce the heat to low and simmer for 5 minutes, uncovered. Remove the glaze from the heat and let cool to room temperature.

2. Brush both the sides of the ribs with two to three coats of the glaze. Arrange the ribs in the slow cooker. If you have a round cooker, stack the ribs. Cover and cook on LOW until tender and the meat starts to separate from the bone, 8 to 10 hours. Serve immediately.

Country Ribs with Onions, Apples, and Sauerkraut

W hile sauerkraut, literally "sour cabbage," is thought of as a European culinary tradition, it was a staple food more than 2,000 years ago in China, where it was fermented in stoneware crocks with rice wine and salt. It made its way to Europe along the spice route, and the countries along the North Sea, especially Germany and Poland, adopted it. Sauerkraut has a sour tang that complements the sweetness of pork perfectly. Do not buy canned or jarred sauerkraut; opt for the fresh kraut in bags, found in the deli section. Serve these ribs with mashed or boiled parsley potatoes, cranberry sauce, and some creamy horseradish.

● *Serves 4*

COOKER: Large round or oval
SETTING AND COOK TIME: LOW for 8 to 9 hours

2 to 3 pounds country-style pork ribs
Salt and freshly ground black pepper to taste
2 medium-size white onions, sliced ¼ inch thick
2 medium-size tart cooking apples, peeled, cored, and sliced ¼ inch thick
2 pounds fresh sauerkraut, rinsed and drained
½ teaspoon caraway seeds
½ cup apple juice or dry white wine
¼ cup beef or vegetable broth

Grease the bottom of the slow cooker with some butter or oil. Season the ribs with salt and pepper. Layer in the onions, apples, ribs, and sauerkraut. Sprinkle with the caraway seeds and pour the juice and broth over everything. Cover and cook on LOW until tender and the meat starts to separate from the bone, 8 to 9 hours. Serve immediately.

Soulfully Good Pork Spareribs with Pineapple and Ginger

Here is another glaze that is ridiculously simple and really delicious. It does require overnight marination, so plan accordingly. ○ *Serves 4 to 6*

COOKER: Large round or oval
SETTING AND COOK TIME: LOW for 8 to 9 hours

One 20-ounce can pineapple chunks packed in juice, drained and ½ cup juice reserved
⅓ cup soy sauce
⅓ cup ketchup
3 tablespoons cider vinegar
2 tablespoons dry sherry
3 tablespoons light or dark brown sugar
2 tablespoons minced or grated fresh ginger
1 clove garlic, minced
4 pounds pork spareribs or baby back ribs, cut into serving pieces of 3 to 4 ribs each,
    or country-style ribs

1. Combine the reserved pineapple juice, the soy sauce, ketchup, vinegar, sherry, brown sugar, ginger, and garlic in a large deep bowl; add the ribs. Cover and marinate overnight in the refrigerator.

2. Grease the slow cooker with some oil and add the ribs and marinade. If you have a round cooker, stack the ribs, alternating them with the reserved pineapple chunks. If you have an oval cooker, put the ribs in the crock and scatter the pineapple around the ribs. Cover and cook on LOW until tender and the meat starts to separate from the bone, 8 to 9 hours. Serve immediately.

Short Ribs of Beef Flavored with Chiles and Beer

T his recipe came from one of our favorite, and surprisingly little known, food magazines, *Chile Pepper*. Yep—every recipe has chiles in it. This one is so tasty, you might never head over to a rib joint again. You can eat these ribs right out of the cooker or finish them off on the grill for a really fast and easy barbecue party where the guests are not waiting around for hours for your ribs to cook through. Serve with coleslaw and margaritas. Don't be put off by the large amount of ribs. This recipe is designed for entertaining, but you can cut the amounts in half with no problem. ○ *Serves 10 to 14*

COOKER: Large oval or round
SETTING AND COOK TIME: LOW for 7 to 9 hours

Two 12-ounce bottles beer
¼ cup firmly packed light brown sugar
2 teaspoons dry mustard
2 teaspoons garlic powder
4 cups barbecue sauce of your choice, homemade (pages 390–392) or prepared
½ cup rice vinegar
½ cup yellow mustard (not too hot)
½ cup honey
1 orange, cut into ¼-inch-thick rounds
1 medium-size white onion, cut into ¼-inch-thick slices
4 pickled jalapeños, cut into ¼-inch-thick rings
2 canned chipotle chiles in adobo sauce, drained and chopped
12 pounds beef short ribs
Sea salt and freshly ground black pepper to taste

1. Combine the beer, brown sugar, mustard, and garlic powder in a medium-size bowl and stir until well blended. Add the barbecue sauce, vinegar, mustard, and honey and stir until smooth.

2. Put the orange, onion, jalapeños, and chipotle peppers in the slow cooker. Season the ribs with salt and pepper and arrange them on top. Pour on the sauce, completely covering the ribs. Or, if you have a round cooker, stack the ribs, alternating them with sauce. Cover and cook on LOW until tender and the meat starts to separate from the bone, 7 to 9 hours.

3. Transfer the ribs to a platter and set aside. Let the sauce cool a bit, then spoon the liquid fat off the top and discard. Serve immediately or place the ribs on a hot grill to finish off and give the ribs more color. Strain the sauce through a fine-mesh strainer and serve on the side.

Red Wine Short Ribs of Beef

T his beef rib recipe is based on the first one Beth ever made. Though it was good, browning the ribs first in a Dutch oven was a lot of work. The slow cooker completely eliminates that step, but still serves up beef ribs that are meaty and juicy. ○ *Serves 4 to 5*

COOKER: Large round or oval
SETTING AND COOK TIME: LOW for 7 to 8 hours

1 cup red wine, such as Merlot
⅔ cup ketchup
3 tablespoons soy sauce
2 cloves garlic (optional), crushed
2 tablespoons light or dark brown sugar
½ teaspoon freshly ground black pepper
4 pounds beef short ribs
2 medium-size yellow onions, chopped

1. Combine the wine, ketchup, soy sauce, garlic, if using, brown sugar, and pepper in the slow cooker and mix until smooth. Add the ribs, submerging them in the sauce. If you have a round cooker, stack the ribs. Distribute the onions over the ribs. Cover and cook on LOW until tender and the meat starts to separate from the bone, 7 to 8 hours.

2. Transfer the ribs to a platter and set aside. Let the sauce cool for a bit, then spoon the liquid fat off the surface and discard. Pour the sauce over the ribs and serve immediately.

The Easiest Beef Short Ribs

 This is fast, easy, and delicious.
o *Serves 4*

COOKER: Large round or oval
SETTING AND COOK TIME: LOW for 7 to 8 hours

1 tablespoon unsalted butter or olive oil
1 medium-size yellow onion, finely chopped
¾ cup ketchup
¼ cup soy sauce
3 tablespoons cider vinegar
3 tablespoons light or dark brown sugar
3 to 4 pounds beef short ribs

1. In a small skillet, heat the butter over medium heat until melted, then cook the onion, stirring, until softened and golden, about 5 minutes. Add the ketchup, soy sauce, vinegar, and brown sugar, stir until smooth, and heat for 5 minutes.

2. Place the short ribs on a broiler pan and broil until well browned. Arrange the ribs in the slow cooker. If you have a round cooker, stack them. Pour over the sauce, distributing the onions over all the ribs. Cover and cook on LOW until tender and the meat starts to separate from the bone, 7 to 8 hours.

3. Transfer the ribs to a platter. Let the sauce cool a bit, then spoon the liquid fat off the surface and discard. Pour the sauce over the ribs and serve immediately.

Peking Honey Chicken Wings

hese wings are nice party food, salty and sweet at the same time. Or serve them with rice for a casual dinner. ● *Serves 4 as a main dish, 10 as an appetizer*

COOKER: Large round or oval
SETTING AND COOK TIME: HIGH for 1½ to 2 hours

4 pounds chicken wings, cut into joints, with bony wing tips reserved for stock
   or discarded; or 3 pounds chicken drumettes
1 tablespoon vegetable oil
½ cup soy sauce
¼ cup dry sherry
¼ cup cider vinegar
¼ cup hoisin sauce
½ cup honey
¼ cup orange marmalade
6 green onions (white and green parts), finely chopped
2 cloves garlic, minced
A few splashes of hot pepper sauce, such as Tabasco

1. Coat the slow cooker with nonstick cooking spray. Rinse the chicken and pat dry.

2. Heat the oil in a large, heavy skillet over medium-high heat. Brown the wings nicely, in batches if necessary, 3 to 5 minutes per side. As they brown, transfer to the cooker.

3. Whisk together the remaining ingredients in a medium-size bowl, and pour over the wings; stir the wings to coat evenly. Cover and cook on HIGH for 1½ to 2 hours. If possible, stir gently halfway through cooking with a wooden spoon, pushing the wings on the top to the bottom to coat with sauce. Serve hot or warm.

Orange-Dijon Chicken Wings

 These tangy wings were the tasters' favorites.

○ *Serves 4 as a main dish, 10 as an appetizer*

COOKER: Large round or oval
SETTING AND COOK TIME: HIGH for 1½ to 2 hours

4 pounds chicken wings, cut into joints, bony wing tips cut off and reserved for
    stock or discarded; or 3 pounds chicken drumettes
1 tablespoon olive oil, or more as needed
3 shallots, finely chopped
½ cup orange marmalade
3 tablespoons Dijon mustard
2 tablespoons cider vinegar
2 teaspoons Worcestershire sauce
1 tablespoon firmly packed light brown sugar
Pinch of salt

1. Coat the slow cooker with nonstick cooking spray. Rinse and pat dry the wings.

2. Heat the oil in a large heavy skillet over medium-high heat. Brown the wings
nicely, in batches if necessary, 3 to 5 minutes per side. As they brown, transfer to
the cooker.

3. Lower the heat to medium, and if necessary, add 1 to 2 teaspoons more oil to the
skillet. Add the shallots and cook, stirring, until softened, 3 to 4 minutes; stir in
the remaining ingredients.

4. Remove from the heat and pour over the wings; stir the wings to coat evenly.
Cover and cook on HIGH for 1½ to 2 hours. If possible, stir gently halfway through
cooking with a wooden spoon, pushing the wings on the top to the bottom to coat
with sauce. Serve hot or warm.

Chicken Wings with Apricot Sauce

This sweet glaze is also excellent on pork ribs. It is adapted from one that was featured in our "Home Plates" column in the *San Jose Mercury News*, which was in turn adapted from a recipe in a 1999 issue of *Gourmet* magazine.

● *Serves 4 as a main dish, 10 as an appetizer*

COOKER: Large round or oval
SETTING AND COOK TIME: HIGH for 1½ to 2 hours

4 pounds chicken wings, cut into joints, with bony wing tips reserved for stock
    or discarded, or 3 pounds chicken drumettes
1 tablespoon olive oil, or more if needed
⅔ cup apricot preserves
2 cloves garlic, pressed
½ cup fresh lime juice (from 5 to 6 limes)
⅓ cup soy sauce
¼ cup sugar

1. Coat the slow cooker with nonstick cooking spray. Rinse the wings and pat dry.

2. Heat the oil in a large, heavy skillet over medium-high heat. Brown the wings nicely, in batches if necessary, 3 to 5 minutes per side. As they brown, transfer to the cooker.

3. Combine the remaining ingredients in a food processor and process until smooth. Pour over the chicken; stir the wings to coat evenly. Cover and cook on HIGH for 1½ to 2 hours. If possible, stir gently halfway through cooking with a wooden spoon, pushing the wings on the top to the bottom to coat with the sauce. Serve hot or warm.

Fish and Shellfish

In this chapter we include a few recipes for preparing fish and shellfish in the slow cooker. Please take careful note that fish cooks much more quickly than other foods, so cooking it in the slow cooker is never an all-day affair unless you are making a sauce that will act as a base. Our recipes use techniques that depart from the "all-day" format, so pay particular attention to the short cook times. What you'll find in this chapter are flavorful seafood stews and a revolutionary steaming technique—cooking the fish on HIGH for a short time—that is so convenient, we think you will use it over and over again.

Crab Cioppino

C ioppino is a communal tomato and seafood stew that is somewhat of a tradition around the San Francisco Bay Area in the restaurants of North Beach, as well as in homes. It is nicknamed "fisherman's stew" for its popularity in the Italian and Portuguese fishing communities, partly because it is based on leftovers from the daily catch. Many families enjoy it as their Christmas Eve dinner, which comes smack-dab in the middle of the West Coast Dungeness crab season. Serve it in a shallow serving bowl with tongs and a ladle for all to portion out their shares, and provide bibs, crab crackers, and lots of napkins. This is a meal you eat with your fingers, along with sourdough bread to sop up the sauce. This recipe can easily be doubled; just remember to allow half a crab for each person.

o *Serves 6*

> **COOKER:** Large round or oval
> **SETTINGS AND COOK TIMES:** LOW for 4 to 6 hours,
>   then HIGH for 20 to 30 minutes (when crab is added)

¼ cup olive oil

1 medium-size yellow onion, finely chopped

2 cloves garlic, minced

One 15-ounce can tomato sauce

Two 28-ounce cans whole plum tomatoes, drained a bit (if packed in purée, don't drain)

1 cup dry white wine

1 bay leaf

1 tablespoon dried basil, or 3 tablespoons chopped fresh basil

1 teaspoon red pepper flakes

½ teaspoon dried oregano

Salt and freshly ground black pepper to taste

3 steamed whole crabs, cracked and cleaned (ask your fishmonger to do this)

1. In a medium-size skillet, heat the oil over medium heat, then cook the onion, stirring, until softened, about 5 minutes. Add the garlic and cook, stirring, for 2 minutes. Transfer to the slow cooker and add the tomato sauce, tomatoes, wine, bay leaf, basil, pepper flakes, and oregano. Break up the tomatoes with the back of a spoon. Cover and simmer on LOW for 4 to 6 hours.

2. Season with salt and pepper. Add the crab, cover, and cook on HIGH for 20 to 30 minutes to heat the crab through. Serve immediately.

Mixed Seafood Cioppino: In place of the crabs, substitute 1 pound of medium-size (16 to 20 count) shrimp with their tails left on, peeled and deveined; 2 cracked and cleaned steamed crabs; ½ pound large sea scallops; and 1 pound white-fleshed fish fillets, such as red snapper, sea bass, halibut, or monkfish. Add to the hot tomato sauce during the last 20 to 30 minutes of cooking.

Tips for Cooking Seafood in the Slow Cooker

- Buy fresh fish, but look for deals on frozen shrimp, scallops, and calamari, which work perfectly in the slow cooker. Fresh fish should smell clean and sweet, never fishy or unpleasant. Avoid slimy or dried out fish; it should look firm, moist, and translucent. And avoid delicate fish, which will fall apart in the cooker. If you are using clams, oysters, or mussels, they should be alive and clean, and their shells should be intact and tightly closed.

- Store all seafood in the refrigerator until ready to use.

Shrimp Creole Stew

H ere is that holy trinity of Creole cooking: onion, celery, and green pepper. Filé powder (pronounced FEE-lay) or sassafras root, is a seasoning characteristic of Creole cooking. It tastes woodsy with a hint of root beer. It is added at the end of cooking to thicken as well as to enhance flavor. ○ *Serves 6*

COOKER: Medium round or oval
SETTINGS AND COOK TIMES: LOW for 5 to 6 hours, or HIGH for 2½ to 3 hours

One 14.5-ounce can diced tomatoes, with their juice
One 14.5-ounce can chicken broth
1½ cups chopped onions
1 cup seeded and chopped green bell pepper
1 cup thinly sliced celery
2 cloves garlic, minced
1½ teaspoons paprika
½ teaspoon freshly ground black pepper
¼ teaspoon salt
¼ teaspoon hot pepper sauce, such as Tabasco
1 bay leaf
One 6-ounce can tomato paste
1½ pounds raw medium-size shrimp (31 to 35 count), peeled and deveined
1 medium-size bunch green onions (white part and a few inches of the green), chopped
1 tablespoon filé powder

FOR SERVING:
3 cups hot cooked white or pecan rice
Hot pepper sauce, such as Tabasco

1. Combine the tomatoes with their juice, the broth, onions, bell pepper, celery, garlic, paprika, black pepper, salt, hot pepper sauce, and bay leaf in the slow cooker; stir in the tomato paste. Cover and cook on LOW for 5 to 6 hours or on HIGH for 2½ to 3 hours.

2. Discard the bay leaf. Stir the shrimp, green onions, and filé powder into the hot tomato-vegetable mixture, cover, and cook until the shrimp are cooked through, about 5 minutes. Serve immediately over hot cooked rice with a bottle of hot pepper sauce on the side.

Confetti Seafood Chowder

An elaboration of the corn chowder on page 70, this seafood chowder is a colorful meal-in-a-bowl. Chowder is a gift to the culinary world from the fishermen of France; it is a communal stew made with the catch of the day. The fish stew was cooked in a heavy iron pot called a *chaudière,* the root of the word "chowder." We like to make it with the individually quick-frozen mixed seafood that is sold in convenient 1-pound bags in one of our local specialty markets. We keep a bag or two in the freezer so that we can make this chowder anytime. The blend we buy consists of calamari rings, peeled shrimp, and scallops, but we've seen other blends that include fish chunks, clams, and crab. Or design your own combination of shellfish and/or mild white fish fillets based on what is available. If you are using fresh seafood, the final cooking step will go more quickly.

● *Serves 4 to 6 as a main course*

COOKER: Medium or large round
SETTINGS AND COOK TIMES: LOW for 5 to 6 hours, then HIGH for 1 hour or less

1½ tablespoons unsalted butter

1 small yellow onion, finely chopped

3 ribs celery, finely chopped

1 large or 2 small red bell peppers, seeded and finely chopped

2 medium-size russet potatoes, peeled and cut into ½-inch dice

2 cups chicken broth

½ bay leaf

⅛ teaspoon paprika

1 teaspoon dried thyme or 1 tablespoon chopped fresh thyme

¼ teaspoon freshly ground black pepper

½ teaspoon salt or to taste

2 cups whole milk

1 cup half-and-half

2 cups frozen corn kernels, thawed

1 pound shellfish, white-fleshed fish fillets, or a combination
    (choose fresh or individually quick-frozen shellfish), cleaned or
    shelled and cut into chunks, if necessary

1. In a medium-size skillet, heat the butter over medium-high heat. Add the onion and celery and cook, stirring a few times, until the onion is transparent, 2 to 3 minutes. Add the bell pepper and cook until it begins to soften, 2 to 3 minutes longer.

2. While the vegetables are cooking, put the potatoes in the slow cooker.

3. When the vegetables are ready, scrape them into the cooker along with any remaining butter. Add the broth, bay leaf, paprika, thyme, and black pepper. If the broth is unsalted, add the ½ teaspoon salt. Stir the top layer of the ingredients very gently, trying not to disturb the potatoes, which should stay submerged. Cover and cook on LOW until the potatoes are fork-tender, 5 to 6 hours.

4. Add the milk, half-and-half, corn, and seafood and stir to combine. Cover and cook on HIGH until the chowder is heated through and the seafood is just cooked through, about 1 hour longer. Taste for salt and pepper. Remove the bay leaf before serving.

Chicken and Shrimp Jambalaya

Jambalaya is a hallmark of regional Creole cooking and there must be a version for every restaurant in New Orleans. It is a complex one-pot dish, composed of rice, onions, green peppers, tomatoes, a cured meat such as ham or bacon, poultry, and shellfish, or any combination thereof. ○ *Serves 4 to 6*

COOKER: Medium or large round or oval
SETTINGS AND COOK TIMES: LOW for 5 to 6 hours, or HIGH for 2½ to 3 hours, then HIGH for 10 to 15 minutes (when shrimp and green pepper are added)

1 large yellow onion, chopped
1 cup thinly sliced celery
One 14.5-ounce can diced tomatoes, with their juice
One 14.5-ounce can chicken broth
3 ounces tomato paste (half of a 6-ounce can)
1½ tablespoons Worcestershire sauce
1½ teaspoons Cajun seasoning
1 pound boneless, skinless chicken breast halves or thighs, cut into ¾-inch pieces

1½ cups converted rice

8 ounces raw large shrimp (16 to 20 or 21 to 30 count), peeled and deveined

¾ cup seeded and chopped green bell pepper

FOR SERVING:

French bread

Butter

1. Combine the onion, celery, tomatoes with their juice, broth, tomato paste, Worcestershire, and Cajun seasoning in the slow cooker. Stir in the chicken and rice. Cover and cook until most of the liquid is absorbed, the chicken is cooked through, and the rice is tender, on LOW for 5 to 6 hours, or on HIGH for 2½ to 3 hours.

2. Stir in the shrimp and green pepper, cover, and cook on HIGH for 10 to 15 minutes, until the shrimp is cooked through. Serve immediately in shallow bowls with fresh French bread and butter.

Huachinango à la Veracruzana

When Beth traveled in Baja, California, there were many restaurants, often large like cafeterias, that specialized in *mariscos,* or seafood. One of the most common dishes on the menu was *huachinango Veracruzana* (snapper in tomato sauce), named for the city on the Caribbean east of Mexico City, that at one time received most of the merchant ships arriving from Spain. Mexican capers are not usually available in the United States, so just use the plumpest, largest ones you can find on the supermarket shelf. Also use Mexican oregano, which is mellower than Greek oregano and a favorite herb. Traditional recipes recommend serving this with chopped green or black olives, a touch we find optional. Accompany it with Spanish rice and warm corn tortillas. ◦ *Serves 4 to 5*

COOKER: Medium or large oval

SETTINGS AND COOK TIMES: LOW for 5 to 6 hours, then HIGH for 20 to 30 minutes; or HIGH for 3 to 3½ hours total; fish added during last 20 to 30 minutes

1 small to medium-size yellow or white onion, finely chopped

2 cloves garlic, pressed

½ teaspoon dried oregano

Pinch of ground cinnamon

2 tablespoons olive oil

2 tablespoons minced fresh flat-leaf parsley or cilantro

1 to 2 jalapeños, to your taste, seeded and finely chopped

One 28-ounce can diced tomatoes, drained

½ cup bottled clam juice

1 pound snapper fillets

3 tablespoons fresh lime juice

1 tablespoon large capers, rinsed and drained

2 limes, sliced, for serving

1. Combine the onion, garlic, oregano, cinnamon, olive oil, parsley, jalapeños, tomatoes, and clam juice in the slow cooker. Cover and cook until the sauce is bubbling hot and well blended, on LOW for 5 to 6 hours or on HIGH for 2½ to 3 hours.

2. Lay the fish in the sauce; if the fillets are thick and you have an oval cooker, lay them flat and slightly overlapping. If you have a round cooker, roll up the fillets and set them in the sauce. Spoon some of the sauce over the fillets; drizzle with the lime juice and sprinkle with the capers. Cover and cook on HIGH until the fish is cooked through and flakes when prodded with a fork, 20 to 30 minutes. Do not overcook.

3. Serve immediately, garnished with lime slices.

Baccalà alla Fiorentina

B*accalà* is cod that has been salted and dried, probably one of the oldest ways of preserving fish. It is a hallmark of provincial European cookery. Every province of Italy has its own salt cod stew cooked in earthenware. The French counterpart is *brandade,* and the Spanish is *bacalao al ajo.* Here we use olives, capers, pine nuts, and raisins and dredge the milk-soaked cod in flour, which thickens the stew. This version of *baccalà* is found in Florence, an area of

Italy not on the seacoast. The salt cod must be soaked in cold water for 12 hours before preparing the dish, so plan accordingly the day before. Serve this with boiled potatoes and spinach or turnip greens on the side and crusty Italian bread.

○ *Serves 4 to 6*

COOKER: Medium round or oval

SETTINGS AND COOK TIMES: HIGH for 1 hour, then LOW for 3 to 4 hours; pine nuts added during last 20 minutes

2 pounds salt cod

Milk

¼ cup all-purpose flour or whole wheat pastry flour

Salt and freshly ground black pepper

¼ cup olive oil

16 white boiling onions, peeled and cut in half

4 medium-size ripe tomatoes, peeled, seeded, and chopped;
    or 1 cup chopped canned tomatoes, drained

¾ cup pitted ripe olives of your choice, drained

½ cup golden raisins

¾ cup chicken or vegetable broth

3 tablespoons tomato paste

3 tablespoons balsamic vinegar

3 tablespoons chopped fresh flat-leaf parsley or celery leaves

2 tablespoons nonpareil capers, rinsed and drained

⅓ cup pine nuts (optional), toasted lightly in a dry skillet over medium heat
    until light brown

1. Wash the salt cod, place in a bowl, and cover with cold water. Cover and refrigerate for about 12 hours, pouring off the water and refilling 3 times. Drain and rinse in a colander under cold running water and pat dry with paper towels. Remove the skin and cut the fish into 2-inch chunks. Put in a bowl and cover with cold milk. Cover and refrigerate for about 2 hours. Rinse the salt cod again in a colander under cold water and pat dry. Put the flour on a plate, season with salt and pepper, and coat each chunk of fish with the flour.

2. Heat 2 tablespoons of the oil in a large, heavy skillet over medium-high heat and quuickly brown the cod on both sides. Transfer to the slow cooker. Add the remaining 2 tablespoons of oil to the skillet and quickly cook the onions, stirring, for

5 minutes only, until limp. Transfer to the cooker. Add the tomatoes, olives, raisins, broth, tomato paste, vinegar, parsley, and capers to the cooker. Cover and cook on HIGH for 1 hour.

3. Turn the cooker to LOW and cook until the onions are tender, 3 to 4 hours.

4. Stir in the pine nuts during the last 20 minutes of cooking. Serve hot ladled out of the crock.

Crock-Poached Salmon Steaks

The oval cooker works best for this simple recipe; the naturally high fat content of the fish means it is forgiving of being slightly overcooked. Be sure to pour the boiling liquid around the fish, not over the top. This recipe also works perfectly with halibut or swordfish steaks. Serve with tartar sauce. ○

Serves 4

COOKER: Medium or large oval
SETTING AND COOK TIME: HIGH for 1½ hours

Four 8-ounce salmon steaks or fillets, rinsed and blotted dry
1 cup chicken broth or water
½ cup dry white wine
Sea salt to taste
2 black peppercorns
1 sprig fresh dill
1 thick slice onion
3 sprigs fresh flat-leaf parsley

FOR SERVING:
Lemon wedges
Cold tartar sauce

1. Coat the slow cooker with nonstick cooking spray and arrange the salmon in it. The steaks can be set tightly side by side; tuck the ends of fillets under themselves to even out the thickness of the fish so it can cook evenly.

2. Heat the broth and wine in a saucepan or the microwave until boiling. Pour around the salmon. Sprinkle the steaks with some salt, then add the peppercorns, dill, onion slice, and parsley to the liquid around the steaks. Cover and cook on HIGH until the salmon is opaque and firm to the touch, about 1½ hours.

3. Carefully lift the salmon out of the cooker with a rubber spatula or pancake turner. Serve immediately while still hot or cool until lukewarm in the poaching liquid and refrigerate until cold. Accompany with lemon wedges and tartar sauce.

Nancyjo's Crock-Poached Salmon with Hollandaise Sauce

O ur friend Nancyjo Riekse serves slices of cooked salmon on a bed of steamed baby bok choy. We like it with hollandaise as well. ● *Serves 4 to 6*

COOKER: Medium or large oval
SETTING AND COOK TIME: HIGH for 1½ hours

One 2- to 3-pound skinned thick center-cut salmon fillet, rinsed and blotted dry
Salt and freshly ground black pepper to taste
1 lemon, sliced
1 cup vegetable broth
2 tablespoons unsalted butter

HOLLANDAISE SAUCE:
4 large egg yolks
1 tablespoon fresh lemon juice
Dash of salt and white pepper
1 cup (2 sticks) unsalted butter, melted and kept hot
⅓ cup sour cream (reduced fat is okay)

1. Coat the slow cooker with nonstick cooking spray and arrange the salmon fillet in it, tucking the ends of the fillet under to even out the thickness of the fish so it will cook evenly. Season the fish lightly with salt and pepper, then arrange the lemon slices over the top.

2. Heat the broth and butter together in a saucepan or the microwave until boiling. Pour around the salmon. Cover and cook on HIGH until the salmon is opaque and firm to the touch, about 1½ hours.

3. To make the sauce, put the egg yolks, lemon juice, salt, and white pepper in a food processor and process to combine. With the motor running, add the hot melted butter, drop by drop at first, then in a slow, steady stream through the feed tube, until the sauce is creamy and emulsified. Transfer to a bowl and whisk in the sour cream. Pour the sauce into a deep container that can stand in a hot water bath until serving or into a Thermos-type container.

4. Carefully lift the fish out of the crock with a large rubber spatula or pancake turner. Serve immediately with the hollandaise on the side for individual pouring.

Citrus Sea Bass

 You can substitute other firm fish such as halibut or grouper for the sea bass. ◦ *Serves 4*

COOKER: Medium or large oval
SETTING AND COOK TIME: HIGH for 1½ hours

1½ pounds sea bass fillets, rinsed and blotted dry
Sea salt and white pepper to taste
1 medium-size white onion, chopped
¼ cup minced fresh flat-leaf parsley
1 tablespoon grated lemon, lime, or orange zest or a combination
3 tablespoons dry white wine or water
1 tablespoon olive oil or Asian sesame oil

FOR SERVING:
Lemon wedges
Lime wedges
Cold tartar sauce

1. Coat the slow cooker with nonstick cooking spray or butter and arrange the fish in the crock. Season lightly with salt and white pepper, then add the onion, parsley, and zest. Drizzle with the wine and oil. Cover and cook on HIGH for 1½ hours.

2. Carefully lift the fish out of the cooker with a plastic spatula or pancake turner. Serve immediately with lemon and lime wedges and tartar sauce.

Trout in White Wine

T rout is a member of the salmonid family, which means it is related to salmon, as well as rainbow and steelhead trout. This is a popular method of preparing trout. Serve it hot from the crock with a *beurre blanc,* the delicious French white butter sauce that is a reduction of shallots, vinegar, and wine. Or remove the fish from the crock, let cool, refrigerate, and serve cold with tartar sauce. Either way will complement the dry texture of the fish. ○ *Serves 6*

COOKER: Medium or large oval
SETTING AND COOK TIME: HIGH for 45 minutes to 1¼ hours, depending on size of fish

6 boned trout, head and tail left on, each about 1½ pounds
Salt and freshly ground black pepper to taste
2 tablespoons unsalted butter
2 medium-size shallots, chopped
¼ cup chopped fresh flat-leaf parsley
1 lemon, sliced
1½ cups dry white wine

1. Coat the slow cooker with nonstick cooking spray. Sprinkle the inside and outside of the fish with salt and pepper and arrange the trout in the cooker; they can be lying against each other.

2. In a small skillet over medium heat, melt the butter, then cook the shallots until softened, 3 to 4 minutes; stir in the parsley and stuff the mixture inside each trout. Arrange the lemon slices on top.

3. Heat the wine in a saucepan or the microwave until boiling. Pour around the trout. Cover and cook on HIGH until the fish is tender, 45 minutes to 1¼ hours.

Slow Cooker Coquilles

F resh scallops have a sweet, clean smell and are very perishable. Like other seafood, scallops, known as *coquilles Saint Jacques* in French, steam until tender quickly in the slow cooker, so stay in the kitchen for this recipe. Since scallops are different sizes, the cook time will be slightly different each time. Rinse and drain them just before cooking. Serve this as a first course with French bread or as a main dish with a steamed green vegetable, such as peas or asparagus. If you want the scallops browned, sprinkle them with Swiss cheese and place under the broiler until melted and browned. Thanks to fellow slow cooker aficionado Lora Brody for turning us on to cooking scallops in the cooker. o

Serves 4 as an appetizer

COOKER: Medium round
SETTING AND COOK TIME: HIGH for 45 minutes to 1¼ hours;
scallops added during last 30 to 45 minutes

2 tablespoons unsalted butter
2 tablespoons minced shallots
¼ cup dry vermouth
6 slices lemon
1⅓ pounds bay scallops (or sea scallops, halved), rinsed and blotted dry
Pinch of sea salt
Pinch of white pepper
2 tablespoons minced fresh flat-leaf parsley (optional)
¼ cup crème fraîche (optional)

1. Combine the butter, shallots, vermouth, and lemon slices in the slow cooker. Cover and turn to HIGH until the butter is melted, 15 to 30 minutes. It is very important to heat the poaching liquid first or the scallops will not cook properly.

2. Add the scallops and salt, tossing the scallops to coat with the poaching liquid. Cover and cook on HIGH until opaque and firm, 30 to 45 minutes. Watch carefully so they don't overcook.

3. Discard the lemon slices and add a sprinkling of white pepper. Lift the scallops out of the poaching liquid and divide among 6 scallop shells or little ramekins. Serve as is sprinkled with a bit of parsley or add ¼ cup crème fraîche to the reserved poaching liquid to make a divine and decadent sauce. Spoon over the scallops.

Calamari Fra Diavolo

Beth worked at India Joze restaurant in Santa Cruz in the 1980s. One of the restaurant's features was a calamari festival every September. Even though Beth was a pastry chef, at around noon every day during the festival, the backroom baking table was covered in plastic and a team of part-time workers arrived just to clean squid. Beth joined in and for two weeks personally cleaned tens of pounds of squid with a Chinese cleaver. There were also cooking classes.

There are two distinct methods of cooking calamari. One is to flash sauté it in a frying pan or wok with some nice sauce. The second is to cook it for about 45 minutes at a very low simmer. Any method between these two extremes will give you chewy flesh and tentacles. Fra diavolo—a spicy tomato sauce—is a very common way to present calamari to diners who have never had it before. You can chop the tentacles into smaller pieces, or leave them whole since they are small. Serve this with fresh crusty bread or over spaghetti. ○ *Serves 4*

COOKER: Medium round or oval
SETTING AND COOK TIME: LOW for 2¼ to 3 hours; squid added during last 45 minutes to 1 hour

¼ cup olive oil

1 large yellow onion, diced

1 clove garlic, crushed

2 cups chopped canned plum tomatoes or peeled fresh tomatoes

2 tablespoons tomato paste

¼ to ½ teaspoon red pepper flakes, to your taste

¼ teaspoon dried oregano

1½ cups dry white wine

2 pounds squid, or 1¾ pounds if it has already been cleaned

2 tablespoons chopped fresh flat-leaf parsley

Salt to taste

1. Heat the oil in a medium-size, heavy skillet over medium heat and quickly cook the onion, stirring, until softened, about 5 minutes, then add the garlic and sauté a few minutes longer. Transfer to the slow cooker and add the tomatoes, tomato paste, red pepper, and oregano. Pour the wine into the skillet, and turn the heat to high. Bring to a boil and reduce the wine by one-third, to about 1 cup; add to the crock. Cover and cook on LOW for 1½ to 2 hours.

2. To clean the squid, if necessary, first pull off the head and remove the insides and ink sac that come with it. Peel off the outer speckled skin from the body by pulling off the fins; it will slide off. Remove the cellophane-like spine from the inside of the back of the body. Squeeze out the insides, and you will have a cone shape. Rinse well with cold water, blot dry with paper towels, and coarsely chop or slice into rings. Take the head section and cut off the tentacles below the eyes. Remove the hard beak located where the tentacles are connected together. Leave the tentacles whole or chop so they won't look so scary. Cover and refrigerate until needed.

3. When the tomato sauce is ready, add the calamari and parsley, cover, and continue to cook on LOW until the calamari is tender, another 45 minutes to 1 hour. Taste for salt.

Fettuccine with Smoked Salmon

T his is a rich, elegant, and oh-so-easy pasta that you can serve as an appetizer or, in larger portions, as a main course. Because the fish is salty, you won't need to add any additional salt. ○ *Serves 4 as a main dish, 6 to 8 as an appetizer*

COOKER: Small or medium round
SETTING AND COOK TIME: LOW for 1 to 2 hours

2 cups heavy cream
3 to 4 ounces top quality lox or smoked salmon, chopped or flaked into ½-inch pieces
1 pound fresh fettuccine, regular egg or spinach flavored
2 tablespoons olive oil (optional)
Freshly ground black pepper to taste

1. Combine the cream and the lox in the slow cooker. Cover and cook on LOW until very hot, 1 to 2 hours.

2. Meanwhile, cook the fettuccine in boiling water until tender to the bite, about 3 minutes. Take care not to overcook. Toss with the olive oil if the pasta is to stand for over 5 minutes. Add the fettuccine to the hot sauce and toss to coat evenly. If your cooker is large enough, just add the pasta to the cooker; if not, pour the sauce over the pasta in shallow, heated bowl. Garnish with a few grinds of black pepper and serve immediately.

Seafood Pasta

 variation on Slow Cooker Coquilles (page 416), here is a combination of scallops, shrimp, and crab to serve over fresh fettuccine. ○ *Serves 4*

COOKER: Medium round
SETTING AND COOK TIME: HIGH for 45 minutes to 1¼ hours;
    seafood added after 15 to 30 minutes

2 tablespoons olive oil
2 medium-size shallots, chopped
¼ cup dry vermouth
8 ounces bay scallops (or sea scallops, halved), rinsed and blotted dry
8 ounces medium-size shrimp, peeled and deveined
8 ounces crabmeat
2 teaspoons minced fresh tarragon
Pinch of sea salt to taste
1 pound fresh fettuccine

1. Combine the olive oil, shallots, and vermouth in the slow cooker. Cover and cook on HIGH for 15 to 30 minutes, until hot. It is very important to heat the poaching liquid first or the seafood will not cook properly.

2. Add the scallops, shrimp, crabmeat, tarragon, and salt, tossing to coat the seafood with the poaching liquid. Cover and cook on HIGH until opaque and firm, 30 to 45 minutes. Watch carefully so the seafood doesn't overcook.

3. At the end of the cooking time, cook the pasta in boiling salted water until tender to the bite. Pour through a colander, then rinse briefly with some hot water and drain. Divide the pasta among 4 warm plates and spoon the seafood over the pasta. Pass the pepper grinder.

Cheesy Tuna-Stuffed Potatoes

 Here is a light main dish for lunch or supper. Because the canned tuna is salty, we find no additional salt is needed. ● *Serves 4*

COOKER: Medium or large round or oval
SETTINGS AND COOK TIMES: HIGH for 3¾ to 6 hours; or LOW for 6 to 8 hours, then HIGH for 45 minutes to 1 hour

4 medium-size Idaho or russet potatoes, scrubbed and left dripping wet
¾ cup finely shredded cheddar cheese
¼ cup milk
One 6-ounce can water-packed tuna, drained
½ cup sour cream (reduced fat is okay)
1 green onion (white and some of the green), thinly sliced

1. Prick each dripping-wet potato with a fork or the tip of a sharp knife and pile them into the slow cooker; do not add water. Cover and cook until fork-tender, on HIGH for 3 to 5 hours or on LOW for 6 to 8 hours.

2. Remove the potatoes from the cooker with tongs and cut in half lengthwise. Scoop out the center of each half with a large spoon, leaving enough potato to keep the shell intact. Put the potato flesh in a bowl and add ½ cup of the cheese, the milk, tuna, sour cream, and green onion. Mash the filling with a fork and spoon it back into the shells, mounding it high. Return to the slow cooker, setting down the stuffed potatoes in a single layer if possible so that they touch each other. Sprinkle with the remaining ¼ cup of cheese. Cover and cook on HIGH for 45 minutes to 1 hour. Remove carefully from the cooker and serve immediately.

Slow Cooker Puddings, Cakes, and Breads

We start out here with desserts that are a bit sublime, puddings, and then bridge the gap to cakes and steamed cake breads with rustic, hearty bread puddings. These are the desserts that work nicely in the slow cooker without fuss or special equipment. As you read through our recipes, enjoy your sense of anticipation. Sweets are just like that—something to look forward to.

Sponge puddings are the best of both worlds—they have a creamy pudding sauce on the bottom and a delicate, soufflé-like cake on top. They separate into two layers during the baking process.

The slow cooker makes beautiful, creamy-sweet dessert puddings such as tapioca and rice pudding, delightful old-fashioned desserts. Anywhere in the world that there is rice or bread, there is some sort of rice or bread pudding. The practice of using leftover starch as an ingredient in a sweet concoction probably dates from the time humans first cooked a grain mush such as oatmeal or cornmeal. Slow-cooked Indian Pudding (page 434) is pure Americana, with its delightful molasses fragrance. You can use either whole pearl tapioca or quick-cooking tapioca (whole tapioca run through a machine like a coffee grinder) in slow cooker recipes.

The key to perfect silky puddings, especially rice pudding, is not to overcook them. And using the slow cooker provides a great way to avoid that problem. The starch in the rice breaks down during the cooking process and, along with eggs, gently thickens the mixture. Our recipes

often call for short- and medium-grain rice such as the Italian Arborio or Japanese glutinous rice to make a nice, creamy pudding. Long-grain rices don't have enough starch to thicken puddings as easily. Serve your rice puddings warm. Remember that chilling hardens the starch in the rice kernel and you end up with a stiffer pudding after refrigeration.

Bread puddings, containing milk and eggs, are usually cooked on the HIGH setting, which is still lower than if you were cooking in a regular oven. You don't want the mixture to sit at too low a temperature for a long period, or you risk spoilage. The puddings must be watched carefully at the end to prevent burning or overcooking.

The slow cooker world of cake baking has its boundaries. The cooker will not make sponge cakes, traditional pies in a crust, meringues, or cookies, but it has its genre of desserts all its own, which are delicious and old-fashioned. While there are pans that can be inserted to turn your slow cooker into a minioven for baking cakes and breads in the slow cooker (Rival has a small aluminum baking pan), we looked for recipes that could be made di-

Make your pudding cakes in a round slow cooker; they tend to burn in an oval cooker.

rectly in the crock without any special equipment. We found quite a few. This is the realm of simple one-layer cakes, steamed puddings, dense fruitcakes, and quick breads.

We especially like the slow cooker for steaming puddings as an alternative to the stove top. Depending on the mold, you can use a trivet under it or not; the heating element is around the sides in the cooker, so there is no bottom contact with direct heat, as there is on a stove top.

Our quick breads and cakes are cooked directly in the crock. These desserts are especially convenient if you are in a kitchen with no oven, or in a facility with limited appliances, such as on a sailboat or in a studio room without any kitchen. Don't pass up our fruit and spice steamed puddings, which are very moist cakes. They are not overly sweet and hark back to our ancestors, who did not have the lux-

ury of baking in a slow cooker and made do with an open fire.

Our single layer cakes take on the shape of the bottom of your cooker crock. Applesauce cake, carrot cake, and gingerbread—nothing fancy, just plain cake. The blueberry cake is as good for breakfast or a snack as it is for dessert. All have a firm enough batter to hold up in the cooker. We like to put a round of parchment in the bottom for easy removal. You can serve the cakes with one of our sauces, whipped cream, a favorite frosting, powdered sugar sprinkled on top, or just plain.

Then we found we could bake some dense-batter cornbreads in the crock. These pair nicely with our beans, soups, and chilis. Please note that most of the baking recipes are cooked on the HIGH heat setting; the LOW setting will not be able to set the texture of breads and cakes.

•• About Baking Yeast Breads ••
in the Slow Cooker Crock

The slow cooker crock is made from high temperature glazed ceramic material that works perfectly as a baking pan for making yeast breads in a conventional oven. If you have a slow cooker with a removable crock, it produces a lovely browned loaf in a flowerpot shape with a domed top. All types of bread doughs work well.

The crock should be well greased before putting in the dough to prevent sticking, then covered with greased plastic wrap during the rising phase. When the dough has doubled in bulk, or as directed in the recipe, remove the plastic wrap and place in a preheated oven with the oven rack on the lowest rung to leave room for the crock to fit with plenty of room between the top of the crock and the oven ceiling. Upon removal from the oven, take care to use heavy oven mitts and grip firmly under the crock rim for secure removal; the crock will be very hot. Place on a folded cloth towel on the counter to cool, not directly on the cold counter, the top of the stove, or a wire rack; ceramic does not like fast changes in temperature, which can cause it to crack.

You can use a 1- to 1½-quart crock, soufflé dish, or 6-inch springform pan in place of an 8 x 4-inch rectangular loaf pan, or a 2- to 2½-quart crock for a standard 9 x 5-inch rectangular loaf pan. Use a 3½- to 4-quart crock to bake the volume of dough for 2 standard loaves, increasing the baking time by 15 to 30 minutes. This is a nice alternative for breads often made in a standard 10-inch Bundt, such as monkey bread and special holiday coffee cakes. Russian kulich, which is traditionally made in a tall mold, can be made in a 3½- to 4½-quart crock.

Some home bakers use their medium and large slow cooker crocks just to raise the bread dough, as you would a crockery bowl or plastic rising bucket. The narrow crock with its high sides is perfect for coaxing the dough to rise perfectly in an upward motion, rather than spreading horizontally. You can then transfer the dough to a work surface, deflate it, divide into portions, shape them, and bake in regular bread pans.

Hot Fudge Spoon Cake

Normally baked in a hot water bath for slow, even baking, the pudding cake is one of the best desserts to make in the slow cooker. It separates during baking, forming a custard-like sauce on the bottom and a sponge layer cake on top. You serve it right out of the slow cooker (with an oversized spoon) warm, room temperature, or chilled. If you can't find the ground chocolate, you can use cocoa powder; if all you've got is unsweetened cocoa, increase the sugar to ⅔ cup. ◦ *Serves 4 to 6*

COOKER: Medium round
SETTING AND COOK TIME: HIGH for 2 to 2¼ hours

¾ cup all-purpose flour
¼ cup sweet ground chocolate, such as Ghirardelli
¼ cup sugar
1½ teaspoons baking powder
¼ teaspoon salt
½ cup milk
¼ cup (½ stick) unsalted butter, melted
1 teaspoon vanilla extract

TOPPING:
¼ cup sweet cocoa powder, such as Ghirardelli
¼ cup granulated sugar
¼ cup firmly packed light brown sugar
1½ cups boiling water
Vanilla ice cream or coffee frozen yogurt for serving

1. Coat the slow cooker with butter-flavor nonstick cooking spray.

2. In a medium-size bowl, whisk together the flour, ground chocolate, sugar, baking powder, and salt. Make a well in the center, add the milk, melted butter, and vanilla, stir the liquid ingredients until well blended, and continue stirring in widening circles, gradually incorporating the dry ingredients, until you have a smooth batter. It will be thick. Spread evenly in the cooker.

3. To make the topping, combine all the ingredients in another medium-size bowl and whisk until smooth. Gently pour over the batter in the cooker; do not stir. Cover and cook on HIGH until puffed and the top layer is set, 2 to 2¼ hours.

4. Turn off the cooker and let stand, covered, for at least 30 minutes before refrigerating or serving right out of the cooker.

5. To serve, scoop the cake into individual bowls. Add a scoop of vanilla ice cream or coffee frozen yogurt alongside the cake. Spoon some of the fudgy pudding at the bottom over the cake and ice cream.

Chocolate Peanut Butter Pudding Cake

This is one of the oldest slow cooker desserts circulating and could be nicknamed Chocolate Goober Pudding Cake. The mixture is cooked directly in the cooker on HIGH, the temperature it needs to bake properly; do not attempt it on LOW. When you assemble the cake, the batter goes on the bottom and the pudding on top. But after it has baked, when you take off the lid, you will discover that the pudding has sunk to the bottom, and the gooey, chocolatey cake is on top! This can be served warm, at room temperature, or chilled. ● *Serves 6 to 8*

COOKER: Medium round
SETTING AND COOK TIME: HIGH for 2 to 2¼ hours

1 cup all-purpose flour
2 tablespoons unsweetened cocoa powder
½ cup sugar
1½ teaspoons baking powder
Pinch of salt
½ cup whole milk or chocolate milk
2 tablespoons canola, peanut, or walnut oil
1 tablespoon vanilla extract
½ cup smooth or chunky peanut butter (natural or hydrogenated)
½ cup semisweet chocolate chips

TOPPING:
3 tablespoons unsweetened cocoa powder
¾ cup sugar
1½ cups boiling water

Vanilla ice cream for serving

1. Coat the slow cooker with butter-flavor nonstick cooking spray.

2. In a medium-size bowl, whisk together the flour, cocoa, sugar, baking powder, and salt. Make a well in the center, add the milk, oil, and vanilla, and stir until well blended; continue stirring in widening circles, gradually incorporating the dry ingredients, until you have a smooth batter. Stir in the peanut butter (warm it in the microwave if thick and sticky from refrigeration); the batter will be thick. Stir in the chocolate chips. Spread evenly in the cooker.

3. To make the topping, in another medium-size bowl, combine the cocoa and sugar; pour in the boiling water and whisk until smooth. Gently pour over the batter in the cooker; do not stir. Cover and cook on HIGH until puffed and the top layer is set, 2 to 2¼ hours.

4. Turn off the cooker and let stand, covered, for at least 30 minutes before serving.

5. To serve, scoop the cake into individual bowls. Add a scoop of vanilla ice cream alongside the cake. Spoon some of the fudgy pudding over the cake and ice cream and serve.

Lemon Buttermilk Sponge Pudding

I n this dessert, we use one of our favorite products: Boyajian citrus oil. The company's oils, made from the rinds of fresh lemons, oranges, and limes, are pungent and so pure tasting. You need only a little bit for a fabulous lemon flavor. Look for the oils in individual bottles, or in a boxed set, in gourmet markets. Or buy them online at www.boyajianinc.com. Here in California, we have easy access to the juicy, sour-sweet Meyer lemon, the "backyard lemon," which is now becoming more widely available commercially. Its juice is truly delightful in this recipe.

This pudding cake is more refined than the chocolate ones. The sponge cake layer on the top is pale and delicate and the lemony pudding underneath is smooth and abundant. The amaretto gives a nice almond flavor, but you won't taste the alcohol. Serve this plain or with fresh berries. ○ *Serves 4 to 6*

COOKER: Medium round
SETTING AND COOK TIME: HIGH for 1½ to 2 hours

1 cup sugar

¼ cup all-purpose flour

¼ teaspoon salt

1 cup buttermilk

¼ cup fresh lemon juice, preferably from Meyer lemons

¼ teaspoon Boyajian lemon oil or ⅛ teaspoon lemon extract

1 tablespoon amaretto

3 large eggs, separated

1. Coat the slow cooker with butter-flavor nonstick cooking spray.

2. In a medium-size bowl, whisk together the sugar, flour, and salt. Make a well in the center, pour in the buttermilk, lemon juice and oil, and amaretto, and stir until well blended; continue stirring in widening circles, gradually incorporating the dry ingredients, until you have a smooth batter. In a small bowl, whisk the egg yolks until pale, then whisk into the batter.

3. In a medium-size bowl, using an electric mixer, beat the egg whites until stiff but not dry. Gently whisk about one-third of the beaten egg whites into the batter. Add the remaining egg whites and fold in gently with a rubber spatula. Pour the batter into the cooker. Cover and cook on HIGH until the cake is puffed and the top is set, 1½ to 2 hours; it will be browned around the edges.

4. Turn off the cooker and let stand, covered, for at least 30 minutes before serving.

5. To serve, scoop the warm cake and the pudding-like sauce into individual bowls. Top with fresh berries if desired.

Vanilla Bean Rice Pudding

Rice puddings are pure comfort food. For as long as rice has been cultivated, some sort of rice pudding has been made. The use of the evaporated milk is important; it keeps the milk from breaking down during the cooking process.

○ *Serves 8*

COOKER: Medium round

SETTING AND COOK TIME: LOW for 3 hours; eggs, cream, zest, nutmeg, and raisins added during last 30 minutes

²⁄₃ cup medium-grain white rice, such as Calrose, or a risotto rice,
    such as Arborio, rinsed briefly and drained

One 12-ounce can evaporated milk

2½ cups whole milk

¾ cup sugar

Pinch of salt

1 vanilla bean

2 large eggs, lightly beaten

½ cup heavy cream

1 teaspoon grated lemon zest

½ teaspoon freshly grated nutmeg

½ cup golden or dark raisins (optional)

Fresh or canned fruit or whipped cream (optional) for serving

1. Coat the slow cooker with butter-flavor nonstick cooking spray. Combine the rice and evaporated milk in the cooker.

2. In a large, heavy saucepan over medium-high heat, combine the whole milk, sugar, and salt. Heat until bubbles appear around the edges to dissolve the sugar. Remove from the heat.

3. Split the vanilla bean down the center and scrape out the seeds with the tip of a small knife; add the bean and the seeds to the cooker. Pour the hot milk into the cooker and stir with a whisk. Cover and cook on LOW until the milk is absorbed and the custard is set, about 2½ hours. While cooking, the milk will be gently bubbling. Remove the vanilla bean, rinse, and dry to save for another use.

4. In a medium-size bowl, whisk together the eggs, cream, lemon zest, and nutmeg. Add about ¼ cup of the hot pudding to the egg mixture and beat well to prevent curdling; slowly pour the mixture into the pudding in the cooker, stirring constantly until well combined. Stir in the raisins, if using. Cover and cook on LOW for 30 minutes more.

5. Turn the cooker off and let the pudding cool, partially covered, for up to 30 minutes. Serve warm or spoon into small dishes, cover with plastic wrap, and refrigerate to eat cold. If you like, serve with canned or fresh fruit or a dollop of whipped cream.

Jasmine Rice Pudding with Coconut Milk

Fragrant jasmine rice pairs naturally with coconut; it seems to accentuate the aroma of the nut. Remember to stir gently so as not to make mush out of the delicate cooked rice. The pudding will thicken considerably as it cools. Serve with sliced fresh mangoes or peaches. Whipped cream or a pool of heavy cream is optional and very decadent. ○ *Serves 8*

COOKER: Medium round
SETTING AND COOK TIME: LOW for 3 hours

¾ cup jasmine rice
One 14-ounce can unsweetened coconut milk
1 quart half-and-half
½ cup sugar
2 teaspoons vanilla extract
1 teaspoon coconut extract
1 to 2 ripe mangoes or peaches (optional), peeled, pitted, and chopped (1 to 2 cups)
Whipped cream or heavy cream (optional) for serving

1. Coat the slow cooker with butter-flavor nonstick cooking spray. Combine the rice and coconut milk in the cooker.

2. In a large heavy saucepan over medium-high heat, combine the half-and-half and sugar. Heat until bubbles appear around the edges to dissolve the sugar. Pour the hot cream into the cooker and stir with a whisk. Cover and cook on LOW until thick, about 3 hours. While cooking, the milk will be gently bubbling.

3. Gently stir in the extracts. Turn off the cooker and let the pudding cool, partially covered, for at least 30 minutes. Fold in the mangoes or peaches, if using. Serve warm, at room temperature, or cold, with the cream, if desired.

Kheer

The creamy, aromatic Indian rice pudding known as *kheer* is a real favorite of ours, something we only had enjoyed in restaurants before we learned to prepare it at home. You may have to go to a gourmet market or an Indian or Middle Eastern store to find rosewater and whole green cardamom pods. The green cardamom pods are not the same as the white pods used in Scandinavian cooking. You also don't want hulled or ground cardamom. Green cardamom pods can also be ordered from Penzeys Spices (800-741-7787; www.penzeys.com). You can make a rich version of *kheer* with whole milk, a lean one with skim milk, or an in-between version with lowfat milk. ○ *Serves 6*

COOKER: Medium or large round
SETTINGS AND COOK TIMES: LOW for 4 hours, then HIGH for 30 minutes

⅔ **cup white basmati rice**
⅔ **cup sugar**
One 12-ounce can evaporated milk
2½ **cups milk**
4 green cardamom pods
¼ **cup golden raisins, or more if desired**
1 teaspoon rosewater
3 tablespoons shelled pistachios, toasted in a dry skillet over medium heat until
   fragrant, then coarsely chopped

1. Coat the slow cooker with butter-flavor nonstick cooking spray.

2. Rinse the rice in a fine-mesh strainer and drain it well. Put the rice, sugar, evaporated milk, 1½ cups of the milk, and the cardamom pods in the cooker; stir well. Cover and cook on LOW for 4 hours. If you are at home, stir the *kheer* once or twice during this time.

3. Stir in the remaining 1 cup of milk. Cover and cook on HIGH for 30 minutes.

4. Turn off the cooker and let the *kheer* cool, covered, until lukewarm; stir in the raisins and rosewater. Cover and refrigerate until serving time.

5. To serve, spoon the *kheer* into small dishes, and sprinkle each serving with some of the pistachios.

Tapioca Pudding

apioca pudding is back again—although, for many hardcore pudding lovers, it never left—and even turns up in the refrigerator case at our supermarkets. Once you've made it at home in your slow cooker, though, you'll never go back to store-bought! Sure, tapioca is a bit fussy to make on the stove, but it is ever so easy in the slow cooker. This version is smooth, creamy, and rich tasting, even when you make it with low-fat milk. For a richer pudding, use whole milk or milk and half-and-half. Be sure not to use instant, or minute, tapioca in this recipe. You can double or triple the quantity, but move up to a medium-size cooker. The cook time in step 2 will increase to 2½ to 3 hours if you're doubling. ○ *Serves 4*

COOKER: Small round
SETTING AND COOK TIME: LOW for 2 hours; egg added during last 30 minutes

2 cups milk (low fat is fine)
½ cup sugar
¼ cup small pearl tapioca (not instant)
1 teaspoon vanilla extract
1 large egg
Fresh or canned fruit or whipped cream (optional) for serving

·· Chocolate Tapioca Pudding ··

If you love tapioca pudding and you love chocolate, treat yourself to chocolate tapioca pudding. It's a snap! When either of the tapioca puddings (this page and next) is finished, add semisweet chocolate chips (¼ cup for each 2 cups of liquid in a recipe). Gently stir until the chocolate is melted and evenly distributed throughout the pudding. Serve warm or let cool, cover, and refrigerate to serve cold. Chocolate tapioca pudding is great with strawberries, sweetened whipped cream, or nondairy dessert topping.

1. Coat the slow cooker with butter-flavor nonstick cooking spray.

2. Combine the milk, sugar, tapioca, and vanilla in the cooker; stir well with a whisk. Cover and cook on LOW until the milk is absorbed, the pudding thickened, and most of the tapioca balls are completely transparent, about 1½ hours. Some of them will still have a white dot at their centers; that is okay. While cooking, the milk will be gently bubbling.

3. Beat the egg in a cup or small bowl. Stir the tapioca thoroughly to break up any clumps. Spoon a few tablespoons of the hot tapioca into the egg and beat well; pour the mixture into the cooker and stir well with a spoon or spatula to combine. Cover and cook on LOW for another 30 minutes.

4. Turn off the cooker and let the pudding cool, partially covered, for 30 minutes. Serve warm or pour into individual bowls, cover, and chill. Serve plain or with fruit or whipped cream on top. Store, covered, in the refrigerator.

Nondairy Tapioca Pudding

The profusion of soy, grain, and nut milks means there are so many new options for those who don't or can't drink milk. This tapioca pudding incorporates vanilla soy milk. Because soy milks vary in sweetness from brand to brand, you may need to adjust the amount of sugar in this recipe. ○ *Serves 4*

COOKER: Small or medium round
SETTING AND COOK TIME: LOW for 2½ hours; egg added during last 30 minutes

2 cups vanilla soy milk
⅓ cup firmly packed light brown sugar
¼ cup small pearl tapioca (not instant)
½ teaspoon vanilla extract
1 large egg
Fresh or canned fruit or nondairy dessert topping (optional) for serving

1. Coat the cooker with nonstick cooking spray. Combine the soy milk, brown sugar, tapioca, and vanilla in the slow cooker. Cover and cook on LOW until the milk is absorbed, the pudding has thickened, and most of the tapioca balls are completely transparent, about 2 hours. Some of them will still have a white dot at their centers; that is okay.

2. Beat the egg in a cup or small bowl. Stir the pudding thoroughly to break up any clumps of tapioca. Spoon a few tablespoons of the hot tapioca into the egg and beat well. Pour the egg mixture back into the cooker and stir well to combine. Cover and cook on LOW for another 30 minutes.

3. Turn off the cooker and let the pudding cool, partially covered, for 30 minutes. Serve warm or pour into a bowl, let cool, cover, and chill. Serve plain or topped with fruit or a nondairy dessert topping.

Indian Pudding

When Beth was growing up in the 1950s, every night there was a planned dessert, which was how she got her start in cooking. Nothing fancy, just simple, homey desserts—puddings of all sorts, chilled fruit cocktails, Jell-O parfaits, golden and chocolate layer cakes with smooth frostings, gingerbread with real whipped cream, pound cake, New York cheesecake with frozen sweetened strawberries poured over the top, and Indian pudding made from a recipe in the original Betty Crocker cookbook. Indian pudding has probably been made by American cooks as for as long as corn has been cultivated. A traditional New England dessert, it was simply cornmeal mush mixed with imported molasses from the Indies, milk, butter, and eggs. A sort of a sweetened polenta, it was slowly baked in a wood fire oven all day or all night in an earthenware crock. Betty Crocker had us baking it in a very slow oven for 3 hours. Here is the slow cooker version, every bit as good as it can be. Indian pudding is traditionally served warm out of the crock the day it is made, with vanilla ice cream melting all over it.

○ *Serves 6*

COOKER: Medium round
SETTING AND COOK TIME: LOW for 8½ to 9 hours

3¼ cups whole milk

½ cup medium- or fine-grind yellow cornmeal

¼ cup light or dark molasses

3 tablespoons light or dark brown sugar

½ teaspoon ground cinnamon

½ teaspoon ground nutmeg

⅛ teaspoon baking soda

Pinch of salt

1 teaspoon vanilla extract

1 large egg

1 large egg yolk

3 tablespoons unsalted butter, cut into pieces

½ cup light cream or evaporated milk

1. In a medium-size saucepan, heat 2¾ cups of the whole milk over medium heat. In a small bowl, combine the remaining ½ cup of milk with the cornmeal and whisk until smooth. Pour the cornmeal mixture into the hot milk, whisking constantly. Cook until it begins to thicken, stirring constantly to avoid lumps. Whisk in the molasses, brown sugar, cinnamon, nutmeg, baking soda, salt, and vanilla. Beat the whole egg and yolk together in a small bowl; add a spoonful of the hot cornmeal mixture and beat well to avoid curdling. Add another spoonful of the hot mixture, stir, then pour the egg mixture into the saucepan and whisk to combine. Remove from the heat.

2. Grease the slow cooker with 1 tablespoon of the butter. Pour the cornmeal pudding mixture into the cooker and stir in the remaining 2 tablespoons of butter until melted. Pour in the light cream in a circular motion; do not stir. Cover and cook on LOW until the pudding is set, 8½ to 9 hours.

3. Serve warm, spooned into individual bowls.

Raisin Bread Pudding
with Calvados and Pecans

A s far as we're concerned, there is no brandy that can come close to *vieux* (aged) Calvados. At first sip, you might be disappointed; although it is made from apples, it does not taste like apples. It tastes like a super strong brandy. But what it does in cooking! It melds the flavors of apples and dried fruit in this delicious bread pudding made with old-fashioned raisin bread. ○ *Serves 6*

COOKER: Medium round
SETTING AND COOK TIME: HIGH for 2½ to 3 hours

1 cup pecans, coarsely chopped
8 slices raisin bread, crusts removed and diced
2 medium-size tart cooking apples such as pippin, or firm pears, peeled, cored, and thinly sliced
2 cups half-and-half
3 large eggs
½ cup honey
¼ cup Calvados or another brandy
1 teaspoon ground cinnamon
½ teaspoon ground nutmeg
¼ cup (½ stick) unsalted butter, melted
Vanilla ice cream (optional) for serving

1. Preheat the oven to 350°F. Spread the pecans on a baking sheet pan and bake until golden, 8 to 10 minutes, stirring a few times.

2. Coat the slow cooker with butter-flavor nonstick cooking spray. Place the bread cubes in the cooker and sprinkle with the toasted pecans and apples; toss to combine. In a medium-size bowl, combine the half-and-half, eggs, honey, Calvados, cinnamon, and nutmeg and whisk to mix well; pour over the bread in the cooker. Drizzle with the melted butter. Cover and cook on HIGH until the apples are tender when pierced with a fork and the custard is set, 2½ to 3 hours. An instant-read thermometer inserted in the center should register 190°F.

3. Turn off the cooker and let the pudding stand, covered, for at least 15 minutes before serving warm or at room temperature with vanilla ice cream, if desired.

Fresh Raspberry Bread Pudding

 Here is a sumptuous simple vanilla bread pudding. You can substitute blueberries or blackberries for the raspberries. ○ *Serves 6 to 8*

COOKER: Medium round
SETTING AND COOK TIME: HIGH for 2½ hours, plus 15 minutes uncovered

5 to 6 cups coarsely crumbled or diced stale French bread, challah,
    or rich white bread, crusts removed
½ pint fresh raspberries
2 cups heavy cream
2 cups whole milk
1¼ cups sugar
6 large eggs
1 tablespoon vanilla extract
Whipped cream for serving

1. Coat the slow cooker with butter-flavor nonstick cooking spray.

2. Layer half of the crumbled bread in the slow cooker, and sprinkle with half of the berries. Repeat the layers, ending with the berries on top. In a large bowl, whisk together the cream, milk, sugar, eggs, and vanilla until smooth. Pour into the cooker over the bread cubes and berries, and gently push down the bread to evenly moisten. Cover and cook on HIGH until puffed and a knife inserted in the center comes out clean, about 2½ hours. An instant-read thermometer inserted in the center should register 190°F.

3. Remove the lid and cook on HIGH for another 15 minutes.

4. Cover, turn off the cooker, and let the pudding stand to cool slightly. Serve warm or at room temperature, with whipped cream, if desired.

Chocolate Bread Pudding

T his is really a triple chocolate pudding: you have melted bittersweet bar chocolate incorporated into the custard, cocoa powder, and bits of chopped chocolate dispersed throughout the pudding. Check the pudding at 2½ hours; you may need more time if it was refrigerated most of the day. Serve it warm with vanilla ice cream or crème fraîche, although it needs no garnish whatsoever. This pudding can be reheated in a 200°F oven for 20 to 30 minutes or eaten cold out of hand in chunks. Use a good-quality chocolate, such as Valrhona. ○ *Serves 6*

COOKER: Medium round
SETTING AND COOK TIME: HIGH for 2½ to 3 hours, plus 15 minutes uncovered

1¼ cups whole milk
12 ounces bittersweet chocolate, broken into pieces
4 to 4½ cups cubed good-quality day-old white bread or
    challah (1 medium-size loaf) with crusts removed
3 large eggs
2 large egg yolks
¾ cup plus 2 tablespoons granulated sugar, or
    ¾ cup granulated sugar plus 2 tablespoons raw sugar
1½ teaspoons vanilla extract
3 tablespoons Dutch-process unsweetened cocoa powder
1¼ cups heavy cream
3 tablespoons cold unsalted butter, diced
1 cup crème fraîche (recipe follows) or sour cream
2 tablespoons confectioners' sugar

1. In a medium-size saucepan over medium heat, warm the milk just until you can see bubbles forming around the edge of the pan. Remove from the heat, add 8 ounces of the chocolate, and let stand until the chocolate has melted; whisk until smooth.

2. Coat the slow cooker with butter-flavor nonstick cooking spray. Put the diced bread in the cooker. With a whisk or electric mixer, vigorously beat together the whole eggs and yolks, ¾ cup of granulated sugar, vanilla, and cocoa in a medium-size bowl until pale and thick. Slowly drizzle in the warm chocolate mixture and cream. Pour into the cooker over the bread cubes and push down the bread to moisten evenly. Cover and refrigerate for 30 minutes, or up to 8 hours, to soak the bread.

3. Fold in the remaining 4 ounces of broken-up chocolate. Dot with the butter and sprinkle with the remaining 2 tablespoons of granulated or raw sugar. Cover and cook on HIGH until the pudding is puffed, wiggles slightly in the center, and a knife inserted into the center comes out mostly clean, 2½ to 3 hours. An instant-read thermometer inserted in the center should register 190°F.

4. Remove the lid and cook on HIGH for another 15 minutes.

5. Turn off the cooker, cover, and let stand for at least 15 minutes before serving warm or at room temperature. When ready to serve, combine the crème fraîche and confectioners' sugar in a small bowl and beat with a whisk or hand-held electric mixer until soft peaks are formed. Spoon the pudding onto dessert plates and serve with a dollop of the crème fraîche.

Chocolate Custard Bread Pudding with Fresh Cherries: Toss 12 pitted fresh Bing cherries with the bread cubes before pouring the custard over.

Crème Fraîche

There are many ways to make homemade crème fraîche, a thickened cream, but this is the simplest and most successful. Crème fraîche is used in place of sour cream or heavy cream in recipes. This recipe can be doubled or tripled with no problem. It is really tasty stuff and will not separate when stirred into a hot liquid, such as a soup. ◗ *Makes 1½ cups*

1 cup heavy or whipping cream (not ultra-pasteurized, if possible)
⅓ cup regular sour cream (not reduced fat or imitation), or buttermilk
2 tablespoons plain yogurt containing acidophilus cultures

1. In a small bowl, combine the heavy cream, sour cream, and yogurt; whisk until smooth. Leave in the bowl or pour into a clean jar or small crock, preferably cleaned well in the dishwasher. Cover with plastic wrap. Let stand at room temperature until thickened, 6 to 8 hours. Let stand a few hours longer if you want it a bit thicker.

2. Cover and refrigerate the crème fraîche until ready to use. It will continue to thicken as it chills. The crème fraîche will keep in the refrigerator up to 1 week, if it lasts that long!

Natalie's Pumpkin Bread Pudding

N atalie" is Natalie Haughton, food editor of the *Los Angeles Daily News* and author of *The Best Slow Cooker Book Ever* (Harper Collins, 1995), one of the first really comprehensive slow cooker cookbooks. She absolutely loves pumpkin and makes an amazing number of recipes with it. She made her favorite custard bread pudding and added a can of pumpkin purée, then baked it in the slow cooker with great success. Here is her wonderful recipe. Do not cook this on the LOW setting. ● *Serves 6*

COOKER: Medium round
SETTING AND COOK TIME: HIGH for 2½ hours, plus 20 minutes uncovered

3 cups cubed (¾ inch) good-quality white French bread with crusts removed
One 15-ounce can solid-pack pumpkin
3 large eggs
2 cups whole milk
3 tablespoons cream sherry
1½ teaspoons ground cinnamon
½ teaspoon ground nutmeg
¼ teaspoon ground cloves
¼ teaspoon ground ginger
¾ cup sugar
Whipped cream (optional) for serving

1. Coat the slow cooker with butter-flavor nonstick cooking spray.

2. Put the diced bread in the cooker. In a large bowl, whisk together the pumpkin, eggs, milk, sherry, spices, and sugar until smooth. Pour into the cooker over the bread cubes and push down the bread to evenly moisten. Cover and cook on HIGH until puffed and a knife inserted into the center comes out clean, about 2½ hours. An instant-read thermometer inserted in the center should register 190°F.

3. Remove the lid and cook on HIGH for another 20 minutes.

4. Turn off the cooker, cover, and let the pudding stand for 15 minutes. Serve warm or at room temperature with whipped cream, if desired.

Honey and Apple Bread Pudding
with Golden Raisins

This is a milk-free, egg-free bread pudding and it is every bit as good as the custard-based ones. Because there are no dairy products, the pudding is cooked on LOW heat instead of HIGH. The amount of honey you use will depend on the tartness of your apples. ● *Serves 4 to 6*

COOKER: Medium round
SETTING AND COOK TIME: LOW for 5 to 6 hours

8 slices of your favorite bread
¼ cup (½ stick) unsalted margarine, softened
3 cooking apples, such as Golden Delicious or Gala, peeled, cored, quartered, and sliced
¾ cup golden raisins
1¼ cups unfiltered apple juice
¼ to ½ cup honey, to your taste
2 tablespoons fresh lemon juice
1 tablespoon grated lemon zest
1 teaspoon ground cinnamon
½ teaspoon ground nutmeg
Ice cream, whipped cream, or nondairy whipped topping for serving

1. Coat the slow cooker with butter-flavor nonstick cooking spray. Preheat the broiler.

2. Butter the bread on both sides and place on a parchment paper–lined baking sheet. Place under the broiler and lightly toast both sides; cut the warm toast into chunks. Put the bread in the cooker, then add the apples and raisins. In a small bowl, whisk together the apple juice, honey, lemon juice and zest, and spices; pour into the cooker and stir to moisten the bread evenly. Cover and cook on LOW for 5 to 6 hours. If possible, gently stir halfway through the cooking process. Pierce the apples with the tip of a knife to make sure they are soft.

3. Turn off the cooker and let stand, covered, for about 15 minutes. Serve warm or at room temperature with ice cream, whipped cream, or nondairy whipped topping, if desired.

Old-Fashioned Applesauce Cake with Walnuts

A pplesauce cake is wildly old-fashioned. Many of the old recipes from World War II contain no butter or eggs, which were rationed, but the cake was still a treat. It is a dense, moist cake by nature, so baking it in the slow cooker works beautifully. Eat it plain, with hot applesauce poured over, or with whipped cream. ● *Serves 6*

COOKER: Medium or large round
SETTING AND COOK TIME: HIGH for 2¼ to 2½ hours

1½ cups all-purpose flour
½ cup firmly packed light brown sugar
1 teaspoon ground cinnamon
½ teaspoon ground cloves
¼ teaspoon ground nutmeg
Pinch of ground allspice
1 teaspoon baking soda
½ teaspoon baking powder
¼ teaspoon salt
1 cup unsweetened applesauce
¼ cup buttermilk
5 tablespoons unsalted butter, melted
1 large egg
½ cup chopped walnuts

1. Line the bottom of the slow cooker with a round of parchment paper. Coat the paper and the sides of the cooker, one-third of the way up, with butter-flavor nonstick cooking spray, or grease with butter.

2. In a medium-size bowl, whisk together the flour, brown sugar, spices, baking soda, baking powder, and salt. In a small bowl, combine the applesauce, buttermilk, melted butter, and egg; beat until smooth. Add the applesauce mixture to the dry ingredients and beat until smooth and fluffy. Stir in the walnuts. Spread the batter evenly in the cooker. Cover and cook on HIGH until puffed and a cake tester inserted into the center comes out clean, 2¼ to 2½ hours.

3. Turn the cooker off, remove the lid, and let stand for 30 minutes to cool. To remove the cake, run a knife around the inside edge of the cooker and lift it out with a large rubber spatula. Cut into small wedges and serve warm or at room temperature.

Slow Cooker Carrot Cake

C arrot cake has perennial appeal. It never goes out of style. Serve plain, sprinkled with powdered sugar, with some whipped cream or ice cream, or with cream cheese icing slathered all over. ✿ *Serves 4 to 6*

COOKER: Medium or large round
SETTING AND COOK TIME: HIGH for 2¼ to 2½ hours

1½ cups all-purpose flour
¾ cup sugar
1 teaspoon ground cinnamon
¼ teaspoon ground nutmeg
1 teaspoon baking powder
½ teaspoon baking soda
¼ teaspoon salt
¼ cup water
½ cup light olive oil
2 large eggs
1¼ cups shredded carrots (2 to 3 medium)
3 tablespoons drained canned crushed pineapple or finely chopped nuts

1. Line the bottom of the slow cooker with a round of parchment paper. Coat the paper and the sides of the cooker, one-third of the way up, with butter-flavor non-stick cooking spray, or grease with butter.

2. In a medium-size bowl, whisk together the flour, sugar, spices, baking powder, baking soda, and salt. In a small bowl, combine the water, oil, and eggs, beating until smooth. Add the liquid ingredients to the dry, beating until smooth and fluffy. Stir in the carrots and pineapple. Spread the batter evenly in the cooker. Cover and cook on HIGH until puffed and a cake tester inserted into the center comes out clean, 2¼ to 2½ hours.

3. Turn the cooker off, remove the lid, and let stand for 30 minutes to cool. To remove the cake, run a knife around the inside edge of the cooker and lift it out with a large rubber spatula. Place it on a small serving plate and cut into small wedges. Serve warm or at room temperature.

Banana Cake with Pineapple

While bananas only grow in the tropics, thanks to the gigantic fruit import business that has flourished since the Civil War, we in the temperate zones consider bananas a staple, just as they do around the equator. Bananas are not categorized botanically as a fruit, but rather as a berry—a long, skinny, plump berry. Is there anyone who does not love the taste of bananas and banana cake? We think not. ○ *Serves 6*

COOKER: Medium or large round
SETTING AND COOK TIME: HIGH for 2¼ to 2½ hours

½ cup vegetable oil
1 cup sugar
2 large eggs
1 teaspoon pure vanilla extract
3 medium-size to large overripe bananas, slightly mashed
1¼ cups all-purpose flour
1 teaspoon baking soda
¼ teaspoon salt
⅓ cup canned crushed pineapple, drained on a double layer of paper towel

1. Line the bottom of the slow cooker with a round of parchment paper. Coat the paper and the sides of the cooker, one-third of the way up, with butter-flavor non-stick cooking spray, or grease with butter.

2. In a medium-size bowl, combine the oil and sugar. Beat hard with a whisk or electric mixer until light colored and creamy, about 1 minute. Add the eggs and vanilla and beat again until well combined. Add the mashed bananas and beat until smooth. Add the flour, baking soda, and salt and stir to combine. Beat well to make a creamy, well-blended batter. Fold in the pineapple and spread the batter evenly in the cooker. Cover and cook on HIGH until the top is firm to the touch and a cake tester inserted into the center comes out clean, 2¼ to 2½ hours.

3. Turn the cooker off, remove the lid, and let stand for 15 minutes to cool. To remove the cake, run a knife around the inside edge of the cooker and lift it out with a large rubber spatula. Let cool on a rack. Wrap the cake tightly in plastic wrap and chill for 8 hours, or up to 3 days before serving.

Crock-Baked Cornbread with Green Chiles and Corn

This is from Nancyjo Rieske, who likes to use freshly roasted chiles and fresh corn in season, though the bread is still very good when canned chiles and frozen corn must do. ● *Serves 4 to 6*

COOKER: Medium round
SETTING AND COOK TIME: HIGH for 2¼ to 2½ hours

1½ cups all-purpose flour
⅔ cup sugar
½ cup medium- or fine-grind yellow cornmeal, preferably stone-ground
1 tablespoon baking powder
½ teaspoon salt
1 cup whole milk
2 large eggs
⅓ cup canola, sunflower, or corn oil
3 tablespoons unsalted butter, melted
1¼ cups thawed frozen white baby corn kernels or fresh corn kernels, roasted in a 350°F oven until slightly browned
One 4-ounce can diced green chiles, drained, or 2 fresh Anaheim chiles, roasted, peeled, seeded, and diced (see Note on page 117)
Butter for serving

1. Line the bottom of the slow cooker with a round of parchment paper. Coat the paper and the sides of the cooker, one-third of the way up, with butter-flavor nonstick cooking spray, or grease with butter.

2. Whisk together the flour, sugar, cornmeal, baking powder, and salt in a medium-size bowl. Make a well in the center and add the milk, eggs, oil, and melted butter. With a large spoon or dough whisk, give a few vigorous strokes to blend the liquid and dry ingredients. Stir in the corn and chiles carefully, making sure not to overmix. Spread the batter evenly in the cooker. Cover and cook on HIGH until a cake tester inserted into the center comes out clean, 2¼ to 2½ hours.

3. Turn the cooker off, remove the lid, and let stand for 30 minutes to cool. To remove the cornbread, run a knife around the inside edge of the cooker and lift it out with a large rubber spatula. Cut into pieces and serve with butter.

Crock-Baked Hominy Cornbread

W e adore canned hominy and are always looking for good ways to incorporate it into our baking. This is a nice, moist cornbread, excellent with chili or a stew. ○ *Serves 4 to 6*

COOKER: Medium round
SETTING AND COOK TIME: HIGH for 2¼ to 2½ hours

1¼ cups medium- or fine-grind yellow cornmeal, preferably stoneground
¾ cup all-purpose flour
¼ cup whole wheat pastry flour
2 tablespoons sugar
1 tablespoon baking powder
1 teaspoon salt
2 large eggs
¾ cup canned golden or white hominy, rinsed and drained
1 cup whole milk
6 tablespoons (¾ stick) unsalted butter or leaf lard, melted

FOR SERVING:
Butter
Strawberry jam

1. Line the bottom of the slow cooker with a round of parchment paper. Coat the paper and the sides of the cooker, one-third of the way up, with butter-flavor nonstick cooking spray, or grease with butter.

2. Whisk together the cornmeal, flours, sugar, baking powder, and salt in a medium-size bowl. Make a well in the center and add the eggs, hominy, milk, and melted butter. With a large spoon or dough whisk, stir the dry ingredients into the liquid center until all the ingredients are moistened and thoroughly blended; take care not to overmix or break up the hominy too much. Spread the batter evenly in the cooker. Cover and cook on HIGH until a cake tester inserted into the center comes out clean, 2¼ to 2½ hours.

3. Turn the cooker off, remove the lid, and let stand for 30 minutes to cool. To remove the cornbread, run a knife around the inside edge of the cooker and lift it out with a large rubber spatula. Cut into small wedges and serve warm with butter and jam.

Steamed Breads and Puddings

Steamed puddings are wildly popular in Britain, and a "pud" is a must for ending winter holiday meals. English cookbooks offer dozens of recipes. In the New England colonies, the steamed pudding tradition continued with Boston brown bread, made with cornmeal. Steaming is one of the oldest methods for baking, long preceding the enclosed oven, and could be performed over an open fire in a covered large cauldron. Steamed breads and puddings were once heavy with suet, but modern versions are more like a steamed sponge cake or sweet quick bread, light and flavorful from fall fruits such as cranberries, pumpkin, and persimmon.

Steamed puddings and breads are a cross between cakes and bread. Moist and sweet, they sometimes have an accompanying sauce and are slightly dense in texture because of the steaming.

Traditionally they are baked in flowerpot-like ceramic bowls, known as English china pudding molds or basins, which look surprisingly like the round slow cooker crock.

The mold is of paramount importance here. Modern pudding molds are made of tin or another metal and have tight-fitting lids that slip over the top to keep water from dripping down onto the batter. Most of the molds fit nicely into a large slow cooker crock. We use beautiful clip-top, fluted metal pudding molds, easily available from Williams-Sonoma (800-541-2233; www.williams-sonoma.com), La Cuisine (800-521-1176; www.lacuisine.com), or Sur La Table (800-243-0852; www.surlatable.com). You can also use a fluted tube pan or tall one-pound mold, since the slow cooker is deep. We recommend the 1½-quart (6-cup) round melon shape, Corinthian column, or wreath pattern shape, or a metal kugelhopf tube mold.

Look for a pudding mold or heat-proof ceramic bowl, such as a soufflé dish, that fits into your slow cooker and allows the lid to close completely. You should have at least an inch of clearance all around. If there is no lid on your chosen container, you can cover the top tightly with two sheets of aluminum foil or a sheet of greased parchment paper and a sheet of aluminum foil, tying them securely with string. While watching a British cooking show on TV one Christmas, Beth saw the host deftly tie a little handle with the string so as to lower and remove the crock easily from the steamer.

And what if you can't find a bowl of the proper depth and size? You can use a small slow cooker crock for steaming as well; it will fit into a medium or large cooker. If you have an oval cooker, a casserole dish or soufflé dish can be a good substitute. Just be aware that your pudding may cook a bit more quickly because it will not be as tall.

The technique for steaming is simple. The mold is buttered and filled up to two-thirds but never more, to allow for expansion. Snap on the lid or cover and lower it into the slow cooker. Fill the slow cooker with the hottest tap water you can manage so it comes about 2 inches up the sides of the mold. You can check the water level through the glass lid, but we found no evaporation with the slow cooker.

Warm steamed puddings should have a complementary sauce, ice cream, or liqueur-flavored whipped cream to proclaim them ready to eat. Steamed breads are good with butter, jam, and spreadable cheeses. Here are a few of our favorites.

Steamed Brown Bread

Steamed brown bread is one of those old-timey American foods that hardly anyone makes anymore. What a shame! It is the age-old Colonial favorite to serve with Boston Baked Beans (page 194). You can mix it up in just a few minutes and let it steam to moist perfection unattended. The only trick is finding a small pudding mold or heat-proof bowl that will fit inside your slow cooker with an inch or so of clearance all around. That space is necessary to allow the steam to circulate properly. A deep stainless-steel or ceramic bowl, about 1½ quarts in capacity, is perfect for this recipe. Whatever you choose to use as a mold, do not fill it all the way to the top. Your bread needs room to expand.

Some people shy away from recipes that call for molasses because it can be frustrating—and messy—to work with. If you have trouble getting the molasses *into* your measuring cup, warm it up to make it easier to pour. Put the open jar in the microwave and heat on HIGH for about 10 seconds, depending on your microwave. (Keep watch to avoid a boil-over.) To make it easy to get the molasses *out* of the measuring cup, grease the cup first with a few drops of oil or a bit of nonstick cooking spray. Then the molasses will pour right out. ◦ *Serves 6*

COOKER: Medium or large round or oval
SETTING AND COOK TIME: HIGH for 2 to 2½ hours

1 large egg
½ cup sugar
½ cup light molasses
1 cup whole milk
1 cup whole wheat pastry flour
1 teaspoon baking soda
½ teaspoon salt
¼ teaspoon ground nutmeg

1. Grease and flour a 1½-quart (6-cup) pudding mold, heat-proof bowl, or small slow cooker crock that will fit inside your slow cooker with an inch or so of clearance all around.

2. In a medium-size bowl, beat the egg with a whisk. Add the sugar and molasses and continue to beat until thoroughly mixed. Beat in the milk. In a small bowl, whisk together the flour, baking soda, salt, and nutmeg, then add to the molasses mixture and stir just until the ingredients are thoroughly combined. Pour the batter into the prepared mold. Place the cover on the mold or, if you are using a bowl, cover it tightly with a double layer of aluminum foil; tie a string around the rim of the bowl to hold the foil in place.

3. Lower the mold into the slow cooker and carefully add enough hot water to come about 2 inches up the sides of the mold. Cover and cook on HIGH for 2 to 2½ hours. To determine if the bread is done, carefully remove the lid or foil from the mold and gently touch the center of the bread. It should spring back into place. If your finger leaves an impression, re-cover the bread and cooker and continue to steam, checking the bread at 30-minute intervals.

4. When the bread is done, carefully transfer the mold to a rack and let the bread cool, uncovered, for 10 minutes. Run a table knife around the inside of the mold to loosen the bread. Invert onto a rack to remove the mold, then turn the bread right side up to cool. To serve, cut into wedges or slices.

Steamed Winter Squash Bread

The winter squash acts as part of the liquid in this firm, not-too-sweet loaf, a variation on steamed brown bread. Use leftovers of your own cooked winter squash, such as hubbard or butternut, or any type of pumpkin. You can use canned pumpkin if you need to with no loss of flavor. This bread is excellent smeared with cream cheese for breakfast or served with beans or chili for lunch or dinner. ○ *Serves 6*

COOKER: Medium or large round or oval
SETTING AND COOK TIME: HIGH for 2 to 2½ hours

1 large egg
½ cup honey
¾ cup winter squash or pumpkin purée
½ cup whole wheat flour
½ cup all-purpose flour

⅓ cup fine- or medium-grind yellow cornmeal

1 teaspoon baking soda

½ teaspoon salt

¼ cup chopped pitted dates

¼ cup chopped walnuts

1. Grease and flour a 1½-quart (6-cup) pudding mold, heat-proof bowl, or small slow cooker crock that will fit inside your slow cooker with an inch or so of clearance all around.

2. In a medium-size bowl, beat the egg and honey together with a wooden spoon, then beat in the squash. In a small bowl, whisk together the flours, cornmeal, baking soda, and salt. Add the dry ingredients to the squash mixture and stir just until thoroughly combined. Stir in the dates and walnuts. Pour the batter into the prepared mold. Place the cover on the mold or, if you are using a bowl, cover it tightly with a double layer of aluminum foil; tie a string around the rim of the bowl to hold the foil in place.

3. Lower the mold into the slow cooker and carefully add enough hot water to come about 2 inches up the sides of the mold. Cover and cook on HIGH for 2 hours. To determine if the bread is done, carefully remove the lid or foil and gently touch the center of the bread. It should spring back into place. If your finger leaves an impression, re-cover the bread and cooker and continue to steam, checking at 30-minute intervals.

4. When the bread is done, carefully transfer the mold to a rack and let cool, uncovered, for 10 minutes. Run a table knife around the inside of the mold to loosen the bread. Invert onto a rack to remove the mold, then turn the bread right side up to cool. Cut into wedges or slices and serve.

Steamed Molasses Brown Bread

A real old-fashioned brown bread, such as this one, is a whole wheat, rye, and cornmeal molasses loaf made with no eggs. This turns out moist and is the perfect accompaniment to your bean and chili dishes. • *Serves 6*

COOKER: Medium or large round or oval

SETTING AND COOK TIME: HIGH for 2 to 2½ hours

⅓ cup light molasses

1⅓ cups buttermilk

½ cup whole wheat flour

½ cup medium rye flour

½ cup medium- or fine-grind yellow cornmeal

1¼ teaspoons baking soda

½ teaspoon salt

⅓ cup raisins

1. Grease and flour a 1½-quart (6-cup) pudding mold, heat-proof bowl, or small slow cooker crock that will fit inside your slow cooker with an inch or so of clearance all around.

2. In a medium-size bowl, beat together the molasses and buttermilk with a wooden spoon. In another medium-size bowl, whisk together the flours, cornmeal, baking soda, and salt. Add the dry ingredients to the molasses mixture and stir just until thoroughly combined. Stir in the raisins. Pour the batter into the prepared mold. Place the cover on the mold or, if you are using a bowl, cover it tightly with a double layer of aluminum foil; tie a string around the rim of the bowl to hold the foil in place.

3. Lower the mold into the slow cooker and carefully add enough hot water to come about 2 inches up the sides of the mold. Cover and cook on HIGH for 2 hours. To determine if the bread is done, carefully remove the lid or foil and gently touch the center of the bread. It should spring back into place. If your finger leaves an impression, re-cover the bread and cooker and continue to steam, checking at 30-minute intervals.

4. When the bread is done, carefully transfer the mold to a rack and let cool, uncovered, for 10 minutes. Run a table knife around the inside of the mold to loosen the bread. Invert onto a rack to remove the mold, then turn the bread right side up to cool. Cut into wedges or slices and serve.

Steamed Bran Muffin Bread

This is an adaptation of an old Mable Hoffman recipe; she is the pioneer of slow cooker cookbook writers. We love this steamed in a 2- or 2½-quart slow cooker crock. ● *Serves 6 to 8*

1¾ cups buttermilk
1 large egg
½ cup dark molasses
¼ cup canola oil
2 cups All-Bran cereal
1 cup whole wheat flour
1 cup all-purpose flour
2 teaspoons baking powder
1 teaspoon baking soda
½ teaspoon salt
¾ cup chopped dried apricots, or a combination of dried cherries and golden raisins
½ cup shelled raw sunflower seeds

1. Grease and flour a 2-quart (8-cup) pudding mold, heat-proof bowl, or small slow cooker crock that will fit inside your slow cooker with an inch or so of clearance all around.

2. In a large bowl, stir together the buttermilk, egg, molasses, and oil. Add the cereal and let stand 15 minutes to soften. Add the flours, baking powder, baking soda, and salt. Stir just until thoroughly combined. Stir in the dried fruit and seeds. Pour the batter into the prepared mold. Place the cover on the mold or, if you are using a bowl, cover it tightly with a double layer of aluminum foil; tie a string around the rim of the bowl to hold the foil in place.

3. Lower the mold into the slow cooker and carefully add enough hot water to come about 2 inches up the sides of the mold. Cover and cook on HIGH for 3 to 3½ hours. To determine if the bread is done, carefully remove the lid or foil and gently touch the center of the bread. It should spring back into place. If your finger leaves an impression, re-cover the bread and cooker and continue to steam, checking at 30-minute intervals.

4. When the bread is done, carefully transfer the mold to a rack and let cool, uncovered, for 10 minutes. Invert onto a rack to remove the mold, then turn the bread right side up to cool. Cut into wedges or slices and serve.

Steamed Ginger Brown Bread

We love recipes made with commercial mixes that taste like a whole lot more. Here we use gingerbread mix. This will be more tender than our other steamed brown breads, so be sure to serve at room temperature to let it firm up a bit. ○ *Serves 6*

COOKER: Medium or large round or oval
SETTING AND COOK TIME: HIGH for 2 hours

One 14-ounce package gingerbread mix
¼ cup medium- or fine-grind yellow cornmeal
Grated zest of 1 small orange
Pinch of salt
1½ cups whole milk
2 tablespoons finely chopped crystallized ginger

1. Grease and flour a 1½-quart (6-cup) pudding mold, heat-proof bowl, or small slow cooker crock that will fit inside your slow cooker with an inch or so of clearance all around.

2. In a medium-size bowl, combine the gingerbread mix, cornmeal, orange zest, salt, and milk, stirring just until thoroughly combined. Stir in the chopped ginger. Pour the batter into the prepared mold. Place the cover on the mold or, if you are using a bowl, cover it tightly with a double layer of aluminum foil; tie a string around the rim of the bowl to hold the foil in place.

3. Lower the mold into the slow cooker and carefully add enough hot water to come about 2 inches up the sides of the mold. Cover and cook on HIGH for 2 hours. To determine if the bread is done, carefully remove the lid or foil and gently touch the center of the bread. It should spring back into place. If your finger leaves an impression, re-cover the bread and cooker and continue to steam, checking at 30-minute intervals.

4. When the bread is done, carefully transfer the mold to a rack and let cool, uncovered, for 10 minutes. Invert onto a rack to remove the mold, then turn the bread right side up to cool. Cut into wedges or slices and serve.

Steamed White Fruitcake

Both French and English fruitcakes often begin with a pound cake base, to which lots of dried fruit and nuts are added. While glacé, or candied dried fruits, are nice when you can get them, we use regular dried fruits, easily found in the supermarket, and a commercial pound cake mix. Voilà! You have a wonderful, very moist cake to serve right out of the steamer, requiring no aging, although you may brush it all over with dark rum, Cognac, Calvados, or another brandy as it is cooling. This fruitcake is also nice with some custard sauce. ○ *Serves 8 to 10*

COOKER: Medium or large round or oval
SETTING AND COOK TIME: HIGH for 2 to 2½ hours

One 16-ounce package pound cake mix
½ teaspoon ground nutmeg
Pinch of ground allspice
2 large eggs
¾ cup whole milk
One 7-ounce package chopped mixed dried fruit
⅓ cup chopped mixed candied peel, such as lemon or orange
¼ cup golden raisins
2 tablespoons chopped blanched almonds
2 tablespoons dark rum, Cognac, Calvados, or another brandy (optional)
3 tablespoons apricot jam or orange marmalade (optional), heated until liquid

1. Line the bottom of a 2½-quart (10-cup) pudding mold, heat-proof bowl, or small slow cooker crock that will fit inside your slow cooker (with an inch or so of clearance all around) with a round of parchment paper. Grease and flour the paper and the sides of the mold.

2. With an electric mixer on medium speed, beat together the pound cake mix, spices, eggs, and milk in a medium-size bowl until creamy and smooth, about 5 minutes. Fold in the mixed dried fruit, candied peel, raisins, and nuts until uniformly distributed throughout the batter. Pour into the prepared mold. Place the cover on the mold or, if you are using a bowl, cover it tightly with a double layer of aluminum foil; tie a string around the rim of the bowl to hold the foil in place.

3. Lower the mold into the slow cooker and carefully add enough hot water to come about 2 inches up the sides of the mold. Cover and cook on HIGH for 2 hours. To determine if the cake is done, carefully remove the lid or foil and gently touch the center of the fruitcake. It should spring back into place. If your finger leaves an impression, re-cover the cake and cooker and continue to steam, checking at 30-minute intervals.

4. When the fruitcake is done, carefully transfer the mold to a rack and let cool, uncovered, for 10 minutes. Run a table knife around the inside of the mold to loosen the cake. Invert onto a rack to remove the mold, then turn the cake right side up to cool. Brush with the rum or brandy, if desired, then with the jam, if you want to glaze the fruitcake. Let cool completely. Cut into wedges or turn it on its side to cut round slices. Store in the refrigerator or at room temperature for up to 4 days. You can freeze the unglazed fruitcake up to 2 months.

Steamed Persimmon-Ginger Pudding with Pecans

Y ou can buy two types of persimmons in the fall—the larger, pointed Hachiyas and the smaller, more rounded Fuyus. Fuyu persimmons are firm when ripe, but don't try eating a Hachiya until it is jelly-soft. Ripen Hachiya persimmons at room temperature, which can take days, or even weeks. Fortunately, you can freeze the ripe persimmons, whole, unpeeled, and wrapped, for up to 3 months. This pudding is moist and spicy, as well as sweet, with its double hit of ginger. Serve it with softly whipped sweetened cream (add a bit of rum if desired) or vanilla ice cream. For real ginger lovers, serve with our extra-quick, fantastic ginger ice cream (recipe follows). ☉ *Serves 10*

COOKER: Large round or oval
SETTING AND COOK TIME: HIGH for 2½ to 3 hours

3 ripe Hachiya persimmons
1 cup all-purpose flour
1 teaspoon baking powder

1 teaspoon baking soda

½ teaspoon salt

½ teaspoon ground cinnamon

¼ teaspoon ground cardamom

¼ teaspoon ground ginger

⅛ teaspoon ground nutmeg

3 large eggs

½ cup firmly packed light brown sugar

½ cup granulated sugar

½ cup (1 stick) unsalted butter, melted and cooled

2 tablespoons golden or dark rum

⅓ to ½ cup chopped crystallized ginger, to your taste

1 cup chopped pecans

1. Grease and flour a 2- to 2½-quart pudding mold with a lid or a heat-proof bowl that will fit inside your slow cooker with at least an inch of clearance all around.

2. Cut the persimmons in half, and scoop the jelly-like pulp into a large strainer set over a bowl. Use a spoon to push the pulp through the strainer, discarding any seeds or fibrous bits that will not go through. Measure 1 cup of pulp and set aside. Discard the rest or reserve for another use.

3. Whisk together the flour, baking powder, baking soda, salt, and spices in a small bowl. Set aside.

4. With an electric mixer, beat together the eggs and both sugars in a medium-size bowl until smooth and creamy. Beat in the melted butter and rum. Add the dry ingredients and stir just until combined. Stir in the reserved persimmon pulp and fold in the chopped ginger and pecans. Pour the batter into the prepared mold. Cover with a lid or a double layer of aluminum foil, secured with string.

5. Lower the mold into the slow cooker and carefully add enough hot water to come about 2 inches up the sides of the mold. Cover and cook on HIGH for 2½ to 3 hours. Check the pudding; it should feel firm, rather than jiggly, yet slightly moist. A cake tester inserted in the center should come out clean.

6. When the pudding is done, carefully transfer the mold to a rack and let cool, uncovered, for 10 minutes. Invert onto a serving plate and let the pudding slide out. Serve slightly warm or at room temperature, cut into wedges.

Quick Ginger Ice Cream

Makes 1 quart

¼ cup crystallized ginger, chopped
¼ cup water
1 quart vanilla ice cream

1. In a small saucepan or nonstick skillet over medium-low heat, simmer the ginger in the water until softened; the liquid will evaporate and thicken a bit. Set aside to cool to room temperature.

2. Set the ice cream in the refrigerator until soft and malleable but not melted, 15 to 30 minutes. Transfer the ice cream to a medium-size bowl. With an electric mixer or by hand, beat the ice cream quickly until just creamy. Add the ginger pieces and their liquid and blend until evenly distributed. Working quickly, scrape the ice cream back into the carton with a large spatula. Return the ice cream to the freezer to firm up for at least 6 hours before serving.

Fruit Desserts, Sauces, and Compotes

Desserts made in the slow cooker fall into two categories: some are cooked directly in the crock, and others steam in a mold inside the crock, which acts like a water bath. For this chapter we offer fruit desserts that are made directly in the crock, including baked fruit desserts, fresh and dried fruit compotes, fruit sauces, and poached fruits.

We really enjoy using seasonal fruit in our menus. Fresh warm fruit, aromatic sweet spices, a crumb top to soak up the juices, some fresh cream, and we are in dessert heaven. The wholesome, fruit-based desserts known as crumbles, crisps, buckles, cobblers, and the like are nostalgic and homey. Without the added step of making and rolling out a crust, they're quicker than pies to put together.

We have a number of fresh fruit crumbles, the British version of American crisps with a slightly heavier topping, which usually includes rolled oats. Remember that baking in the slow cooker crock does not encourage browning, so the crumbly top will be pale, but cooked through. We offer one for winter and one for summer, and with these recipes as templates, you can substitute your own fruit combinations.

Then we have some cobblers: stewed fruit with a tender cake or biscuit topping. They are also called grunts and buckles, a throwback to old-fashioned American country home baking. Remember that these fruit mixtures should not be thick,

like canned pie filling, but juicy. We have a nice, yellow, cake-like topping to complement a variety of fresh fruit, as well as our variation of the brown Betty, the brown Bethy, a layering of bread and fruit. Please use a rich, tender egg bread if you can. It makes the difference in texture and taste.

Like savory slow cooker preparations, fruit desserts made in a crock need some liquid to cook properly; it can be just a dash of liquid or full submersion. Stewed, baked, and poached fruit desserts are wonderful in the cooker since they are cooked in varying amounts of liquid. None of them are left to cook all day since they are too delicate. You must be around to supervise the timing. You want whole fruit to retain its shape and not end up like apple or pear sauce.

We love simple fruit sauces, such as applesauce, pear sauce, and peach sauce. They are tasty breakfast food, and so we offer several recipes here. These preparations need only a few tablespoons of liquid; the fruit itself has plenty and when it breaks down in the cooking process, you get a nice, naturally thick purée of fruit. No stirring is necessary because the slow cooker will not allow the fruit to burn.

The slow cooker, with its gentle even heat source, makes lovely fruit desserts such as gently spiced compotes and poached fresh whole fruit, which for some reason are dismissed as too old fashioned or simple for today's diners. We disagree. They are pure comfort food—softly cooked, warm, and sweet. These are not elaborate desserts, just soothing simplicity.

Poached fresh and dried fruits have a charm all their own. They are still appreciated at European tables, and most bistros and trattorias offer some type of poached fruit with a bit of syrup. Depending on the type of fruit, they can be poached whole, halved, or in pieces, in a thick or thin sugar syrup. You can make a compote out of a single fruit or a combination of two or more, which is called a *compote composée*. They are just plain gorgeous in a serving bowl surrounded by their syrup. Fruits can be poached in water, wine, or fruit juice, or a combination thereof. The slow cooker does so gently, even though we poach most fruits on the HIGH setting. Poached prunes are the most familiar cooked dried fruit, sadly restricted to the breakfast table, but all sorts of other dried fruits lend themselves well to the gentle cooking and sweet aromatic bath required for a nice compote. A glass or porcelain raised footed bowl made just for serving compote is called a *compotier,* and it makes an elegant presentation. Simply put the fruits in the bowl with a slotted spoon and pour the syrup over them.

Cooked fruits are traditionally served while still warm or at room temperature with whipped cream, but they are also good cold as a topping for vanilla cheesecake and a battery of plain old-fashioned cakes such as angel food cake, sponge cake, gold cake, and pound cake.

Orchard Crumble

F ruit crumbles are homey desserts that manage to pack a delightful array of flavors and textures into each fork full: smooth, soft, tart fruit; a sweet and chewy topping; honey-like syrup; and, if you are lucky and there is some in the freezer, the cold, creamy shock of vanilla ice cream. This crumble does the usual apple version one better, adding the gentle sweetness of pears and the bright flavor and color of cranberries or cherries. What a delightful way to use up those bags of cranberries stashed in the freezer! ● *Serves 6 to 8*

COOKER: Medium round or oval or large round
SETTINGS AND COOK TIMES: HIGH for 30 minutes, then LOW for 2½ to 3½ hours

FRUIT MIXTURE:
3 firm Bartlett pears, peeled, cored and thickly sliced
2 large tart cooking apples, peeled, cored, and sliced
1½ cups fresh or frozen cranberries, or 2 cups fresh sweet cherries, pitted, or frozen sweet pitted cherries, thawed
½ teaspoon ground cinnamon
½ cup granulated sugar
2 tablespoons cornstarch

TOPPING:
1 cup all-purpose flour
½ cup quick-cooking rolled oats
1 cup firmly packed light brown sugar
½ teaspoon ground cinnamon
½ cup (1 stick) cold unsalted butter, cut into pieces

Vanilla ice cream or whipped cream for serving

1. Coat the slow cooker with butter-flavor nonstick cooking spray or grease with butter. To make the fruit mixture, put the fruit in the cooker; sprinkle with the cinnamon, granulated sugar, and cornstarch and toss to coat the fruit. Cover and cook on HIGH for 30 minutes.

2. Meanwhile, make the topping. Combine the flour, rolled oats, brown sugar, and cinnamon in a small bowl or food processor. Cut in the butter with two knives, or your fingertips, or pulse to make coarse crumbs. After the 30 minutes, spread the topping evenly over the fruit, leaving a ½-inch border without topping to prevent burning. Cover, set the heat to LOW, and cook until the fruit is tender, 2½ to 3½ hours. Test by sticking a knife into the center of the crumble; when it passes through the fruit with little resistance, the crumble is done.

3. Uncover and let cool for 10 minutes before serving. If desired, top each serving with ice cream or whipped cream.

Peach Crumble

F or peach lovers, peaches mean summer. They were once considered a luxury food because they were so rare, and royalty would plant their own orchards of trees. Columbus brought the first peach trees to the New World on his voyage of discovery, and the first governor of Massachusetts asked for peach trees to be brought from England. They flourished so nicely that the peach is sometimes thought to be native to America. ❍ *Serves 6 to 8*

COOKER: Medium round or oval or large round
SETTINGS AND COOK TIMES: HIGH for 30 minutes, then LOW for 2½ to 3 hours

2 pounds firm-ripe peaches, peeled, pitted, and thickly sliced

TOPPING:
¾ cup quick-cooking rolled oats
¾ cup all-purpose flour
¾ cup firmly packed light brown sugar
1 teaspoon baking powder
½ teaspoon ground cinnamon or apple pie spice
Pinch of ground nutmeg
¼ teaspoon salt
½ cup (1 stick) cold unsalted butter, cut into pieces

Vanilla ice cream or whipped cream for serving

1. Coat the slow cooker with nonstick cooking spray or grease with butter. Put the fruit in the cooker, cover, and cook on HIGH for 30 minutes.

2. Meanwhile, make the topping. Combine the rolled oats, flour, brown sugar, baking powder, cinnamon, nutmeg, and salt in a medium-size bowl and cut in the butter with two knives or your fingertips. Or combine the dry ingredients in a food processor and cut in the butter with a few pulses. After the 30 minutes, spread the topping evenly over the fruit, leaving a ½-inch border without topping to prevent burning. Cover, set the heat to LOW, and cook until the fruit is tender, 2½ to 3 hours. Test by sticking a knife into the center of the crumble; when it passes through the fruit with little resistance, the crumble is done.

3. Uncover and let cool for 10 minutes before serving. If desired, top each serving with ice cream or whipped cream.

Blueberry Grunt

A grunt is another Colonial American dessert, stewed fruit topped with a drop biscuit dough that steams like a dumpling. It was originally made in a cast-iron skillet or Dutch oven on the stove top. Even in its traditional form, the topping never browns, so the slow cooker is perfect for this recipe. The "grunt" in the recipe title is a reference to the sound the fruit makes while cooking. This is also good made with blackberries, or a combination of berries and nectarines. If you use half blackberries and half blueberries, call it black and blue grunt.

○ *Serves 4 to 6*

COOKER: Medium or large round
SETTINGS AND COOK TIMES: LOW for 5 hours, then HIGH for 30 minutes

STEWED FRUIT:
2 pints fresh blueberries, picked over for stems, or one 16-ounce package individually frozen blueberries (not packed in syrup), thawed
½ cup sugar
½ cup water, warm if using frozen blueberries
2 tablespoons instant tapioca

DUMPLING TOPPING:
2 cups all-purpose flour
2 tablespoons sugar

2½ teaspoons baking powder

½ teaspoon salt

¼ cup (½ stick) cold unsalted butter

½ cup cold milk

1 large egg

Cold heavy cream for serving

1. Coat the slow cooker with butter-flavor nonstick cooking spray or grease with butter. Combine the blueberries, ½ cup of the sugar, water, and tapioca in the cooker, stirring gently to evenly coat the berries. Cover and cook on LOW until the berries have formed a thick sauce, about 5 hours.

2. To make the topping, in a medium-size bowl, whisk together the flour, 2 table-spoons of sugar, baking powder, and salt. Using a pastry blender or two knives, cut in the butter until the mixture resembles coarse meal. In a small bowl, beat the milk and egg together; stir into flour mixture with a few strokes to form a soft dough.

3. Turn the cooker to HIGH and remove the lid. Drop the dough by heaping table-spoonfuls on top of the hot blueberries. Cover and cook until the topping is firm and a toothpick inserted in the center comes out clean, about 30 minutes; the topping will not brown.

4. Turn the cooker off, remove the lid, and let the grunt rest for 10 minutes. Spoon into individual bowls and pass the pitcher of heavy cream.

Pear Brown Bethy

T his warm baked winter fruit dessert, similar to a crumble or crisp, has been a popular American pudding since Colonial times. Be sure to use pears that are ripe, but still nice and firm, or they will disintegrate when cooked. This can also be made with apples. It is important to use a fine bread, such as a French brioche or a challah, for a good finished flavor. Serve this with a pitcher of heavy cream on the side. It is best eaten the day it is made. ● *Serves 6*

COOKER: Medium or large round
SETTING AND COOK TIME: HIGH for 2½ to 3 hours

1 pound fresh white bread, challah, or brioche, crusts removed, and cut into ½- to ¾-inch cubes

10 tablespoons (1¼ sticks) unsalted butter

½ cup firmly packed light brown sugar

½ cup granulated sugar

1 tablespoon all-purpose flour

2 teaspoons ground cinnamon

½ teaspoon ground allspice

¼ teaspoon ground nutmeg

Pinch of ground ginger

2½ pounds firm pears (about 8), such as Bartlett or Bosc, peeled, cored, and thickly sliced

3 tablespoons fresh lemon juice

¼ cup apple or pear juice or water

1. Coat the slow cooker with nonstick cooking spray or grease with butter. Preheat the oven to 350°F. Place the bread cubes in a single layer on a baking sheet and bake until golden and dry, about 10 minutes. Set aside.

2. Melt the butter in a large skillet over medium heat. Add the bread cubes and stir to moisten with the butter. Transfer to a large bowl to cool. Then add the sugars, flour, and spices and toss to coat.

3. In another large bowl, toss the sliced pears with the lemon juice.

4. Put one-third of the spiced bread in the cooker. Layer in half of the pears and pour over the juice. Top with half of the remaining spiced bread, and then layer in the remaining pears. Finish with the remaining bread cubes. Cover and cook on HIGH until bubbly and the fruit is tender, 2½ to 3 hours. Serve hot, scooping out the Bethy with an oversized spoon. Or let stand in the crock, with the lid off, until cool and serve at room temperature.

Applesauce

W e love our homemade applesauce—the jarred stuff doesn't even come close. And we don't get fussy about the type of apple we use; every type of apple on hand, especially when cleaning out the produce drawer in the refrigerator, goes into the slow cooker. If the price is right, we will also pick up a big bag at the market just for sauce. You can add the sugar or not; Julie likes hers sweet, Beth likes hers without sugar but with a swirl of butter at the end. Serve it for breakfast with yogurt, alongside pork chops for dinner, on toast with cottage cheese, or warm with a scoop of vanilla ice cream for dessert. ○ *Makes about 4 cups*

COOKER: Medium or large round
SETTING AND COOK TIME: HIGH for 3 to 3½ hours, or LOW for 5 to 6 hours

8 to 10 apples, peeled, cored, and quartered
2 tablespoons fresh lemon juice
2 tablespoons water, as needed
Sugar to taste

1. Put the apples in the slow cooker and toss with the lemon juice. If the apples seem unusually dry, add the water to the cooker. Cover and cook until the apples are extremely tender and falling apart, on HIGH for 3 to 3½ hours or on LOW for 5 to 6 hours.

2. Purée the cooked apples in a food processor, or in the cooker with a handheld immersion blender, or pass them through a food mill fitted with the medium or large blade. Add sugar to taste, if desired. Serve immediately or refrigerate and serve cold. The applesauce will keep, tightly covered, for 2 weeks in the refrigerator.

Cinnamon Applesauce: Put one 4- to 6-inch cinnamon stick in the cooker along with the apples. After cooking, discard the cinnamon stick before puréeing the apples.

Orange Applesauce: Using a vegetable peeler or paring knife, remove the zest from 1 orange in long strips, leaving the white pith behind. Put the zest in the cooker along with the apples. After cooking, discard the zest before puréeing the apples.

Cran-Apple Peach Sauce

O ur literary agent was visiting her sister in Detroit, and in the mail came an article on slow cookers by Heart Smart, the Henry Ford Hospital Heart and Vascular Institute. This simply fabulous recipe by program representative Darlene Simmerman, R.D., is excellent, and we are happy to include it here (with less sugar). Make it with fresh peaches, please. If you can find McIntosh or Rome Beauty apples, both of which have a very short season at the end of summer, do use them because they make wonderful sauce. ○ *Makes about 4 cups*

COOKER: Medium or large round
SETTING AND COOK TIME: HIGH for 3 to 4 hours, or LOW for 5 to 7 hours

8 to 10 cooking apples, peeled, cored, and quartered
4 ripe peaches, peeled, pitted, and chopped
½ cup dried cranberries
¼ cup firmly packed light brown sugar or granulated sugar, or a combination of both (optional)
½ cup water
2 tablespoons fresh lemon juice
2 teaspoons ground cinnamon

1. Put the apples, peaches, cranberries, brown sugar if using (you can leave this out and still get delicious sauce), water, lemon juice, and cinnamon in the slow cooker. Cover and cook until the apples are extremely tender and falling apart, on HIGH for 3 to 4 hours or on LOW for 5 to 7 hours.

2. Beat to make a coarse mash, or use a handheld immersion blender for a smoother sauce. Serve immediately or refrigerate and serve cold. The applesauce will keep, tightly covered, for up to 2 weeks in the refrigerator.

Apple and Pear Sauce with Ginger

This is a good fruit sauce for winter, combining apples, pears, and ginger. You can use any firm, ripe pear, such as Bosc (a great cooking pear), Winter Nellis, or Anjou. We like the big tart Granny Smith apples if you can find them; otherwise, any other tart green apple will do. ● *Makes about 4 cups*

COOKER: Medium or large round
SETTING AND COOK TIME: HIGH for 3 to 3½ hours, or LOW for 5 to 6 hours

6 cooking apples, peeled, cored, and quartered
6 firm pears, peeled, cored, and quartered
¼ cup sugar or honey (optional)
½ cup water
2 tablespoons fresh lemon juice
1 chunk fresh ginger, about 3 inches long, peeled and minced
3 tablespoons unsalted butter

1. Combine the apples, pears, sugar (you can leave this out and still get delicious sauce), water, lemon juice, and ginger in the slow cooker. Cover and cook until the fruit is extremely tender and falling apart, on HIGH for 3 to 3½ hours or on LOW for 5 to 6 hours.

2. Beat to make a coarse mash or use a handheld immersion blender for a smoother sauce. Stir in the butter. Serve immediately or refrigerate and serve cold. The fruit sauce will keep, tightly covered, for up to 2 weeks in the refrigerator.

Crock-Stewed Dried Apricots

 f you love apricots, you will make this recipe often because it is so versatile. ○ *Serves about 6*

COOKER: Medium round
SETTING AND COOK TIME: LOW for 3 to 4 hours

One 12-ounce package dried apricots
1 strip lemon or orange zest

1. Put the apricots and citrus zest in the slow cooker and add water to cover. Cover and cook on LOW until plump and tender, 3 to 4 hours.

2. Turn off the cooker, remove the lid, and let the apricots cool. Transfer to a storage container, and refrigerate. Serve cold with a dab of sour cream or crème fraîche, or purée to make a sauce. The apricots will keep, tightly covered, for a week in the refrigerator.

Rhubarb-Strawberry Compote

 his is an unbelievably delicious compote to make for early summer brunches or desserts when fresh rhubarb is in season. ○ *Serves 6*

COOKER: Medium round
SETTING AND COOK TIME: LOW for 3 to 4 hours

¼ cup water or orange juice
1 cup sugar
1 pound fresh rhubarb, trimmed of leaves and cut into 1½-inch chunks (about 4 cups)
2 teaspoons fresh lemon juice
2 pints fresh strawberries, hulled and cut in half

1. Combine the water, sugar, and rhubarb in the slow cooker. Cover and cook on LOW until soft, 3 to 4 hours.

2. Mash the rhubarb a bit with a fork or the back of a large spoon. Add the lemon juice and strawberries and stir once to distribute. Turn off the cooker and let the fruit cool a bit. Serve warm or at room temperature. Or transfer to a storage container, refrigerate, and serve chilled, ladled into dessert bowls. The compote will keep, tightly covered, for 4 days in the refrigerator.

Rum-Butterscotch Bananas

his is a simplified version of bananas Foster, which, unlike the original, is not flambéed. An American dessert created in New Orleans at Brennan's Restaurant in the 1950s, bananas Foster is served hot over a scoop of vanilla ice cream. Use light brown sugar, with its more subtle flavor, rather than dark, to complement the bananas. ◦ *Serves about 4*

COOKER: Small or medium round
SETTING AND COOK TIME: LOW for 1¼ to 2½ hours;
    bananas added during last 15 to 20 minutes

½ **cup (1 stick) unsalted butter**
½ **cup firmly packed light brown sugar**
¼ **cup dark rum**
2 large, firm, ripe bananas
Vanilla ice cream for serving

1. Combine the butter, brown sugar, and rum in the slow cooker. Cover and cook on LOW for 1 to 1½ hours. Stir with a whisk until smooth.

2. Just before serving, peel the bananas, cut in half lengthwise, and cut each piece in half crosswise to make 4 pieces per banana. Add to the hot sauce. Cover and continue to cook on LOW until heated through and coated with the sauce, 15 to 20 minutes.

3. Serve immediately over scoops of vanilla ice cream

Stewed Blueberries

Blueberries are a common sight on American tables from June to September. They take well to being stewed, and this is a favorite way to cook them. Rock-hard frozen berries will take longer to cook than fresh. This is wonderful served with vanilla gelato. ○ *Serves 4*

COOKER: Medium round
SETTING AND COOK TIME: LOW for 3 to 4 hours

4 cups fresh or frozen blueberries
½ cup sugar
⅓ cup orange juice
3 slices lemon

1. Add all the ingredients to the slow cooker insert and stir to combine. Cover and let stand at room temperature for 15 minutes or in the refrigerator for an hour to give the berries a chance to exude some liquid (this is especially important for the frozen berries).

2. Cook on LOW for 3 to 4 hours. Turn off the cooker, remove the lid, and let the blueberries cool a bit. Serve warm or at room temperature. Or transfer to a storage container, refrigerate, and serve chilled, ladled into dessert bowls. The blueberries will keep, tightly covered, for 4 days in the refrigerator.

Poached Cots

Our editorial colleague at the *San Jose Mercury News* is Rebecca Salner. While working on a story for the "Merc" about poached fruits, she poached fresh apricots to rave reviews. Once more a basic, simple dessert, originally from the *James Beard Cookbook,* was the top winner (we left the Cognac measured in jiggers the way Beard wrote it; a jigger is 1½ ounces or 3 tablespoons). So we adapted the recipe for the slow cooker. We have the apricots poached whole, but you can poach halves as well; just use the lesser amount of time and leave in the pits while cooking. In a short time, you will have plump, tender fruit and a decadent sauce to eat alone or over ice cream. You can use this recipe to poach whole fresh figs as well. ○ *Serves 4*

COOKER: Medium round or oval
SETTING AND COOK TIME: HIGH for 2 to 3 hours

1 cup water
1 cup sugar
Juice of ½ small lemon
12 firm, ripe fresh apricots, dipped in boiling water with a slotted spoon
    for 5 seconds and skins slipped off
1 to 2 jiggers Cognac, to your taste

1. Combine the water, sugar, and lemon juice in the slow cooker. Add the apricots; they will float. Cover and cook on HIGH for 2 to 3 hours. Do not stir at any time during the cooking in order to avoid bruising the fruit. Check the consistency of the apricots by piercing their flesh with the tip of a small knife; you want them firm, but slightly soft. They will soften a bit more as they cool. Remove from the liquid with a slotted spoon to a serving bowl.

2. With the lid off, cook the liquid down a bit; stir in the Cognac. Pour the sauce over the fruit and serve warm or cold.

Crock-Baked Apples

B aked apples can be a healthful and simple dessert or a stupendous breakfast. We really can't understand why hardly anyone makes them anymore. This is a perfect autumn and winter fruit dessert, served hot or warm with vanilla ice cream, whipped cream, crème fraîche, or just some plain heavy cream thickening the aromatic cooking liquid. For breakfast, try these apples cold, or warm them in the microwave to take the chill off. The cooking time will vary, depending on the size and firmness of your apples. The bigger and firmer the apples, the longer the cooking time. ○ *Serves 6*

COOKER: Medium or large round or oval

SETTING AND COOK TIME: HIGH for 2½ to 3½ hours
(time will vary somewhat depending on the apple)

6 large firm baking apples (about 8 ounces each), such as Golden Delicious, Granny Smith, Rome
Beauty, or Fuji
⅔ cup firmly packed light or dark brown sugar
½ teaspoon ground cinnamon
About 2 tablespoons unsalted butter, cut into 6 pieces
½ cup apple juice, apple cider, or water

1. Grease the slow cooker with some butter or coat with butter-flavor nonstick cooking spray.

2. Using a paring knife, vegetable peeler, or corer, remove the cores of the apples, leaving ½ inch of flesh at the bottom. Peel off a strip of skin around the top of each apple. Mix the brown sugar and cinnamon together in a small bowl and pack each core with the mixture. You will have some left over. Arrange the apples in the cooker, right side up. Fit as many apples as possible around the bottom, then stack the rest on top, offset, not squarely on top of the others. Place a dab of butter on top of each apple and sprinkle with any leftover brown sugar mixture. Pour the apple juice into the cooker. Cover and cook on HIGH until the apples are soft when pierced with the tip of a small knife, 2½ to 3½ hours; you want them firm, but slightly soft. They will soften a bit more as they cool.

3. Turn off the cooker, remove the lid, and let the apples cool a bit. Serve hot, warm, or room temperature with some of the cooking juices spooned over the top. To serve cold, refrigerate the apples in their liquid, covered, for at least 4 hours. The apples will keep, covered, for 3 to 4 days in the refrigerator.

Caramel Apples

Buying already-made caramels and melting them in the slow cooker created the most luscious melted candy for dipping fresh apples just like the ones you get at a fair or circus. Use a small cooker for this; it allows the caramel to achieve some depth for proper dipping. Leave the dipped apples at room temperature to set; do not refrigerate or the caramel will harden and be difficult to sink your teeth into. ● *Makes 8 apples*

COOKER: Small round
SETTING AND COOK TIME: LOW for 1 to 2 hours

14 ounces caramel candies
½ cup water
8 medium-size firm, crisp apples, thoroughly washed and dried

1. Put the caramels and water in the slow cooker, cover, and cook on LOW until the caramels are melted and smooth, 1 to 2 hours; stir a few times with a wooden spoon. The mixture will be thick when completely melted. Add some hot water to adjust the consistency if necessary.

2. Meanwhile, prepare the apples for dipping. Line a baking sheet with parchment paper and rub with butter or coat with butter-flavor nonstick cooking spray; set aside. Remove the stems from the apples and turn them upside down; the stem end will be wider and flatter and will be the top of the caramel apple. Insert a wooden stick into the blossom end of each apple, right into the center, pushing only two-thirds of the way into the apple; set aside near the cooker.

3. Turn off the cooker and remove the lid. If your crock is removable, use oven mitts to take it out of the cooker and place it on a folded tea towel. Tip the crock to make the mixture deep enough for dipping a whole apple and coat it with the caramel, holding it by the wooden stick, and turning to coat all surfaces up to the base of the stick. Hold the apple above the crock and let any extra caramel drip back in. Place the apple on the parchment-lined baking sheet, with the stick pointing up. Repeat with the remaining apples, spooning the last of the caramel over the last apple at the end. Do all the dipping at once, or the caramel will begin to cool and harden. Let the apples cool at room temperature and set up for 1 to 2 hours.

4. Butter or spray a few sheets of waxed paper and cut into pieces large enough to wrap around each apple and twist around the wooden stick to secure. Caramel apples keep for 2 to 3 days at cool room temperature.

·· Caramel Corn ··

Makes about 10 cups

14 ounces caramel candies
2 teaspoons vanilla extract
½ cup water
½ cup unpopped popcorn kernels or 12 to 14 cups already popped popcorn

1. Melt the caramel as directed in step 1 of Caramel Apples recipe (page 475), stirring in the vanilla extract and the water. Pop the corn if necessary.

2. Preheat the oven to 250°F. Line several large baking sheets with parchment paper and rub them with butter or coat them with butter-flavor nonstick cooking spray. Spread the popcorn over the prepared sheets. Pour the hot caramel over the popcorn and toss gently with 2 wooden spoons or flat spatulas until all the popcorn is coated. Place in the oven and bake for 45 minutes, stirring every 15 minutes. Remove the pans from the oven and place on racks to cool completely on the pans. Transfer the caramel corn to a bowl or an airtight container. Store at room temperature for up to 1 week.

Fruit Butters, Jams, and Chutneys

When you want to capture the fresh tastes of summer fruit and vegetables for the winter, what do you do? Make your own jams, fruit butters, preserves, chutneys, and marmalades. If you have never tasted homemade strawberry or apricot jam, you are missing out on one of life's great gustatory experiences. And commercial chutneys just do not come close to homemade ones.

Too much trouble, you say? Not anymore. The slow cooker is an excellent way to put up small batches of jams, preserves, marmalades, and chutneys without lots of stirring (maybe once or twice) or fussing with a thermometer; there is little risk of scorching and you can be sure the fruit will not react with the pot and get an off taste or discolor. If you are a first time jam maker, this method is most certainly for you.

If you like to make larger batches and put up pints and pints of your own jams, be sure to refer to a reliable canning book; we skipped that step here. We like to keep small batches in the refrigerator or freezer and make more as needed.

When loading your ingredients, be sure that you have plenty of room in the slow cooker; jams can bubble up to almost four times their volume and you want to avoid messy spillovers. There are two schools of thought regarding the size of cooker to use: according to one, the crock should be at least half full so that the heating element can reach the entire mixture efficiently, and therefore a medium or small cooker is best. The other school believes a large cooker with plenty of room is what is needed. We found both ways work fine; it is your choice.

"All the recipes I use for jams are exactly the same ones I used when I made them in the pot on top of the stove," says one of our testers who makes all her jams in the slow cooker. "The only difference is the slow cooker cooks longer at a slightly lower temperature than on the stove top. The benefit is you don't need to stand over them and they don't burn, but you do need to keep an eye on them the last 2 hours just to make sure. The first 2 hours cooking on LOW gets all the ingredients to turn mushy. Stir once or twice. Then for the last 2 to 4 hours, cook with the top off to reduce and cook off. I personally never strain nor use pectin since I don't like the solid stiff stuff that pectin makes. I enjoy the more soft yummy stuff; that's why the cooking time depends on the consistency you like and on the condition of the fruit—soft cooks longer, a firm consistency cooks shorter."

We have tried to be as precise as possible when giving times for cooking. You will notice in some recipes you will cook covered on LOW for a few hours, then uncover and cook on HIGH to evaporate the accumulated fruit juices until the preserve is the consistency you desire, just as our tester recommended. This will be different for each person, hence the wide time range. We recommend you stay at home while the slow cooker is uncovered and cooking on HIGH. Even though each of our testers used the same recipe, every single person reported a slightly different cooking time. This had to do with the climate, condition of the fruit, and model of the slow cooker. Within one to two batches we are certain you will find your perfect cooking time. Please note it for future reference.

•• Do You Know Your Jams from Your Jellies? ••

We know how much we love a bit of sweet on our toast, but what are they and what is the difference between them all? Well, while all jams and condiments are technically called preserves, they all call for a varying amount of sugar; each has a different proportion of it in relation to the amount of fruit and a slightly different method of preparation. Here is a glossary of terms to help you differentiate each type. Please note that jellies are not included here and are not recommended for preparation in the slow cooker.

Jam: A jam contains one or more fruits that are chopped or crushed and cooked rapidly with sugar. Jams are slightly firm, always softer than jelly, but do not hold the shape of the jar unless they contain pectin. They are best made in small batches.

Marmalade: Similar to preserves, marmalades contain small pieces of fruit and peel suspended in a transparent jelly. Orange is the most famous in this category, but marmalade can also be made from lemons or limes.

Preserves: Preserves are made just like jam or marmalade but the whole fruit retains its shape and becomes tender. The most common preserves are made with berries. Since most of the fruit is whole, the syrup stays clear and becomes the consistency of honey. Preserves are best made in small batches.

Conserve: A conserve is also made like a jam, but it contains at least two fruits and often raisins and nuts.

Butter: A fruit butter is made by slow-cooking together mashed or puréed fruit, sugar, and sometimes spices to a make a gloriously thick spread.

Chutney: A chutney is a raw or cooked condiment served with meals. Cooked chutney, known as a preserved chutney, is a combination of fruit, sugar, vinegar, and spices and has a thick consistency ranging from chunky to smooth. While chutneys can be fiery hot or sweet, the ones with a bit of both are delicious spreads for bread or accompaniments for bread, cheese, and pâtés. The slow cooker makes fabulous chutneys.

·· What Makes It Gel? ··

Pectin is a water-soluble substance that is found in fruit. When introduced to heat, sugar, and an acid, pectin will thicken like gelatin, a process called gelling. Commercial pectin is available in two forms, liquid and dry. The liquid is natural pectin concentrate from apples and the dry is derived from apples or citrus fruits.

Fruits High in Natural Pectin

This category includes tart apples, blueberries, blackberries, cranberries, currants, Concord grapes, papayas, damson plums, and quinces. The peels of lemons and oranges have a lot of natural pectin. Under-ripe fruit contains more natural pectin than overripe fruit. Fruits high in pectin will set up and become thick without any added pectin after slow cooking.

Fruits Low in Natural Pectin

Apricots, bananas, cherries, mangoes, nectarines, peaches, pineapple, raspberries, rhubarb, strawberries, and all overripe fruit are low in natural pectin. They need some commercial liquid or dry pectin and a bit more sugar to gel properly.

·· Sterilizing Jars and Glasses for Preserving ··

It is best to have sterilized jars even if you are not using the traditional canning method to preserve fruit. Always check their condition by running your finger around the rim to check for cracks or chips. Always use new lids, but bands can be reused. Wash your jars with hot, soapy water and rinse in scalding water. Place the jars in a deep kettle or stockpot filled with water, cover, and boil for 15 minutes (use a timer) from the moment the steam emerges from the pot. You can use a jar lifter if you like. You must keep the water boiling. Turn off the heat and let the jars stand in the hot water. When your jams or preserves are ready, remove the jars with tongs and place upside down on a clean kitchen towel to dry. Many cooks use the dishwasher to sterilize jars instead. If you prefer that method, make sure the heat cycle for drying is turned on.

Fill the jars while they are still hot, leaving 1 to 2 inches of headroom. Toss the lids into the pot with the hot water and boil for at least 5 minutes; they will be easy to put on hot. Refer to the manufacturer's instructions that are printed on every lid box or to a manual with instructions for canning from the U.S. Department of Agriculture and state extension agents.

Apple Butter

Everyone loves old-fashioned apple butter. In the oven or on the stove top, apple butter needs a watchful eye. And it is a messy process as well. Not so with slow cooker apple butter, one of the best uses of your 4- to 6-quart cooker. Be sure to use unpeeled apples, since the pectin in the skins will help make the butter nice and thick. The yield will vary, depending on how thick you like your butter.

○ *Makes 5 to 8 cups*

COOKER: Large round
SETTING AND COOK TIME: LOW for 12 to 20 hours; cooker is uncovered at 10 to 12 hours

5 pounds tart cooking apples, unpeeled, cored, and cut up, or enough apples to fill your cooker
2 cups sugar
1 cup apple juice or cider (optional; see step 1)
1¼ teaspoons ground cinnamon
¼ teaspoon ground cloves
¼ teaspoon ground nutmeg
¼ teaspoon ground allspice
Pinch of salt

1. Coat the slow cooker with nonstick cooking spray. Fill with the apples, almost to the top; the exact amount is not critical. As you load in the apples, sprinkle with the sugar in layers. Cover and let stand at room temperature all day; the apples will exude some of their own juice and collapse slightly. If you want to skip this step, just add the apple juice.

2. Add the spices and salt and toss the apples with a large wooden spoon. Cover and cook on LOW for 10 to 12 hours, or overnight.

3. In the morning, remove the lid and let the apple butter cook an additional 2 to 8 hours on LOW to reach the desired thickness.

4. Turn off the cooker and let cool to room temperature in the crock. Transfer to a blender or food processor, or use a handheld immersion blender right in the crock and purée the butter until completely smooth. Scrape with a rubber spatula into spring-top glass jars (or use screw tops with new lids). Store, covered, in the refrigerator for up to 2 months. Or transfer to small plastic storage containers and freeze for up to 3 months. Serve cold or at room temperature.

Pumpkin Butter

T ime to go beyond pumpkin pie and make some more delicious things with pumpkin. Pumpkin butter cooks up quite quickly and is spicy sweet. Here we use canned pumpkin for ease, but you can cook any winter squash and use it instead; you will want about 3 cups smooth cooked purée. Pumpkin butter is good on toast, English muffins, and pancakes, or dabbed as a topping for yogurt. Don't be tempted to add more spices; they really intensify during the slow cooking process. ○ *Makes about 3¾ cups*

COOKER: Medium round
SETTING AND COOK TIME: HIGH for 2½ to 3 hours;
    cooker is uncovered during last 30 minutes to 1 hour

One 29-ounce can pumpkin purée
1¼ cups firmly packed light brown sugar
½ cup mild honey
Juice of 1 lemon
1 tablespoon cider vinegar
¾ teaspoon apple pie spice or pumpkin pie spice

1. Put all the ingredients in the slow cooker and stir with a spatula until well mixed. Don't worry if there are some lumps in the sugar; they will melt into the butter during cooking. Use the spatula to scrape down the sides. Cover and cook on HIGH for 2 hours, stirring occasionally.

2. Remove the lid and let cook on HIGH for an additional 30 minutes to 1 hour to reach the desired thickness.

3. Turn off the cooker and let the pumpkin butter cool to room temperature in the crock. Scrape with a rubber spatula into spring-top glass jars (or use screw tops with new lids). Store, covered, in the refrigerator for up to 6 weeks. Or transfer to small plastic storage containers and freeze for up to 3 months. Serve cold or at room temperature.

Chestnut Butter

T he chestnut is a sweet and starchy low-fat nut that appears in the fall. The United States once had a glut of chestnut trees, so old cookbooks usually have recipes for chestnut jam. In the early part of the last century there was a chestnut blight, which spelled the end of the chestnut glut. Trees from Europe have been replanted in Texas, as well as in home gardens, so chestnuts have once again appeared in the supermarket. But getting those little buggers peeled is some work, so here we use canned chestnuts packed in water, imported from France. They are available in the jam section of most well-stocked supermarkets. You certainly may peel your own, but this spread is convenient and exotic at the same time, with no loss of flavor. Use good vanilla; you will taste it here. Serve this on breakfast toast with honey, or with butter cookies and fresh fruit. ● *Makes about 2 cups*

COOKER: Small or medium round
SETTING AND COOK TIME: HIGH for 2 to 2½ hours

One 15-ounce can whole chestnuts packed in water
½ cup granulated sugar
¼ cup firmly packed light brown sugar
1¼ teaspoons pure vanilla extract or ½ split vanilla bean

1. Combine the chestnuts and their water in a food processor and process until smooth and creamy.

2. Transfer to the slow cooker and add the sugars and vanilla; stir with a rubber spatula until well mixed. Don't worry if there are some lumps in the sugar; they will melt into the chestnut butter during cooking. Use the spatula to scrape down the sides. Cover and cook on HIGH for 2 to 2½ hours until thick and spreadable, stirring a few times.

3. Remove the vanilla bean, if using. Turn off the cooker and let the chestnut butter cool to room temperature in the crock. Scrape with a rubber spatula into spring-top glass jars (or use screw tops with new lids). Store, covered, in the refrigerator for up to 6 weeks. Or transfer to small plastic storage containers and freeze for up to 3 months. Serve cold or at room temperature.

Fresh Peach Jam

P each jam is a favorite in the jam world, but it is difficult to find commercially. Use slightly underripe firm fruit for the most pronounced peach flavor. Some peaches are very juicy, and the jam will cook up softer than for firmer fruit. Peach jam is an excellent addition to your homemade barbecue sauce. You can double this recipe easily, but always be sure to use a large cooker. ○ *Makes about 5 cups*

COOKER: Medium or large round
SETTINGS AND COOK TIMES: LOW for 2½ hours,
    then uncovered on HIGH for 2 to 3 hours

About 2 pounds slightly underripe peaches (7 to 8 large)
¼ cup fresh lemon juice
One 1.75- or 2-ounce box powdered pectin (optional)
3 to 4 cups sugar, to taste

1. Peel the peaches by dipping them into a pan of boiling water to loosen the skin, then immediately cool them by holding under cold water. The skins will slip off. Remove the pits. In a large bowl, coarsely crush by hand with a potato masher or pulse a few times in a food processor; you'll have about 5 cups of pulp. Combine the peaches and lemon juice in the slow cooker; sprinkle with the pectin, if using. Let stand for 20 to 30 minutes.

2. Stir in the sugar. Cover and cook on LOW for 2½ hours, stirring twice.

3. Remove the lid, turn the cooker to HIGH, and cook 2 to 3 hours longer, until the jam achieves the desired consistency.

4. Ladle the warm jam into clean spring-top glass jars (or use screw tops with new lids); let stand until cool. Store, covered, in the refrigerator for up to 2 months. Or spoon into small plastic storage containers and freeze for up to 3 months.

Nancyjo's Peach and Pluot Jam

A Pluot, a name that sounds like a newly discovered planet, is a cross be-tween a plum and an apricot and is now appearing in supermarkets and in even greater numbers at farmers markets. Its taste is exactly what you would expect, a cross between the two fruits. Our friend Nancyjo Riekse doubles this recipe since she likes to put up a lot of jam if she makes a batch. It is a delicious summer spread. ○ *Makes about 5 cups*

COOKER: Medium or large round
SETTINGS AND COOK TIMES: LOW for 2½ hours, then uncovered on HIGH for 2 to 3 hours

1½ pounds slightly underripe peaches (about 3½ cups)
1½ pounds Pluots (about 3½ cups)
5 to 6 cups sugar, or to taste
3 tablespoons fresh lemon juice

1. Peel the peaches and Pluots by dipping them into a pan of boiling water to loosen the skin, then immediately cool them by holding under cold water. The skins will slip off. Remove the pits. In a large bowl, coarsely crush by hand with a potato masher or pulse a few times in a food processor. Combine the peaches, Pluots, sugar, and lemon juice in the slow cooker. Cover and cook on LOW for 2½ hours, stirring twice during cooking.

2. Remove the lid, turn the cooker to HIGH, and cook for 2 to 3 hours longer, until the jam reaches the desired consistency.

3. Ladle the warm jam into clean spring-top glass jars (or use screw tops with new lids); let stand until cool. Store, covered, in the refrigerator for up to 2 months. Or spoon into small plastic storage containers and freeze for up to 3 months.

Fresh Apricot Jam

Beth spent her early teens growing up in the Santa Clara Valley, in Northern California, under the boughs of apricot trees. In this premier fruit-growing region, apricot trees covered most of the valley. Unfortunately, the trees were gradually pulled out to create Silicon Valley, but delicious fruit is still picked from backyard trees and appears at farmers markets. Apricot jam is luscious and is the second most popular homemade jam, after strawberry. ● *Makes about 5 cups*

COOKER: Medium or large round
SETTINGS AND COOK TIMES: LOW for 2½ hours, then uncovered on HIGH for 2 to 4 hours

3 pounds peeled, pitted, and chopped fresh apricots (about 4½ cups)
2 tablespoons fresh lemon juice
One 1.75- or 2-ounce box powdered pectin (optional)
3 cups sugar, or to taste

1. Combine the apricots and lemon juice in the crock. Sprinkle with the pectin, if using. Let stand for 20 to 30 minutes.

2. Stir in the sugar. Cover and cook on LOW for 2½ hours, stirring twice during cooking.

3. Remove the lid, turn the cooker to HIGH, and cook for 2 to 4 hours longer, until the jam achieves the desired consistency.

4. Ladle the warm jam into clean spring-top glass jars (or use screw tops with new lids); let stand until cool. Store, covered, in the refrigerator for up to 6 weeks. Or spoon into small plastic storage containers and freeze for up to 3 months.

Fig and Ginger Jam

Figs were brought to the New World by the Spanish and have flourished, especially in California. They are sometimes hard to find in a supermarket; you have to go to a produce stand or farmers market, or even beg from a neighbor with a productive tree. Fig jam is something you make when you have lots of fresh figs and have tired of eating them out of hand. You can use either the Black Mission or yellowish-green Calimyrna, a fig that gets its name from California and Smyrna, Turkey, where it originates. Fig, lemon, and ginger is a great flavor combination. ◦ *Makes about 3 cups*

COOKER: Medium or large round
SETTINGS AND COOK TIMES: LOW for 2½ hours, then uncovered on HIGH for 2 to 3 hours

2 pounds fresh figs, stemmed, peeled, and quartered
1½ cups sugar
½ cup water
1 thin-skinned lemon, quartered and thinly sliced (remove any seeds)
2 tablespoons chopped crystallized ginger

1. Combine the figs, sugar, water, lemon, and ginger in the slow cooker. Cover and cook on LOW for 2½ hours, stirring twice during cooking.

2. Remove the lid, turn the cooker to HIGH, and cook for 2 to 3 hours longer, until the jam reaches your desired consistency.

3. Ladle the warm jam into clean spring-top glass jars (or use screw tops with new lids); let stand until cool. Store, covered, in the refrigerator for up to 2 months. Or spoon into small plastic storage containers and freeze for up to 2 months

Fresh Bing Cherry Jam

T his recipe, adapted for the slow cooker, comes from our local cherry grower, Deborah Olson, of Sunnyvale, California, whose family has tended their orchards of Bing cherries for more than 100 years. To pit the cherries, use a cherry pitter, which is a great tool if you are a cherry lover. Or with a small paring knife, cut each cherry in half, and pick out the pit with the tip of the knife. Those little splatters go with the process, so be sure to wear an apron. ◦ *Makes about 5 cups*

COOKER: Medium or large round
SETTINGS AND COOK TIMES: LOW for 2½ hours, then uncovered on HIGH for 2 to 3 hours

4 cups pitted fresh Bing cherries from about 2 pounds of cherries
   (you will have both whole and pieces of cherries)
2 cups sugar
2 tablespoons fresh lemon juice
Pinch of salt
3 tablespoons powdered pectin

1. Combine the cherries, sugar, lemon juice, and salt in the slow cooker. Let stand for 15 minutes to dissolve the sugar.

2. Sprinkle with the pectin. Cover and cook on LOW for 2½ hours, stirring twice during cooking.

3. Remove the lid, turn the cooker to HIGH, and cook for 2 to 3 hours longer, until the jam reaches your desired consistency.

4. Ladle the warm jam into clean spring-top glass jars (or use screw tops with new lids); let stand until cool. Store, covered, in the refrigerator for up to 2 months. Or spoon into small plastic storage containers and freeze for up to 2 months.

Fresh Strawberry Jam

U se a combination of overripe as well as underripe berries in this jam. After purchasing, store berries, unwashed, wrapped in two layers of paper toweling, in a closed plastic bag in the refrigerator. Because they absorb water quickly, never float berries in water to clean them, just rinse under running water right before using. You can double this recipe with no problem, but again, be sure to use a large cooker. ● *Makes about 5½ cups*

COOKER: Medium or large round
SETTINGS AND COOK TIMES: LOW for 2½ hours, then uncovered on HIGH for 2 to 3 hours

4 pints fresh strawberries (about 2 pounds), rinsed in a colander, drained, and hulled
2 tablespoons fresh lemon juice
One 1.75- or 2-ounce box powdered pectin (optional)
3 to 4 cups sugar, to your taste

1. In a large bowl, coarsely crush the berries by hand with a potato masher or pulse a few times in a food processor, leaving a few whole berries or chunks; you'll have about 8 cups. Transfer to the slow cooker. Add the lemon juice and sprinkle with the pectin, if using. Let stand for 10 minutes.

2. Stir in the sugar. Cover and cook on LOW for 2½ hours, stirring twice during cooking.

3. Remove the lid, turn the cooker to HIGH, and cook for 2 to 3 hours longer, until the jam reaches the desired consistency.

4. Ladle the warm jam into clean spring-top glass jars (or use screw tops with new lids); let stand until cool. Store, covered, in the refrigerator for up to 2 months. Or spoon into small plastic storage containers and freeze for up to 3 months.

Blackberry Jam

We often pass up the strawberries and raspberries to get to the blackberries. They are a member of the rose family and have plenty of thorns and brambles. There are a multitude of varieties, so if you see different sizes of blackberries in the store at different times of the year, that is because they are grown in different parts of the country, from Oregon to Louisiana and New York to Virginia. To make a seedless jam, push the cooked hot jam through a mesh strainer or hand-cranked food mill. ○ *Makes about 3 cups*

COOKER: Medium or large round
SETTINGS AND COOK TIMES: LOW for 2½ hours, then uncovered on HIGH for 2 to 3 hours

2 pints fresh blackberries, rinsed in a colander
2 to 3 cups sugar, or to taste
3 tablespoons fresh lemon juice

1. In a medium-size bowl, coarsely crush the berries by hand with a potato masher or pulse a few times in a food processor, leaving a few whole berries or chunks. Transfer to the slow cooker. Stir in the sugar and lemon juice. Cover and cook on LOW for 2½ hours, stirring twice during cooking.

2. Remove the lid, turn the cooker to HIGH, and cook for 2 to 3 hours longer, until the jam is nice and syrupy.

3. Ladle the warm jam into clean spring-top glass jars (or use screw tops with new lids); let stand until cool. Store, covered, in the refrigerator for up to 2 months. Or spoon into small plastic storage containers and freeze for up to 2 months.

Tomato Jam

omato jam is virtually unknown in this country, but British cookbooks are replete with recipes for this jam, a favorite in Europe. While we are used to tomatoes in savory concoctions, they are technically a fruit. This should be made with sweet summer tomatoes for the best flavor. Serve with cream cheese and whole grain bread or scones. ○ *Makes about 4 cups*

COOKER: Large round

SETTINGS AND COOK TIMES: LOW for 2½ hours, then uncovered on HIGH for 2 to 4 hours

2 pounds ripe tomatoes
4 cups sugar
One 1.75- or 2-ounce box powdered pectin (optional)
Grated zest of 2 lemons
Grated zest of 2 oranges
1 tablespoon fresh lemon juice
1 chunk fresh ginger, about 4 inches long, peeled and grated
2 cinnamon sticks

1. Peel, core, seed, and slice the tomatoes. Combine the tomatoes with the sugar, pectin, if using, lemon and orange zests, lemon juice, ginger, and cinnamon sticks in the slow cooker. Cover and cook on LOW for 2½ hours, stirring twice during cooking.

2. Remove the lid, turn the cooker to HIGH, and cook 2 to 4 hours longer, until the jam reaches the desired consistency. Discard the cinnamon sticks.

3. Ladle the warm jam into clean spring-top glass jars (or use screw tops with new lids); let stand until cool. Store, covered, in the refrigerator for up to 4 months. Or spoon into small plastic storage containers and freeze for up to 2 months

Orange Marmalade

O range marmalade was made famous by the Dundee manufacturers in Scotland, and it ranks as one of the most popular of all fruit spreads. Normally you must soak the peels before cooking; this slow cooker method eliminates the soaking time. You won't need any pectin since the citrus has plenty of natural pectin and the marmalade will set up on its own. Our tester Nancyjo Rieske cooks her batch of marmalade overnight. "After the long cooking it will be reduced and ready to put into jelly jars. I love that part; you don't have to worry ever about it scorching. You can go to a movie, read a book, or go to bed." This is an adaptation of her recipe, which she makes in larger batches. ● *Makes about 3½ cups*

COOKER: Medium or large round
SETTINGS AND COOK TIMES: HIGH for 2 hours, then LOW for 6
   hours, then uncovered on HIGH for 1 to 2 hours

1¼ pounds Valencia oranges (2 to 4)
4 cups water
Juice of 1 regular or Meyer lemon
3 to 4 cups sugar, as needed

1. Wash, quarter, and seed the oranges, separating the peel from the pulpy center, and cutting the peel into very small shards. Or chop the whole oranges in a food processor until chunky (just make sure you don't overprocess). Transfer the orange pulp and peel to the slow cooker and add the water and lemon juice. Cover and cook on HIGH until simmering, about 2 hours.

2. Add the sugar and mix well; you want the sugar to equal the amount of boiling orange stock. Stir often until you are sure the sugar has dissolved. Then cover, turn the cooker to LOW, and cook for 6 hours, stirring every 2 hours to check for consistency. The peel will be translucent when the marmalade is ready for the next step.

3. Remove the lid, turn the cooker to HIGH, and cook for another 1 to 2 hours, or even longer (Nancyjo cooks for up to 6 hours more), until you have a nice syrupy consistency.

4. Ladle the warm marmalade into clean spring-top glass jars (or use screw tops with new lids); let stand until cool. Store, covered, in the refrigerator for up to 2 months.

Quince Marmalade

The word "marmalade" is from the Portuguese word *marmelo,* a type of quince. Marmalades of all kinds have been popular since the Middle Ages. At that time marmalades were made exclusively from quince. Old-fashioned and aromatic, the astringent pale yellow fall fruit is difficult to peel and chop because it is almost rock hard. It must be cooked a long time to be edible, and old recipes all recommend long, slow cooking. The quince, which has lots of natural pectin, is incredibly beautiful when cooked, turning a surprisingly deep golden pink color. This luscious recipe is adapted from award-winning pastry chef Stephen Durfee of the French Laundry restaurant in the California Napa Valley. While it is a delicious breakfast spread for buttered toast, brioche, or croissants, it is just as good as a condiment for roast poultry. ○ *Makes about 2½ cups*

COOKER: Medium round
SETTINGS AND COOK TIMES: LOW for 5 to 7 hours,
    then longer uncovered on HIGH (optional)

1½ pounds fully ripe quince (4 small or 2 large)
¾ cup water
1 cup sugar
½ vanilla bean, cut in half lengthwise and still attached at the end
Grated zest and juice of 1 lemon

1. Halve the quince, remove the seeds, and core with a melon-ball cutter or sharp paring knife. Peel the quince, then cut into a small dice, or use the large shredding disk on a food processor (the easiest method).

2. Combine the quince, water, sugar, vanilla bean, and lemon zest and juice in the slow cooker. Cover and cook on LOW for 5 to 7 hours. The quince will be very tender and make a beautiful rosy purée. Discard the vanilla bean. If you would like a thicker marmalade, turn the cooker to HIGH and remove the lid; continue to cook until the marmalade achieves the desired consistency.

3. Turn off the cooker and let the marmalade stand in the crock until cool. Scrape with a rubber spatula into clean spring-top glass jars (or use screw tops with new lids). Store, covered, in the refrigerator for up to 2 months.

Plum Chutney

Chutney is from the Sanskrit word *chatni*, which means "for licking." Made with American ingredients, this is a luscious jam-like fruit chutney. Make it in the late summer when the fruit is ripe and plentiful. It is good with vegetable dishes, in chicken salad, and with roasted poultry and game. ○ *Makes about 4 cups*

COOKER: Medium or large round
SETTING AND COOK TIME: HIGH for 4 to 5 hours;
cooker uncovered during last 30 minutes

2½ to 3 pounds dark firm-ripe plums, such as Santa Rosas,
    cut in half, pitted, and quartered
½ cup golden raisins
1 chunk fresh ginger, about 2 inches long, peeled and grated
1 medium-size white onion, chopped
1 jalapeño, seeded, and slivered
1½ cups sugar
¾ cup cider vinegar
½ teaspoon ground cinnamon
½ teaspoon ground coriander
½ heaping teaspoon curry powder, preferably Madras
Pinch of salt
¼ teaspoon cayenne pepper, or to taste
2 tablespoons minced crystallized ginger

1. Combine all the ingredients, except the crystallized ginger, in the slow cooker. Cover and cook on HIGH for 4 to 4½ hours, until the chutney reaches a jam-like consistency.

2. Remove the lid and let the chutney cook on HIGH an additional 30 minutes to evaporate excess juice and thicken, if necessary. Stir in the crystallized ginger.

3. Turn off the cooker and let the chutney cool to room temperature in the crock. Scrape with a rubber spatula into clean spring-top glass jars (or use screw tops with new lids). Store, covered, in the refrigerator for 2 weeks *before* using to allow the flavors to mellow. The chutney will keep in the fridge for up to 2 months. Serve cold or at room temperature.

Mango and Pineapple Chutney

Mangoes were once considered exotic and very special. We would encounter them on our travels to Mexico, India, and South America, where they are as common as an American apple. They are eaten raw, after you cut through the leathery skin to get to the juicy, bright-colored flesh, and they are cooked in sweet and savory preparations. Now they seem to be a common fruit here as well, available in most supermarkets. The fresh pineapple, another tropical fruit, is a must in this chutney, which is positively euphoric in both aroma and flavor. ● *Makes about 3 cups*

COOKER: Medium or large round
SETTING AND COOK TIME: HIGH for 4 to 4½ hours;
  cooker is uncovered during last 1½ hours

1 large ripe pineapple, trimmed, peeled, eyes cut out, quartered,
  and cut into 1-inch chunks
1 large firm-ripe mango, peeled, pitted, and coarsely chopped
1 medium-size white onion, finely chopped
½ cup raspberry vinegar
1 cup firmly packed light brown sugar
1 medium-size chunk fresh ginger, about 2 inches long, peeled and grated
Grated zest and juice of 1 lime
1 to 2 cloves garlic, to your taste, mashed
1 jalapeño, stemmed, seeded, and minced
One 4-inch cinnamon stick

1. Combine all the ingredients in the slow cooker. Cover and cook on HIGH for 3 hours, until the chutney reaches a jam-like consistency.

2. Remove the lid and let the chutney cook on HIGH for an additional 1½ hours to evaporate excess juice and thicken.

3. Turn off the cooker and let the chutney cool to room temperature in the crock. Scrape with a rubber spatula into clean spring-top glass jars (or use screw tops with new lids). Store, covered, in the refrigerator for up to 2 weeks. Serve cold or at room temperature.

Mango, Lime, and Date Chutney

ere is another mango chutney, but with a totally different flavor and texture than our Mango and Pineapple Chutney (page 494) because this one contains dates, which melt right into the hot mixture. Mangoes are a venerated fruit. There is a legend from India telling of a gift from a wealthy landowner of a mango grove to the sage Buddha so that he and his followers might meditate under the lush tree's shade. ○ *Makes about 3½ cups*

COOKER: Medium or large round
SETTING AND COOK TIME: HIGH for 4½ to 5 hours;
cooker is uncovered during last 30 minutes

3 to 4 large ripe mangoes, peeled, pitted, and coarsely chopped

8 ounces pitted dates, chopped

1½ cups dark raisins, or a combination of golden raisins and dried cherries

1 chunk fresh ginger, about 3 inches long, peeled and grated

1 large white onion, chopped

2 limes, diced, including the rind

1½ cups cider vinegar

1½ cups firmly packed dark brown sugar

¾ cup granulated sugar

2 teaspoons yellow mustard seeds

1½ teaspoons ground cinnamon

1 teaspoon vanilla extract

1 teaspoon chili powder

1 teaspoon ground coriander

1 teaspoon ground allspice

½ teaspoon turmeric

¼ teaspoon ground nutmeg

½ teaspoon red pepper flakes

1. Combine all the ingredients in the slow cooker. Cover and cook on HIGH for 4 to 4½ hours, until the chutney achieves a jam-like consistency.

2. Remove the lid and let the chutney cook on HIGH for an additional 30 minutes to evaporate excess juice and thicken, if necessary.

3. Turn off the cooker and let cool to room temperature in the crock. Scrape the chutney with a rubber spatula into clean spring-top glass jars (or use screw tops with new lids). Store, covered, in the refrigerator for up to 3 months. Serve cold or at room temperature.

Peach and Dried Apricot Chutney

(T)here is no better condiment than a stone-fruit chutney. It has a great fresh flavor enhanced with pungent spices. This is a variation of a nectarine chutney made by Narsai David, which we used to buy. When it disappeared from the market, it was time to make our own. The chutney must be chunky, dark, hot, and sweet all at the same time. This pairs well with Indian food, barbecued meats, pork, pâté, and meat loaf. ○ *Makes about 4 cups*

COOKER: Medium or large round
SETTING AND COOK TIME: HIGH for 4½ to 5 hours;
    cooker uncovered during last 30 minutes

About 2½ pounds slightly underripe fresh peaches (6 or 7), or
    frozen unsweetened peach slices, thawed
1 chunk fresh ginger, about 3 inches long
1½ cups chopped dried apricots
1 medium-size white onion, diced
1½ cups cider vinegar
1½ cups firmly packed dark brown sugar
2 teaspoons ground ginger
2 teaspoons ground coriander
½ teaspoon ground cumin
1 teaspoon salt
Pinch of red pepper flakes
½ cup raisins or dried cherries

1. Peel the peaches by dipping them into a pan of boiling water to loosen the skin, then immediately cool them by holding under cold water. The skin will slip off. Pit, then coarsely chop into chunks and transfer to the slow cooker. Peel the ginger and mince to make 2½ tablespoons, more or less, depending on how hot you want the chutney. Add the apricots, onion, vinegar, sugar, spices, salt, and pepper flakes to the cooker. Cover and cook on HIGH for 4 to 4½ hours, until the chutney achieves a jam-like consistency. Add the raisins towards the end of the cooking time.

2. Remove the lid and let the chutney cook on HIGH for an additional 30 minutes to evaporate excess juice and thicken to the final desired consistency.

3. Turn off the cooker and let cool to room temperature in the crock. Scrape the chutney with a rubber spatula into clean spring-top glass jars (or use screw tops with new lids). Store, covered, in the refrigerator for up to 3 months. Serve cold or at room temperature.

Apple and Dried Fruit Chutney

One of Beth's most outspoken and talented cookbook copyeditors was Sharon Silva. She wrote a great book devoted solely to apples with Frank Browning called *An Apple Harvest* (Ten Speed, 1999). Her recipes are glorious. This is Sharon's apple chutney, adapted for the slow cooker. This is a great house gift as well as good in have in your own fridge. ○ *Makes about 3½ cups*

COOKER: Medium or large round
SETTING AND COOK TIME: HIGH for 4 to 5 hours;
　　cooker uncovered during last 30 minutes

**5 large Granny Smith, pippin, fuji, or other tart cooking apple, peeled, cored, and coarsely
　chopped**
½ cup chopped dried apricots
½ cup chopped dried pears
½ cup chopped dried peaches
⅓ cup golden raisins
1 chunk fresh ginger, about 2 inches long, peeled and grated
5 to 7 cloves garlic, to your taste, mashed
2½ cups sugar
1¼ cups white wine vinegar
1½ teaspoons salt
½ to 1 teaspoon cayenne pepper, to your taste

1. Combine all the ingredients in the slow cooker. Cover and cook on HIGH for 4 to 4½ hours, until it achieves a jam-like consistency.

2. Remove the lid and let the chutney cook on HIGH an additional 30 minutes to evaporate excess juice and thicken, if necessary.

3. Turn off the cooker and let cool to room temperature in the crock. Scrape with a rubber spatula into clean spring-top glass jars (or use screw tops with new lids). Store, covered, in the refrigerator for 2 weeks *before* using to allow the flavors to mellow. It will keep in the fridge for up to 2 months. Serve cold or at room temperature.

Cranberry-Apple Chutney

E very holiday season Beth's friend Joan Briedenbach makes quarts of this bright cranberry chutney, conceived by the creative food writer Peggy Fallon, to give as gifts. Serve with poultry or pork, as a spread for sandwiches, or as a condiment with cheese. ○ *Makes about 4 cups*

COOKER: Medium round
SETTING AND COOK TIME: LOW for 4½ to 5 hours;
   cooker is uncovered during last 30 minutes

2 large shallots, peeled
Zest of 1 large orange, cut off the fruit in strips with a small knife
One 12-ounce bag fresh cranberries, rinsed and picked over for stems
2 large tart apples, such as Granny Smith, cored and finely chopped
   (you can peel or leave on the skin)
1½ cups firmly packed dark brown sugar
½ cup dried currants or golden raisins or finely chopped dried apricots
1 chunk fresh ginger, about 1 inch long, peeled and grated
½ teaspoon curry powder
¼ teaspoon ground cloves
¼ teaspoon ground allspice
⅓ cup cider vinegar or raspberry vinegar
⅓ cup slivered almonds (2 ounces), toasted in a 325°F oven until pale gold and chopped

1. Coarsely chop the shallots and orange zest in a food processor.

2. Combine all the ingredients, except the almonds, in the slow cooker. Cover and cook on LOW for 4 to 4½ hours, until the chutney achieves a jam-like consistency.

3. Remove the lid and let the chutney cook on LOW for an additional 30 minutes to evaporate excess juice and thicken, if necessary.

4. Stir in the almonds. Turn off the cooker and let the chutney cool in the crock to room temperature. Scrape with a rubber spatula into clean spring-top glass jars (or use screw tops with new lids). Store, covered, in the refrigerator for up to 6 weeks. Serve chilled or at room temperature.

Cranberry-Ginger Compote

B eth's mother got this recipe, which we adapted for the slow cooker, from her antique dealer, Alan, who is a constant source of inspiration in the kitchen. He cooks every day and it is always something inventive and fabulous. You can add the crystallized ginger at the end or during the cooking, when it will melt into the compote. Serve this with all sorts of roasted meats such as poultry, pork loin, and ham. ○ *Makes about 2¼ cups*

COOKER: Medium round
SETTING AND COOK TIME: HIGH for 2 to 2½ hours

1 chunk fresh ginger, about 5 inches long
One 12-ounce bag fresh cranberries, rinsed and picked over for stems
1 cup sugar
¼ cup water
Grated zest and juice of 1 large orange
⅛ teaspoon ground cloves
½ cup walnuts, chopped
¼ cup chopped crystallized ginger (optional)

1. Peel and coarsely grate the ginger. Take the grated ginger in your fist and squeeze out as much of the juice as you can into the slow cooker; discard the pulp.

2. Leave two-thirds of the cranberries whole and chop the rest. Add all the cranberries to the cooker, along with the sugar, water, orange zest and juice, and cloves. Cover and cook on HIGH for 2 to 2½ hours; the whole cranberries will have popped open.

3. While still hot, stir in the walnuts and crystallized ginger. Turn off the cooker, remove the lid, and let the compote cool in the crock to room temperature. Scrape with a rubber spatula into clean spring-top glass jars (or use screw tops with new lids). Store, covered, in the refrigerator for up to 3 weeks. Serve chilled or at room temperature.

Slow Cooker Cranberry Sauce

C ranberries come from the same botanical family as blueberries, rhododendrons, and heather. Fresh cranberries arrive in stores in late fall and can be frozen in their original wrapping for use in the spring and summer. Use bags of fresh cranberries within two weeks of purchase so that they don't get mushy or shriveled. If you use frozen cranberries, do not defrost them, but plan on an extra 30 to 45 minutes in the cooker. Try the lime zest; it is a smashing flavor combination with the cranberries. ◦ *Makes about 2 cups*

COOKER: Medium round
SETTING AND COOK TIME: HIGH for 2 to 2½ hours

One 12-ounce bag fresh or frozen cranberries, rinsed and picked over for stems
1 cup sugar
½ cup water
Grated zest of 1 orange or lime

1. Combine the cranberries, sugar, and water in the slow cooker. Cover and cook on HIGH for 2 to 2½ hours; the cranberries will have popped open.

2. Stir the zest into the hot sauce. Turn off the cooker, remove the lid, and let cool in the crock to room temperature. Scrape with a rubber spatula into clean spring-top glass jars (or use screw tops with new lids). Store, covered, in the refrigerator for up to 3 weeks. Serve chilled or at room temperature.

Cranberry Sauce with Red Wine and Oranges

 he red wine tends to intensify, as well as complement, the flavor of the cranberries. Serve, of course, with all types of poultry. ○ *Makes about 3 cups*

COOKER: Medium round
SETTING AND COOK TIME: HIGH for 2 to 2½ hours

One 12-ounce bag fresh cranberries, rinsed and picked over for stems
1½ cups sugar
1 cup dry red wine, such as Cabernet Sauvignon
1 cinnamon stick
Grated zest of 1 orange, and fruit cut in half
4 cloves

1. Combine the cranberries, sugar, wine, cinnamon, and zest in the slow cooker. Stud the orange halves with 2 cloves each; submerge in the cooker. Cover and cook on HIGH for 2 to 2½ hours, until the berries have popped.

2. Discard the cinnamon stick and the oranges. Turn off the cooker, remove the lid, and let cool in the crock to room temperature. Scrape with a rubber spatula into clean spring-top glass jars (or use screw tops with new lids). Store, covered, in the refrigerator for up to 1 week. Serve chilled or at room temperature.

New-Fashioned Apple and Pear Mincemeat

A tradition on both sides of the Atlantic for the holidays, you either love mincemeat or hate it. Those who do indulge love it and wait all year for the fruit cooked with a strong blend of spices and soaked in spirits. Mincemeat has a reputation for being an insipid food, but the mass-produced commercial version just is not nearly as good as homemade. Mincemeats widely vary—the British like mock versions with no meat, the French and Americans like beef sirloin or corned beef in theirs. Early Americans used rabbit or other game, such as venison. Here is our version, no meat or suet, and just as satisfying. It cooks nice and slow to meld all the flavors. This makes a batch big enough for 2 double-crusted mince pies. ● *Makes about 2 quarts, enough for 2 deep-dish pies*

COOKER: Large round

SETTING AND COOK TIME: HIGH for 3½ to 4½ hours; cooker is uncovered during last 2 to 3 hours

3 large apples, peeled, cored, and coarsely shredded

3 firm Bosc pears, peeled, cored, and coarsely shredded

2 cups pear or apple juice

4 ounces dried apples, chopped

1 cup golden raisins

1 cup dried currants

¾ cup dark raisins

¾ cup dried cranberries

¾ cup chopped dried apricots

¾ cup finely chopped candied orange peel

1 cup firmly packed dark brown sugar

¼ cup dry sherry

¼ cup brandy

¼ cup cider vinegar

½ cup (1 stick) unsalted butter

1 teaspoon ground cinnamon

1 teaspoon ground allspice

1 teaspoon ground nutmeg

1 teaspoon ground mace

1 teaspoon ground cloves

Pinch of salt

1 large orange, cut in half

¼ cup brandy for topping mincemeat in jars

1. Combine all the ingredients, except the orange and topping brandy, in the slow cooker. Put the whole orange in a food processor and pulse to chop the fruit and rind; add to the cooker. Stir the ingredients to combine. Cover and cook the mince-meat on HIGH for 1½ hours, bringing the mixture to a full boil.

2. Remove the lid and continue to cook on HIGH, stirring a few times, until the fruits are soft and the mixture has thickened considerably, 2 to 3 hours.

3. Transfer the hot mincemeat to 2 clean, hot, 1-quart Mason jars or a covered bowl and let cool completely. Pour 2 tablespoons of the brandy into each jar or pour the entire amount over the bowl to cover the mincemeat. Cover and refrigerate overnight, or up to 1 week, to meld the flavors before serving. Mincemeat keeps in the refrigerator for up to 6 months. Use cold, directly out of the refrigerator.

Sweet and Spicy Red Grapes

Beth's friend Robert Lambert handcrafts a line of preserved fruits and sells it at Dean and Deluca and other gourmet outlets. When Beth tasted his pickled grapes in a sweet, winey syrup, she went nuts; they are so delicious. Here is a simple version that re-creates those wondrous orbs. We know: picking them off the stem and cutting grapes in half is kinda wild, but be sure to do it. It is easiest to get the largest seedless red grapes you can find. Red Flames, which are Tokay grapes, are known for their beauty and appear in the fall. Be sure to get a great red wine vinegar, such as a Zinfandel or Cabernet. Stored in two pint-size Mason jars, these will keep in the refrigerator for weeks. Serve with poultry, game, or meats as a condiment. ○ *Makes about 4 cups*

COOKER: Medium round
SETTINGS AND COOK TIMES: HIGH for 45 minutes to 1 hour,
    then LOW for about 1½ hours; grapes added during last 30 minutes

One ½-inch knob fresh ginger, sliced
1 small chunk of fresh nutmeg
One 4-inch stick cinnamon, broken in half
¼ teaspoon whole cloves
½ cup excellent red wine vinegar, such as Zinfandel or Cabernet
½ cup fruity red wine, such as a Merlot, Chianti, or Zinfandel
1½ cups sugar
2 pounds Red Flame seedless grapes, washed, dried, stemmed, and cut in half

1. Put the ginger, nutmeg, cinnamon, and cloves in a piece of cheesecloth and tie shut. Put in the slow cooker and add the vinegar, wine, and sugar. Cover and cook on HIGH for 45 minutes to 1 hour to bring to a boil and dissolve the sugar.

2. Stir, then cover, turn the cooker to LOW, and cook for 1 hour.

3. Discard the spice bag. Add the grapes to the cooker, cover, and continue to cook on LOW for another 20 to 30 minutes; you want the liquid to return to a simmer and just heat the grapes through, not cook them or have the skins fall off.

4. Turn off the cooker, remove the lid, and let the grapes cool in the crock to room temperature. Pour the grapes into clean glass jars. Store, covered, in the refrigerator for up to 5 weeks. Serve chilled or at room temperature.

Confit of Green Tomato

This recipe is a cross between a mincemeat and a condiment such as chutney or cranberry sauce. Green tomatoes are simply unripened tomatoes, often the ones that are still on the vine at the end of the season, when you are ready to pull out the plant in anticipation of the first killing frost. The recipe is adapted from one by Stephen Durfee, who served for years as pastry chef at the famous French Laundry restaurant. He would make a cornmeal cake and maple sugar ice cream and serve this confit on the side. We like it with pound cake and vanilla ice cream just fine. It's even good piled on toast with cottage cheese or alongside poultry or pork. Lots of people don't bother peeling the tomatoes, but it makes for a smoother confit. ○ *Makes about 3 cups*

COOKER: Medium round

SETTING AND COOK TIME: HIGH for 3½ to 4 hours; cooker is uncovered during last hour

6 medium-size hard green tomatoes (it's okay if they have some blush on them)
2 large apples, peeled, cored, and chopped
1½ cups firmly packed light brown sugar
½ cup water
1 cinnamon stick
1 chunk fresh ginger, about 1 inch long, peeled and lightly crushed
Grated zest and juice of 2 oranges

Grated zest and juice of 2 lemons
Grated zest and juice of 2 limes
½ cup golden raisins
½ cup chopped dried apricots or dried peaches
2 tablespoons sherry vinegar

1. Prepare the tomatoes by placing them on a baking sheet and broiling a few inches below the flame to char the skin; this can also be done on a gas grill. Wash off the skin under cold running water, cut in half, then squeeze out most of the seeds. Dice the tomatoes and transfer to the slow cooker. Add the remaining ingredients, except the vinegar, to the cooker. Stir to combine. Cover and cook on HIGH for 2½ to 3 hours.

2. Remove the lid and continue to cook on HIGH, stirring a few times, until the fruits are soft and translucent and the mixture has thickened to the desired consistency, about 1 hour more. If you want a looser consistency, one more like applesauce, you do not have to cook with the lid off.

3. Discard the cinnamon stick and ginger and stir in the vinegar. Transfer the confit to a clean, hot, 1-quart Mason jar or covered bowl and let cool completely. Cover and refrigerate for up to 1 week. Serve chilled or room at temperature.

Quick and Easy Tomato Ketchup

This tangy condiment is a snap when made with canned tomato purée, an improvement from spending the entire day laboriously peeling tomatoes that eventually cook down to less than a quart We make enough for short-term refrigerator storage in a glass spring-top jar without the fuss of preserving. Today's commercial brands can't compare with your own batch of ketchup. Be sure to make a meat loaf or meat pie the night you make this ketchup; it is great to serve warm. ○ *Makes about 3¼ cups*

COOKER: Medium round
SETTING AND COOK TIME: HIGH for 2½ to 3½ hours;
cooker is uncovered during last 30 minutes to 1 hour

One 28-ounce can tomato purée

1 small yellow onion, coarsely chopped

1 medium-size shallot, chopped

½ cup cider vinegar

¼ cup firmly packed light or dark brown sugar

½ teaspoon dry mustard, such as Coleman's

¼ teaspoon ground allspice

¼ teaspoon ground cinnamon

¼ teaspoon ground mace

¼ teaspoon ground ginger

¼ teaspoon ground cloves

¼ teaspoon ground red pepper flakes

Sea salt to taste

A few grinds of black pepper

1. In a food processor, combine the tomato purée, onion, and shallot and process until just smooth. Add the vinegar, brown sugar, mustard, allspice, cinnamon, mace, ginger, cloves, and pepper flakes and pulse to combine. Pour the tomato mixture into the slow cooker. Cover and cook on HIGH for 2 to 2½ hours, stirring occasionally.

2. Remove the lid and continue to cook the ketchup on HIGH, stirring a few times, until the mixture has thickened to the desired consistency, 30 minutes to 1 hour. You want it to be able to plop off a spoon. Season with salt and pepper.

3. Turn off the cooker and let the ketchup cool to room temperature in the crock. Scrape with a rubber spatula into a clean spring-top glass jar (or use a screw top and a new lid). Serve warm, at room temperature, or chilled. Store, covered, in the refrigerator for up to 2 months.

Slow Cooker Manufacturers

Applica (Windmere)
800-557-9463
www.applicainc.com

Corningware
www.worldkitchen.com

General Electric
877-207-0923
www.gehousewares.com

Hamilton Beach (Proctor-Silex)
800-851-8900
www.hamiltonbeach.com

Rival
800-557-4825
www.crockpot.com

West Bend
800-821-8821
www.westbend.com

Index